THE MAKINGS OF A DIPLOMATIST

THE MEMOIRS OF ALEXANDER QUAISON-SACKEY

Foreword by Kwaw Ansah

Completed & Edited by Awo Aferba Quaison-Sackey

AWO A. QUAISON-SACKEY

DigiBooks

Published by Digibooks Ghana Ltd.

P. O. Box BT1, Tema, Ghana

Tel: +233-303-414-720 / +233-246-493-842

Email: admin@digibookspublishing.com

Website: http://www.digibookspublishing.com

Cover Design: Koku Dotse

DEDICATION

To M'maa and M'paa

CONTENTS

FOREWORD

Istudied in the United States in the years 1963 to 1967. During this time, I would visit my cousin, Alex Quaison-Sackey, at his residence in New Rochelle – always invited by M'paa and M'maa (as everyone called Alex and Elsie Quaison-Sackey) to spend time with them and the children. There was always a festive air on those visits with M'paa saying to me *"Kwaw, dzidzi, dzidzi. Wo mame nnye ha!"* admonishing me to "eat, eat. Your mother is not around." As a poor, young student in a foreign land I appreciated and took advantage of the invitations.

I was an intern at the United Nations in 1964 working on the switchboard. At that time, switchboard operators would direct the calls to the recipient. A call came in from Kwame Nkrumah asking for Alex Quaison-Sackey. I stayed on the call in order to disconnect it when completed. Dr. Nkrumah called him "Quai-Son" with emphasis on the "Son". He asked how the campaign for President of the General Assembly was going. M'paa replied that there were so many obstacles being put in his way, that the United States was working to muddy the waters by encouraging several African delegates to stand for the Presidency and thereby obfuscating the election through a divide-and-conquer strategy. Dr. Nkrumah replied, "Quai-Son, if you do not become the first black African President of the General Assembly, do not call me Kwame Nkrumah!"

There was a gap in what happened next until Chris Hesse later filled in the blanks for me. Chris Hesse was with Kwame Nkrumah at the time when Nkrumah made that call to M'paa. Apparently, Dr. Nkrumah picked up the phone and called the then President of Sudan and said "my brother, my brother, for the first time an African south of the Sahara is to become the president of the United Nations and look at the resistance. Look at what they are doing to us. They want to stand in our way." All I was witness to at the time was that soon after the telephone call between Dr.

Nkrumah and M'paa, I heard the telex machine printing a telex to be delivered. The telex was from the President of Sudan to the Ambassador from the Sudan to the United Nations and said something to the tune of: "your excellency, if you do not step down in the race for the President of the General Assembly, you can call yourself Ambassador of no country."

The kind of celebration I saw in the diaspora when Alex was elected showed how proud everyone was. In fact, even the black Americans at the time saw this as their victory. Maya Angelou in her book "The Heart of a Woman" refers to this pride in Chapter 3 of the book when she says "One Hundred and Twenty-Fifth Street was to Harlem what the Mississippi [River} was to the South ... Clever appliance-store owners left their TV sets on the channels broadcasting U.N. affairs. I had seen black people standing in front of the stores watching the faces of international diplomats ... The mood was hopeful, as if a promise was soon to be kept. The crowd tightened, pulled itself closer together and toward the window, as a small dark figure appeared on all the screens at once. The figure was that of an African wearing a patterned toga, striding with theatrical dignity toward the camera. The sidewalk audience was quiet but tense. When the man's face was discernible and the part in his hair distinct, the crowd began to talk. "Hey, Alex, Hey, brother." ..."He's a good-looking thing." ..."That African walk like God himself." She talks about the self-congratulatory pride felt by the black Americans in Harlem.

Another example of this is when we in the diaspora travelled to Brunswick to meet Captain Techie-Menson who had brought one of our ships to NY. When we got there, the black Americans were already there. They pushed us out of the way to get to Captain Techie-Menson and they raised him on their shoulders and carried him in jubilation.

When I returned to Ghana later and people were saying that Dr. Nkrumah was jealous of "Quai-Son", I knew that he had supported M'paa and there was no jealousy there. When I heard people saying the M'paa had betrayed Dr. Nkrumah and had been paid off by the CIA, I knew that he had always done what he thought was best for Ghana, and that while the CIA had been behind the 1966 coup d'etat, M'paa had been ignorant of the events happening behind the scenes. In fact, my understanding was that "they" later apologized to M'paa for not letting him know that this was in the works. At the time of the coup, M'paa had been in office as the Minister of Foreign Affairs for just a few months. He did not have to return to Ghana from Hanoi, he chose to do so for the love of his country and his family and not as an intentional betrayal of the man with whom he had shared a vision. On M'paa's return to Ghana, getting off the plane at gunpoint, when he was asked why he returned, he said "I returned because I love my wife". That statement nullified and minimized his prior contributions to Ghana and the world. I know for a fact that M'maa herself did not like that he made that statement. I personally wish he would have said what I know was the truth for him: that he had been serving his country the entire time he was Ambassador to the United Nations, President of the General Assembly and then Minister of Foreign Affairs through Dr. Kwame Nkrumah; and that his return was as a continuation of his service to the country that he loved so much.

In 1996, my friend, the Hollywood actor and director Danny Glover asked me to assist him with some items related to the film "Deadly Voyage". He came to look at the MV Accra and to meet the crew on the ship. We were introduced to a young lady as the captain but I don't think Danny heard. When we got to the end of the line, he asked where the captain of this large vessel was. I explained that we had met her at the front of the line. He looked at me quizzically and we went back to the front of the line. He asked the young lady if she was the captain. She said yes. He asked her how long she had been doing this. She said 20 years. He grabbed her in a bear hug lifting her off the ground, and with tears in his eyes, he said "and they say Africa is a jungle. I do not think that I can ever see this in the United States." He was talking about a black female as the person in charge!!

That is the Ghana that M'paa was helping Dr. Nkrumah to bring to the world stage, the Ghana we can be proud of. It is that essence of who we are that continues to give me hope and is the impetus for Bisa Abrewa, my museum in Takoradi that pays homage to all that has come before, to all that has gotten us here and all that will be the foundation that takes us into the future to fulfil our destiny.

Kwaw Ansah
Film-maker
Accra
December 2021

ACKNOWLEDGEMENTS

I have to acknowledge my mother first: Alex's wife, Mrs. Quaison-Sackey, Elsie Annie, Anamoaba, M'maa. It is a result of the legacy gifts I was bestowed from her that this project has been completed. I cannot even begin to recite the "M'maa-isms" that encouraged, cajoled and provided needed pressure along the way. Thank you for everything.

Then last but not least is my son, Awenate Cobbina, who is always encouraging of my projects and actions, never misses an opportunity to help me and provide support no matter what the next thing is that I take on. When I told him that I was typing M'paa's memoirs, he was extremely positive, and never in the 28 ensuing years, made any comment about how long it was taking! Thank you for everything.

In between are so many other people. Kabral Blay-Amihere and D. K. Osei of the Council on Foreign Relations read the manuscript when I finished typing it, and gave a thumbs up. Kabral has been very generous with his time, lending his expertise and guidance since I have never had anything published before. Thank you for everything.

Jeffrey Akowuah-Amankwah and Solomon Debrah, two young people that I have had the pleasure of working with, did the major research and initial proofreading. It was gratifying that this was a learning experience for them as they did not know much about the slice of history that is covered in the book. Thank you so much for spending all those weeks and Zoom meetings to collaborate with me in getting this work done. Thank you for everything.

Thank you to Koku Dotse for bringing his eagle eye to the final proofreading, and then, more importantly, his artistic eye to the artwork for the cover. In addition, we are working on an accompanying coffee table book of additional photographs, and Koku has again applied his design abilities to make that project come to life. Stay tuned!

And then there are my siblings who each provided of their expertise in this project: Nenyi, the family archivist and glue, who made sure that we had all the photographs that he has painstakingly scanned in order to preserve the images; K.B., who read huge portions of the manuscript as I was typing and proofread and corrected as we went along; and Yaaba, our prayer maven and "story teller" who was the only one in Ghana with Alex and Elsie in his final years, and so recounted tales that the rest of us could not have known about.

With all my gratitude and appreciation to all. All glory to God – we are blessed, I am blessed.

Love,
Awo Aferba

INTRODUCTION

M'paa, as a lot of people called our father, was a charming, fun man. There are so many words that are used to describe him. Between the ages of 5 and 10 years old, we lived in New Rochelle, New York at the residence of the Ambassador from Ghana to the United Nations. I was the third child with two older brothers, Egya and Nana. My younger brother, K.B. was a baby. During those days, I thought I was my father's favorite. Nenyi and Yaaba were born later, and I was the only girl in those days. I would call my father during the day to tell him that Egya and Nana were calling me names. He was always ready to say something to make me feel better and special. I was oblivious to what I was interrupting when I called. In typing his manuscript, I now see how it might have been for him to be in the middle of some kind of deliberations or important conversation, getting the message that your young daughter is on the phone, and taking the call in order to help her deal with her latest sibling conundrum.

He was known for a lot of things: at or near the top of the list was his love of banku and his love of having lots of people around. Regardless of what he ate during the day, he had to have his banku before the day ended. My mother used to joke that he was "come to my party". There were always people in our home.

M'paa passed away on December 21, 1992. At that time, he had written most of the manuscript and wanted to make sure that it was completed and published. He had left it with me, and I had promised I would get it typed up for him. We were interacting as though there was going to be a lot of time ahead to get this done. So, you will find that the manuscript ends with the period just after the February 24, 1966 coup d'etat, clearly unfinished.

There was no time to write about how he was able to put his life back together after the coup, getting permission from the then government to leave Ghana for London where he completed his legal education and came back to Ghana to practice law, first with Quarshie-Idun, and then with his partner E.B.O. Anderson at Sackandah Chambers, and then with Japan Motors for the remainder of his life. He didn't have a chance to write about becoming Ambassador of Ghana to the United States and Mexico from 1978 until 1980. He didn't have time to write about his leadership roles with the Methodist Church of Ghana.

And he never wrote about how he felt about life after what turned out to be the pinnacle of his career – the first black President of the General Assembly. To have reached one's peak as early as the age of 40 ... I can now appreciate (not having had the maturity to have these discussions while he was alive) the difficult choices he had to make in 1965 after the year as President of the General Assembly, to return to his homeland to serve. And the difficult decision to once again return to his homeland a few months later on February 24, 1966 against the instruction of his boss, the deposed President Dr. Kwame Nkrumah. I believe there was never any question for my father. His dedication to Ghana and Winneba were the reason why my brothers, sister and I, at a time when it was not "fashionable" to give your children Ghanaian first names were named Egya Akumbia, Nana Bordoh, Awo Aferba, Kweku Bondzi Asiedu, Nenyi Embi, and Yaaba (I guess my parents were too tired by this time to give her any additional names, so she took Alberta as her middle name in honor of our paternal grandmother). It is the reason why my sister and I were given criteria for the men we should marry — which criteria when you boiled it down translated into "someone from Winneba".

One of his closest friends was Kow Nkensen Arkaah. They grew up together in Winneba. The Arkaahs were part of our "family". When M'paa died, we went to see Mr. Arkaah and Auntie Marian Arkaah, his wife. Mr. Arkaah told us stories about growing up with M'paa. One that sticks with me is how they would go to the beach instead of going to school. He said they would jump off the rocks into the ocean, shouting "when I grow up, I am going to be like ..."; and they would fill in the blank with the great men they had learned about such as Alexander the Great, Socrates, and others. This ambition was realized for both of these young men in spite of having come from very humble beginnings. When my paternal grandfather passed away and we were sorting through his belongings, we found letters that M'paa had written to his father from Mfantsipim, asking for a pen or a pair of shorts or some other basic supply. In those letters, he would say something like "what if I am destined to become somebody great but I am not able to write my exams because I do not have a pen"? This young man was determined to make something of himself.

Why publish this now? After all, M'paa died in 1992 – over 28 years ago. We believe there is more than a passing interest in this slice of history. We feel that it is important that people know and not take for granted the world that we have been born into. There are people who fought for this nation to be born. We may even understand from reading this book, that each one of us can also take a stand for something that we believe in.

I learned a great deal typing up this manuscript about M'paa, our family, myself, and especially Ghana. I learned that he was named Alexander Quaison Sackey with Quaison as his middle name in honor of his maternal grandfather. Later in life he hyphenated the name to Quaison-Sackey. I had grown up thinking it was the family name. I learned that the transition to independence and self-determination was in the end deliberate and planful when one compares Ghana to other African nations going through their journey. The selection and training of the first ambassadors was impressive in its structured approach. The hope and vision of the time is palpable in what he writes. But even so, there is paper in the manuscript where he is clearly trying out various titles and they all speak to the disappointment of what has come after. Potential titles such as "Ghana – The Country of Broken Dreams", "Ambition that Failed", "A Dream that Went Sour" bespeak some hope that did not materialize. I would say that hope was captured in his first book published by Praeger in 1963 when Ghana was still a toddler – "Africa Unbound". While I am sure some of that refers to his own career having been cut short, there is also the sadness of independence not having led to the realization of the high hopes of the time.

I believe we have reason to be optimistic. The nation has not lost its capability to fight for what is right and what is for the benefit of the citizens of the country. There are still those that are committed to public service for public gain rather than merely individual gain. There is hope. The future is ours to create in honor of those who went before, and for the benefit of those yet to come.

Awo Aferba Quaison-Sackey (b.1954)
January 1, 2021
Accra

On behalf of Elsie Anamoaba Quaison-Sackey (b.1927 – d.2003) and the Quaison-Sackey children: Egya Akumbia (b.1951 – d.1994), Nana Bordoh (b.1952 – d.1990), Kweku Bondzi (b.1959), Nenyi Embi (b. 1962), Yaaba (b.1967)

CHAPTER 1

EARLY LIFE AND EDUCATION

I was born at Winneba in Ghana, then known as the Gold Coast at 10:00 p.m. on August 9, 1924. My mother, Ekua Kwesiwa, was baptized and christened as Alberta Quaison at the Catholic Church in Sekondi where she was born on October 17, 1905. Her father was Joseph Edmundson Quaison, alias Kodwo Bordoh born in 1884 at Ewusiajo near Sekondi, in the Western Region of Ghana. Her mother was Nana Yaaba of the Royal Anona family of Apowa also near Sekondi-Takoradi in the Western Region. Thus, my mother was of the Ahanta tribe, who inhabit all that vast area from Shama to Dixcove and Busua in the Western Region. My maternal grandmother died when my mother was nine years old. Therefore, my grandfather, Mr. Quaison, took my mother and her two younger sisters with him wherever he went on transfer. Grandpa Quaison was a Sanitary Inspector-cum-dispenser, specially trained in those days to assist in the combating of yellow fever, smallpox, and malaria.

When my mother was ten years old, her father was transferred from Sekondi to Saltpond and then to Winneba. Mr. Quaison brought his three daughters along with him to Winneba. He and his daughters were Roman Catholics. Unfortunately, there was no Catholic Church in Winneba at that time, and so my mother was encouraged to join the Wesleyan Methodist Church where she was confirmed. She liked to sing and so she threw herself, body and soul into the Singing Band. I have been informed by her contemporaries that my mother had a beautiful treble voice and she used to sing solos in church. She was also attractive and

1

beautiful. There were several suitors who did not dare approach her because she was under the eagle eyes of "Papa Town Council" as my grandfather was affectionately called.

Sanitary Inspectors in those days had the authority to enter homes to make sure that drinking water was free from bacteria and that the environment was kept clean. My grandfather worked directly under the British Medical Officer of Health for Winneba. People in Winneba were therefore in awe of him and held him in high esteem. He remained a staunch Catholic to the end. He retired from the Civil Service in 1935 as a Senior Health Inspector, one of the first Africans to have held such a "European" post. He later became a member of the Sekondi-Takoradi Municipal Council, and then Treasurer and Paymaster of the Ahanta Confederation. He died in January 1964 at the age of eighty.

My father was Alex Emmanuel Sackey, alias Kweku Sekyi. His father was Emmanuel Kodwo Sackey, alias Kodwo Sei who was a carpenter by trade but became quite wealthy through the fishing business. He was reputed to have introduced dragnet and seine fishing to Winneba, innovations which were very unpopular amongst Winneba fishermen in 1900. My father's mother was Adwoa Aferba, a fishmonger and trader who established a flourishing trade in salted fish and trotters (salted pig feet).

My father was born in Winneba on July 24, 1902. He attended the Methodist Elementary School where he passed the Standard Seven School Leaving Certificate Examination. He continued his education at the West African College of Music and Commerce established and run by Professor Charles Graves, a noted educationist, at Cape Coast where he specialized in music, accountancy, and bookkeeping. He was a good chorister and continued as a member of the choir on the completion of his secondary education. It was while he was a chorister that he met my mother. He was attractive to young ladies and was quite a *bon vivant*.

His courting of my mother was vigorously opposed by my grandfather, Mr. Quaison, who was very much attached to his daughters and was suspicious of young men who tried to court his daughters. He wanted to be sure that any young man who married any of his daughters would take good care of them.

At this time in 1923, the Paramount Chief of Winneba was my father's elder brother. Therefore, when my grandfather became unbending and difficult, my father who was really in love with my mother, solicited the assistance of his elder brother. The Chief, Nana Ayirebi-Acquah III, popularly known as Kow Sackey, intervened by sending a delegation to seek the hand of my mother in marriage. My mother told me that she was also in love with my father. One day, when she saw a group of people coming to her father's residence: two elderly men, one holding a linguist stick, and two old ladies, she knew that her fate was going to be decided. The delegation duly conveyed the greetings of Nana Ayirebi-Acquah III and explained the purpose of their visit to Mr. Quaison. Mr. Quaison was then staying at the house of Mr. Kwamena John Ghartey, son of King Ghartey IV of the Fante Confederacy fame, who had been Chief of Winneba from 1871 to 1897. Certain customary rites were performed and my grandfather agreed to convey his reply in due course. In the meantime, he was discreetly advised to vacate his opposition because he could not possibly turn down the Chief's request without incurring his displeasure. He therefore sent delegation of elders to the Chief with the customary drinks conveying his reply in the affirmative. My grandfather had yielded, but not until he had been given a firm assurance that, if he was transferred from Winneba, my mother Alberta Quaison would be in safe hands. It so happened that Nana Ayirebi-Acquah III belonged to the Anona Clan, the same clan as my mother's. Thus, as traditionally persons of the same clan regard themselves as brothers and sisters, my mother's safety and security were guaranteed. And so, after all the customary rites of betrothal were performed, my father and mother got married. There were eight children of this marriage, five of whom were female. I am the first child of that marriage. My father turned out to be a polygamist, in the tradition of his fathers and brothers. When he died in January 1972, he left behind seven men and eleven women as his offspring.

3

And so, it was that I saw the light of day at Papa Kwamena John Ghartey's house at Winneba. After my birth, my mother moved to join my father at my paternal grandfather's house, popularly known as "Adanse"[1] where I grew up under very congenial conditions.

Winneba itself lies forty-three miles west of Accra, the capital of Ghana. It is a coastal town nestling around a bay and boldly facing the Atlantic Ocean. The inhabitants call it Simpa, after the founder and first Chief called Nana Osimpan or Tumpa. But the Europeans called it Winneba. The name Winneba is said to be derived from "Windy Bay", so-called by the Europeans who found the sea at Winneba rather windy. Jean Barbot, a Huguenot,[2] was supposed to have sailed by the "Windy Bay" in 1679 and to have seen some fifty huts.

Winneba must have been inhabited about the 16th century. According to Professor A. W. Lawrence who was formerly a Professor of Classical Archaeology at Cambridge and subsequently became a Professor of Archaeology at the University of Ghana and also the Director of the National Museum and Monuments in Ghana, the British built and completed a fort in Winneba around 1727. In his book, *Trade Castles and Forts of West Africa*, Professor Lawrence wrote at page 68 "The people of Winneba, where the English eventually (1812) destroyed their fort in disgust, after the murder of the Commander, had roused the Governor in Council twenty years earlier (that is in 1792) to declare: "the Winneba people have not only now, but for many years past behaved themselves in a manner that requires the severest punishment; they having at all times (within my recollections) acted as if they would be master and not subjects to the English nation."

---

1   Adanse remains a popular area that is well known at Winneba for Nana Ayirebi-Acquah III and his royal lineage. Adanse is from an Akan word, *"Odansew"* which means it is unique.

2   Huguenots were French Protestants who held to the Reformed, or Calvinist tradition of Protestantism. The term has its origin in early 16th century France. It was frequently used about those of the Reformed Church of France since the Protestant Reformation.

The people that the "Governor in Council" was referring to in 1792 are the Effutu people, being a mixture of Fantes and Guans, of which I am one. The Commander of the fort at Winneba referred to by Professor Lawrence was James Meredith. According to our history, the Chief and the people of Winneba got news of an impending attack by the Ashanti warriors. Therefore, they collected all their gold, jewelry, and other valuable possessions and took them to James Meredith for safekeeping, while their able-bodied men sallied forth to face the Ashantis. After the skirmishes were over, which resulted in the routing of the enemy, the Winneba Chief and people returned to claim from Meredith what they had left behind in the fort for safekeeping. Our history tells us that James Meredith had sent all the gold and other valuables to England and had refused a refund or compensation. And so, on one Saturday morning, the people assembled before the fort and drummed all night, warning Meredith that they would kill him the following day, being a Sunday, if he did not produce the gold and other valuables. In the meantime, the grasslands near the "Munyi" Lagoon at Winneba had been burnt. On Sunday, the Commander was seized and taken to the prickly grasslands, where he was made to walk barefoot while the people beat drums and chanted war songs. Meredith died as a result of this harsh treatment. News of this torture eventually reached Freetown, Sierra Leone, and a "Man of War" was dispatched to Winneba to destroy not only the fort but the whole of Winneba.

After the destruction of the fort, the Chief and his elders went to the "Man of War" by canoes to plead for peace. The peace offering was made by tendering gold to the captain of the ship. Today, Meredith Street in Winneba remains as a reminder of the former Commander of the fort. In the place of the fort, a Methodist Chapel was built. Once every year the people drum the same message to James Meredith on that fateful Saturday in 1812 "tomorrow we shall kill James" (*okyena Kwesi, yebokum*

James[3] – repeated many times), during the annual Deer Hunt Festival.[4]

The main occupation of the Winneba people is fishing and so the town is essentially a fishing port.[5] It was a busy seaport by the middle of the 19th century. Ocean liners and merchant ships anchored about one mile away. They brought imported goods like gunpowder, textiles, salted fish, salted beef, rice, alcohol, different types of canned goods, building materials and so on from Europe while they took away cocoa beans in sacks, cola, palm oil, palm kernel, spices, and other tropical products from the hinterland.

When I was a little boy, I saw "Albion" lorries loaded with cocoa and other products plying Commercial Street, then the principal thoroughfare at Winneba, towards the beach. These loads were carried in open canoes to the ships. They returned loaded with imported cargo. The beach was a real hive of activity. Warehouses, the offices of the Elder Dempster Lines (a shipping company), Lighterage offices, and the Customs Department were all located near the beach. There was also a busy Marine Police office.

The population of Winneba in 1924 was quite sizeable, with European and Syrian traders. The reigning Chief, Nana Ayirebi-Acquah III had been installed in 1919. He had attended Mfantsipim Secondary School and was to have been ordained as

---

3 Tomorrow Sunday, we shall kill James.
4 Winneba is widely known for its rich cultural heritage and nobody talks about Winneba without referring to its unique Deer Hunting Festival, popular among all festivals celebrated in the world and ranked number one by great historians. The 'Aboakyir Festival' is held in the first week in May and is one of a kind. A deer is hunted in the forests along the Munyi Lagoon by the two main parties: Twafo Asafo company No. 1 dressed in white, and Dentsefo Asafo company No. 2 dressed in red. Hunting for the deer is a competition between the two Asafo companies, and whoever catches the deer first has its unique interpretation. According to history and oracle, there will be more food from the forest if the Asafo company No. 1 catches the deer first. There will be more fish from the sea if Asafo company No. 2, should catch the deer first. The deer is taken to a big durbar ground, where seated is the chief and his sub-chiefs of the Effutus, his elders, guests, foreigners, and the subjects of Simpa both young and old. The chief rewards the young brave men and women who belong to the Asafo companies with money for bringing a deer home which make the festival a memorable one. The deer is a demand by the god of the Effutu, Nana Penkye Otoo. The deer is slaughtered and the blood is poured for the god and the meat is shared among the royal family.
5 The people of Winneba also cultivated onions along the Munyi Lagoon due to the seasonal nature of fishing.

a Methodist minister when he succeeded his uncle, Chief Acquah II who had died in 1916. As an educated Chief, he encouraged commerce by personally inviting his British friends to set up businesses in Winneba. He hobnobbed with Colonial Governors and District Commissioners. He was extremely fluent in English and for 12 years, was a member of the Legislative Council. This is why he attracted a lot of European firms and government establishments to Winneba. Under his leadership, much progress took place. Winneba boasted of coal-tarred roads, two hospitals, pipe-borne water supply and electricity, schools, modern markets, tennis courts, and even a nine-hole golf course, with a flourishing European Club. This was at a time when very few places in Ghana could boast of such amenities. The Europeans and Syrians living in Winneba carried on commerce, while some were of government departments. For a long time, the Syrians and Lebanese were referred to as "Portuguese". Because of the flourishing business, many people from other parts of Ghana and elsewhere were attracted to Winneba. The Methodist Church which had been established about 1835 provided a great meeting place and forum for the people. The schools were good, and it was at the time when the sons of fishermen were literally forced to attend school.

Today, Winneba has about 80,000 inhabitants. It boasts of 6 primary and middle schools, a number of day nurseries and preparatory schools, one secondary school, a nursing training school, the Specialist Teacher Training College, the Advanced Teacher Training College[6] and the National Academy of Music[7] Incidentally, the premises of the Advanced Teacher Training College were built and known as the Kwame Nkrumah Ideological Institute. The first President of Ghana, Osagyefo Dr. Kwame Nkrumah wanted the Institute to produce ideologues steeped in the socialist ideology, not only for Ghana but for other parts of Africa. In fact, freedom fighters from East, Central, and Southern Africa came to be indoctrinated at this Institute

---

6   Advanced Teacher Training College, is now a full-fledge Universty Of Education, Winneba under the 1992 Ghana Constitution.
7   The National Academy of Music (NAM) Central Campus, is now a department within the University Of Education, Winneba.

which they regarded as the Mecca of African Socialism. In 1965, Ministers of State and top senior civil servants were directed to come to Winneba to imbibe socialist ideas so that, according to the President of Ghana, they could understand the direction towards which the country was being steered. It was a moot question of whether they learned anything. After the coup d'etat which overthrew the Nkrumah government, the place was turned into a Teacher Training College. Even Dr. Kwame Nkrumah's statue embedded in a fully constructed marble column was destroyed under the personal supervision of Colonel Kotoka, the architect of the coup.

I spent my childhood and boyhood days at Winneba which a German friend years later described as "a large beach village". I was always at the beach. The problem in those days was that pipe-borne water was sold. There were also several wells at Winneba but the private owners sold the water, albeit more cheaply than pipe-borne water. Therefore most people, especially boys, had to sea-bath. I really enjoyed the sea. There was always the danger of boys playing truant at the beach and not caring to go to school the whole day. I had myself begun schooling at Winneba and continued at Agona Swedru some fifteen miles inland from Winneba to the north, where my father was engaged in the cocoa trade: buying cocoa from the cocoa producing areas like Nyakrom, Nkum, Odoben, Esikuma and Duakwa for his principals, F. A. Swanzy Limited. My parents were concerned about the standard of education at Swedru which was not as reputable as the Winneba Methodist School. What was more, they were worried about my unauthorized bathing in the local river called "Akora". One day I nearly drowned. I was lucky to be rescued by a Hausa man who was selling *kyinkyinga*, the local equivalent of *shish-kebab*. The Hausa man was one of the many spectators on the bridge who saw me being carried away by the river which was in full flood. All I can remember was that as I was swallowing mouthfuls of water and was completely helpless, I was suddenly seized by some firm hands and taken to land. The Hausa man saved my life. I was then seven years old. My parents were naturally agitated by this drowning episode and they immediately sent me back to Winneba. I was taken to the infant class one of the Methodist Elementary School.

Soon after, my mother and father returned to Winneba. By 1931, the Great Depression which was global in nature had had a telling effect on the cocoa industry. My father was personally affected and was on the verge of bankruptcy. He had received from his principals, huge sums of money which he had paid out to farmers. But the cocoa product had become useless for lack of effective demand in the face of the depression and so all that money had gone down the drain. My father's assets were sold. He later joined the Lighterage Company in Winneba and then the G. F. Overbeck, a German trading company in 1933 until 1939 when the Second World War broke out.

To take up the story of my education, I settled down at the Methodist school in Winneba. My teachers and friends called me Alex, as I had been baptized as Alexander in the Methodist Church at Winneba. Customarily, I had been named Kodwo Sei after my paternal grandfather. My father was never tired of telling me that the Sackey or Sekyi family was intelligent. He used to refer to my grandfather's younger brother, Kwamena Gyate, who became a notable Methodist Minister, known as Rev. Ebenezer Amos Sackey, whose eldest son, Dr. Ebenezer Amos Sackey trained in Faraday House and rose to become the first Ghanaian Chief Electrical Engineer. Even at that young age, I was being urged to be serious in whatever I did. But I could not help being a boy. Boys will be boys they say, and I enjoyed swimming and playing the truant. My maternal grandfather was also concerned about my education and liberally assisted my father financially. As a favor to the old man who never had male children, my father decided that Quaison should be added to my name – hence the Quaison-Sackey.

As I have pointed out earlier, like most boys of my age at Winneba in those days, the sea was my first love. Every morning most schoolboys had a sea bath before they went to school. I would go to the beach, armed with a bottle of fresh water. I would swim, clean my body with sand which acted like a sponge, swim again

9

and then come to firm land to wash myself with my bottle of fresh water, that is if my bottle had not meanwhile been stolen by some other boy! This daily ritual was scrupulously followed until I was about eleven years old when pipe-borne water was free. School usually started at eight o'clock in the morning and woe to a boy or girl who came to school late. You would certainly be punished, and teachers in those days did not spare the cane.

I enjoyed attending the Winneba Methodist Elementary School, perhaps because of the challenges posed to me. I got caned for going late to school. I got caned for failing to attend choir practice. I even got caned for missing a church service on a Sunday. Discipline was strict, and many a boy or girl who could not cope with the rigors of school discipline simply dropped out. I was determined to complete my elementary school education and tried as much as possible not to be caught in the meshes of school regulations. Looking back, I sometimes wondered why I persisted in going to school against many odds. Perhaps it was because of the many challenges. For one thing, most of my playmates were children of fishermen who did not go to school because their parents could not afford the school fees which, in my time, amounted to two shillings and six pence for the lower classes and three shillings and six pence from Standards Four to Seven, at which Standard you had to pass the School Leaving Examination. For another, there were too many distractions for a boy. One could easily play the truant, playing at the beach, searching for mangoes or climbing coconut trees, a feat in which I excelled.

But I was lucky. My parents and my aunts who were my guardians in the absence of my parents tried very hard to restrain me from becoming wayward. And the fact that I became a chorister instilled in me some amount of discipline. I was also lucky to have teachers who were really dedicated and took their jobs rather seriously, in every sense of the word. They were disciplinarians of the highest order and very devoted indeed. In those days, one teacher was in charge of one class. He taught all subjects, including English, arithmetic, writing, civics, Bible knowledge and nature study. Before classes began at eight in the morning and when the school closed for the day at four in the evening, it was the practice for the whole school to assemble, sing and pray together. Once a week, a day was set aside to teach the pupils hymns and songs. For Arts and Crafts, there was a specialist teacher who taught the boys handicrafts, drawing, painting and clay modeling, basket weaving, door-mat making with coconut fiber or sisal hemp, rope making, and carpentry. The girls had a Domestic Science teacher to teach them cookery, needlework, sewing, and a host of other things which now go by the nomenclature of Home Economics. Each pupil belonged to one of five sections into which the whole school had been divided: red, green, blue, gold, and grey. Competitions were held periodically to decide which section kept the best garden and/or flower plots. End of term sports competitions were also held. I belonged to the green section throughout my elementary school days. No wonder then that green has been my favorite color. I was not particularly good at handicrafts and my drawing was atrocious. I did quite well, however, in subjects like reading, arithmetic, English, and history. As far as extra-curricular activities were concerned, I played football reasonably well but I did not make the school team. My forte in sports was high jumping.

It is difficult for me to forget my teachers who influenced my life and career in later years. Teacher Arkorful taught me in Class One and, of course, he taught me how to add and to subtract and multiply, divide, and spell. Another teacher who had a profound influence on me was Teacher Yanney in Class Three. In those days, it was considered a feat to jump from junior school to a "higher grade". Teacher Yanney gave us a sound grounding and made it possible for me to pass to the Standard One "A" where the veteran Master J. W. Quainoo prepared pupils for higher things. I got my love of history and languages from Master Quainoo who had been Headmaster of the Methodist School at one time. As I write, he is an old man of 92, alert and spritely. I was then a 10-year old when I was in Master Quainoo's class and I was first in his class in order of merit during the third term. There were no quick promotions in those days, but I did so well in Standard One that I was promoted from Standard One to Standard Three. However,

11

my father did not like this jump, so I had to move back to Standard Two. In Standard Four, I was taught by Teacher C. T. Yeboah who had come to the school in 1937 fresh from Wesley College where he had trained as a teacher after completing Mfantsipim School. It was Teacher C.T.Y., as we affectionately called Mr. Yeboah, who drummed into me the existence of a secondary school called Mfantsipim. He did have a tremendous impact on me. After two terms, he had to leave for a higher assignment at Mfantsipim. His place was taken over by another Mfantsipim Old Boy, Teacher S. A. Amoah. Before turning 13 years, I sat and passed the entrance examination to Mfantsipim Secondary School, but my father insisted that I had to complete my elementary schooling by hook or by crook. There was an erroneous notion in those days that it was better to possess a Standard Seven School Leaving Certificate than to have nothing at all so that if your parents were unable to sponsor you for secondary school education, you would have something to hold on to. There could also be financial mishaps in the family while one was at the secondary school, and my father felt that if I possessed a Standard Seven Certificate, a mere white sheet with the imprimatur of the Director of Education, I could always brandish it and it would secure me a job as a clerk or some village letter writer.

I, therefore, continued to Standard Seven in 1940, where a bright old boy of the Methodist School who had performed brilliantly at Wesley College was the teacher, Mr. Robert R. Okyne, a dedicated and good teacher, had come to teach in Standard Seven the previous year and his pupils had done better than in previous years. Teacher Okyne was an effective teacher but he was a martinet. He instilled in us his love of school, love of Winneba, and love of the Gold Coast. He did not spare the cane at all. He tended to focus his attention on his bright students and singled them out for harsh punishment when they made, what he considered to be, unpardonable mistakes. The one great thing I learned from Teacher Okyne was precision in thought and deed. He had rented a flat in my aunt's house and so I was privileged to carry his books to school every morning. He insisted on our writing good essays. He seemed to like Dickens and so, some of us tried to read books like *A Tale of Two Cities* to acquire the

"Dickensonian" style. At the end of the day, Teacher Okyne had given us a solid foundation. It, therefore, did not come as a surprise that the Class of 1940 broke all previous school records by obtaining four distinctions. The color of the distinction certificate was blue and any student who obtained it had his or her name placed on the honors board of the Methodist School. The four boys who scored distinctions were David Adwoku Barnes who proceeded to Achimota Teacher Training College and subsequently became an Assistant Director of Education in the Ghana Education Service. He also served in Zanzibar as an Education Advisor loaned by the Ghana Government. Then there was Atta Annan Mensah who continued his education at Mfantsipim, Achimota, Trinity College of Music in London and Northwestern University in Evanston, and subsequently became Professor of Music at the Universities of Cape Coast in Ghana and Ilorin in Nigeria. The third person was Richard S. Essandoh who also went to Mfantsipim and Belfast University and subsequently became a Doctor of Medicine. The fourth person is the writer who went on to Mfantsipim, Achimota, Exeter College, Oxford and the London School of Economics, and subsequently became a Ghanaian diplomatist, rising to become Ambassador for Ghana at the United Nations, Cuba, Mexico, and the United States, crowning his career as President of the United Nations General Assembly and then the Foreign Minister of Ghana.

My boyhood days at the Methodist School and at home were exciting. Discipline at home was not as strict as at school. My father and mother were stern, and as a boy, I was in great awe of my father. My mother petted me somewhat, but she became mad at me when I showed insubordination or played the truant. She would either threaten that she would report me to my teacher or she would give me a surprise smack. I was a playful, but not a bad, boy. I tried to perform all my assigned daily chores before I went to school. They included sweeping the two bedrooms and a sizable hall and verandah which was all that my father's house contained. He had built this house in 1927 after moving out of his own father's house at "Adanse". My other tasks were to fetch water and fill the coolers, made of earthenware, and make my father's bed. When I came home from school at half-past four

13

in the evening, that is if I did not loiter around at school, (the school normally closed for the evening at four), I had to fetch more water, usually from a central pipe stand serving the people of a section of Winneba. As there were not many pipe stands in my time, there were usually long queues.

And so, my boyhood days went by. But I must point out that my home did not have as much influence on my character as my school and church. Most boys of my age and coming from so-called "educated" homes, looked up at the school as the very repository of everything that was worthwhile in the society. School teachers were regarded as paragons of excellence. Parents, themselves, mostly relied on teachers to mold the characters of their children or wards. And with the Methodist or any other mission school, the role of the church was all-pervading.

In the very important book, *The Roots of Ghana Methodism* written by my old master at Mfantsipim, Mr. Francis Lawrence Bartels (former Headmaster of Mfantsipim and subsequently Ghana's Ambassador to the Federal Republic of Germany), a lucid and detailed account has been given of the role of the Methodist Church in Ghana. Writing about the work of the Methodist District Synod of 1904 under the Chairmanship of the Rev. A. T. R. Bartrop, who had arrived from England on October 4, 1903. Mr. Bartels quotes the following passage at page 153: "The first duty of the Church is to make the great heathen populations "disciples" of Jesus Christ, and to teach them those things which make for true manhood and womanhood, and create a noble character and pure life. The well-being of the land, which its sons and daughters love so dearly, depends primarily not upon the success of the gold mines, the volume of its commerce, the condition of its industries and agriculture, or even upon a wise and just government. All these are important factors, but the very basis of prosperity is in the character of the people. If that be truly Christ-like, all else that is good and desirable will follow. This, the Synod recognizes, and to this end, it directs attention to those elements in preaching, teaching, and discipline, which present and maintain the nature, ethics, and duties of the Kingdom of God as well as its privileges; and which secure simplicity of worship, purity in Church life, and the loyal observance of our rules.

Education has always held a front place in the Methodist Church. It is part of the Great Commission and is another method of preaching. We may save the nation by saving the children. The Synod, therefore, urges that every effort be made to secure good educational results. There is a need for drastic reform in many ways; but in the endeavor to perfect secular instruction, the Synod emphasizes the fact that religious instruction must have even greater attention than heretofore. An educated brain and an unchanged, untrained heart make a worse and not a better child."

This re-examination of the evangelical and educational policies of the Methodist Church made by the Synod in 1904 must have had a profound influence on the subsequent goals of the Church. There was no doubt that boys and girls of my early days felt the full rigors of the discipline of the Church. Methodist elementary schools in the country were regarded as first-rate and, I feel proud that it was the Methodist School at Winneba that nurtured me and laid the foundations of my Christian upbringing and education. I was also lucky that from Winneba, I went on to Mfantsipim School at Cape Coast, a Methodist foundation which has turned out most of the men of whom Ghana can proudly boast.

Alex Emmanuel Sackey, alias Kweku Sekyi, Alex's father

The original Kodwo Sei after whom Alex was named

Alex E. Sackey to the far right.

Alex with his mother, Alberta Quaison, and his siblings

Nana Ayeribi Acquah, brother to Alex E. Sackey, Alex's father

Elsie with Nana Ayeribi Acquah in 1964 when he visited New York City

CHAPTER 2

FIVE YEARS AT MFANTSIPIM

In 1941 I entered the portals of Mfantsipim Secondary School situated on Kwabotwe Hill in Cape Coast. Mfantsipim's nickname is "Kwabotwe".

Mfantsipim had a rather chequered history before it got going on November 12, 1907, with the arrival of the Rev. W. T. Balmer. The School was established on April 3, 1876, as Wesleyan High School. In 1891, it became known as Wesleyan Collegiate School. The first principal was James Picot, who was about eighteen years old then and possessed only the College of Preceptors Certificate. James Picot was the brother of the Rev. Thomas R. Picot who was then Chairman of the Methodist District of Ghana (then the Gold Coast).

As the fortunes of the school waned, two illustrious old boys, J. Mensah-Sarbah, who later became one of the greatest Ghanaian jurists, and William Edward Sam, decided to do something to save it and found a truly national school. The "Fante Public Schools Ltd." was formed by several stalwart Methodists and the school was formally opened on April 3, 1905, as Mfantsipim. According to Mr. F. L. Bartels in his *Roots of Ghana Methodism*, pages 165 –167, the opening service was conducted by the Rev. A. W. Parker of Methodist fame. "The hymn "O God of Bethel" which remains the opening hymn of the school's Founder's Day Service was followed by the reading of Job 28 by "Father" Brown, President of the Aborigines' Rights Protection Society. "The school motto", said J. Mensah-Sarbah, when he rose to

23

speak, "is not in Latin or English, but in plain Fante, '*Dwen Hwe Kan*' (Think and look ahead). Three months later, it was decided on the initiative of Bartrop (the Reverend Chairman of the Methodist District) that the new foundation and the older Collegiate School should be amalgamated under the name of Mfantsipim. Mfantsipim began again, this time with 17 pupils, but soon got into difficulties in the face of keen competition from the Cape Coast Grammar School which was to continue until Egyir Assam (a former Assistant Headmaster of the Collegiate School who had retired in 1898) decided to rejoin the Methodist Ministry. On November 12, 1907, the Rev. W. T. Balmer, Principal of Richmond College, Freetown, reached Cape Coast on a commission of inspection of Wesleyan Schools on the West Coast, the aim: to promote the educational work of the Church, particularly in the matter of establishing secondary education on a firm footing, and to formulate a plan whereby the Methodist districts in West Africa could work together and feed a central college, in which ministers and laymen would be trained. Balmer found eight boys at Mfantsipim, whom he christened "The Faithful Eight". The School had only eight names upon its roll, and there was no staff – the last headmaster, the Rev. J. Delaney Russell, having left the country for his leave in England on July 18. These boys were meeting for mutual help. Balmer had found little support for his work at Richmond College, Freetown, most of whose students had, in any case, come from Ghana; but here, in Cape Coast, were "The Faithful Eight", as encouraging a group for him as were the Bible Band of thirteen for Dunwell (the first Methodist Missionary to arrive in Ghana in 1835) and with the added persuasion of Bartrop, he remained as the headmaster and built alongside Mfantsipim a Richmond College where the training of ministers was restarted."

When I went to Mfantsipim in 1941, it had already established its reputation as the oldest and best secondary school my country could boast of. For Ghana, Mfantsipim is the ancient seat of learning. Our main rival was Adisadel College (formerly called St. Nicholas Grammar School) and as Oxford regards Cambridge as "the other place" so does Mfantsipim look upon Adisadel.

I was quick to learn that the motto of Mfantsipim is *"Dwen Hwe Kan"*. Most "greenhorns" (that is how newcomers to Mfantsipim are called) would translate the motto, which is in the Fante language, as "Aim High" which did not earn them any marks at all. It is the literal translation as handed down by the great J. Mensah-Sarbah which was acceptable. The motto means "Think and Look Ahead" which underlines the ambitions and purposes of the founders and all those who struggled hard to build a great educational institution for Ghana. As my master, Mr. F. L. Bartels makes clear in his book to which I have referred, Africans like Egyir Assam, J. Mensah-Sarbah, W. E. Sam, R. A. Harrison, J. E. Biney and D. Myles Abadoo, and Europeans like James Picot, Rev. A. T. Bartrop, Rev. W. T. Balmer, and the Rev. R. A. Lockhart looked upon Mfantsipim as a precious gem possessed by Ghana. As Principal Balmer once wrote in a letter to the great J. Mensah- Sarbah, "I want to raise a generation of men in the Mfantsipim School who will be brave enough to face the problems of their continent, practically and unselfishly."

For a whole year, I was considered a "greenhorn" as was the tradition. On my arrival at Kwabotwe, I was directed to carry my boxes to Freeman House, which was to remain my house for the next four years. There were in my time four houses on the Hill. Freeman, which sported the green color; Sarbah, red; Balmer, blue; and Lockhart, yellow. Every "greenhorn" had to learn quickly the history of the school, the nicknames of the masters, and their foibles and susceptibilities. It was a must for a "greenhorn" to learn about "The Faithful Eight" but for whose tenacity of purpose Mfantsipim would have collapsed. It did not take me much time to learn that Sarbah House was named for J. Mensah-Sarbah, an old boy, by whose efforts the "Fante Public Schools Ltd." was promoted to found a truly national school named Mfantsipim. It was Sarbah who announced the motto of the school and explained its meaning. Sarbah was a great benefactor to whom Mfantsipim owes an eternal debt. Freeman House was named after Thomas Birch Freeman, one of the greatest Methodist missionaries whose length of service from 1838 to 1890 must have surpassed any other missionary's in 19th century Ghana. His work extended to various parts of the country. He first went to Kumasi on April 1, 1839, and his work in Ashanti was monumental. Balmer House was named after the Rev. W. T. Balmer who discovered "The Faithful Eight" in 1907. Inspired by those eight boys he decided to stay on instead of returning to Richmond College in Freetown and become one of the most effective headmasters Mfantsipim has known. One of "The Faithful Eight" was William Essuman Gwira Sackey. He was later known as Kobina Sekyi, a barrister, philosopher, and politician who became an ardent Ghanaian nationalist and a member of the Aborigines Rights Protectionist Society (APRS). He was the author of "The Blinkards" a play lampooning senseless imitation by Ghanaians of everything English. The fourth house was named after the Rev. R. A. Lockhart who became headmaster of Mfantsipim from February 1925 to March 1936. He was known as a fearless fighter for the rights of Mfantsipim in the face of the colonial government's partiality towards Achimota School. He was an effective administrator and a brilliant leader. He infused into Mfantsipim boys including Old Boys, love of school, and the need to maintain the highest of standards. Under him, Mfantsipim examination results were the best year by year throughout West Africa. According to Mr. F. L. Bartels in his book under reference page 200, "To Lockhart more than to any other person does Mfantsipim owe its unique position; founders of secondary schools in Ghana in the first half of the twentieth century wanted the new institutions to be modeled on Mfantsipim; among those were Accra Academy and Wesley Grammar School in the east, Fijai in the west and Tamale in the north."

There was a healthy rivalry among the four houses in sports – athletics, football, hockey, and cricket – in cleanliness, through Wednesday afternoon, inspections by the Senior Housemaster sometimes accompanied by the Headmaster himself, and in academic results. Freeman House was noted for providing the "Scholar of the Year" in my time at Mfantsipim. No "greenhorn" could settle down at Mfantsipim until he has been formally initiated into the school by the Senior Prefect or SP as Mfantsipim Head Boys were called. I still remember the day I was initiated on a Saturday night in January 1941 at the Assembly Hall.

The School Prefect in 1941 was Paa Kayper Mensah, who later read the Natural Sciences Tripos at Cambridge and became an accomplished poet and educationist. In the afternoon, all "greenhorns" were put in classrooms and were requested to give written answers dealing with the history and current events and gossip of the school. We were made to feel that our continued stay at Mfantsipim depended on the results of the examination. Many a weak-kneed "greenhorn" fainted for failing to answer the questions, convinced that they would be "sent down" for failing.

In the evening, each of us carried a broomstick and a bucket, and clothed in white bedsheets we paraded on the stage before the full glare of all assembled. The School Prefect, Mr. Kayper Mensah, moving around like some High Priest then intoned. Then the whole school assembled sang the traditional song welcoming "greenhorns" to Mfantsipim, ending in the chorus "O Greenhorns, Greenhorns, Greenhorns, Greenhorns!" We had been accepted as full members of the school, and from then on, we could walk around with our chests out as proud Mfantsipim boys. Of course, the bullying of "greenhorns" continued. Senior boys, that is, those in Forms 5 and 6 sent you on various errands, washing their towels and handkerchiefs or preparing *gari*[8] for them. And any boy who entered the school a year before a "greenhorn" could bully. I remember an incident on the very day of my arrival when a tall boy ordered me to carry his box to his dormitory and, generally, threw his weight about, asking me questions about Mfantsipim which he knew I could not provide the answers; "Who is 'Bui-buo'? Have you seen Caliban around?" Later on, I discovered that this particular boy had been in Form One and had just been promoted to Form 2B. I was placed in Form 2A! Apparently "Bui-buo" was a nickname given to Mr. Obeng-Addae who taught me English in Forms 2 and 3: and "Caliban" a character in Shakespeare's *Tempest* referred to Mr.

---

8 Gari is made from fresh cassava, which is grated and the excess liquid squeezed out. The remaining cassava is then fried over an open fire, on a broad metal pan that has been greased with a little palm oil, vegetable oil or other oil. The resulting product is crisp and crunchy to taste, and can be eaten with stews, soups, or shito (a local pepper condiment) and fish. Alternatively, it can also be soaked with water, milk and sugar and eaten as a sweet.

Quarshie who taught me geometry in Form 2. Mr. Quarshie is now a doctor of medicine.

I spent five glorious years at Mfantsipim. Unlike the elementary school where one teacher was in charge of one class, at Mfantsipim, there was a teacher for each subject. My first impression at school was to see boys from different parts of the country, moving in groups and speaking their languages. There were Fantes, Twis, Gas, Ashantis, Ewes,[9] Nigerians and so on, all at "Kwabotwe". What linked us together was English which we all spoke in our different intonations. I quickly made many friends, some of whom have remained friends to this day, like David Darko- Mensah (D. D. as we called him), Atta Annan Mensah who had been a friend from Winneba, E. K. Newman, Heman-Ackah, Napoleon Tamakloe, Kodwo and Kweku Haizel, Nana De-Graft Johnson, K. Y. Arkaah and K. N. Arkaah, Archie Ocran, and many others who still communicate with me on occasion. Such was the close bonds that Mfantsipim forged among its boys.

At Mfantsipim I learned how to use the library, thanks to Mr. F. L. Bartels, who taught me English Literature and Bible Knowledge in Form 2. It was really in Form 2 that a firm foundation was laid for us. I remember even now our Latin master, Mr. Michael F. Dei-Anang, taking those of us in Form 2A to the Assembly Hall to demonstrate and explain to us the four configurations in Latin. He would walk around the stage shouting *"ambulo"* — *ambulo* meaning "I am walking", "I am walking"; then he would sit down and say *"sedeo"* meaning "I am sitting down"; then he would get up and say *"surgo"* meaning "I rise"; he would then continue "ambulating" and then turn and walk towards the chair and say *"revenio"* meaning "I am returning. " Mr. Dei- Anang taught us Latin until we got to Form 4. By the end of Form 4, I was able to do "Unseens"[10] given to the higher forms. At the Cambridge School Certificate examination, I obtained an A which meant that I had a distinction in Latin and came top in that

---

9   Fantes, Twis, Gas, Ashantis, Ewes are Akan tribes who can be found within the 16 regions of Ghana.
10 The phrase "Seeing the Unseen" evokes the idea of the supernatural, and being able to see things which are outside of human perception. Thus being able to execute something you have not been taught or trained in.

subject. I have singled out Latin to show how Mfantsipim made sure that the boys started on a firm footing from Form 2. In Form 2, we had Mr. C. M. O. Mate, the then Senior Housemaster and Sports master to teach us History. Mr. Mate later left the school to become a government inspector of schools.

Apart from my masters; Mr. Bartels, Mr. Dei-Anang and Mr. Mate whom I have mentioned, other masters who taught me and made a lasting impression were Mr. Charles Quaye (History in Forms 5 and 6), Mr. Hugh Mills (Algebra and Geometry), Mr. George Ackumey (English Language and Literature in Forms 5 and 6) and Mr. Walton (Fante and Bible Knowledge). All Mfantsipim masters were dedicated and as most of them were themselves Old Boys, they insisted on excellence and inspired us to aim at great achievements. My favorite subjects were History, Latin and English Literature. Although I did well in Mathematics and General Science, I was certain by the time I got to Form 4 that I would plump for the Arts and not Science. As far as extra-curricular activities were concerned, I played cricket for my house and school (I was supposed to be a fast bowler), football, hockey, and table tennis for my house. I was also a high jumper and hurdler for my house and hurdled for the school at the Inter-Collegiate Sports Competition. I was not excellent at any of the sports, except table tennis which I played very well. After leaving Mfantsipim, I was tried in the Oxford Three to face Cambridge. I did not make it!

At Mfantsipim in those days, there were two particular clubs, Kwabotwe Circle and the Study Club, membership of which was considered prestigious. Kwabotwe Circle generally attracted those boys who were interested in history and public affairs. It was reputed to be the breeding ground for future politicians. Members were privileged to invite political stalwarts to Mfantsipim to speak to them. A notable politician and philosopher whom we invited or whose house we were permitted to visit was Kobina Sekyi, a Barrister-at-Law who was well known for his being an outspoken and uncompromising critic of the then colonial government of Ghana. Through the Kwabotwe Circle, I learned a lot about the characters in *Gold Coast Men of Affairs*, a book written

29

by Mr. Magnus Sampson who had received his Bachelor of Arts degree from Fourah Bay College, Sierra Leone, and had become Secretary of the Joint Provincial Council of Chiefs. Learning about the life and work of men like J. Mensah-Sarbah, J. E. Casely-Hayford (also an Old Boy who was the founder of the Congress of West Africa), and Dr. Nanka-Bruce influenced my political thinking to a very large degree.

The Study Club, which in my time, was under the chairmanship of Mr. F. L. Bartels, concerned itself with the Arts and Sciences. It was high-brow and like the Kwabotwe Circle, a boy was thoroughly vetted before he got admission. One memorable talk was by Dr. Hall, an English Medical Officer at Cape Coast, who spoke to us on "the human machine." It was more of a lecture on physiology but the treatment of the subject was exciting and must have decided some students to take up medicine as a career.

I belonged to these two clubs. I was particularly active in the Kwabotwe Circle and in looking back, my profound interest as a student of political history and international affairs stemmed from my humble membership in that club.

In my last year in 1945, I became the Senior Prefect (SP) of Mfantsipim. In those days, there was a convention that any boy who became the Secretary of the Saturday Night Entertainment Committee (SNEC) would invariably become SP the following year. Of course, it was not so in every case, and in 1943 a Day Boy, Mr. Joe C. De-Graft became the SP in 1944. My immediate predecessor, George Odamten, who spoke rather fluent English, was also a surprise choice for SP. The point about the secretaryship of SNEC was that the whole school voted by ballot to elect the secretary. I was so elected in 1944 as secretary. But the choice of the boys would not be the person preferred by those who chose the SP. The choice was made by a "College of Electors" comprising the Headmaster, the Senior Housemaster, Housemasters, and other members of Staff and the outgoing House Prefects led by their SP. The Headmaster would have someone in mind different from the Senior Housemasters or the outgoing SP's. To choose an SP, there were several considerations: the person must be academically sound, that is, he must be considered excellent by his peers (his classmates), his character must be good, he must be a good leader or have the makings of one and, above all, he must be courteous and must speak good English.

When my name was announced before the school assembled by the Acting Headmaster, Mr. F. L Bartels, after having announced the names of prefects and their assistants for the four houses, it was received with thunderous acclamation by the boys. It was on one morning in December 1944. At once, I became the acclaimed leader of Mfantsipim boys and upon my shoulders rested the discipline and general demeanor of all the boys at school. The House Prefects who were elected to assist me in the discharge of my responsibilities were: E. K. Newman assisted by P. E. Paintsil for Balmer House; D. D. Mensah assisted by J. Assami for Freeman House; T. C. Addo assisted by S. E. Attafuah for Lockhart House and A. A. Armattoe assisted by E. G. Biney for Sarbah House.

The crowning point of my stay at Mfantsipim was at the Speech and Founders Day in November 1945. I delivered the Senior Prefect's speech. From all accounts, it went down well. By that time, a new Headmaster had arrived in 1945 to take over from the Acting Headmaster, Mr. Bartels. He was the Rev. Alec A. Sneath who had been Headmaster of the school before in 1911. He told me after my speech that he would like me to be a minister of the Gospel. He had been impressed and he thought I had a gift of advocacy which should be put to the service of the Methodist Church. The general comment from the boys was that they were pleasantly surprised my stammer completely vanished during my speech because I used to stutter a bit. Suddenly, I had become Demosthenes, the ancient Greek orator who was himself a stammerer! Of course, the school was delighted that I was able to wrench from the Headmaster two days' holidays, instead of the traditional one after a Speech Day. Soon after the Speech Day, came the Cambridge School Leaving Certificate Examinations. There were forty-nine boys in my class of 1945, having started in Form 2 with 103 of us. A lot had fallen by the wayside. Some had left school because their parents could not afford to continue paying their school fees. Some had to repeat their classes. Others left the school because they simply could not keep up with

31

the pace and spate of work and others had died. Out of the 49 boys who were presented by the school, only one failed. We obtained 37 exemptions from the London Matriculation and the Cambridge Previous. I was one of the four boys who obtained five distinctions (i.e. "A"s) and three credits. The others were E. K. Newman, who is now Doctor of Medicine, Mr. J. A. Owusu (later to be called Owusu-Acheampong) who became Ghana's Chief Auditor and then High Commissioner to Australia, and Mr. Kow Esiboa De-Graft Johnson who became Professor of Sociology at the Universities of Ghana and Kenya.

And so, I had spent five years as a boarder at Mfantsipim! However, as we were about to leave the school, Mr. Bartels invited me, Mr. E. K. Newman, Mr. K. E. De-Graft Johnson, Mr. K. Y. Arkaah and Mr. E. G. Biney to return to the school for special studies. That great man was looking ahead and must have seen in each of us some potential that must be developed. Mr. Bartels never gave us any reasons for the invitation. All I knew was that I had become an SP and, perhaps I had become someone to be watched.

When we returned to school in 1946, we spent one term in a bungalow which was known to the school as Bungalow No. 4. Mr. Bartels gave us a reading list, and under his guidance we read and discussed literature and current issues. Unfortunately, after a term, Mr. Bartels left for the United Kingdom to be groomed to take up the Headmastership of Mfantsipim which at the time had been occupied by ordained ministers. We dispersed. Mr. Biney left Ghana for Manchester University at the instance of his father. My other colleagues left for their homes. I was invited to teach at Mfantsipim. It was a great privilege to become Assistant Housemaster of Sarbah House with Mr. Mante, now a Medical Officer, who was the substantive housemaster. I taught Latin, English, and Bible Knowledge in Forms 2 and 3. Meantime, I sat and passed the entrance examination to Achimota to further my studies for the London University Intermediate Arts degree (Inter B.A.). My class was called Inter '48 (Arts). Incidentally, I met at Achimota, my classmate and friend, Mr. E. K. Newman who had also passed the entrance examination to do Inter B.Sc.

Sekondi Students at Mfantsipim

Freeman Senior Dormitory 1945

The Study Circle 1945

Mfantsipim Athletes 1945

The Ahanta Group at Mfantsipim 1943

The Kwabotwe Circle 1945

CHAPTER 3

TWO YEARS AT ACHIMOTA

In 1919 a new Governor arrived in Ghana who from all accounts was a capable administrator with a great vision. He had been the head of the Survey Department in Nigeria before the outbreak of the First World War (WWI), and in 1914 he was the director of the Public Works Department in Ghana. This Governor was no other person than Brigadier-General Sir Gordon Guggisberg, KCMG, DSO. He was a progressive Governor who understood and respected the aspirations of the people of Ghana. Today, Takoradi Harbor, Korle Bu Hospital, and Achimota School stand as living monuments to the foresight and capability of Guggisberg. He regarded education in Ghana as the keystone to the progress and prosperity of the people. He, therefore, conceived Achimota College as an institution which would provide education for boys and girls from kindergarten to the university. Thus, the Governor gave the colonial government full backing to Achimota. Funds were readily available for the asking. No wonder, Dr. J. B. Danquah, the then doyen of Ghanaian politics, a philosopher and jurist, was moved to refer in a speech in the Legislative Council in the 1940s that Achimota had been the spoilt darling of the Government. He then said, "a golden key had been used to open Achimota."

And so at the time, I completed my secondary school education, Achimota College was the only place which provided post-secondary education leading to the Intermediate degree of the London University in Arts, Science and Engineering, Commerce and Economics. Such provision became available from the 1930s but because of the limited accommodation available at Achimota, it was not easy to enter the so-called "Intermediate" Department of Achimota. There was no university in Ghana at that time and the idea of the sixth form pre-University education was to become a reality in about 1949. I counted myself privileged to have been admitted to Achimota College after a competitive examination. As at Mfantsipim, I had met bright boys, some of whom had also obtained Distinctions in the Standard Seven Leaving examinations, so at the Intermediate Department of Achimota were some of the best students from the various secondary schools then in existence. I met students from Achimota School, like Samuel Sey, Alex Kwapong, Henry Richardson, Patrick D. Anim, and Sylvanus Amegashie; from St. Augustine's College, Cape Coast, I met Patrick K. K. Quaidoo and Kobina Bucknor; from Accra High School, I met Kenneth Kweku S. Dadzie and Daniel Annan; from Accra Academy, I met J. K. Okine; and from my own school, Mfantsipim, were E. K. Newman, A. T. Darko and Moni Heman-Ackah. All these and others from my Achimota days were destined to play important roles in the development of Ghana.

I shall mention, among those who have distinguished themselves, Samuel Sey who after graduating from the University College of Hull and the University of California at Berkeley rose to become Professor of Agricultural Economics at the Ghana University of Science and Technology, Chairman of the Ghana Cocoa Marketing Board, Deputy Governor of the Bank of Ghana, and Chairman of Barclays Bank (Ghana) Ltd. Alex Kwapong went on to King's College, Cambridge where he distinguished himself in Classics and subsequently became the Vice-Chancellor of the University of Ghana (actually the first black and Ghanaian Vice-Chancellor of the University of Ghana) and sub-Rector of the United Nations University at Tokyo, Japan. R. Sylvanus Amegashie went on to Newcastle University and became a chartered accountant and rose to become the Head of the School of Administration at the University of Ghana and Commissioner of Industries and, then, Lands and Mineral Resources. He later became a rather opulent businessman. Patrick K. K. Quaidoo proceeded to Bristol University for his degree and subsequently taught at St. Augustine's Secondary School in Latin and Mathematics before being returned to Parliament in 1954 and became an upright Minister of Trade in the First Republic of Ghana. Patrick D. Anim went on to Selwyn College, Cambridge where he read the History Tripos. He was subsequently called to the Bar at the Middle Temple. He became a High Court Judge, Commissioner of Foreign Affairs in the first military regime, and later a Justice of the Supreme Court of Ghana. J. K. Okine became a distinguished headmaster of his old school, Accra Academy. Dan Annan, after graduating in law at the University of Hull, was called to the Bar at the Inner Temple. He entered the Judicial Service of Ghana and rose to become a Justice of the Court of Appeal and subsequently became a Deputy to the Flight Lieutenant J. J. Rawlings, who seized power on December 31, 1981, and established the ruling Provisional National Defense Council (PNDC). E. K. Newman became a noted gynecologist at the Korle Bu Teaching Hospital. Ours was a generation bound to be involved in the making of the new nation of Ghana.

At Achimota, we were called "inter" students ("inter" being the shortened form of intermediate) and treated as university undergraduates. We were in reality reading London University subjects for the first and second years. We were all ambitious young men, highly motivated. During my time, only three ladies were reading for the Intermediate Arts degree and two studying science to become medical students. Miss Gloria Addae (later to become Mrs. Gloria Nikoi) read and passed "inter" Arts and went on to St. Andrews University to graduate in Economics. She became a distinguished Foreign Service Officer and later became Commissioner for Foreign Affairs in 1978-9. Miss Hayfron-Benjamin, one of the two science students, went on to become a doctor of medicine.

As the highest academic institution then available, the Intermediate department of Achimota offered a student great opportunities for academic, moral, and spiritual upliftment. A student could order his life the way he liked, provided he behaved decently within college regulations. There was no monitorial system as obtained in secondary schools. There was the Junior

41

Common Room (JCR) with its own President, and relations between Staff and students were correct and harmonious. For my part, I took part in many extracurricular activities. The JCR was an open forum for discussions on a variety of current topics. Seldom did we meet in the JCR as a student body. When we did meet, it was to debate portentous matters. One such occasion was when in 1948, in my last year, the leaders of the United Gold Coast Convention (UGCC), the so-called "Big Six" were arrested by the colonial government on the ground that they had incited the people of Ghana to riot and that their being at large was not conducive to the public good.

The UGCC was established at Saltpond in August 1947 as a national movement. The founders were George Alfred Grant, a wealthy timber merchant from Axim popularly known as "Paa Grant", Dr. J. B. Danquah, to be later dubbed affectionately as "the doyen of Ghana politics", Mr. Edward Akuffo-Addo, a noted barrister-at-law, who became Chief Justice in 1967-69 and ceremonial President of Ghana in 1970, Dr. Ernest Ako Adjei, a barrister-at-law who became Ghana's first substantive Minister of Foreign Affairs from 1958 – 1962; Mr. William Ofori Atta, later a barrister-at-law and Foreign Minister (1970-1973) and Mr. Obetsebi Lamptey, also a barrister-at-law. The Convention initially appointed Mr. Ako Adjei as the General Secretary. But, as a legal practitioner, Ako Adjei did not have much time to travel around the country to spread the news of the new awakening and so, he himself suggested to his colleagues that they should recruit a full-time General Secretary. On his recommendation, his friend, Kwame Nkrumah who was then studying law in England was appointed General Secretary, and money was duly sent to Nkrumah to return home after twelve years in America and the United Kingdom.

According to Kwame Nkrumah, "In December 1947 I returned to my country after twelve years in America and the United Kingdom. I had been asked to become general secretary of the United Gold Coast Convention, a political organization set up to secure independence in the shortest possible time. The UGCC was slow to make much impression on the country as a whole, probably because it was composed mainly of business and professional men, especially lawyers. My task as general secretary was to widen the membership and to form the UGCC into an active popular movement." (I Speak of Freedom by Kwame Nkrumah, page 1).

By January and February 1948 the national movement had caught on like wildfire. The economic situation at this time was serious with rising prices and inflation. Nii Kwabena Bonne II, Mantse of Osu Alata, who was himself a businessman, organized a boycott of textiles throughout Ghana. On Thursday, February 5, 1948, crowds of demonstrators marched through the streets of Accra carrying placards saying "we will not buy; wait until prices are reduced; time and tide wait for no man." The fever of rising expectations had afflicted the masses. The explosion came on February 28, 1948. On that fateful Saturday, a group of ex-servicemen determined to present their petition to the Governor at Christiansborg Castle, outlining their grievances of unemployment and general conditions of living as World War veterans, organized a parade. The government granted them a permit but directed them to follow a certain fixed route to the Castle. They, however, took another route, and at Christiansborg crossroads the police opened fire on these unarmed ex-servicemen, killing Sergeant Adjetey and another leader and wounding several others. The shooting naturally sparked off a pandemonium. There was looting and rioting and the burning of shops owned by European, Lebanese, and Asian commercial establishments in Accra. News of the demonstrations and looting spread to Kumasi and other principal towns where there were similar riots and looting. It was known that in Kumasi, Krobo Edusei, who later became a Cabinet Minister, led the riots. The Governor blamed the leaders of UGCC and proceeded to arrest Danquah, Akuffo-Addo, Ako Adjei, Obetsebi Lamptey, William Ofori Atta and Kwame Nkrumah, who had earlier sent telegrams to Mr. Arthur Creech Jones, the Secretary of State for the Colonies in England to send a special commissioner to Ghana to hand over power to the chiefs and people of Ghana. We the students at Achimota's "inter" department became incensed by the arrest of the "Big Six". Therefore, that special meeting at

43

the JCR was convened at the instance of a third-year engineering student, Anakwa, to decide on a course of action that would help the release of the "Big Six". It was a tempestuous meeting. There was a spontaneous decision to demonstrate on our compound. In the event, our demonstrations continued to the grounds of Achimota School across the road where some enthusiastic secondary school students joined us. I remember that some of us were singing "Ose ye ... Ododo doo dua"[11]; the principal, Charles Deakin, and other lecturers walked along, pleading with us "Don't kill the new University", "return to your rooms", "you are breaking regulations." On the whole, we were peaceful. However, our demonstrations sparked off other demonstrations at Cape Coast, where the students of Mfantsipim, Adisadel, and St. Augustine's had a field day. They could not be restrained and in the end, quite a number of students were dismissed. It was because of these dismissed students that Kwame Nkrumah founded the Ghana National College to enable them to continue their studies.

In 1948, there had been a political awakening whose consequences proved to be far-reaching. For my part, all these events happening in my country fortified me in my conviction that I would in the future have a role to play in the affairs of Ghana, but that I needed to be fully equipped intellectually and ideologically. Already at Achimota, even before the momentous events in the country that I have outlined, I had been nicknamed "the young statesman" and "the young politician" because of my fondness of talking politics. Our "inter" department did not lack in clubs and societies of all kinds. There was the Plato Club whose motto was "The unexamined life is not worth living." I was an active member of this club. We organized debates on current topics and sometimes on political and economic matters; lectures were also organized and we would invite an expert on a particular subject to speak. For example, Mr. Kofi Larbi, a barrister-at-law who had earned a reputation in England as a good criminal lawyer, defending dock workers, spoke to us on the state of the criminal law in Ghana. Dr. Ako Adjei spoke to us on "current issues." I

---

11 Together, we can.

44

remember that on this occasion the Assembly Hall was filled to capacity. Almost every "inter" student was present, as were our lecturers, both black and white. Ako Adjei traced the history of the black American from slavery to emancipation, highlighting his tremendous achievements since emancipation. He then opined that if the black man and woman in the United States of America could make great intellectual, political and economic progress, despite the shackles of racial prejudice and segregation, there was no reason why Africans should remain dormant and inert in our own land. He singled out for mention the achievements of people like Ralph Bunche, Paul Robeson, Dr. Dubois, Marcus Garvey, and Mary McLeod Bethune. It was altogether an inspiring speech, delivered with deliberation, precision, and clear diction. It was at this time in 1948 that I developed an admiration for Ako Adjei whom I regard today as one of my political mentors.

About a fortnight later we decided to invite Kwame Nkrumah to speak. He chose to address us on "dialectical materialism". Once again, we had a crowded hall. A number of British officials also came to listen to this man whom the colonial government had dubbed as a Marxist. He had a rather strange accent and spoke with pungent oratory. He spoke about "Thesis" and "Antithesis" and "Synthesis" and concluded that colonialism and imperialism represented the "thesis", the struggle for freedom and independence represented the "antithesis", and the resultant independence and birth of the new nation of Ghana represented the "synthesis." I remember Dr. Kwame Nkrumah shout that the people of Ghana needed "self-government Now" to manage or mismanage their own affairs. Never in the history of our sojourn at Achimota had we heard a politician speak with such pugnacity. The man was bold and forthright and the whole assemblage of listeners was electrified. In the course of his tirade against imperialism and colonialism, the British civil servants present left the hall one by one. I never forgot the excitement Nkrumah's speech produced among us, and for days on end students continued to discuss the speech, particularly that aspect where Nkrumah opined that "we prefer self-government with danger to servitude in tranquility."

45

It was soon after the visits of Ako Adjei and Kwame Nkrumah to Achimota College that the riots and looting and the arrest of the "Big Six", as I have described earlier, took place. Although the principal of Achimota did not take kindly to our demonstrations, there were no victimizations whatsoever. Students continued to perform their daily tasks and studies uninterrupted.

Apart from the Plato Club, there was the Apollo Choir of which I was a staunch member. Other clubs included the Jazz Club, the Dramatic Society, the Cricket Club, the Table Tennis Club, and the Students Christian Movement (SCM). As I could not be a member of everything, I chose to join the Plato Club because of my love for politics, the Apollo Choir because I liked to sing, the Table Tennis Club because I played the game rather well, and the SCM because I took my Christian religion seriously. The Apollo Choir broke the tedium of reading Latin and other textbooks. It was the vogue then to sing Negro Spirituals because while the times were themselves exhilarating, the words were inspiring: "Same train carry my father, same train, same train, ..."; "Were you there when they crucified my Lord ..."; "Gwine to ride up in the chariot, sooner in the morning..."; and "There were ten virgins when the bridegroom came ..."; these and many other spirituals were favorites. But we also sang some of Professor Amu's compositions. Mr. Ephraim Amu was an illustrious teacher in music at Achimota for many years. His songs like "Yen ara asaase ni";[12] "Asem Yi di ka, hena beka";[13] and "abosomakotre nam brebre"[14] are notable ones known throughout Ghana. In my time, the leader of the Apollo choir was Dr. Gabidou, an engineering student from Sierra Leone. He was a heavily-built man with a deep voice and was often seen around the college campus with a pipe in his mouth. He was ably assisted by Mr. Atta Annan Mensah, my friend, who was then studying at the two-year post-secondary teachers training college at Achimota. The choir was quite popular in Accra. We used to visit hospitals to cheer up patients with our songs.

---

12 This is our own land.
13 The issue needs to be addressed, Who will ?
14 The chameleon walks slowly.

Then there was the Student Christian Movement which brought together a number of students desirous of making a serious study of the Holy Bible. In addition to Bible study, we used to have discussions on topics like Free Will and Predestination, "What is the Will of God ?", and the meaning of the Resurrection and life after death. It was quite a lively Christian movement. Occasionally, we would invite our patron, Mr. Miguel Ribeiro who was a history teacher at Achimota. Mr. Ribeiro later became a Supervisor of Ghanaian students in London, Director of Recruitment, and later Ghana's Ambassador to Ethiopia, the Federal Republic of Germany, the United States, and Italy.

I was an active member of the SCM and rose to become its president. In that capacity, I attended the Ghana SCM annual conference at Aburi in Akwapem, near Accra. There I met students from other institutions, like the Akropong Training College, and made many Christian friends. It was at Aburi that I met Mr. Tony de B. Wilmot, a devout English Christian gentleman who was then an assistant colonial secretary of the Secretariat, the name given to the office of the Gold Coast Colonial Secretary to the Governor. Mr. Wilmot and I became close friends. Our friendship lasted for years.

Life at Achimota was thus full and eventful. Since classes began at 8 in the morning, a student woke up early to do general cleaning before a shower. Whenever I had a shower I would sing hymns at the top of my voice to the annoyance of one particular student who was an ex-serviceman and had been in active service in Burma. Lieutenant Tufuatse Kobina Impraim, whom we affectionately called "Leftie" kept complaining about my singing during the morning shower, not to me but to other students. But one day as I was showering and singing with gusto, "Leftie" shouted at the top of his voice from the veranda "who is that bugger disturbing my peace of mind?" That rebuke was enough to let me reduce my singing to humming. It was also a reason for putting some distance between "Leftie" and me.

Lieutenant T. K. Impraim left Mfantsipim, my old school, in 1936. He entered the civil service as a second division clerk in the political administration. At the outbreak of the Second World War, he enlisted as a private in the Gold Coast brigade which was part of the West African Frontier Force. He became a commissioned officer in the 81st division which saw active service in the jungles of Burma. Lieutenant Impraim was mentioned in dispatches. After the war, he took part in the Victory Parade in London. On his return to the Gold Coast where he was demobilized, he joined our class in 1946 to do a refresher course before he proceeded to Exeter College, Oxford where he did the Honour School in History.

Classes at Achimota ended by two in the afternoon. We would then have lunch, after which a student was free to organize his time, doing homework, preparing notes, playing a game, or indulging in some extra-curricular activity of his own liking. Some afternoons I played table tennis or attended Apollo Choir practice. But at most times I would be reading Latin or Literature or History or Economics, or I would be arguing with my colleague next to my cubicle. He was Mr. J. N. K. Taylor, an engineering student who had a flair for politics. It was a joy to argue with "JNK" as I called him. He had attended schools in Nigeria and had come to Achimota to do engineering. I knew his heart was not in engineering but his father had apparently "decreed" that he should become an engineer. At the time he was full of "Zik", the nickname of Dr. Nnamdi Azikiwe who became the first Governor-General and President of the Federal Government of Nigeria. "JNK" was strong of the opinion that "Zik's" National Council of Nigeria and the Cameroons (NCNC) was bound to gain independence for Nigeria and that "Zik" was the foremost political star in the West African political firmament. Through our arguments, I gained an illuminating insight into the work of the Congress of West Africa led by Casely-Hayford of Ghana, MacCauley of Nigeria, and Wallace Johnson of Sierra Leone. Incidentally, JNK did not become an engineer. I did not know how he fared in his engineering "Inter" examination. All I remember is that I taught in a post-elementary school which was founded by JNK. I later saw him in London reading Law. He subsequently became a State Attorney and a Justice of the Supreme Court. He and I still talk politics!

I must dispel any given impression that the Intermediate Department was an independent institution. It was part of the Achimota College, whose other components were the secondary school and the two-year teacher training department. The Intermediate Department used to share common services with Achimota School. It was in fact housed on the school compound and "inter" students were taught by Achimota School teachers.

During the war, students of Yaba College in Nigeria were brought to Achimota to join the "inter" students. The presence of the Nigerian students enhanced the standing of the "inter" students and gave the impression of a growing university within Achimota. It is now a matter of interest that it was the Yaba College of Lagos which after the war, blossomed into the University College of Nigeria and subsequently became the University of Nigeria, Ibadan.

In 1946, the year that I entered the "Inter" Department, "Inter" students were moved from the school compound to occupy the premises across the road which were used by the British Resident Minister of the Allied General Headquarters in West Africa during the war. The "Inter" Department thus achieved an autonomous status with its own Principal, Bursar, and academic staff, but it was still part of the Achimota complex. Charles Deakin, an engineering graduate from Cambridge, was the Principal and Modjaben Dowuona, an Oxford graduate in Politics, Philosophy, and Economics was the Bursar. It was envisaged that our class of 1946-48 would form the nucleus of a full-fledged university college, thus bringing to a triumphal culmination the dream of Brigadier General Sir Gordon Guggisberg, the Governor, that Achimota would provide education from the primary to the university level.

As I have mentioned, a student sat for the London University Intermediate degree examination after two years at Achimota. If he passed, he obtained what was commonly termed Inter B. A. (Intermediate Bachelor of Arts) for Arts subjects like History, English Language, English Literature, Latin, Mathematics, Greek, Economics, Geography, etc.; or he obtained Inter

49

B.Sc. (Intermediate Bachelor of Science) for Physics, Chemistry, Botany, Mathematics, or Engineering, or he obtained Inter B. Com. for commercial subjects like Accounting, Economics, Banking, Insurance, and so on. The "inter" degree was the highest academic qualification available in an educational institution before the establishment of the University College of the Gold Coast in 1949.

I studied at Achimota History, English Literature, Economics, and Latin. I must say that Latin was easily my best subject and I am certain that I would have read classics had I read Greek in addition at Mfantsipim. But I entertain no regrets as I also had a profound interest in History. At the end of my second year, I successfully obtained Inter B.A., a qualification which in my time was the envy of many a struggling student!

After the "inter" degree, there was no guarantee whatsoever that a student would proceed to a university unless his parents could afford to send him overseas for further studies or he obtained a scholarship bursary for that purpose. What most people did after obtaining the "inter" degree was to seek a job in the civil service or in some commercial establishment, or teach in a secondary school or college. I remember that as a student at Mfantsipim most of my teachers were "inter" degree holders, who were really birds of passage, waiting for an opportunity to go overseas for higher studies. While they were working, some would take correspondence courses for higher qualifications. Wosley Hall and "Rapid Results" correspondence courses were extremely popular in those days.

For my part, I applied to work in the civil service as a second division clerk. Although I had won a government scholarship on entering Achimota College, after passing a competitive entrance examination, yet I was not bound to work for the government. I could have returned to teach at my old school, Mfantsipim, but I considered a year's experience as a teacher quite enough for me. I wanted to know how the machinery of government worked, as I felt that I would be involved in government one day as a politician. Of course, the over-riding consideration was that, if I worked hard and efficiently as a second division clerk, I would have an opportunity of securing a government scholarship. I was, in the event, employed at the Secretariat, where I spent some six weeks learning how to copy-type and later learned how to receive and dispatch letters, file schedule papers, and minutes from desk officers, mostly assistant colonial secretaries. Merely reading minutes and dispatches from these seasoned offices on various topics ranging from rural development to mass education and community development taught me a great many lessons. They became useful in my future career as a diplomatist.

Long before I entered the civil service, there had been a scheme by which some effective second division clerks or junior civil servants, so-called, were sent overseas for various courses to improve their effectiveness and usefulness in the civil service. Scholarships were, in fact, awarded by the colonial administration and missionary institutions to qualified and deserving students to enter British universities for higher studies. I knew that awards were highly competitive, based upon a person's qualifications, school reports, and upon the criteria that the grantee's services would be available to the department of Government or educational institutions making the offer. It was the common practice for a student to sign a bond that after his studies overseas, he would return to Ghana and serve for at least five years.

In 1948, the Colonial Development and Welfare Fund which had been established soon after the Second World War (WWII) for all the colonies of the British Empire was then in operation in the Gold Coast. The purpose of this fund was to make money readily available for the training of graduate teachers, medical doctors, engineers, agronomists, agriculturalists, scientists, and technical experts. There was also established a fund to be administered by the Secretary of State for the colonies for the training of top administrators for the colonial civil service. It was when I was working at the Secretariat that I saw advertised in the Government gazette that any person in possession of the London matriculation or an exemption therefrom could apply for a government scholarship. I applied for a scholarship. I duly

51

received an official invitation to an interview at the Secretariat. I recall that there were about twenty people waiting to be interviewed on the appointed date. Only three awards were made that year. I obtained one.

The other two awards went to Patrick Anim, a classmate of mine at the "inter" department, who was also a Latin scholar, and Kenneth Dadzie who had read "inter" commerce in our year. Patrick Anim's scholarship took him to Selwyn College, Cambridge where he read History and Kenneth Dadzie proceeded to Queens College, Cambridge, where he read Economics.

The year, 1948, was altogether a very exciting and eventful year for me. I had obtained the highest educational qualification available in any institution in my country at the time. I had mastered the typewriter as a typist. Then I obtained the Secretary of State's scholarship to go to Exeter College, Oxford to read Politics, Philosophy, and Economics (PPE). And to crown it all, my parents engaged Miss Elsie Blankson for me to marry on December 18, 1948, which was also her birthday anniversary.

Miss Elsie Blankson, the eldest daughter of Mr. Oman Ghan Blankson and Mrs. Jane Blankson, became my friend when I was about twenty years old. Mr. Blankson was, for over thirty years, the Organist and Choirmaster of the Winneba Methodist Choir and, as a chorister, I used to be one of his favorites. Little did I know that I would one day be his son-in-law. Elsie herself was trained as a teacher at the famous Wesley College in Kumasi. During the school holidays, we met at Winneba.

In those days, that is, in the 1940s, there was a flourishing Students Union at Winneba to which belonged every student at a secondary school or training college, who was a citizen of Winneba or spent his or her holidays at Winneba. One of our aims was to inspire and assist students in the primary schools to further their education at post-primary educational institutions. We awarded bursaries to students who excelled in essay competitions the

Union organized for primary schools. To obtain the funds, we staged plays for entertainment. These were highly patronized and every year the Winneba literate community looked forward to the Union's play.

In 1943, the Union staged the "Buck Basket", a shortened form of Shakespeare's *Merry Wives of Windsor*. I played the role of Falstaff and Elsie had a role in the play as well. In 1944 we staged *Twelfth Night*. I was Orsino in that Shakespearean play while Elsie played Viola. These student activities brought us closer together during our holidays. By this time I was influenced by a book written by R. P. Downes called *From Friendship to Marriage*. I, therefore, entertained in my psyche that any girl who became my steady girlfriend would be my future wife. And so it was on that happy day of December 18, three elderly ladies were sent by my parents to Mr. Blankson's house armed with the usual customary drinks and money to ask for Elsie's hand in marriage to me. As custom would have it, Elsie's parents in turn had to consult the elders of both Mr. Blankson's family and Mrs. Jane Blankson's own family as to whether they accepted my family background and my person. The fact that it did not take more than a week for Elsie's parents to send emissaries to my parents signifying their approval meant that general acceptance of me by Elsie's family was swift. But years later after the engagement, I heard that there had been some opposition from the Blankson family on the grounds that Elsie's paternal grandfather and my paternal grandfather, who had been brothers-in-law, had been at loggerheads before their deaths without reconciliation. However, after there had been agreement all round as to our suitability to marry, a ceremony was performed at Elsie's parents' house which was tantamount to our engagement, at which drinks, a Holy Bible and an engagement ring were given by the emissaries of my parents to Elsie's parents. Elsie and I were properly engaged to marry. The following August 1949, I left the Gold Coast for the University of Oxford.

"The Future Statesmen"

CHAPTER 4

OXFORD DAYS

On August 29, 1949, I left Accra for London with my colleagues, Patrick Anim and Kenneth Dadzie by a BOAC[15] Argonaut airplane called RMA Manton. It took us 24 hours to travel from Accra to London, instead of the 6 hours which today's jumbo jets take to do. It was my first time traveling by air. As the plane was racing to take off, I held my breath with sheer curiosity, but once we were airborne, I felt relaxed without any anxiety. From the way my colleagues suddenly began to converse with me when we were airborne, it was clear that they had also been anxious. The journey itself was smooth with occasional bumps, but the experience was exciting. Over the Sahara, we strained to look out of the glazed window to see miles and miles of sand dunes with occasional oases. The plane touched down at Lagos airport, Kano, Castel Benito (as Benghazi was then called by the Italians), and Rome. Great was our relief when our plane finally landed at the London airport. We had arrived at the great metropolis safe and sound.

We were met by an officer from the Office of the Director of Colonial Students. A coach took us to Victoria Station whence we rode by taxi to Balmoral Hotel, a hostel for students, situated near Earls Court. We were thoroughly briefed about life in England and directed to the Colonial Office where we met the Director of Colonial Students, Mr. Keith. He confirmed that I had a place at Exeter College, Oxford where I could read Politics, Philosophy,

---

15 (BOAC) British Overseas Airways Corporation was the British state-owned airline created in 1939 by the merger of Imperial Airways and British Airways Ltd.

and Economics (PPE). I had hoped that I would be permitted to read Jurisprudence for my degree, but I was politely informed that it was not then the Colonial Government's policy to give scholarships for Law, as there were too many lawyers already in the Gold Coast. What the country needed was an efficient class of administrators, engineers, agriculturalists, and medical doctors.

There was still time before the start of the academic year and so I decided to sight-see London and enjoy its delights. Meantime, I wrote to Mr. T. K. Impraim, who had written to me from Exeter College congratulating me on my admission to his college, that I had arrived in London. He was kind enough to visit me at Balmoral Hotel and to inform me when we could travel together to Oxford.

In London, I did some shopping and bought the necessary clothes for the university. Sightseeing was made easier for me than it would have been by Kweku (Kuuku) Sekyi who insisted on showing me around London. He himself had come on holiday from Cork, where he was studying Philosophy and Law. He was also staying at the Balmoral Hotel and so it was a joy to have some "old coaster" on hand. As I was a newcomer to England, I was called JJC (Johnny-Just-Come) by those who had come to England a year or so before me. Mr. Sekyi and I traveled by "tube", the underground train, to a number of places all over London. We visited Westminster Abbey, St. Paul's Cathedral, the Houses of Parliament, the Tower of London, the Royal Albert Hall, Madame Tussauds[16] and Hyde Park, gallery of criminals in wax was fascinating as well as frightening. The gallery of famous men was really inspiring.

All the places we visited were of great historical interest. As I stood in the House of Commons, I had an instant dream of being a Parliamentarian and the history I had learned about Disraeli, Canning, Pitt the younger, Peel, Gladstone and Asquith kept coursing through my mind. It was an awe-inspiring chamber.

---

16 Madame Tussauds is a museum in London. It was founded by a wax sculptor; Marie Tussauds. It is a major tourist attraction in London which displays waxwork of famous and historical figures as well as popular personalities in the world

As for Hyde Park, I visited the Speakers' Corner a few more times to listen to the soap-box orators. I heard Mr. Kwesi Lamptey and Mr. Joe Appiah at various times making rabble-rousing speeches amidst heckling and booing and clapping. Both were "old boys" of my school, Mfantsipim. Joe Appiah definitely had the gift of the gab and seemed simply unruffled by the incessant heckling from an elderly English gentleman who kept shouting back at Joe, "Can you hold your self-government if we give it to you? Can you? Can you?" and Joe would go on raving and ranting "our forefathers ruled themselves in Ashanti before the white man came;" "we prefer self-government to slavery." I must say that I was attracted by Joe Appiah's raving against British imperialism and colonialism. Paradoxically, Mr. Appiah later became a barrister-at-law and married Peggy Cripps, the only child of Sir Stafford and Lady Cripps. Sir Stafford was a famous Chancellor of the Exchequer in Clement Atlee's Labor Government.

My days in London slowly drew to a close and I had to leave for Oxford. But I had enjoyed my short stay at the Balmoral Hotel. Never had I met so many West African and West Indian students in my life. There was a general solidarity and camaraderie among the students from the various countries. However, what baffled me somewhat was the occasional outburst of acrimonious exchanges of words between West African students, especially Nigerians, on the one hand, and West Indian students, especially Jamaicans on the other. Apparently, West Indians had the silly habit of referring to those of us from West Africa as "bushmen", while West Africans referred to West Indians as "sugar cane men" who did not know their roots. But, of course, this was a simple matter of lack of understanding and a dearth of proper communication. There had been individual friendships which have lasted until today. When I went up to Oxford, I befriended Hector Wynter, who was my year at Exeter College studying Modern Languages, and the redoubtable Dudley Thompson who was reading Jurisprudence at Brasenose College. Both men hailed from Jamaica and they were destined to play vital roles in the affairs of Jamaica. Hector Wynter became Editor of the newspaper "The Gleaner" and was Ambassador to Trinidad and

Guyana for Jamaica while Dudley Thompson became a noted senator and Minister of Foreign Affairs of Jamaica.

The trip to Oxford, my first, I have not forgotten. Mr. Impraim and I took the coach from Victoria Coach Station. Mr. Impraim gave me a running commentary as we passed through Slough, Amersham, High Wycombe, and a number of small towns on the way. We arrived at the Oxford coach station at dusk. From there we took a taxi to college. I remember asking Mr. Impraim, as we drove through Oxford, where the University was. My friend did not answer me at all, because he apparently read my thoughts. I had expected to see a campus a bit outside the city of Oxford with open fields and trees shielding the halls of residence and blocks of lecture rooms. Instead, I saw clusters of buildings and what I thought were church spires, narrow streets, and bicycles upon bicycles with their riders wearing black short-sleeved gowns over their coats.

We entered a gate when we got down from the taxi. We had sent ahead our baggage by train. As soon as we entered the college, Mr. Impraim intoned, as if in some chapel, "This is Exeter College; we are standing in the Porter's Lodge; the green lawn you see in front of you is called the quad. You are a freshman." A quad at Oxford meant quadrangle and a freshman or fresher was a student in his first year at the University of Oxford.

Introductions done, the porter showed me a list where I saw my name against which were written 3:6. I had the 6th room on staircase 3. As I entered the quad and made for my staircase, I felt as if I had come to an ancient monastery. Little did I realize that I had entered a beautiful college, established in 1314 for West countrymen by Walter de Stapledon, the Bishop of Exeter, a distinguished statesman of the reign of Edward II. I was indeed an undergraduate in a famous and ancient seat of learning, whose beauty must be discovered to be appreciated. As I stayed for three years, Oxford grew on me, and then I recalled what a science lecturer and preacher at Achimota College had once said in the Gold Coast, "Oxford is a spirit – you live it."

My two rooms in college suited me. There was a spacious study and a rather smallish bedroom. My study room had two doors, the outer one being an oak door. Tradition had it that a student was not to be disturbed on any account once the oak door had been bolted.

I felt miserable on my first night. It was a cold October night and I was completely unprepared to sleep in a room without a heater, which was what my bedroom lacked. Nobody had advised me to buy a hot water bottle and it was an effort to sleep in cold sheets and once I slept, it was a struggle to come out of bed when my "scout" woke me up the following morning. A scout was the name given to a college servant at Oxford. In Cambridge and Durham, he is called gyp. Tom was my scout. He had been a scout for thirty years before my arrival in college and he used to regale me with anecdotes about the college. He even informed me how students scaled the walls when the college gate was bolted at midnight. It was he who told me that the first Prime Minister of Pakistan, Lingat Ali Khan, lived on my staircase many years before me. Tom liked tiger nuts which I had brought from the Gold Coast and so I lavished them on him in return for favors!!

On my second day in college, I had to meet my Moral tutor, Dr. Dacre Balsdon, a Greats[17] man who had written a book about Oxford and was indeed an institution in the college. When I complained about my cold bedroom, he promptly advised me to procure woolen undershirts and wear them in addition to my pajamas. As he smiled at me, he said "You see why we Englishmen are hardy; we sleep in cold rooms." I did not know whether I had to take what Dacre said as a joke, but I felt my pride pricked. Throughout my stay in England, I did not wear woolen undershirts and underpants beneath my pajamas; I used hot water bottles in my bedsheets.

---

17 Literae humaniores, nicknamed greats, is an undergraduate course focused on classics (Ancient Rome, Ancient Greece, Latin, ancient Greek, and philosophy) at the and some other universities. The Latin name means literally "more human literature" and was in contrast to the other main field of study when the university began, i.e. res divinae, also known as theology. Lit. hum. is concerned with human learning, and Res. Div. with learning that came from God. In its early days, it encompassed mathematics and natural sciences as well. It is an archetypal humanities course.

I also met the sub-rector who was also the Dean in college to discuss my course of study. Mr. W. G. Barr explained the Oxford lectures and tutorials to me. My tutors in various subjects would indicate which lectures were necessary and which were optional. He said Lord Cecil's lectures in English Literature were popular and, as they would broaden my knowledge, I could attend some of them. But Mr. Barr emphasized that tutorials were a must and a diligent approach to them would be rewarding in the end. The College expected me to pass the first university examination or Mods, as Oxford called the first examination, at the end of the second term. In addition, there were "collections" at the beginning of each term. These were college tests which a student must pass in the subjects in which he had been tutored the previous term. I was informed that my tutor in politics would be Mr. H. G. Nicholas, a Fellow of the College. For Philosophy, I was assigned to Professor Kueale, also a Fellow of Exeter College. My Economics tutor was to be Mr. E. Ward-Perkins, Fellow of Pembroke College. I had Dr. Hla Mint, a Burmese economist who was at Medfield College to teach me Colonial Economics (as economics of underdeveloped countries was then called). For Moral Philosophy I had a professor of Magdalene College, while Mr. J. Richardson of Exeter College taught me Economic Organization. For university lectures, my tutors guided me in my choice from a list of topics and lecturers which was promoted for every term.

I found the tutorial system at Oxford very beneficial. I wrote an essay every week. The usual practice at the end of the tutorial was that the tutor who would have read your paper of the previous week would question you on a number of points and you would have to defend your position or some contention made by some author. A lively discussion would ensue at which the tutor would bring up fresh ideas to supplement yours. Your tutor insisted on giving you a long reading list and requested you to read as much as possible on any given subject. My economics tutor wanted me to "produce sparks", meaning I should do some original thinking. I always looked forward to my tutorials. The days on which I had no tutorials I spent reading at the Bodleian

Library or the Radcliff Library, which I found comfortable. At Oxford, an undergraduate was very much on his own and he had to organize his time in such a way that he would find time for other pursuits.

In my very first year, it dawned on me that Oxford education was something much more than lectures, seminars, classes, and tutorials. While these were vital for a degree, a lot more was required of a student – the acquisition of a vigorous independence of mind. Undergraduates bathed in the sea of accumulated knowledge and sifted wisdom of centuries. It was incumbent on them to make the most out of what Oxford offered. I met mature students in my time, some of whom were ex-servicemen or had completed their National Service at some outpost of the British Empire. There was rising expectation everywhere and we all looked forward to a brave new world, where there would be full appreciation of the worth and dignity of the human person. For me, the challenge my studies at Oxford posed was overwhelming. I came from the Gold Coast where there was a new awakening. I had no doubt that I had a vital contribution to make after my studies in the building of a new nation where there would be prosperity, unity, and peace.

The University of Oxford was a veritable beehive of activity. A freshman was often bombarded with invitations to join this or that club or society. My pigeon-hole was inundated with invitations and notices. The Cosmos Club, the United National Students Association, the Socialist Club, the Labor Club, the Tory Club, the West African Students Association, the Oxford Intercollegiate Christian Union (OICCU), the Students Christian Movement (SCM), the Oxford Union usually called The Union, the Majlis Association and other clubs too numerous to mention were all available for an undergraduate to pick and choose from. I still recall the occasion when I was effectively canvassed and convinced to join the Labor Club by Miss Shirley Catlin of Somerville College. She later became Mrs. Shirley Williams and a famous Minister of Education in a Labor Government. She did not see eye to eye with the Labor Party leadership and became one of the Labor party dissidents who resigned to found the

Social Democratic Party, which she represented as a Member of Parliament.

I knew that I could join all these clubs at Oxford, but had to content myself with a select few. I became a life member of The Union and joined the West African Students Union, the Labor Club, and the OICCU. For some reason, my English friend, Tony Wilmot, did not think that the SCM offered the kind of spiritual nourishment I needed and so he suggested that I join the OICCU instead.

I had a full life at Oxford. Both college and university life had their joys and pinpricks. At Exeter College, the communal life was pleasant. We had breakfast, lunch, and dinner in Hall, with its polished wooden tables and benches for college students and a high table for fellows. While breakfast and lunch were not formal and compulsory, college members were expected to dine in and we had to wear our gowns. I wore a Commoners gown, a short gown falling to the waistline with short sleeves and two long straps hanging loosely from each shoulder. Scholars and Exhibitors had their own separate gowns. Apart from dinners, students and fellows wore gowns for lectures, tutorials, and to most college and university official functions.

In those days, we in Exeter College had communal baths and toilets towards Broad Street. This meant that I had to walk across the quad from my staircase to reach these facilities. In winter, I did not cherish the idea of walking all this distance and I must admit that I was happier as far as this aspect of life was concerned when I moved into "digs"[18] in my third and last year. Otherwise, I enjoyed myself immensely in college. I got invited to the Rector's Lodge a few times. The Rector in my time was Dr. Barber, a wily looking intellectual with a patrician but warm personality. On each occasion of my visits, I drank port, a habit which was rather common at Oxford. My Politics tutor, Mr. H. G. Nicholas for his part, served claret which I liked.

---

18 Digs refers to an accommodation system mainly for students. This is accommodation rented by students who wish to stay alone, with friends and even in couples outside college premises.

On one occasion, after my Politics colleagues had had claret at the rooms of our Politics tutor, we got so tipsy that we gave vent to our feelings as we got down to the quad. Unknown to me, my colleagues had conspired to debag me. I was suddenly mobbed. I struggled and got free and I was chased around the quad until I was overpowered. All I knew was that I was being carried shoulder-high like an African chief but without my trousers! We ended up going down the basement to drink beer at the bar. Exeter brewed its own beer.

I played hockey and table tennis for my college. I was even tried for Oxford Three at table tennis. I also did a lot of punting and swimming during the summer. On my first May Day morning at Oxford, I observed tradition by waking up early at five in the morning and joining my friends at Magdalene College. We had commandeered a punt the previous night. At six o'clock in the morning as we sat on the punt, some melodious music sung by the Magdalene College Choir emanated from the top crowds of undergraduates and people milling all around the college and the Magdalene Bridge listening to the singing of the choir, presumably for the first time like me. Of most things at Oxford, you might do it once. The music ended suddenly, and there were picnics all around. My friends got into our punt and I punted them near to some meadows where we had our picnic. Punting was an art in which I was much practiced. It had to be done adroitly, otherwise, you fell into the river if your pole got stuck in the mud and you tenaciously held on to it.

Apart from going on the river during the summer for relaxation, I did some swimming at "Pastor's Pleasure", so-called because the legend was that some part of the river had been reserved for pastors, dons, and Oxford men to swim naked. I heard that there was a counterpart for ladies called "Ladies Delight" but I never ventured in that direction.

I did occasional walking to sample the beautiful spots all around. To walk along Christ Church and Merton Meadows or to stray into the Fellows Gardens at St. John's College or Exeter College was a treat. I was fond of showing off Exeter College Fellows

Gardens to my friends and visitors. I would take them to the garden and stroll up to the walk which was like a parapet. There we viewed Brasenose College (BNC), Radcliffe Library, the Sheldonian Theatre, Hartford College, the spires of the University Chapel, all in one sweep. It was on these occasions that I bathed in the spirit that was Oxford.

I attended the clubs which I had joined rather religiously. At the meetings of the Labor Club, I met budding socialist politicians some of whom became my friends. Through them, I became a member of a small group which met on most Wednesday nights in the rooms of G.D.H. Cole at All Souls. Professor Cole declaimed on workers' participation in industry, sharing ideas with management for the more effective organization of industry, and sharing in the profits accruing. I was fascinated by Professor Cole's Guild Socialism and became a devotee. It was during this period that I considered myself a socialist, vowing that I would one day work with workers and organize them to understand the part they had to play in industry and agriculture and in the general reconstruction of the economy and the society of Ghana.

I took my membership of the Oxford Union seriously. The Union had been the nursery of many English and world politicians and statesmen. I nursed ambitions for office at the Union, but I quickly discovered that to become an officer you had to literally spend all your time at the Union premises, wining, lunching and dining, and speaking "on the paper". To speak "on the paper" was to be listed to speak in a debate, either in support of or against the motion. To be listed to speak in a debate, you must have attracted attention by your powers of oratory or your potential as a good speaker, by making evident interventions from the floor of the "house". In a few cases, the fame of good speakers had gone up to Oxford before them as they came from Eton or Harrow or Winchester or Charterhouse. An African from "one of ours", as an old English lady had once referred to me, had not got much of a chance.

Once or twice after I had made interventions from the floor, I heard a remark that "here is another Nelson-Williams". This was an obvious reference to Mr. Nelson-Williams, an eloquent and debonair Nigerian who had read Jurisprudence at BNC and had risen to the enviable position of Secretary of the Union. I had missed him by a year or so, but my English friends would often mention his name to spur me on. One such friend was Robin Day who became President of the Union.

I did observe that some of the best speakers at the Union gulped some alcoholic beverage before they entered the "house". Like that Queen of the Netherlands, mentioned in Harold Nicholson's delightful book *Diplomacy*, who had insisted that any Ambassador accredited to her Court had "to be capable of absorbing large quantities of intoxicating liquor without being deranged", so did the Oxford Union seem to encourage many a brilliant orator to imbibe some amount of port or sherry or brandy before a speech. A bit of alcohol, it was believed, loosened the tongue! Speakers at the Union tended to imitate members of Parliament in their mannerisms and general demeanor. Such outbursts as "hear, hear", "Mr. President Sir", "shame", "rubbish", "sit down", "point of order" were part of parliamentary behavior which I learnt at the Oxford Union. Years later when I became a member of Ghana's Parliament, I felt very much at home because of my experience at the Union!

A lot of Oxonians whom I knew at the Union emerged as prominent personalities on the British or international scene. I cannot forget William Rees-Mogg of Balliol who was President of the Union when I joined it in the academic year 1949-50. My freshman's impression of him was of a solid and unemotional figure not to be trifled with. Although he was not my friend, I took an interest in what he would do in later life. I was not a bit surprised to learn that he had become the distinguished editor of the *London Times* and had become Sir William. Another Union member I very well remember was Robin Day of St. Edmund Hall (Teddy Hall to Oxonians). He succeeded Rees- Mogg as President of the Union and it was under his presidency that I spoke "on the paper". He became a distinguished member of the British Broadcasting Corporation (BBC) and his program *Panorama* became a popular feature and one which I enjoyed watching when I was working in London as a diplomat. He too became Sir Robin. Then there was Jeremy Thorpe of Trinity College. He was my year. He was superbly eloquent and became an effective President of the Union. That he rose to become the leader of the British Liberal Party and a good Parliamentarian did not surprise me. There was also Keith Kyle of Magdalene College, another eloquent speaker. The last time I saw him was at the United Nations delegates Lounge, where he interviewed me on Africa and the United Nations. He had become a journalist and was a special correspondent for a British paper. Others like Ivan Yates of Pembroke, Dick Taverne of Balliol who became a Labor Member of Parliament and a Cabinet Minister, but later joined, like Mrs. Shirley Williams, the Social Democratic party, and Raghavan Iyer of Magdalene, a brilliant Indian scholar, were notable speakers at the Union, whose gift of the gab stood them in good stead after Oxford.

I must put it on record that it was Robin Day, as President that I got noticed at the Union. I also got invited on occasions to the President's receptions before a debate. On one such occasion, I met Randolph Churchill, son of the famous Sir Winston. He chatted with me and wanted to know all about Africa, of which he knew next to nothing. On another occasion, I met the redoubtable Prime Minister of Southern Rhodesia (now Zimbabwe), Sir Godfrey Huggins. He and I got locked in an animated argument about self-government for the British colonies. He was at pains to make me feel that as an African from the Gold Coast, I was quite different from the African in Rhodesia. I tried to convince him that it was all a matter of opportunity and not a question of any inherent superior qualities that I possessed. He then propounded his "pyramid" doctrine that the white settlers would remain at the apex and offer leadership to the blacks who would form the base of the pyramid. He thought it would take 50 years for the Africans in Rhodesia to start climbing to the top.

This heated argument between me and Lord Malvern as he later became, took place in 1951. Ten years later, in 1961, it was I, as the Permanent Representative of Ghana to the United Nations, that challenged in the General Assembly the British delegation's insistence that the General Assembly could not discuss the question of Southern Rhodesia because it fell within the purview of Article 2 paragraph 7 of the Charter of the United Nations. I argued succinctly before the General Assembly that Southern Rhodesia was a colony, albeit a self-governing one, but the white minority of settlers could not presume to represent the black majority who did not even have a vote. I urged with great success for the General Assembly to accept with a thumping majority that Southern Rhodesia was a colonial issue and should be treated as such. I was also one of the outspoken advocates for the dismantlement of the ill-fated Central African Federation. Like Caliban in Shakespeare's *The Tempest*, I had been taught language by my British masters and I "knew how to curse".

As I have narrated before, it was under Robin Day as President of the Union that I made my maiden speech at the Union. This was during the debate about Seretse Khama's marriage to an English lady typist. What happened was that soon after leaving Balliol College, Seretse Khama, the son of King Khama of the Bamangwato tribe in Bechuanaland (now Botswana) decided to marry an English woman. This was against the express wishes of his people, especially of his uncle Tsekedi Khama, then Regent of the Bamangwatos, who maintained that the marriage was not acceptable as it was a taboo for the tribe. With the connivance of the British Government, which exercised protectorate powers over Bechuanaland, Tsekedi Khama banned his nephew from the tribe and would not permit him to enter Bechuanaland. Seretse Khama was, of course, the heir apparent to the throne. The whole episode was sensational and convulsed Oxford and England at the time. The Oxford Union was seized of the issue and the motion was to the effect that Seretse's marriage to an English woman was proper and that the ban was improper. I spoke against the motion, supporting the ban by Tsekedi. My speech was mentioned by *Isis*, the University journal as follows: "Notable among the speakers was Alex Q. Sackey (Exeter), who spoke with simple fervor". I subsequently became more enthusiastic as a member of the Union, but my other clubs also claimed my attention and time.

The West African Students Union was also a good forum where a student's *tour de force* in speech-making was noticeable. After all, the club was mostly concerned with political and economic matters affecting Africa in general, and West Africa in particular, and it was necessary that members should be abreast of the events occurring in West Africa at the time. Ghana and Nigeria were much in the news with Kwame Nkrumah, Nnamdi Azikiwe, and Awolowo stealing the limelight. We organized debates and discussions on issues which were topical. But we also had discussions on African culture, religion, and social change.

We were 25 students from West Africa reading different subjects and having diverse interests. For example, Ernest Amanor Boateng read Geography. He later became a Professor of Geography at the University of Ghana, Legon, and Vice-Chancellor of the University of Cape Coast in Ghana. Solomon Pratt read Economics and Statistics; he later became an international civil servant in the International Labor Office (ILO) and then Minister of State in Sierra Leone, holding various portfolios. Alex Kyerematen read Social Anthropology; he later became a Minister of Local Government in Ghana and author of the *Panoply of Ghana*, depicting the rich cultural heritage of the Ghanaian people. T. K. Impraim read History; he later became a District Commissioner and a renowned Ghanaian civil servant rising to become Deputy Secretary of the Cabinet and Head of the Civil Service. Eldred Jones read English; he later became Professor of English and then Principal of Fourrah Bay College. Richard Akwei read Politics, Philosophy and Economics (PPE); he later became a diplomatist and Ghana's Ambassador to Switzerland and the European office of the UN in Geneva, then Permanent Representative of Ghana to the United Nations in New York, and later Ghana's Ambassador to the People's Republic of China. Lastly, Tunde Lawson who also read PPE, later became a distinguished Nigerian public servant, rising to become the Secretary to the Cabinet of the Federal Republic of Nigeria. These are notable examples I have given to show the high caliber of the membership of the West African Students Club. I became the President of the Club in my last year with Eldred Jones as the Secretary. On the whole, West African students at Oxford in my time were highly motivated and were destined to play important roles on the African continent. I made many friends at the university, with some of whom I still maintain contacts. Friends like Mervyn Jaspan (now Professor of Social Anthropology) and David Jenkins made me conscious of the issue of race and set me on the track in search of racial harmony. Mervyn came up to Exeter College from South Africa where he had seen apartheid in action. He used to keep me informed of the different racial laws in South Africa and unashamedly told me that he could not invite me to South Africa to stay with him as a friend but only as "a shoe-shine boy." He never tired emphasizing the seriousness of the obnoxious governmental system under which the African was chafing. In the case of David Jenkins (also of Exeter College), he wrote to me a letter from Caux where he was attending a moral rearmament conference, apologizing to me for looking down on me as a black man. He was making this confession in his letter and begging me to forgive him because he had been brought up as a child to look upon Africans as savages. Up to the time I received David's letter we had been good friends, exchanging visits to our rooms and discussing problems together. Afterward, I became conscious, very conscious, that I was an African at Oxford.

Friends at Oxford who are still close to my heart are Heinz Hellin, John Black, and Peter Barker. Heinz Hellin, a college friend, became close to me when the two of us were tutored together in general Philosophy at Magdalene College. He was one year ahead of me but philosophy brought us together. His home in Redhill, Surrey, became my home and his mother looked upon me and my wife as her children. After Oxford, Heinz had a stint as a civil servant and then joined Unilever Brothers serving as a Director in a number of countries including Nigeria, Sri Lanka, and Thailand. It was when he was serving as Marketing Director that he and his wife, Ann, and children visited our home at Winneba, Ghana, and spent a few days with us. I am Timothy's godfather (Timothy is his second son). I have just recently visited him and Ann in Bramwell near Guildford in Surrey, England.

71

John Black read PPE at Trinity College. We became friends in our very first year. It was a purely genuine friendship based on mutual admiration. He was a bit retiring but very warm at heart and he did not think much of a lot of the undergraduates he met. I spent my first Easter holidays with him and his family in Cheltenham. We cycled all the way to Cheltenham from Oxford and back. It was a rare experience, riding through the Cotswolds and enjoying the delights of the English countryside.

It was during the same Easter holidays that John, David Jenkins, and I planned to walk along the Roman Wall. We met at David's home in New Castle, from where we visited Durham University, Hexham Abbey, and the York Minister. We then made for the wilds of Cumberland and walked on the Wall for miles. Each of us had a rucksack on the back containing some clothing, food, and maps. John was a pilot and map reader and he led us to spend our first night at "Once Brewed", a small inn, and then on to "Twice Brewed". At each place, we cooked our own food. I remember cooking groundnut soup and rice. There was some pepper in the soup which was too hot for my two English friends. But they ate it and said it was "lovely." I could sense their agony! We walked all the way from New Castle to Chesters, doing on the average fifteen miles per day. We formed an interesting trio – two Englishmen and an African singing lustily as we walked along. Some motorists became curious and slowed down to gaze at us or offer us a lift to where we had thumbed. We hitchhiked through the Lake District from Chester back to New Castle, where John and I bade *au revoir* to David and took a train to Cheltenham.

John Black became a Professor of Economics at the University of Exeter. Since leaving Oxford, I have visited him in Birmingham and Exeter and he got in touch with me when he and his wife visited New York. I am still in touch with him. Unfortunately, he has not yet visited Ghana to see my home.

Of all my English friends, only Peter Barker has stayed and worked in Ghana. For twenty-eight years he stayed in Ghana, first as editor of a monthly, *The New Nation* and later as a Presbyterian priest.

I first met Peter at an OICCU meeting one afternoon during the first term of my first year. He was reading history at Teddy Hall. He was instantly and genuinely friendly and I reciprocated. I invited him to tea in my college and he in turn invited me to spend my first Christmas holidays in his home at 38 Pope's Grove, Twickenham. He was a chorister at St. Stephen's Church near Twickenham and I joined the choir during the Christmas holidays serenading with carols from house to hospital. My love of the Choir of King's College, Cambridge, was first aroused at Peter's house on December 23, 1949, a day before Christmas Eve. I was sitting by the fireside with Mr. Charles Barker, Peter's father, listening to the radio when there beamed out melodious voices of the Choir singing "Once in Royal David's City". Apparently, it was a processional carol sung as the Choir was entering King's College Chapel. I was enthralled as they sang carol after carol. Papa Barker's "beautiful", "this is beautiful", as the choir sang summed up my own feelings that night. I was particularly overjoyed when the Choir rendered "In Dulce Jubilo". Since that night I have tried to listen to the Choir of King's College every Christmas Eve. If I did not spend my holidays in England, I played the latest carols by the King's College Choir.

Rev. Peter Barker has been an indefatigable Christian worker with the Christian Council, having taught for a number of years at the Okuapeman Secondary School at Akropong. His humanity and his ready assistance to whoever needs his help are outstanding. Whether he came to Ghana because of our friendship or because of the challenge Ghana offered, it has been difficult to surmise. But I can testify from my own experience of his person that he has been a man of God who has served mankind and loved his neighbor as himself, thus fulfilling one of the greatest commandments of our Lord Jesus Christ. He has sacrificed his own welfare, his wife's and his children's, to labor in the Lord's vineyard, without counting the cost. Sometimes, I have felt guilty because he was toiling in my country while I was, for most of the time, my country's envoy abroad. Thanks to God, whenever he could make it, he stayed at our house in Winneba. He has been a great influence in my life.

But apart from such kind friends I have mentioned from whom I have learned a great deal, Oxford itself had a profound influence on me, especially in my outlook and thinking. It was there that I had a peep into the British way of life. It was there that I developed a love of British institutions and British constitutional and political history. It was there that my Christian faith got jolted and I had a mental revolution regarding religion. It was there that my political ambitions got sharpened. It was there that I developed a vigorous independence of mind.

I went up to Oxford thinking that I was a Christian and a budding politician. What happened to my political ambitions will be reserved for a later chapter. But what jolted my Christian faith was a matter of great concern to me.

I had been brought up to regard reverend ministers and priests as models of elegance and perfection. When I discovered that they were fallible and even not up to the standards of conduct inculcated in me in the Gold Coast, I became palpably disenchanted.

At the Methodist elementary school, I was caned when I failed to go to church. At Mfantsipim School, it was compulsory to attend church. We marched to Wesley Chapel every Sunday morning in the sun, a distance of about three miles. If I did not attend Wesley, I had to work in a village near Cape Coast as a member of the Mfantsipim Evangelical Group (MEG), preaching a sermon or dispensing medicine, or cleaning a wound and putting medicated cotton wool on it and bandaging it. At Achimota, I was a staunch member of the SCM. At Oxford, I began to attend the College Chapel and also the local Methodist Church. But I had taken my faith for granted and I had not accepted Christ meaningfully and by faith.

The test of my faith came, when I attended church, especially in the London area, and I found pews empty with a few elderly people around, when I began to observe the behavior of people who claimed to be Christians but did not measure up to standards and when, again outside Oxford, I noticed color prejudice in some churches I visited. True, I had learned years before what Aggrey of Africa had once said that there was a vast difference between Christianity and "Church-i-anity"[19]. And if I had been more introspective and had accepted Christ, I would not have reacted the way I did. I stopped going to church and began to be suspicious of anyone who professed to be a Christian. It was a curious period of doubt and uncertainty and when I began to read moral philosophy, my doubt became complete. In a word, I was in a state of utter confusion. I was in that state until I graduated.

But it seemed that I was not completely beyond the pale of religious reasoning. As soon as I returned to Ghana, I wrote to my friend Tony Wilmot. Although I had followed his prescription by reading my Bible with the guide of Scripture Union daily notes which he had sent me, and read carefully a book Tony also sent to me called *Who Moved the Stone*, I still entertained doubts as to the need for religion at all. Like my friend, John Black who was an avowed atheist, I believed that the Jews of Europe would not have been massacred by Hitler and his cohorts if there had been God. How could six million Jews be killed just like that with God looking on?

As luck would have it, I had to return to England in 1954 barely two years after my return from Oxford to attend a conference on African administration at Cambridge and to undertake a six months' course for Labor Officers from different parts of the Commonwealth. I spent the Christmas of 1954 with John Black and his parents in Birmingham. It was while I was staying with the Black family that I gained an insight into my own religion, which changed my state of mind. Papa Black and I got into a discussion about religion one day. He informed me of his parents' plans for him to become a rabbi, being of the Jewish faith. He was a mathematical wrangler at Cambridge and had read about the various world religions. He reiterated what John,

---

19 Churchianity is "an excessive or narrowly sectarian attachment to the practices and interests of a particular church." For example, a dyed-in-the-wool Methodist who rejects any practice or belief that is not sufficiently "Methodist" in his view is practicing churchianity. The term is a play on the word Christianity; churchianity can become a replacement for true, biblical Christianity.

my friend, had maintained that no God would stand by in the face of Hitler's extermination of six million Jews. However, he went on to say that the Christian religion appealed to him immensely. Christ's precepts to turn the other cheek when you are struck on one cheek, love thy neighbor as thyself, and lastly, obey God and do His will were too profound to be ignored. Unwittingly, the old man had set me to think from a fresh angle. It was clear to me that if I could follow these precepts I would be Christ-like. After all, on reflection, my communion with God was personal and did not require the stamp of approval from any individual. Through an atheist, I had discovered the spirit of truth. I could not love my neighbor as myself if I did not know myself. I began then to examine myself and that was the starting point of my embracing the Christian faith as I know it today.

The last great influence on my life at Oxford was our wedding at the Park Lane Methodist Church in Norwich on April 7, 1951. Elsie, who had been engaged to me on December 18th, 1948, won a Methodist Mission scholarship to do a Diploma in Education at the Norwich Teachers Training College, then affiliated to Cambridge University. She came to Norwich in the summer of 1950. The wedding was conducted by Rev. Mr. Barnes assisted by the Chaplain of the Norwich Training College, Rev. Mr. Cyster. Elsie was given away by the Mayor of Norwich, Mr. Dickson, whose son was an administrative officer in Ghana. It was an exciting moment for me. Friends came to Norwich to attend the wedding from different parts of England. There was Henry K. Richardson and L. Y. Graham from Ghana doing accountancy in Norwich, Kwame Bosque-Hamilton, a good friend from my Achimota days who came from Nottingham to be my best man. My friends John Black and Peter Barker also came to grace the occasion. Elsie's friends from the Training College all came to the wedding, which was widely reported in the local press.

Thus, I spent three full and active years at Oxford. It was not easy to leave friends and well-wishers and tutors who had contributed to my acquisition of knowledge and experience. Mr. Bird and his family took very good care of me in my last year

76

when I moved from college into "digs" at 46 St. John's Street. My room was comfortable and I was privileged to have my breakfast in bed throughout the whole year! After school, I took a leave of the University and went down to London.

My wife also completed her Diploma in Education with distinction in the summer of 1952, and she and our son, Egya Akumbia, who had been born on September 10, 1951, joined me at 16 Park Road, Redhill, Surrey, where I was staying with Heinz Hellin and his mother.

Having completed our studies in England, my wife and I decided to have a real honeymoon on the continent of Europe to supplement the short honeymoon we had enjoyed at Oxford after our wedding in Norwich. Luckily, we had been invited to a Quaker Conference held at Harlem in the Netherlands. Therefore, we left our ten-month-old son with a private nanny who had seven English children under her care at home. It was our first trip to the continent of Europe and we made the most of it. We visited Amsterdam where we had a boat ride, visited F. Hals Museum[20] in Haarlem, and went to The Hague, Volendam, and Edam where we visited the famous cheese market. We saw the Great Dyke and crossed the Zuyder Sea.

The conference itself was useful. The theme was "Peace in our Time". There were young men and women from Yugoslavia, Spain, Greece, France, Germany, Holland, the Gold Coast, the United States, the Republic of China, England, India, the West Indies, Scandinavia, and Latin America. It was a veritable international gathering and by the time the conference was over, we had gained mutual understanding, respect, and the worth and dignity of the human person. At the very beginning, the young delegates from Yugoslavia would not talk to the Spaniards or the Greeks. Soon, there was harmony all round. We were all determined to fight for peace in our time.

---

20 The Frans Hals Museum is a museum located in Haarlem, the Netherlands. The museum was established in 1862. In 1950, the museum was split in two locations when the collection of modern art was moved to the Museum De Hallen (since 2018 called Hal).

From the Hague, Elsie and I took the train to Paris where we spent three glorious days before we crossed over to Dover and London to be reunited with our son. Incidentally, Egya looked healthy and cheerful, but we discovered that his hair was untidy and disheveled. Apparently, the English nanny could not manage the crinkly hair of an African!

At last, we received notification of our bookings on the MV Aureol which would sail from Liverpool in September. It was from Redhill that we left for Liverpool and home. It had been a terrific experience staying in England for three years to be prepared for the task ahead. I had seen something of Britain and Europe. I had acquired some little knowledge. I had received rude knocks of racial prejudice. I had come to appreciate classical music. I had made many friends. I had acquired a wife and got a son. I had had my doubts. Thenceforth, I was ready to face life with confidence.

Staff and students at Oxford University

Part of the tennis team at Oxford University

The Oxford University tennis team

Gold Coast Students' Norwich Wedding

Traditional Gold Coast costumes were worn for the wedding at St. Peter's Methodist Church, Park Lane, Norwich, on Saturday, of Miss Elsie Annie Blankson and Mr. Alexander Quaison Sackey. The bride —here seen about to sign the register—is studying at Norwich Training College, and the bridegroom is preparing for a degree at Exeter College, Oxford. They were formerly members of Winneba Methodist Church on the Gold Coast. (Report on Page 5.)

A press clipping of the marriage ceremony between AQS and EAQS

A colorful African Wedding that was the talk of the town

Punting with friends at Oxford

AQS and some friends at Oxford; all dressed up

Gold Coast Man Speaks At Oxford Union

By A "GRAPHIC" London Correspondent

Alex Sackey is in his second year at Oxford, studying philosophy, politics and economics. He is the eldest son of an Accra business man, and was born in Winneba.

He was educated at Mfantsipim School where he became head boy, and later at Achimota College. After that he spent a year working for the Secretariat in Accra.

Mr. Sackey is keen on sport and played cricket and soccer for Achimota. In Oxford he plays soccer, hockey tennis and table-tennis for his college, and is secretary of the table-tennis club.

Apart from his sporting interests he is keen on music and art, and finds that Oxford has much to offer in this line.

Being interested in politics he joined the Oxford Union,

Alex Sackey

society which has nurt many of the leading s ment of Britain, past and sent, and has spoken ther one of the debates.

He is also the secretary the Oxford University, \ African Students Club, flourishing club with nearl

A newspaper clipping describing AQS' maiden speech at the Oxford Union

86

AQS at dinner with friends from the Oxford days

CHAPTER 5

THE MAKING OF A DIPLOMATIST

LABOR OFFICER

On October 9, 1952, I left Liverpool together with my wife and little son, Egya Akumbia, by the *MV Aureol*, one of the passenger ships belonging to Elder Dempster Lines, bound for Takoradi. The voyage was our first experience of traveling by boat on a long trip, traversing the Atlantic Ocean. With a one-year-old boy on our hands we could not imagine the kind of experience in store for us. Elsie and I had indeed crossed the English Channel before from Dover to the hook of Holland and also from Calais to Dover. On both occasions, we were seasick. We were, therefore, terribly afraid that the long voyage would be irksome for us and our son.

As it turned out, we had the most delightful time on board. There were many West Africans who had completed their studies and were returning home to find jobs or go into professions. There were also British colonial officers returning to the "coast" from furlough. Consequently, Egya became a spoilt darling on board as the only black child among several white children. It was a joy to watch him playing with the other children and make incoherent noises understood only by children.

The first two days were rough at sea. We had a terrible crossing of the Bay of Biscayne. Therefore, some passengers kept to their beds with sea-sickness. Some of the faces I saw were sullen and apprehensive. But soon it was all over and the ship became alive with all sorts of activities.

Competitions were organized for deck tennis, quoits, and table tennis. There were variety nights and dancing parties. In sum, everything was done to make us feel comfortable and oblivious of the fact that we were at sea. Elsie and I enjoyed walking the decks and watching the billows as the ship plied along. Occasionally, we would sight another ship from far away, and, on such occasions, the *Aureol* would hoot a siren in greeting which would be reciprocated by the other ship. I also entered the table tennis competition and won my way to the finals, which I played against a gregarious and fine Nigerian gentleman, Michael Olunnide. I won the competition and got a beer tankard which I still keep. Several years later, Michael and I became golfing companions in New York City. When I saw him again in 1984, he had retired from broadcasting with the Voice of Nigeria and had established a second home near Brighton with his English wife.

The *Aureol's* first port of call was at Banjul, then called Bathurst, in the Gambia. On board the ship, we had become friendly with Mr. Sey, a Gambian policeman, who was returning home to take charge of the Gambian Police Band. He kindly invited us ashore and to his home. There, he treated us to a sumptuous meal of jollof rice. Then he took us around sightseeing before we rejoined the ship.

Our next port of call was Freetown in Sierra Leone. Even before the ship docked, there were several young swimmers performing all kinds of acrobatic feats in the sea. It was exciting to see these boys dive to retrieve coins which passengers threw into the sea from the deck. They were undoubtedly expert divers and gave us free entertainment which from our vantage points resembled the diving of the porpoises we had earlier on watched with admiration.

After Freetown, we began to feel some excitement welling up in us. We would soon see the Gold Coast shores and so, home. Indeed, within three days, the ship docked at Takoradi Harbor.

It had taken us twelve long but exciting days to do the voyage from England. As we disembarked, we sighted a large group of relatives who had traveled from Winneba and Sekondi to meet us. We also heard a brass band playing. But that was not for our benefit. It had been arranged for one of the passengers who had apparently been away from the Gold Coast for ten years and had come back home as a medical doctor! It was a hilarious homecoming for those of us who disembarked at Takoradi. The ship's last port of call would be Lagos (Apapa)[21] where the largest contingent of Nigerian passengers would disembark.

Apart from relatives who had come to take us home by special transport, there was also an official from the Social Welfare Department who had met us to ensure that our luggage was properly handled through customs, and to inform us that we were entitled to one month's disembarkation leave before we reported to the Government authorities.

I was at the time of my arrival in the Gold Coast not certain what I wanted to do. Although I was not bonded by the scholarship I won, I thought it would be wise to let the powers that be know that I had arrived from England. Of course, reports regarding my performance at Oxford had already been forwarded to the Gold Coast by the Colonial Office. I had obtained my B.A. Hons. (Oxon) degree and therefore I was a "scarce commodity" in the labor market. I had an aunt, my father's younger sister, who was insistent that I should apply for a managerial post with the United Africa Company (UAC), as that would afford her an opportunity of obtaining merchandise for her trading purposes. My maternal grandfather, on the other hand, felt strongly that I should re-enter the Civil Service, and gain experience before I plunged into politics, which was really my first choice of occupation. Thus, unlike the generality of my compatriots who found it difficult to find jobs, I was lucky to pick and choose what to do.

---

21 "Apapa" is a Local Government Area in Lagos, located to the west of Lagos Island. Apapa contains a number of ports and terminals operated by the Nigerian Ports Authority (NPA), including the major port of Lagos State and Lagos Port Complex(LPC). It was formally known as Monko Apapa

Frankly, it must be recorded that in those days before independence and even now, to some extent, it was an uphill task for the youth to choose a career. In many cases, he had no option whatsoever. For a young lady, it was the fashion to become a nurse, or midwife, or a telephonist, or a teacher, or a housewife. The young man had rather limited opportunities, especially when he had not succeeded in passing through elementary school, let alone obtain a secondary school leaving certificate.

To be candid, I believe that farming or fishing would have been a laudable and lucrative occupation for any ambitious youth who had completed elementary or secondary school. But the educational system was not really oriented to encourage the youth in the rural areas. The common outlook was that farming or fishing was an occupation fit for the illiterate and the old. Of course, it was the children or nephews of cocoa farmers in those days who became lawyers. There was an unstoppable drift of the youth to the urban centers, creating large pools of underemployment. Even skilled trades like carpentry, bricklaying, blacksmithery, and mechanical fitting were not popular with most school leavers. Not until the establishment of trade schools, like that at Asuamantse, did elementary school leavers feel encouraged to learn skills.

This is not to say that efforts were not made in the elementary schools to inculcate the high ideals of the dignity of labor. In fact, the school timetable provided for school gardening and handicrafts. But what was at stake was that no serious effort at job counseling was made and school leavers roamed at will looking for clerical jobs which were not available. This was to become a disgusting tragedy for Ghana which, since independence has suffered from a real dearth of intermediate skilled workers between the unskilled or semi-skilled workers and the top engineers or technical experts.

Thus, after elementary school, the vast majority of elementary school leavers did not have the benefit of secondary school education. A small percentage of school leavers went to secondary schools, teacher training colleges, or trade schools.

The many technical schools and polytechnics and technical/ secondary schools are latter-day additions to the educational systems to meet the growing demand for intermediate skilled personnel. Such was the limited availability of opportunities and facilities in those days that a school leaver simply had no choice. Financial constraints also played a major role. To relieve their back-breaking drudgery, parents were anxious for their children to find whatever jobs were going in order to earn some regular monthly income.

Amidst all this gloom the bright or intelligent students received scholarships, bursaries, or grants from the central government, a missionary establishment, or some rich and forward-looking local council like the Asanteman Council in Kumasi. What is more, some parents struggled hard to see their children or wards through secondary schools and higher institutions overseas. It is such parents who, long before the 1950s when the central government decided to train solicitors, per se, sent their children overseas since the 19th century to qualify as barristers-at-law. If lawyers then became a privileged group in the Ghanaian society, there should be no complaint. And yet a time came when there was a general outcry against lawyers and other professional men like doctors of medicine, architects, engineers, and accountants.

So far, I have been painting a certain background against which my own training and career could be viewed. I have dealt largely on the period before 1949 when educational facilities were limited and job opportunities were few. After the accelerated educational program introduced by the Nkrumah regime in 1951 and the establishment of the University College of the Gold Coast at Legon in 1949, school leavers could face a brighter future. More and more primary and middle schools reached the rural areas. Teacher training colleges mushroomed to train more teachers for these schools. Technical schools and trade schools were opened and a concerted effort was made to direct elementary school leavers to such institutions. Then there was instituted the Cocoa Marketing Board scholarship scheme from which children and the youth benefited as they received bursaries to secondary schools and universities at home and abroad. It was during the period of Kwame Nkrumah's government that there was a massive drive to educate the youth.

Every home in Ghana was affected by the educational revolution, when students were sent overseas to the Soviet Union and other Eastern European countries, to Germany, Switzerland, the United Kingdom, the United States, and Canada to do medicine, engineering, architecture and all kinds of professional training and trades.

I belonged to the generation before the educational revolution launched by the Nkrumah regime. Even so, my generation reaped the whirlwind of the colonial government's genuine attempts after the Second World War to produce efficient administrators, scientists, and engineers, in an effort to prepare the Gold Coast, so it was said, for independence. But in my time, quite a number of students from the elementary and secondary schools who with some financial assistance could have gone on to greater things, fell by the wayside. A student had to be of scholarship vintage or must have had parents with enough financial resources to help him in his education before he could achieve. Otherwise, lurking ambitions simply did not blossom. Aptly could one quote Thomas Gray:

> "Full many a gem of purest serene,
> The dark unfathomed caves of ocean bear Full many a
> flower is born to blush unseen And waste its sweetness in
> the desert air."

I was one of the few young men on whom fortune smiled. As I have already recounted, soon after leaving Achimota College, I became a second division clerk at the Secretariat at Accra on a salary of 120 pounds per annum which was supposed to be handsome for an African. A European in an executive position earned 450 pounds per annum. My counterpart who started working in the civil service after leaving the secondary school earned 72 pounds per annum.

When I returned from Oxford University on October 21, 1952, I took my grandfather's advice and decided to see Mr. Amishadai

Larsen Adu, who was then Commissioner of Africanisation in the Establishment Department of the Civil Service. This was my first meeting with the man who was bound to influence my career and my life in many respects. He welcomed me warmly and congratulated me on my academic success. He then informed me that I had been slated for the Administrative class and I was to proceed to Ho, in the Volta Region of the Gold Coast as a Cadet Government Agent. I politely asked Mr. Adu whether I could have a choice of department. The point was that my friend, Richard A. Quarshie whom I had met at Oxford where he was doing the Devonshire course for senior civil servants, had suggested the Labor Department to me. He himself was a Senior Labor Officer and he believed that I would be more useful as a Labor Officer.

When I intimated that I would prefer to join the Labor Department, Mr. Adu gave me a kind smile and said that I would be one of only four graduates in that department which was full of ex-servicemen. "But I am sure", Mr. Adu said, "that Jimmy Phillips will be pleased to have an Oxford graduate in the Labor Department. He himself went to Cambridge. Let me ring the Commissioner of Labor." He duly rang the Commissioner, a Welsh Trade Unionist called "Taffy" Jones and, from the conversation, I could gather that I had been accepted at the Labor Department. Mr. Adu gave me a note for Mr. Jones. I was pleasantly surprised that Mr. Adu had not objected to my choice of occupation. The man was perspicacious enough to understand that I had to be occupied where I could give of my best.

My interview with the Commissioner was brief but harmonious. He told me that he needed a young graduate like me in his department and exhorted me to work hard and follow the footsteps of the Senior Labor Officer, Mr. J.V.L. Phillips. He introduced me to the Deputy Commissioner, Mr. J. B. Heigham, a Cambridge graduate who received me readily. The third graduate in the department, also a Senior Labor Officer, was Mr. J. S. Annan, an electrical engineer whose trade union activities in the Gold Coast decided the colonial administration to appoint him a Labor Officer.

I started work on the very day of my interview with the Commissioner. I had to prove myself. I was employed as an Assistant Labor Officer on a salary of 650 pounds per annum in October 1952. After a stint at the head office in Accra, I was posted to Sekondi-Takoradi in January 1953. I worked directly under the Regional Labor Officer, Major S. Mackenzie, an ex-serviceman who was forthright in his manners but was fond of using swear words as was the worst of most soldiers. He was very concerned about youth employment and productivity and he specifically instructed me to pay particular attention to these matters in my work with workers and employers.

Takoradi was a busy port and had attracted quite a large number of school leavers and others from the rural areas. Most of these boys called themselves "pilot boys"[22], whose main ambition was to join a ship and become seamen. Crime, including petty thieving, robbery, and prostitution, abounded in Takoradi like any harbor anywhere. But these boys belonged to one of the most organized unions at the time: the Maritime and Dockworker's Union.

My duties as a Labor Officer were to assist in organizing unions, mostly house unions; conciliate in labor disputes between workers and employers; to inspect workplaces and factories and to check the work of labor inspectors in the Sekondi district which included the Labor Office in Cape Coast in the Central Region.

With the exception of the Gold Coast Miners Workers Union, the Railway Workers Union, and the Maritime and Dockworkers Union, most trade unions in my time were "house unions"[23] confined to their particular employment. My task was to advise workers to think in terms of national unions embracing workers in a specific line of employment. Instead of organizing the Union Trading Company (UTC) Workers Union, for example, all

---

22 **"Pilot Boys"** represents the "go-getters," global thinkers, and those who are ready to be the captains of their lives.

23 **"House Union"** is also known as Labor unions. It gives workers the power to negotiate for more favorable working conditions and other benefits through collective bargaining. Union members earn better wages and benefits than workers who aren't union members.

the workers in the commercial establishments could form the National Commercial and General Workers Union. The workers responded slowly to the prodding of the Labor Officers. It was also my task to explain to workers the necessity of exhausting all avenues open to them for negotiation before they embarked on a strike action. Where they failed to get redress through negotiation, I advised them to permit me to conciliate or request for arbitration rather than go on strike. There could be a trade dispute without necessarily resorting to the strike weapon, which I advised, should be used as a last resort. Thus, in the final analysis, the success of a labor officer depended upon his ability to prevent a strike, or in the event of a strike upon how quickly he could conciliate between workers and employers to enable them to reach an amicable and acceptable settlement of their trade dispute.

Major Mackenzie really gave me a free hand to handle management and the unions, and I only reported where I faced problems, especially from management, which in those days, was mostly expatriate. I often ran the risk of being suspected by both workers and employers: workers because they had heard that I had studied in the United Kingdom and they erroneously believed that I would be on the side of the expatriate employers; and by the employers, because I was an African. I somehow managed to dispel these suspicions quickly by always insisting on justice and fair play and by my personal contacts. I got on mightily with both sides.

One of the most radical unions in the country at that time was the Maritime and Dockworker's Union whose General Secretary was a young man called Kojo Addison. He had affected a Lenin-style beard and was parading as a Marxist. I enjoyed going to his union headquarters on Sarbah Road where there were always crowds of "pilot boys", seamen and girls. I goaded him into discussing Marxism and when he realized that I had strong socialist views, he had complete confidence in me. He consulted me on a number of matters such as registering workers for employment at the docks or for getting assignments to ships, and how to get his union members to pay their monthly dues regularly. There was no trouble from the maritime workers while I was at Sekondi-Takoradi.

But I had trouble from the Sanitary Workers Union, which consisted of workers who weeded public places and cleaned open gutters and removed the "night soil"[24] and rubbish from dust bins. The secretary of the union was a man called "Yaro de man" who I found difficult to handle. He was very much aware of the bargaining strength of his union and tried to exploit it at every turn. One day, Major Mackenzie rang to inform me that the Medical Officer of Health had reported a Wildcat strike[25] by the sanitary workers. I rushed to the scene of action at once and sought for Mr. Yaro. I had always felt that the lot of sanitary workers in the country was miserable and needed amelioration. For one thing, it was a crying shame that the Gold Coast did not have a good sewer system and that the government and the people were still employing workers to remove "night soil" instead of these workers working on farms and producing food or cash crops. The whole system was anathema to the people of the Gold Coast.

Therefore, I was at pains to convince Mr. Yaro that a refusal to remove "night soil" was not enough. It posed a danger to the health of the community, but then if they should go on strike, the objective was to prevail upon the government and employers to introduce a better system of sewage, like septic latrines or flush systems. To strike for more money or for the reinstatement of a dismissed worker did not answer the problem. On this occasion, a worker had, indeed, been dismissed for delinquency. Yaro de man had acquiesced in the cat strike without proper consultations or negotiations. He was a powerful trade unionist, always suspicious and seemingly intractable in his dealings with employers. When I intervened, he was still adamant and stated categorically that the strike would continue until the worker involved had been

---

24 "Night soil" is a historically used euphemism for human excreta collected from cesspools, privies, pail closets, pit latrines, privy middens, septic tanks, etc. This material was removed from the immediate area, usually at night, by workers employed in this trade.

25 **"Wildcat strike"** action, often referred to as a wildcat strike, is a strike action undertaken by unionized workers without union leadership's authorization, support, or approval; this is sometimes termed an unofficial industrial action.

reinstated. I then talked to the head of the health department. He was also adamant: the worker had been delinquent and when questioned, he had shown insubordination to a senior officer. Of course, I pointed out the danger of pollution and an epidemic facing the community. In the premise, I suggested that instead of dismissal, the worker in question should be suspended for a week. This would be a compromise. The health officer agreed. Surprisingly, when I sold the compromise to Mr. Yaro, he also bought it. The strike was thus averted!

By this time, I had spent six months in the Sekondi-Takoradi district and I had settled down to orderly progress in my work. My study of workers' attitudes had convinced me that they were not so much concerned about producing and improving their productivity as they were about survival by way of increased earnings. Therefore, I lectured union members on productivity. If they wanted to improve their bargaining power, they should increase their output of work. What was important was real income that is, what their wages could buy and not what they earned as such. If they organized their unions properly against the background of increased production, they would be stronger. I did not make much headway with them because they did not care about productivity and increased output. In those days, food was abundant and comparatively cheap, and with prudent management, a worker with an industrious wife could make ends meet. My lecture on productivity, minimum wage, strong bargaining power, and subsistence level was all an exercise in futility in the early 1950s.

After six months' stay in Sekondi-Takoradi, I was posted to Tarkwa as a Labor Officer. But before I left, there was a strike on my hands. On the coronation day of Queen Elizabeth II of England, the Municipal and Transport Workers at Sekondi went on strike over the dismissal of two of their colleagues. Thus, instead of sitting by my radio with my family listening to the coronation ceremonial proceedings, I was busy settling a strike. My presence as a Labor Officer at the scene of the strike heightened the pandemonium. But soon I was joined by Mr. Arthur, who later became the Regional Commissioner of the Western Region. Between the two of us we succeeded in getting the Municipal

Council and the workers to agree on a settlement. Actually, we pleaded that the two workers involved should be reinstated with a strong warning to the union that the government would not tolerate strikes without proper negotiation and conciliation, and that workers should exhaust all avenues of reaching a settlement with their employers before they called a strike. Independence, we insisted, was around the corner and the country would need a strong but responsible trade union movement. Two days later, I left for Tarkwa.

Tarkwa and its environs were famous for their mineral wealth. There were gold mines at Tarkwa, Aboso, Abontiaksu, Bogoso, and Prestea; manganese at Nsuta and diamond at Dompim, Simpa and all over the Wassa Fiase traditional area. At Awaso, some eighty miles away was bauxite, mined by the British Aluminium Company. There was also a comparatively smaller gold mine at Bibiani. Apart from the mineral wealth, the Tarkwa area abounded in forests. And so, at Samreboe there was a large, prosperous timber industry, run by the African Plywood and Veneer Company.

The Tarkwa area had, therefore, attracted workers from all over the Gold Coast. Apart from workers in the various mines there were all kinds of people, including Nigerians and other West Africans, who were diamond "diggers" and "winners." There was really a large working population in Tarkwa and also a large contingent of Europeans and white South Africans who had come to Tarkwa looking for the "Eldorado."

Tarkwa was the headquarters of the Gold Coast Mines Workers Union, one of the most powerful and well-organized trade unions in the country. Its President was Mr. Kofi Foevie, easily one of the strongest pillars of the trade union movement. The workers had a reputation for toughness and intransigence. Therefore, the Tarkwa district, as a whole, was manned by seasoned officers. As a Labor Officer, it was a testing place. It could make or mar many an officer.

My family and I were housed at a bungalow on the hill in the Tarkwa residential area. The family consisted of my wife and my two sons (the second boy, Nana Bodo, had been born on December 23, 1952, at Winneba) and myself. We were later joined by my younger brother, Frank, who was at school. We settled down quite comfortably in our new home. What was frightening for us at Tarkwa was the incessant thunder and lightning. When there was thunder, it really thundered, shaking the whole place. And when it rained, it was a real tropical downpour.

Life was generally supportable. We were lucky in our colleagues from other Government establishments. For our next-door neighbors, we had Theophilus Tawia and his delightful family. Dr. Tawia was a lively and jovial gentleman who was the Health Superintendent of the Tarkwa District. Dr. Emmanuel Evans-Anfom was the Medical Officer. He and his wife Leo became our good friends. The Superintendent of Police was Mr. E. T. Madjitey, who eventually became the first Ghanaian Commissioner of Police and ended up as a Member of Parliament and the Leader of Opposition during the Second Republic of Ghana. The Assistant Superintendent of Police was Mr. John Harley, who also rose to become the Commissioner of Police and the first Inspector General of Police (IGP). He became the chief schemer and architect in the overthrow of Dr. Kwame Nkrumah, the first President of Ghana on February 24, 1966. The Police Inspector at this time was Mr. Ben Forjoe. He became the Director of Passport when I was Minister of Foreign Affairs and in 1979 when Flight Lieutenant Rawlings seized power for the first time, Mr. Forjoe became the Minister of Interior! It was at Tarkwa, therefore, that we started to have a solid family life, having moved from place to place at short intervals.

Alas! As it had happened, we had to stay at Tarkwa for about a year. But it was a busy period for me as a Labor Officer. Apart from the big mines and timber industries dotted around, there were the small businesses and factories which demanded the attention of the Labor Officer. Thus, in addition to trade union organization, negotiation, conciliation, and arbitration duties, I was also a factory inspector and had to supervise the Employment Exchange which, in my time, was in the very capable hands of Mr. Akumia.

In the course of inspecting factories, I had to go down a gold mine to look at the safety devices and other measures taken to ensure the safety and protection of workers. I went down a shaft in a big elevator at Abontiakom, accompanied by a South African foreman. We got down to about two thousand feet and went on a trolley on a trail which took us to several parts of the underground. We entered a mine with its roof supported by solid sticks. Dynamite was used to blast the rock and the stones were scooped out leaving a space like a cave. My South African companion and I crawled on our bellies in one of such caves, wearing steel helmets and finding our way by torch lights. We crawled a few yards but for me it felt like having crawled a whole fifty yards. It was an ordeal by choice. Since then I had nursed a lot of reverence for miners.

My duties entailed quite a lot of "trekking". In those days, most of the roads were laterite and some were quite rough which we dubbed as corrugated roads. I used to drive a Vanguard Estate car which had specifically been designed for rough roads. I had quite a sizable area to cover as my jurisdiction – from Tarkwa to Bogoso, Asankragua, Samreboe, Prestea, Awaso, Bibiani, Dunkwa-on-the-Offin, Sefwi Wiawso, Sefwi Bekwai, Enchi, Half-Assini, and Atuabo. Very often, I slept the night at some outlandish rest house. Sometimes, I had two punctures on one journey and I had to solicit the help of timber truck drivers to take me to the nearest vulcanizer. Invariably, I was returned home laden with red dust. It was all a great challenge for me.

I found time during my stay at Tarkwa to be a lecturer for the People's Education Association (PEA) in Government and Economics. I held classes at Tarkwa and Simpa. Some of my students gained by the lectures I gave and proceeded to further their education abroad during the scholarship boom of the Nkrumah era.

As I lectured, I also wrote. One of the articles I wrote for the dailies in 1954 was about the constitution of an independent Gold Coast. I was then concerned about the role our chiefs should play in politics. I thought that there was in the Gold Coast a traditional authority represented by the chiefs and an elected authority represented by politicians. Therefore, in my article which was fully published by the Ashanti Pioneer, I advocated that the Prime Minister should perforce be a politician, an elected representative, but the Head of State should be a ceremonial President held by a Paramount Chief. I wrote that the post of President should rotate every four years among the presidents of the various regional houses of chiefs in the country. I suggested that the first ceremonial President or Head of State should be the Asantehene (the King of the Ashanti); after four years, he should be succeeded by the president of the central region house of chiefs, and so on in alphabetical order of regions.

The article caused a furor among the politicians and my name was mentioned in the National Assembly as having arrogated to myself the role of a constitutional expert. Quite naturally, the Commissioner of Labor was questioned about me and he sent me a warning through the regional labor officer that as a civil servant, I should not meddle in politics. I could not fathom, quite frankly, how an expression of a constitutional opinion could be regarded as meddling in politics. But I had to succumb to superior authority.

I cannot possibly end this part of my career as a Labor Officer without mentioning two important national assignments which I undertook before I left Tarkwa. One was my appointment as the Secretary of an Arbitration Committee appointed by the Government to arbitrate the Bibiani Gold Mines dispute and report. The Chairman was Mr. Gwira, a noted Barrister-at-Law, and the members were the Chief of Shama, Nana Kow Freku, and Mr. F. E. Techie-Menson, a trade unionist. The Government felt compelled to appoint this committee because, as a result of a strike by the Bibiani Mines Workers, the employers had closed the mine completely, pleading unprofitability of the mines as an excuse. With such a large labor force laid off when the General

103

Elections of 1954 were in the offing, Dr. Kwame Nkrumah, the Leader of Government Business had to act swiftly. Nkrumah's Convention People's Party (CPP) faced a strong challenge by the opposition United Party (UP) which had a massive following in the Ashanti Region.

The task of the committee was to investigate root causes of the dispute, settle it through arbitration, and report to the Government. As Secretary of the Committee, I was responsible for all arrangements of its sittings and for writing the report based on the proceedings. We held meetings at Sekondi and Bibiani. The Mines Workers Union had engaged the services of Mr. James Mercer, a renowned barrister-at-law at the Sekondi Bar, and the Mines Employers engaged a firm of solicitors, Giles Hunt & Co. Both sides put their cases succinctly. It was clear that the workers were really receiving shabby treatment from their white foremen and that, in most cases, the top management did not know what was going on, as far as industrial and human relations were concerned. It was also true that the Bibiani Mines had become less and less profitable. The issue was how to save the mines by an infusion of investment and how to increase productivity.

However, the Committee was overtaken by events. General Elections had meantime been held and the CPP had won a landslide victory. Mr. F. E. Techie-Menson, the trade unionist member of the Arbitration Committee had been returned unopposed to Parliament by the Dunkwa constituency. With the establishment of a new CPP cabinet, I had to submit an interim report to the Commissioner of Labor for onward transmission to Government. I received instructions from my Commissioner to prepare for an overseas labor officers' course. As far as I can remember, the Bibiani mines remained closed for some time.

The other assignment proved the more difficult of the two. The bauxite workers at Awaso went on strike, claiming a wage increase, which the British Aluminium Company, the employers, had refused to countenance. There had been no proper attempt at negotiations. I traveled to Awaso. There I met the management

104

who claimed that the wages and salaries they had paid their employees compared favorably to what the mines paid their workers with similar skills and training. I then met the Union leaders. They told me that the workers needed a wage increase because they did not receive any bonus paid for excellent work and their living conditions were poor as compared to other mines. They agreed with me that what they should demand was the payment of the annual bonus and the provision of better amenities at their living quarters.

Armed with the workers' new stance, I arranged a meeting between the executive of the union and the management. A settlement was hammered out which satisfied both sides. I was pleased with my success, because strikes at the mines had an uncanny means of spreading or protracting. I had contained this one. I returned to Tarkwa.

No sooner had I settled down to other duties than I was summoned to Sekondi to meet Major Mackenzie, my regional boss. He informed me that he had been contacted by the management of the British Aluminium Company that there had been a fresh outbreak of a strike at Awaso. Apparently, one of the workers had been called a "black monkey" by a white foreman. Because of this insult, the other workers in the same workshop as the person insulted had "downed their tools" in retaliation without reference to the union executive or the management. News of this workshop incident had spread like wildfire and all the workers at Awaso had stopped work in sympathy. Major Mackenzie admitted that I faced an ugly situation and so, if necessary, I should solicit the help of a veteran trade unionist by name Anthony Kobina Woode who at that time resided at Esikado in Sekondi.

Mr. Kobina Woode was a CPP activist in addition to being a trade unionist. I had known and assessed him when I served at Sekondi-Takoradi. He was a shrewd politician full of native wit, but like most party activists during that period, he could only survive politically by indulging in back-stair intrigues. He had, however, come to grief when I contacted him about the troubles at Awaso.

105

Mr. Woode and his close associate and comrade, Mr. Turkson Ocran, had been sent by the CPP as delegates to a Socialist International conference in Vienna, but had proceeded to Eastern Europe without authorization from Accra. At that time, the Colonial Office, which controlled the external affairs of the Gold Coast, did not take kindly to this adventure by the two CPP activists into the communist camp and informed the Governor of the Gold Coast. Kwame Nkrumah, then Leader of Government Business, did not like this open adventure of the young men, as it might upset plans for the independence of Ghana, and so he ordered that the passports of Mr. Woode and Mr. Ocran should be seized. They were put on the carpet! Mr. Woode had not quite recovered from this jolt to his career when I approached him to accompany me to Awaso to help me settle this "black monkey" strike.

We traveled to Awaso only to discover that the strike had become complicated by a demand of the workers engaged in by one of their number, named Mr. Kofi Darkwa, that the company should pay the local chief an increase in the royalty paid yearly for mining the bauxite on their chief's ancestral land. Mr. Darkwa happened to be a CPP activist who nursed high political ambitions. He was taking advantage of an otherwise explosive situation to feather his own nest, because payment of a royalty was a completely different matter and could not be the cause of an industrial dispute, or so I thought. I would learn later that where politics is involved any issue could be exploited.

For sure, no employer, white or yellow, had any right to insult an African worker or any other African at all as a "black monkey". I was myself cut to the quick by this insult, but I was a labor officer determined to bring about harmonious industrial relations and, in this case, proper race and human relations. This incident naturally made me to recall Mr. David Jenkins's letter of apology that he had been brought up as a child to look down upon people of color. After all, as research sponsored by the United Nations Educational, Social and Cultural Organization (UNESCO) have proved, "race is less a biological fact than a

106

social myth."[26]The African's courtesy, tolerance, ready smile, and warmth of friendship towards other peoples should not be construed as servility. The white foreman at the British Aluminium Company had clearly overstepped his bounds. He had no understanding of the dignity and worth of the human person. I was determined to point out the damage he had caused to the smooth working of his company, but I equally decided that the question of royalty was purely a matter between the Chief's Council and the Company.

Mr. Woode and I had arrived in the evening but we quickly arranged for the members of the executive of the Awaso branch of the Mines Workers Union to meet us at the rest house where I had stayed. As it transpired later, my bungalow was the last place I should have met the union leaders, because they were later accused of having sold out. The leaders, in any case, had agreed that the workers should resume work on condition that the white foreman rendered a qualified written apology to the worker whose pride and personality had been wounded. I was also requested by the union to berate him for bad manners and to ask him to desist from using such insults in the future. As regard the question of royalty, the union leaders maintained that the Company had cheated the African for too long and they should be made to increase the rate of royalty paid to the chief and his people, even though they had been paying some taxes to the Central Government. After much heated discussion, the Union leaders agreed to advise the chief and his elders to initiate negotiations with the British Aluminium Company, provided I was prepared to render assistance to the chief, if necessary.

On the following day, I met the company's representatives, including the General Manager. They readily agreed that an awkward situation had been created by the foreman's calling the African employee "black monkey". The foreman concerned explained that he had been using such swear words to his African friends, but on that particular occasion when he used the expression complained of, he had been provoked. In fact,

26 UNESCO Man Changing the Concept of Race, 1945-65 VBN.

the African who had been insulted, had also used the term "white monkey" in the ensuing altercations between him and the workers present at the workshop. His explanation was not accepted and the Company ordered him to write the written apology as demanded by the Union.

As regards the payment of an increase in royalty to the chief, the Company informed me that the payment of royalty had already been agreed by the Company and the chief's ancestor, and there was no way by which either party to the agreement could renege on their undertaking. *Pacta servanda sunt* ("agreements must be observed") was their stand and they would not budge. I pointed out to the Company that a number of the workers were citizens of Awaso and also subjects of the chief and so the Company stood to gain, in the long run, if they agreed to a frank discussion on the issue with the chief and his elders. The Company agreed to talk to the chief.

Fortified in my conviction that the workers' demands had all been met, I decided to address the Union in conclave. The turnout was big. The workers and even officious bystanders gathered to hear what this Labor Officer had up his sleeve. Flanked by the Union leaders on a makeshift platform, I began to explain issues. I had barely uttered two sentences when someone shouted, "We no hear Oxford English." It was Mr. Darkwa, the party activist. People began to clap and shout. Having learnt the trick at a similar gathering of workers elsewhere, I shouted back "Make I broke um" – (may I speak "broken" or pidgin English?). There was a thunderous shout in reply: "Broke um" (speak pidgin English). I mustered all the ingenuity and courage at my command and spoke slowly in a language which must have been understood by all, because there were intermittent applauses and shouts of approval as I explained the agreement concluded between the Union leaders and the Company. Most of the workers were illiterate and came from various parts of the country, particularly northern Ghana, which was called the Northern Territories (NTS) before the independence of Ghana.

108

However, not all was smooth. In the course of my explanation of the agreement, the same Mr. Darkwa shouted at the Union leaders, "Stooges". He had apparently tried to convince the workers before the rally that the executive committee members had met me and Mr. Woode the previous night at my bungalow and so they had been "bought." I countered it by telling the workers that as a Labor Officer I had the workers' supreme interest at heart but it was also my duty to maintain good human and industrial relations with the workers, in the interest of the mines' operations and the country. I explained that the Company had been annoyed by the abusive words used by the foreman and had sternly warned him. He had been ordered to write to the worker concerned conveying his apology. I then waved the letter of apology amidst shouts of approval. I also explained that the chief and his elders on the one hand, and the Company on the other, had agreed to start negotiations on the increase in royalty. There was a great cheer. Many workers rushed to greet and shake my hand. The strike was over. I returned to Tarkwa.

Apparently after I had returned to my station the worker/politician who was, in fact, a strong activist of the local branch of the Convention Peoples Party did not rest on his oars. He was determined to take over the leadership of the Union. I thought Mr. Darkwa would create difficulties for the Company in the matter of the increase in royalty to the chief with whom Mr. Darkwa was on close terms. I soon heard that Mr. Darkwa had been elected General Secretary at an emergency meeting of the Union, contrary to union rules, because branch elections had to be held once annually. But then the workers had been urged to express a vote of no confidence in their executive committee and fresh elections had been held. As soon as Mr. Darkwa got into the saddle, he got the workers to demand that the white foreman should be deported because the insult of "black monkey" rankled. As for the increase in royalty the workers, with the connivance of some politicians, demanded that the increase in royalty should be paid promptly so that social amenities could be provided for the people by the traditional council.

I had by this time received a letter from the new Ministry of Labor, set up after the 1954 General Elections, that I had been nominated by the Government to proceed to the United Kingdom initially to attend a conference on African administration at Cambridge University in August 1954 and afterwards undertake the Labor Officers' course for three months organized at the instance of the colonial office. As I was about to leave Tarkwa, news reached me of a fresh outbreak of a strike at Awaso in which the newly-appointed Minister of Labor, Mr. A. E. Inkumsah had personally intervened. Politics had crept into the Awaso industrial relations but mercifully, I was out of the scene.

Whilst I was a Labor Officer at Tarkwa, I was at pains to impress upon the mine's employers and other big industrial establishments like the African Plywood and Veneer Company at Samreboi, the need for the provision of improved social amenities for the workers. The gold mines and the manganese mine at Nsuta provided accommodation for their workers but living conditions I found were abominable. It was an eyesore to find a family of six crammed into one room. No wonder productivity was low all over. As compared to housing provided for the European or white South African in the mines or other business establishments, the African's accommodation was poor. There were veritable slums in the mining areas, with all the attendant evils of drunkenness and prostitution. The British Aluminium Company at Awaso erred in the provision of adequate and decent housing for their employees. I had urged them during my visits to help workers educate their children and to provide better social amenities. Therefore, I was not surprised that Mr. Darkwa who was really intelligent and a concerned citizen took advantage of the prevailing conditions of inertia and indifference on the part of the aluminium company at Awaso. There was a protracted strike which must have hurt the company a lot, whatever huge profits that had been garnered in over the years.

The Conference on African Administration was duly held at King's College Cambridge in the third week of August 1954. It was a great privilege for me to be part of the Gold Coast (Ghana) delegation of four, ably led by Mr. A. L. Adu, the Permanent

Secretary of the Establishment Department. The conference lasted for two weeks. Among a number of matters dealt with by the conference were central planning and its role in budgeting and economic development; the structure of the civil service, the importance of the general orders (G.O.s) and civil service procedures, and the relationship that had to subsist between civil servants and political heads of Ministries (that is, Ministers of State). The colonial territories in the British Empire sooner than later would attain independence and it was necessary that there should be in each territory an effective civil service manned by well-trained personnel. There were going to be conflicts between permanent or principal secretaries and Ministers of State, unless civil servants understood their roles in the new body politic.

One could only guess what would happen for, as Mr. A.L. Adu himself wrote later in the introduction to his book, *The Civil Service in New African States*: "The complexities of policies in all spheres of government which results from the establishment of new nationalist governments demand the fashioning and installation of a new structure and machinery of government. This could not help but have the profoundest influence on the Civil Services, their organization, and structure. The changes that have had to take place have, unfortunately, had to be so rapid as to make carefully considered long-term planning impracticable. It was impossible to foresee the pattern that would be forced on the services by constitutional developments mainly because these were themselves forced on the colonial powers and because also of the rapidity of changes." The Cambridge Conference on African Administration had anticipated what was bound to happen.

For me, the highlight of the conference was a visit to Harlow New Town, which was then under construction. What impressed me most of all was the construction of the infrastructure – streets, water, gas, electricity and other utilities, telephones, shops, a school, a hospital –before the residential houses were built. A few months later when I was in charge of manpower services in the Department of Labour at Accra, I was able to discuss meaningful suggestions with the town planners and architects of the new Tema township and

111

port near Accra. The Conference itself was useful and instructive. I had met a number of administrative officers from all parts of the Commonwealth whose experiences and views were to be of immense help to me in my civil service career.

After the Cambridge Conference, I returned to London to attend the Labour Officers course. There were Labour Officers from Cyprus, Trinidad, Northern Rhodesia (now Zambia), Nigeria, Kenya, and Tanganyika. We attended lectures on the British Trade Union movement. The Transport and General Workers Union and the National Union of Mines Workers (N.U.M.) were singled out for mention as two of the best run unions in Britain at the time. Experts talked to us on the art of negotiation, conciliation, and arbitration. We also studied the operation of manpower services with special emphasis on youth employment, to which friend and senior in the Labour Department, Mr. J. V. L. Philips, had requested me to pay particular attention during the course. We spent six weeks in the London area, learning all about industrial relations, factory inspection, and employment services, including workmen's compensation, wages policy, and productivity. After the course in London, we were sent to various parts of Britain to see things for ourselves and acquire practical experience. We regrouped in London after six weeks in the "provinces" for an assessment of the course, before our departure to our various countries.

The tour outside London took me to Scotland – Edinburgh, Glasgow, Perth, and Aberdeen. At the Labour Offices of these places, I performed various duties to acquire practical experience. I visited mines, factories, youth employment offices, and some branch unions. I sat in and watched conciliation and arbitration at work. What I saw was not different from similar efforts at home, except that union leaders in Scotland behaved like experts at their work and faced employers at arm's length with confidence and astuteness.

In all, I stayed in Scotland for six weeks. I was highly impressed by the friendliness of the Scots. I learnt that the youth formed a vital part of the community, and came away convinced that any nation which neglected their youth did so at their own peril. Not only were they future leaders, but the quality of their training determined the kind of society that would in future emerge. As I was supposed to pay particular attention to youth employment in Britain, I devoted much of my studies and work to youth recruitment, training within industry, and prospects open to those youth that did not have the benefit of higher education. I found that the standard of education in Scotland was very high, despite the large influx of Irish workers who were mostly untutored.

But all was not work. Whilst I was in Scotland, I had an opportunity to attend musical performances, visit pubs, and see old friends. In Edinburgh were my friends Leo and Emmanuel Evans-Anfom, who it will be recalled, had been at Tarkwa while I was a Labour Officer there. Dr. Anfom had returned to Edinburgh, his old university, to do his fellowship of the Royal College of Surgeons. He and Leo were very fond of music and they took me to a few concerts. There was also E. Kofi Newman, my classmate at Mfantsipim doing medicine. In Glasgow, I met another classmate from Mfantsipim, Harry Bart-Plange, and then Kwamena Derban, from Winneba; both were studying medicine at Glasgow University. They have since become accomplished specialists in the medical field.

The Labour Officers Course over, I returned to London for the final assessment together with my Labour colleagues who had returned from other parts of Britain. The three months' course had been useful. We had filled in the various chinks in our armor, consolidated our experiences, and acquired fresh ideas for future work.

I spent the Christmas of 1954 in Birmingham with my friend, John Black, and his parents. That was the period that by God's amazing Grace, I had a serious discussion on religion with John's father, resulting in my return to accept the Christian faith with conviction. After three years of remaining in a religious state of suspended animation and critical self-examination, I was born again as a Christian. It was with a warm and delightful heart that

I left England in January, 1955 to return to the Gold Coast, my family, and my daily chores as a Labour Officer.

I had a delightful voyage on the motor vessel *Accra* belonging to the Elder Dempster Lines. I shared a cabin with a delightful person, Dr. Louis Simango, who had completed his medical course in England and was returning to Ghana. He was a quiet but amusing gentleman who insisted on our having "a quiet drink" before supper every evening of our twelve days' voyage to Takoradi from Liverpool. As if providence had wanted us to continue our friendship, his first posting as a medical officer was at the Winneba General Hospital. The voyage itself was smooth and happy. On arrival, I was met by my wife and my six months old daughter, Awo Aferba, who had been born on August 31, 1954 whilst I was at the Cambridge conference. The arrival of a daughter after my first two boys, Egya and Nana Bodo, was a very welcome event indeed.

I was posted to the Labour Department at Accra where I had to act in the place of Leslie Saigh, a Senior Labour Officer in charge of manpower services who had returned to his native England on furlough. At the same time, I was to become Secretary to the newly-formed Cabinet Committee on Employment. But once again, God had something else in store for me. Barely six months after settling down to my new assignment, I was selected as one of eight officers from the Civil Service to be trained as diplomats for the future Foreign and Commonwealth Service of Ghana. This was in June 1955 and nobody in the Gold Coast knew the exact date when the Gold Coast would attain independent nationhood within the Commonwealth.

The Gold Coast was then passing through a transitional period from internal self-government to a fully independent and sovereign state. Dr. Kwame Nkrumah's CPP had swept the polls in 1954 and he was poised to become the first Prime Minister of the first country in sub-Saharan Africa to become independent from colonial rule. He cooperated with Sir Arden Clarke, the colonial governor, who was an astute politician and an able administrator. At this time, the Trade Union Congress, whose members, especially the Railway Employees Union and the Mine Workers Union had supported the CPP to the hilt, had become restive. It was the task of the Ministry of Labour to help build a responsible and independent trade union movement. But then the conflict between the World Federation of Trade Unions (WFTU) and the International Confederation of Free Trade Unions (ICFTU) on the international scene had manifested itself within the ranks of the unions in Ghana. The WFTU which was supposed to be communist-inspired was spreading literature full of Soviet anthology of hate. It was our task as Labour Officers to steer the trade unions in the Gold Coast to the side of the ICFTU which was western-oriented.

Therefore, at the elections for the presidency of the TUC in Kumasi, it was our back-stair prodding that helped secure the presidency for Mr. F.E. Techie-Menson, then Secretary of the Posts and Telegraphs Workers Union which was patently pro-ICFTU. The candidate put forward by some unions at the instance of the extreme left of the CPP was John Tettegah, who was pro-WFTU. At the time of writing, Mr. John Tettegah is the Ghana Ambassador to Moscow, sent there by the Rawlings regime.

It would be recalled that it was soon after his appointment as a member of the Bibiani Mines Arbitration Committee that Mr. Techie-Menson was elected President of the TUC and was returned to Parliament unopposed. He was thus a heavyweight in every respect – a strong CPP member of Parliament, a close associate of Dr. Nkrumah, the Prime Minister, the President of the TUC, and he weighed sixteen stones!

I was a Labour Officer for nearly three years. I learnt during that period that a labour officer had to win the confidence of both employers and workers, a difficult feat the best of times, which yielded much fruit if accomplished successfully. I was then a socialist on the far left with the fire of social justice burning in my belly. I entertained no doubts that the Gold Coast worker needed a new deal and that the point of departure was his education. Almost to a man, the unskilled worker was illiterate. He had to be tutored to appreciate his rights as well as his responsibilities.

He had to understand that by his efforts the reconstruction of his country was going on apace. Above all, he had to know that productivity was the key to economic development. I had, as a part-time lecturer for the Peoples Education Association attempted to impart such lessons to the workers in the industrial, mining, and timber areas of the Tarkwa district. I had myself gained from my duties. I had learnt workers' aspirations and the gnawing anxieties of employers and entrepreneurs. But certainly, I had learnt the art of diplomacy in my dealings with workers and employers. I had, indeed, come to have a full appreciation of the human nature.

It had been my plan that I would plunge into active politics after five years' stay at the Labour department. But this did not materialize. For now, I had been chosen for training as a diplomatist, when I would study the art and science of diplomacy and practice it as well.

AQS with EAQS and family

AQS and EAQS: new parents with their first child

AQS and his young family on the boat back to Ghana after the Oxford Years

CHAPTER 6

TRAINEE FOR THE FOREIGN SERVICE OF GHANA

In 1955, there was a rising expectation that my country would sooner than later attain full independence. Since 1951, there had been a Legislature comprising some members directly elected from the municipalities of Accra, Cape Coast, Sekondi-Takoradi and Kumasi; some members elected through electoral colleges, some members, Chiefs and non-chiefs, elected by the traditional provincial councils of chiefs; some members representing special interests like the Chamber of Commerce, and the Chamber of Mines, and ex-officio members like the Financial Secretary, the Attorney General, and Colonial Secretary, representing the Governor. I have already made mention of Sir Arden Clarke, the Governor, during this crucial period; an intelligent, pragmatic and sympathetic colonial Administrative Officer who had evolved a good working relationship with Dr. Kwame Nkrumah, the Prime Minister.

After the 1954 General Elections which resulted in a landslide victory for Nkrumah's CPP indirect elections, all the electoral colleges, special and traditional interests, and ex-officio members had been swept aside. With Dr. Kwame Nkrumah and his all-African Cabinet fully in the saddle, it became clear that a solid and effective plan had to be laid to usher the country into independence. At independence, the Gold Coast would need to have its own foreign policy and handle its external relations. It was, therefore, considered necessary to establish a Foreign and Commonwealth service with adequate personnel, properly and competently trained for it.

It was with that view in mind that the Colonial Office sent to the Gold Coast Sir Francis Cumming-Bruce (now Lord Athlone), a seasoned diplomat in the Commonwealth Relations Office (CRO) in London to advise the Governor on the task of recruiting and training personnel for a future Foreign Service. Sir Francis was ably assisted by Mr. A. L. Adu. I have already referred to Mr. Amishadai Larsen Adu (affectionately called Yaw by friends) as the foremost civil servant at this time. He later became the Permanent Secretary of the new Ministry of Foreign Affairs at Ghana's independence and then Secretary to the Cabinet and Head of the Ghana Civil Service. From Ghana, he became the Secretary-General of the East African Common Services Organization and then the Regional Representative, United Nations Technical Assistance Board (now the United Nations Development Programme – UNDP) in East Africa. When the Commonwealth Secretariat was established in 1965 he became the Deputy Secretary-General from which post he retired and returned to Ghana as Resident Director of the Consolidated African Selection Trust (CAST). He had become my boss in the Ghana Foreign Service. When he retired to Ghana, he became my Wednesday partner at golf, a game which he relished and which gave him that composure and equanimity of mind which he needed in his retirement. But again, his services as a public servant were in demand, and, against the entreaties of his friends like me, he felt obliged to accept for two years the Vice-Presidency of the International Civil Service at the United Nations headquarters in New York. He died in harness in New York.

He was a superb civil servant, competent, and adroit. He knew how to handle people. A whole generation of civil and public servants passed through his hands and I count myself fortunate that after my university education, it was Yaw Adu who interviewed me and gave me guidance in my choice of a government department. In 1955, Yaw and Cumming-Bruce had to interview more than fifty officers from which number, eight had to be selected in the first instance to start training as diplomatists.

The requirement was that each of the eight must have graduated from a recognized university and must have served for at least three years in the civil service.

The eight young men selected were Richard Akwei who had graduated in Philosophy, Politics, and Economics from Oxford (Christ Church); Harry R. Amonoo, a graduate in History from the University of Ghana; Frederick S. Arkhurst, a graduate in Economics from Aberdeen University; Frank E. Boateng, a graduate in History from the University of Ghana; Kenneth K. S. Dadzie, a graduate in Economics from Cambridge (Queen's College); Ebenezer Moses Debrah, a graduate in History from the University of Ghana; Abraham B. B. Kofi, a graduate in Geography from the University of Southampton; and the writer. We came from different departments of the Civil Service. Each of us was given a memorandum in which had been set out our course of training. It consisted of six weeks of an intensive course of lectures and seminars at the British Foreign Office and the Commonwealth Relations Office (CRO), one academic year of post-graduate studies in International Relations and International Law at the London School of Economics, a six months' attachment at the British Embassy, and a three to four months French language course at Tours in France. At the end of it all, there was to be an examination to determine the grade of each officer, which would also take into consideration reports on the officers from the Foreign Office in London.

Seven of us left Accra by air in August 1955 for the Foreign Office in London where we were joined by Fred Arkhurst who had been undergoing a training course in mass communication in the United States, under the auspices of the United States Information Services (USIS). Another recruit, Henry Van Heen Sekyi, joined us straight from Cambridge, where he had read Classics at King's College. He had not been in the Civil Service at all but must have possessed the qualities required. And so, the nine of us from the Gold Coast together with six trainees from Pakistan and India began our diplomatic training.

Our training course at the Foreign Office (FO) was organized and directed by Sir Henniker Major, who was then Head of the Personnel Department of the FO. In those six weeks, we had different speakers to talk to us on their own experiences as Ambassadors or Consuls, on political reporting, consular and commercial work, security aspects of the Foreign Service, the evolution of diplomatic practice or method, and the impact of newspapers and the mass media on foreign policy and diplomacy.

Recommended books like Lord Strang's *The Foreign Office*; Harold Nicholson's *Diplomatic Practice*; Sir Ernest Satow's *Guide to Diplomatic Practice*; Francois de Calliere's *De la Manier de negocier avec les Souverains* (On the Manner of Negotiating with Princes) — all of these and others like Charles Thayer's *Bears in the Caviar* and Lord Kelly's *The Ruling Few* provided me with a great deal of knowledge and insight into what diplomacy is all about and what qualities a diplomatist should possess. I learnt the diplomatic method of the Greek City- States through the Roman period, the Byzantine era, the Italian Renaissance period to the French Diplomatic method which had been universally applied throughout Europe for three centuries since the 17th century until after the First World War 1914-1918 when the so-called new diplomacy emerged.

During the period of the Greek City-States, the sending and receiving of embassies was of a temporary nature. It was in the 15th century that the Italians became the first to establish permanent embassies. Ambassadors of the Greek City- States were appointed by the Assemblies which also received Ambassadors' reports. A mission was usually composed of two Ambassadors representing factions of the Assembly, and those Ambassadors could be acting at cross purposes and in fact, prosecuted each other as when, for example, Demosthenes indicted his former colleague, Aeschines. Greek negotiations were conducted publicly, but they lacked permanency and, in many cases, where the negotiated agreement was repudiated by the Assemblies, Ambassadors responsible for the negotiations were thrown into jail or had their properties confiscated. Thus, the Greek diplomatic method from 800 BC demonstrated the futility of reconciling popular democratic control of foreign policy with effective negotiation or diplomacy.

It was, however, during the Roman period that some order was introduced into diplomatic method. Instead of an Ambassador showing his credentials in the receiving State when challenged as during the period of the Greek City-States, the Romans insisted on a foreign envoy remaining outside the City gates until his credentials had been scrupulously examined and his right to diplomatic status verified. Of course, today before any country sent an Ambassador it must first seek the "agremént" or the consent of the receiving country. The Romans also established the principle of the sanctity of international treaties. The assumption was that an Ambassador who had the full authority of his sovereign to negotiate an agreement should not have the agreement, thus negotiated, repudiated. The case of President Woodrow Wilson, negotiating the compact for the establishment of the League of Nations, who did not get the support of the Congress of the United States has become a sad example in recorded history.

With the rise of Byzantium, diplomatic method involved much protocol and ceremonial. There was evolved a practice by which an Ambassador could bring enough merchandise from his native country to sell in order to defray his expenses at post. The Italians, on the other hand, who were greatly influenced by the Byzantines, were the first to require their Ambassadors to send home periodic reports. And it was in 1450 that the Duke of Milan, Francesco Forza sent Ambassador Nicodemus dei Pontramili, called "Sweet Nicodemus" by his contemporaries, to the first resident embassy at Genoa. Machiavelli's *The Prince* was a guide for diplomatic practice during the Italian Renaissance period.

Diplomacy thus evolved over a number of centuries until the 17th century when Cardinal Richelieu of France brought in a number of reforms. Harold Nicolson, in fact, credits Richelieu as being "the first to establish that the art of negotiation must be a permanent activity and not merely a hurried endeavor". Richelieu also taught that "the interest of the State was primary and eternal ... if national interest demanded an alliance with an obnoxious, even with a heretic state, then no feelings of what one liked or what one disliked should be permitted to blur that necessity. In moments of danger, one should choose one's allies, not for their integrity or charm, but for their physical or even geographical value". This principle of national interest adumbrated by Richelieu presaged Lord Palmerton of England's "permanent interests" and not permanent friends.

On the whole, the French brought order and procedures into a diplomatic method which, though eroded by circumstances of today, still remain relevant and poignant. Under the French system, the Secretary of State for Foreign Affairs became a permanent member of the Cabinet, a Foreign Office was established which blossomed into the Quai d'Orsay and by 1685 permanent embassies of France were seen in more than ten countries. It was the French who also introduced the system of written instructions and made French the language of diplomacy. They settled the problem of precedence.

I have taken some time to delve a bit into the history of the evolution of diplomatic practice just to show how far the art of diplomacy has traveled in order to reach its present state.

When we studied the qualities of a diplomatist during the Foreign Office course, I drew heavily on Francois de Calliere's book *De la Manier de negocier avec les Souverains* (On the Manner of Negotiating with Princes) first published in 1716 which, according to the famous Harold Nicolson, "remains to this day the best manual of diplomatic method ever written." De Calliere wrote that "the good diplomatist must have an observant mind, a gift of application which rejects being diverted by pleasures or frivolous amusements, a sound judgment which takes the measure of things as they are, and which goes straight to the goal by the shortest and most natural paths without wandering into meaningless refinements and subtleties ... The diplomatist must be quick, resourceful, a good listener, courteous and agreeable. He should not seek to gain a reputation as a wit, nor should he be so disputatious as to divulge secret information in order to clinch an argument. Above all, the good negotiator must possess enough self-control to resist the longing to speak before he has thought out what he intends to say. He must not fall into the mistake of supposing that an air of mystery, in which secrets are made out of nothing and the merest trifle exalted into an affair of state, is anything but the symptom of a small mind. He should pay attention to women but never lose his heart. He must be able to simulate dignity even if he does not possess it, but he must at the same time avoid all tasteless displays. Courage also is an essential quality, since no timid man can hope to bring a confidential negotiation to success. The negotiator must possess the patience of a watch-maker and be devoid of personal prejudices. He must have a calm nature, be able to suffer fools gladly, and should not be given to drink, gambling, women, irritability, or any other wayward humors and fantasies. The negotiator moreover should study history and memoirs, be acquainted with foreign institutions and habits, and be able to tell where, in any foreign country, the real sovereignty lies. Everyone who enters the profession of diplomacy should know the German, Italian, and Spanish languages as well as Latin, ignorance of which would be a disgrace and shame to any public man since it is the common language of all Christian nations. He should also have some knowledge of Literature, Science, Mathematics, and Law. Finally, he should entertain handsomely. 'A good cook is often an excellent conciliator'."

Such high qualities expected of a good diplomatist posed a great challenge for me and my colleagues, and at that stage of our training, we could only hope that in time, we would have attained the highest standards needed in our profession. We had observed the manners of the speakers, most of whom had been seasoned diplomatists and had acquired a great wealth of experience through practice. I agree that Francois de Calliere's prescriptions given in the 18th century are as valid and useful today as they were then. But of course, he could not have fathomed the vast changes that were bound to occur with the rise of two super powers, the Soviet Union and the United States, and with the emergence of so many independent, sovereign states on the international scene. Today, Arabic, Russian, and Chinese are important languages worth knowing, while Economics is a vital subject to understand. Today, diplomacy by conference is prevalent, although the age-old quiet diplomacy practices in the past is still very relevant and necessary for the conclusion of bilateral and multilateral agreements. Throughout my diplomatic career, de Calliere's prescriptions remained fresh in my mind and I tried to maintain high standards in my dealings with people and governments.

At the Foreign Office, we had ample opportunity of meeting seasoned British diplomatists, some of whom regaled us with interesting anecdotes in their careers. We also met trainee diplomats from Pakistan and India some of whom have remained friends. I remember Mohammed Akram Zaki from Pakistan. He was as robust as he was witty. The last time I met him, he was the Pakistani Ambassador to Nigeria. He looked as seasoned and as relaxed as ever.

Of all the anecdotes, the one I still recall is the one about a telegram sent by a British Ambassador in one of the Balkan states to the Foreign Office. Apparently, monks in a monastery on the island of Athos had sworn never to leave the monastery under any circumstances. During the war, the monastery was sacked and the monks thrown out. When the telegram was received by the desk officer who was supposed to be none other than the famous diplomatist, Harold Nicolson, it read "Today, the Bulgars have attacked Athos and driven out the monks, thus making them violate their cows"; thereupon, Harold Nicolson, noticing that cows had been typed instead of vows wrote in the margin "what a clerical error?" and passed the telegram on to the Foreign Secretary who was supposed to be Lord Grey, who also wrote at the bottom, "This calls for a Papal Bull." I thought that was a clear manifestation of British wit!

We completed the Foreign Office training full of confidence and high hopes. The training was indeed as intensive as it was comprehensive, covering every facet of foreign policy and diplomatic method.

After this course, Debrah, Kofi, Sekyi and myself were admitted to the London School of Economics (LSE) in October 1955 for one academic year, while the other colleagues were sent off to various British Embassies for six months' attachment training before entering the London School of Economics.

At LSE, I attended lectures on International Law by Professor Schwartzenberger whose book *Power Politics* provided a good background for the study of International Relations. Professor Manning was my professor on International Relations. At his seminars, we spent some time discussing whether international relations should be considered as a subject and taught as such or whether an understanding of international relations could not be readily obtained by a thorough study of the history of nations. My own view had been that while the study of history, especially European history, and British Empire history, was useful, it was difficult to gain an insight into the foreign policy of different states, or into negotiations leading to agreements or treaties; or methods of diplomacy and international institutions unless we studied international relations. History, I maintained could be a useful guide for the future. I also sat at the feet of Professor Godwin who was my tutor. Under him, I studied international institutions and how they impinge on relations between states. Professor Hancock, a specialist on Commonwealth studies, organized seminars on the Commonwealth on Saturdays which I had to attend. It was at one of these seminars that my paper on "The Foundations of a Gold Coast Foreign Policy" was read and discussed. Years later, I found out that this paper had been kept in the archives of the Institute of Commonwealth Studies and made available for research workers like Scott Thompson of the Fletcher School of Diplomacy who made reference to it in his book on *Ghana's Foreign Policy before 1966*.

At the end of the academic year, I left LSE and in May, I received an official intimation from the FO that I had to proceed to Rio de Janeiro in Brazil to serve as Attaché of Embassy at the British Embassy. I was also informed that arrangements had been made for Elsie to join me in Rio. The idea was that while I was learning at post the intricacies of diplomacy, writing draft dispatches, telegrams, minutes, and attending diplomatic receptions, my wife had to acquire first-hand knowledge of what a diplomatists' life would be like. Apart from gaining an insight into diplomatic practices, she had to learn how to organize her own parties. In time, she had to be exposed to diplomatic life before I embarked on my career. The wives of my colleagues, I learned later, had to undergo the same kind of exposure and training at their posts.

Brazil in 1956 was a delightful country. I embarked on the steamship *Alcantra* from Southampton to Rio de Janeiro. Tenerife had been our first port of call and then we touched Recife in Brazil. I enjoyed the sightseeing at both places, especially at the Canaries where a garland of flowers was put around my neck by a fair damsel. But it was at our next stop in Bahia that I saw the glory that was Brazil's. I was impressed by the mixed population which was predominantly black. The confidence of the people, their ever-smiling faces, and open friendliness were overwhelming. I felt at home readily. The Governor, who was as dark as myself, was completely bowled over when he learnt from the British Consul that I came from the Gold Coast and that I was going to be trained as a diplomatist at the British Embassy in Rio. My own joy was unbounded when I visited a church in Bahia. Its glittering interior was a sharp reminder to me of the commercial intercourse between my country and Portugal between 1472 and 1482 when the Portuguese took away a lot of alluvial gold from Elmina in the Gold Coast where the Portuguese had built their castle in 1481.

And then we anchored at the harbor in Rio de Janeiro one afternoon. Without much mincing of words, Rio was for me the most beautiful city I had seen at the time, having seen London, Paris, and Geneva. The felicitous combination of hills, lakes, skyscrapers, and *favelas* (shanty houses) at the brow of the hills was overwhelming. The impression I got was that man was trying hard to destroy what God has provided by way of natural beauty. As I drove home to Peter Parfitt (Peter was the third Secretary at the British Embassy in Rio de Janeiro in 1956) apartment in Rue Senador Jusebio, I was further enthralled to see the mixed population of Portuguese, Indians, and Africans. I was to learn in due course that the beautiful people I had seen in Rio were called *"Carioca"*. The Africans were mostly descendants of West Africans, notably Nigerians. Up to now, the delightful impression I had of Brazil pervades.

When after a fortnight in Rio de Janeiro I had obtained a flat at Rue Senador Eusebio, I was joined by my wife. We entered smoothly into the diplomatic life of Rio. At the time of my attachment to the British Embassy, the Ambassador was Sir Geoffrey Thompson, a tall, patrician-looking career diplomat who was keen on my becoming a good draftsman and therefore saw to it that I initiated as many draft dispatches and/or correspondence as possible. He told me that as Her Majesty's Ambassador on the spot, he was expected to give the full facts of a situation and his own candid opinion or advice. His Counselor of Embassy was Michael Robb and the Head of Chancery was Kenneth James, with whom I shared a room and from whom I had to learn the duties of chancery. Chancery, strictly speaking, should be the place where the Ambassador works and the Embassy where he lives, but modern developments have relegated the term chancery to a place in a present-day embassy where political and administrative work of the whole embassy is coordinated. It is in its present connotation that "chancery" should thus be understood. In fact, whatever went to the Ambassador was supposed to pass through the head of chancery.

Other officers like Peter Parfitt who was in charge of administration and worked up to the head of chancery, Robert John, first Secretary (Commercial), John Hough, first Secretary (Information) and Jock Miller who was responsible for the "diplomatic bag"[27] were all helpful and kind. Although it was with Kenneth James that I worked closely, I had to study the ropes from each of the officers I have mentioned. Each officer in the embassy performed a vital function without which the embassy machine would creak and grind. It was good I paid

---

27 **A diplomatic bag**, also known as a diplomatic pouch, is a container with certain legal protections used for carrying official correspondence or other items between a diplomatic mission and its home government or other diplomatic, consular, or otherwise official entity.

great attention to every aspect of embassy work, because in 1957 when I became the Head of Chancery at the new Ghana High Commission in London (the Gold Coast Commissioner's Office at 13 Belgrave Square automatically became the Ghana High Commission on March 6 1957), I found myself doing my own "bags", doing the coding and decoding, instituting security measures, coordinating the work of the Information section, the trade section, the recruitment section, and the students unit, all of which came under the control of the High Commissioner.

Socially, the officers of the British Embassy and their wives were helpful. They made sure that we attended as many receptions as possible and that we did not underrate the diplomatic rounds. Kenneth James rammed it hard into me that at any reception it was useful, if not politic, to meet as many local personalities as we could, because some chance statement or information might come our way which we would find of great value. Nor were we to ignore fellow diplomats from other embassies. We learnt that the days were gone when diplomats tried to gain advantages over their colleagues. The diplomatic corps was then a freemasonry and colleagues tried to be helpful.

Our stay in Rio de Janeiro was very eventful. We visited our friends in Ipanema and Copacabana. We had become great friends of the Haitian Ambassador, Roger Dorsinville, and his wife, and of the Indonesian Commercial Counselor, Mr. Hadinoto, both of whom did not fail to invite us to their receptions, lunches, and dinners, whenever they entertained. We visited the Samba School and although we missed the Carnival by the time of our arrival in Brazil, there were a number of outings when we sampled Samba dances and even tasted *Kishasha* and ate shrimps! We saw "diplomatic bag" practices which looked very much like some fetish ceremonies we had seen at home; at an intersection of two cross roads were spread coins, candles, and herbs; a practice which people believed would drive away evil spirits and bring good luck. We visited the "Sugar Loaf" and the "Figure of Christ", which dominated the beautiful scenery of Rio. Both hills were rendezvous for Brazilian lovers and tourists alike. Indeed, we mixed very freely in Rio and had some adventures.

132

Two incidents during our stay in Rio need mentioning. At one of the gatherings of the diplomatic wives of the British Embassy, one of Elsie's friends remarked that were Elsie not to wear her Ghanaian dress, she would be mistaken for a maid, because "all the black women in Rio are maids." Elsie decided to test this statement. She donned her nice European frock and went out "looking for a job." At each door of the ten houses she knocked, except one, the door opened all right, but without her muttering a word, the Brazilian occupant assumed that Else wanted a job and would instantly tell her *"nao occupadio"* (no work). But at one house the lady of the house invited her inside and made conversation. When she found Elsie's Portuguese halting, she spoke passable English to which Elsie responded in English with alacrity. The lady was at once impressed with Elsie's command of English and looked at her closely, watching her demeanor. But even that lady persisted in her thinking that Elsie wanted a maid's job and told her that she did not think a maid's job was suitable for Elsie. She promised to help her find an office job!

The other incident involved myself. I usually walked to the Embassy as we lived close by. One day, as I set out, I found myself being mobbed. A crowd, which grew in number as I proceeded, followed me shouting "Otello, Otello". Not knowing what all that was about, I began to perspire and took longer strides, but the crowd kept surging forward still shouting "Otello". I was convinced that I had done nothing to merit this treatment. I literally ran up the embassy steps. Fortunately, the Head of Chancery and another officer had heard the shouting and had come to the entrance to find out what was happening. The crowd kept on shouting "Otello ", even when I had entered the embassy and so Kenneth James and Jock Miller, also our Security man, tried to find out the cause of all the shouting. It transpired that Paul Robeson, the famous singer, and actor was, at the time, playing the role of Otello at one of the playhouses in Rio de Janeiro. I had been mistaken for this famous man because of my stature and, of course, my black skin. Four years later we told Paul Robeson and his wife this story when they visited our home in New Rochelle in New York when I was the Permanent Representative (Ambassador) of Ghana to the United Nations.

From Rio de Janeiro we drove to Sao Paolo, where I was to spend six weeks at the British Consulate-General, training in consular work. I learnt how to interview people who needed British passports and visas. There were British subjects and citizens who came to the consulate with their problems. Some had lost their passports, some had separated from their wives or husbands. Some wanted trading connections in Britain; some wanted to have their lost relatives traced in Britain. In fact, it was a really busy Consulate-General and I admired the patience and the painstaking, devoted endeavors of all the officers. I also visited the small consulate in Santos a few times. But the great attraction at Santos was the coffee mart where I went coffee-tasting. It was really in the Sao Paolo area that we visited some *fazendas*[28] (coffee stores), including our friend, Mr. Levy's beautiful *fazenda* a few miles outside the city, and we came closer to knowing the Brazilian political and financial elite.

After our six weeks' stay at Sao Paolo we returned to Rio to put finishing touches to our training. On our return, there was a new Ambassador, Sir Geoffrey Harrison. He went over with me all that I had done at the Embassy and the Consulate-General. He then told me that the Embassy had been officially informed that the Gold Coast would gain full Dominion status within the Commonwealth on March 6, 1957. There were instructions that I should proceed to London and report at the British Foreign Office, and then go to Tours in France for three months.

I must place on record even now that the practical training I received at the British Embassy in Rio stood me in very good stead in my diplomatic career. It was useful to watch British diplomatists at work whether in the Chancery or at receptions. There was one admonition that my Ambassador gave me which I have never forgotten. Sir Geoffrey said "I am paid to give my Government advice as I am their man in Rio. It does not matter whether or not my advice is taken. I must continue to give it". He emphasized to me the value of a reasoned and well-couched political and economic dispatch.

---

28 "Fazendas" A plantation in Brazil which mainly produce coffee and sugar to stores.

Our return to Southampton, England, from Rio de Janeiro was pleasant and smooth. I had bought myself a Spanish guitar in Brazil and onboard I got the ship's baker to teach me how to play it. By the time we had docked at Southampton, I could strum the instrument.

My wife and I spent the Christmas of 1956 at my friend, Peter Barker's house at 38 Pope's Grove, Twickenham, near London. She then returned to Accra by sea while I proceeded to study French at Tours in France at L'Institute de Tourraine, which was part of the University of Poitiers.

On her return to Accra, Elsie was invited by the Ghana Broadcasting Corporation to narrate her experiences in Brazil. From all accounts, she waxed lyrical of Brazil and its multiracial community, drawing comparisons between Brazilian culture and Ghanaian culture. A number of Fante words spoken in Ghana were derived from the Portuguese language, like *asopaatsee* meaning shoe, which is *sapato* in Portuguese; *boodo* meaning dough cake which is *bolo* in Portuguese, and she vividly explained the similarities. In Ghana, gratitude is expressed in terms of the next day, like *"okyena meda wo ase"* meaning "tomorrow I thank you" which is similar to the Brazilian expression *"at manha obrigado"*. We still cherish vivid memories of Brazil.

My own studies in French at Tours were a continuation of lessons I took at the London School of Economics and at Rio de Janeiro, where I had a private French tutor. The British Foreign Office arranged for me to stay with Monsieur and Madame Delise and their three children at 16 Rue Jules Simone at Tours for three months. As the Delise family spoke very little English, I was compelled to make an effort to make myself understood in French. I had to attend French classes at the institute from eight in the morning till midday, had a lunch break and rest until four o'clock in the afternoon, and then I had to continue with my private tuition at Madame Combalbert's house.

Madame Combalbert was a polished and meticulous French teacher steeped in French culture who insisted that I should speak French with a pure, clear accent for which Tours is famous. She was a great admirer of Leopold Senghor, later to become the President of the West African Republic of Senegal, and then a member of the FrenchAcademy. And she never tired of narrating the story of a French lady who had met Senghor at the public library in Tours and had addressed the African, using the expression *"et tois"* instead of *"et vous"*. Apparently, Senghor hit back at the lady in his impeccable French, and later, on learning who Senghor was, she had returned to the library to apologize to him for her rudeness.

It was Madame Combalbert who made me read *Madame Bovary* and Francoise Sagan's books. At the institute itself, I did grammar and construction of French sentences and phrases while I studied French literature and culture at the feet of Madam Combalbert. At home with the Delise family, I observed at first hand the manners of an average middle-class French family. I spoke French at home. Occasionally, when I had not followed what the children said, Madame Delise tried to explain it in English with a typical French accent.

Tours had its attractions and distractions. There were many foreign students including Americans and English whom I met at the coffee bars and in the restaurants and there was always a temptation to speak English. What was more, the presence of my colleague Henry Van Heen Sekyi at Tours was a distraction. He had come to Tours for his French course after completing his attachment training at the British Embassy in Madrid, Spain. We were both determined to speak French to each other, however haltingly, but we often lapsed into English or Fante, our native tongue. For me, the great attractions were the number of chateaux on the River Loire, like Cherneuceax, D'Amboise, and Azez-de-Rideaux, which Henry and I visited, and the wine caves which we frequented, tasting wine. However, all told, it was a marvelous experience to stay at Tours for three months.

I left there in March 1957 with a passable working knowledge of French. Indeed, the course at Tours was meant to help me acquire a basic knowledge to be built upon by dint of constant practice and further reading, with the passage of time.

It was while I was at Tours that I received official intimation that I had to report for duty at the Ghana High Commission in London, my first posting. I was further informed that each of us trainees would be given the rank of Second Secretary on assumption of office on March 6, 1957. Thus, with the French studies over, I had completed the whole training course mapped out for me and my colleagues. It had been a thoroughly intensive training course for us "the faithful nine", as the nine of us, young diplomats who had begun and completed the foreign service training were later to be dubbed. We had, indeed, had a more thorough training than M. de Torcy's six young diplomatists who were called *"Les Messieurs du Cabinet"* trained for the French foreign service at the Political Academy set up in 1712. On looking back, it can be said that the qualities of a diplomatist which were laid down by Francois de Calliere were as rigorous as they were necessary for a successful diplomatic career. Some of these qualities a person could naturally possess; but a lot more could be acquired as the diplomat soldiered on. That was my experience. It was quite evident that when we started operating the Ghana Foreign Service at independence on March 6 1957, there was a solid core of trained diplomatists who could hold their own anywhere. It was a matter of fact that each one of the "faithful nine" had by 1964 become a distinguished and effective Ambassador in some parts of the world. For my part, it was with confidence and a sense of pride that I proceeded to London to start my diplomatic career at the Ghana High Commission with the rank of Second Secretary of Embassy on March 6 1957.

CHAPTER 7

ARTICULATING GHANA'S FOREIGN POLICY

THE GHANA HIGH COMMISSION, LONDON

The independence of Ghana on March 6, 1957, caught me at Tours, France, just when I was completing the study of the French language at the Institute of Touraine. As I had already received instructions to proceed to London on my first posting, I duly arrived at 13 Belgrave Square, London which had housed the Gold Coast Commission, due to be transformed to the Ghana High Commission. I introduced myself in March 1957 to Henry A. H. S. Grant who had been sent to London a few months before the independence of Ghana to act as Secretary to the Gold Coast Commissioner and to supervise the transformation of the Gold Coast Commission to the Ghana High Commission. He informed me that his instructions from Accra were that I had to join him to run the Mission in London but that I could proceed to Accra on leave during which I would organize my domestic affairs, get my wife and children ready to join me in London and acquaint myself with Government policy and Ghanaian affairs generally. Accordingly, I left for Ghana on May 16, 1957.

After six weeks in Ghana where I had extensive discussions with A. L. Adu, the Permanent Secretary of the new Ministry of Foreign Affairs, I returned to London on July 7, 1957. In no time, I was able to find accommodation at 166 Whitchurch Lane, Edgware which was to be our abode throughout my tour of duty in London from July of 1957 to June 1959. Edgware was at that time a quiet suburb of metropolitan London. The atmosphere was

139

on the whole conducive to the training of children. The schools were excellent and we had no difficulty in placing our two sons, Egya (6 years old) and Nana Bordoh (5 years old) at Rayburn School near Harrow. For our little daughter, Awo Aferba (3 years old), we found a decent private nursery school run by an elderly gentleman, Mr. Sharpe, who was very fond of children. He even taught the 3-year-old children to play the piano, which gave Awo a firm foundation for her later exploits in music.

Our house was within easy reach of Canon's Park underground (tube) station. We could also take the 366 or 18 bus right near our doorstep to the Edgware station. At home, our hands were full, what with the upbringing of three children with all their problems, and with numerous visitors, notably Ghanaians. Elsie was up to her neck with various chores, both at home and at diplomatic rounds, attending meetings of wives of Commonwealth officials, and supervising charity bazaars. My own domestic chores were performed mostly at the weekends. During the week, I drove the children to school before proceeding to 13 Belgrave Square. At weekends I mowed the lawn and cut the hedges during the spring and summer days. In the winter I carried wood and coal for the fireplace in the lounge. In those days, central hearing had not caught on in London and we had to make do with coal, electric, and paraffin heating. I must admit that I did not then relish walking in the inclement weather, let alone carrying wood and coal from the garage. I felt really funny in my heavy overcoat, carrying coal or shoveling snow off our pathway. I was once told that I looked like a bear! But it was a fantastic experience for me and I still cherish those halcyon days we spent in London.

At the Ghana High Commission, I performed my duties as Head of Chancery, though designated as Second Secretary, which was the status given to all of us, the "faithful nine" at the start of our diplomatic careers. I was soon joined by Mr. Richard Quarshie, a replacement for Mr. Henry A. H. S. Grant who had been recalled home to work in the Ministry of External Affairs. Mr. Quarshie had had considerable experience in the Civil Service, having worked in the then political administration and risen to a very senior position within the ranks of the Labor Department. He,

Major Seth Anthony, and Mr. Henry A. H. S. Grant had been recruited for their relatively superior civil service experience for the newly established Foreign and Commonwealth Service. The reason given for this recruitment was that, those of us who had been carefully selected and trained for the Foreign Service were not experienced enough to be official heads of posts like London, Washington, or New York. Mr. Quarshie, therefore, had come to London to replace Mr. Grant as the official Secretary of the Ghana High Commission.

I had known Mr. Quarshie at Oxford where he had gone through the so-called Devonshire course for Colonial Administrators. It was he who had persuaded me to join the Labor Department. He had received the rude knocks of the colonial civil service for sixteen years and was none the worse for it in 1957. He was a man of easy manner with a lot of native wit. Above all, he was rather astute and worldly-wise. He and I had been good friends. It was our duty to change the Gold Coast Commission to the Ghana High Commission and prepare the ground for the Head of Mission who had not then been appointed. We also had to find a suitable accommodation to purchase for the High Commissioner. Happily, we were able to buy a nice house in St. John's Wood at 41 Avenue Road, with the assistance of a professional estate dealer and decorator, Mrs. Carter, who had also arranged to have the residence suitably furnished. If my memory serves me right, the cost of the residence together with a spacious garden fringed by a commodious outhouse of two flats facing Townsend Road, in addition to the cost of furnishing, was about sixty-five thousand pounds. Today the same property would fetch some millions of Pounds Sterling.

Thus, before the first High Commissioner arrived in London we were confident that we had fairly prepared the ground for a successful take-off. In the meantime, as Acting High Commissioner, we had Mr. Thomas Hutton-Mills, who had been the Gold Coast Commissioner in London before March 6, 1957. He had been a distinguished legal practitioner and politician of repute, who had been Minister of State as well, in the pre-independence administration of Prime Minister Dr. Kwame

Nkrumah. Mr. Hutton-Mills was an affable person who reveled in his patrician background. He was rather fond of horse-racing and betting, having acquired the habit during his Dulwich School and Cambridge University days.

His deputy was Mr. John E. Jantuah, now known as Kwame Saana Poku Jantuah, a tough politician of the CPP vintage, who had earlier been a Minister of Agriculture before Ghana's independence. Mr. Jantuah was reputed to have been an outspoken critic of the Asantehene, Nana Sir Agyeman Prempeh II, the then occupant of the "Golden Stool" of the Ashanti people. The Asantehene was alleged to be opposed to Nkrumah's Convention People's Party (CPP) and was supposed to be the prime mover of the National Liberation Movement (NLM) based in Kumasi, a virulently organized separatist Ashanti movement. It became a thorn in the flesh of the CPP activists in Ashanti, like Mr. Jantuah. It had been bruited about that he had made certain disparaging remarks about the Golden Stool of Ashanti, and had thus incurred the wrath of the NLM. He himself felt that his life had been in danger. Therefore, his subsequent posting to London was allegedly meant to give him a safe haven. When I assumed duty at the Ghana High Commission, he had been designated Deputy High Commissioner, contrary to expectations within the Ghanaian community in London that he was destined to be named as the Ghana High Commissioner.

The appointment, however, went to another Ashanti, Mr. Edward Okyere Asafu-Adjaye (later to be knighted in 1961 by Queen Elizabeth II). Dr. Kwame Nkrumah had advised the Governor-General, Lord Listowel, to appoint that great son of Ashanti as the first High Commissioner of Ghana to the Court of St. James. Sir Edward Asafu-Adjaye had been a distinguished barrister-at-law and a veteran politician who had represented the Asanteman Council from 1946 to 1954. He had also served as Minister of Local Government in the first government of Osagyefo Dr. Kwame Nkrumah from 1951 to 1954. In 1954, he had been re-elected, however, on the ticket of the CPP to the Legislative Assembly and had continued as Minister of

Local Government for a year before his appointment as Minister of Trade and Labor. It was from that ministerial position that he had come to London as High Commissioner. He had been concurrently appointed as Ghana's Ambassador to France. He thus undoubtedly straddled two horses, as it were, of almost equal strength, might and importance. I reserve my opinion of Sir Edward till later, as my boss for two years. Let me however remark that his arrival in London instantly boosted the standing of the Ghana High Commission at 13 Belgrave Square.

With the appointment of a substantive High Commissioner, Mr. Thomas Hutton-Mills was appointed Ghana's Ambassador to Liberia. His posting to Monrovia was regarded as propitious because he could easily fit into the social milieu of the True Whig oligarchy then ruling Liberia. From all accounts, Mr. Hutton-Mills and President W.S. Tubman hit it off beautifully. They were both suave, debonair, and enjoyed the good things of life. President Tubman had been in firm control of Liberia and it had been said to the credit of Thomas Hutton-Mills that he had helped in bringing about a proper and sympathetic understanding in Liberia, the oldest African Republic, of the *soi-disant* revolutionary ideas of the new nation of Ghana. Unfortunately, Mr. Hutton-Mills did not stay long at his post in Monrovia. He died at a private London clinic in Queensgate, South Kensington in 1958. I had seen and talked with him just before his death.

Sir Edward Asafu-Adjaye's first act on arrival was to find out when he could conveniently present his letters of credence to the Queen. For this and other matters, he summoned to his residence, Mr. Quarshie and myself. We briefed him thoroughly on what we had then been able to do to organize the High Commission. We had set up the Chancery, that is, the political, economic, consular, and administrative sections. There had already been in existence the Trade Commissioner's office, the Recruitment section, the Information section, and the Students Unit, but all these had to be coordinated by the Head of Chancery, that is, by me, so that the High Commissioner could instantly be informed of the conduct of affairs of these sections.

Sir Edward himself laid bare to us his plans for his diplomatic mission, and he left us in no doubt as to the cooperation he was prepared to give to all the members of his staff. Although he did not come to London armed with a set of instructions laboriously written down, as was the diplomatic practice of old, he had been properly briefed as to the broad lines of foreign policy, and so he had entertained no illusions of the immensity of his assignment in Britain and France. As diplomatic staff of the High Commission, our task was to furnish guidance and the best possible advice in consonance with diplomatic practice against the background of policy statements which the Government of Ghana would make from time to time.

However, what was of immediate concern to Sir Edward Asafu-Adjaye was which of the two of us whom he had met in London for the first time ought to proceed to Paris as Charge d'Affaires during his absences from France. True, the then Permanent Secretary, A. L. Adu had advised that as I had only recently completed my study of the French language, I could prove useful as his man in France. On the other hand, when Sir Edward came to Paris, he had been strongly persuaded by A. G. Levantis, who had founded the prosperous Levantis Trading Company in Ghana and had been appointed Commercial Minister in France, to pick Richard Quarshie as Charge. Apparently, Levantis had known Quarshie and had been impressed with his adroitness and experience. In the event, Sir Edward left the matter to the two of us. I instantly deferred to my senior colleague, Richard. He chose to go to Paris, but unfortunately, with the erroneous notion that, like the High Commissioner, he would control both the Chancery in Paris and the one in London. His effort became apparent when he jibbed at my application for an acting allowance as the Official Secretary at the Ghana High Commission according to the rules. Of course, the Ministry of External Affairs ruled in my favour, as I had been indeed, the *de facto* counselor to the High Commissioner for six months and nothing but glowing reports (as I was informed later) had been given about my work by the High Commissioner. In the event, I held the position of Official Secretary to the High Commissioner from December 1957 to June 1959.

The basis of our diplomatic operations in London was, of course, the foreign policy of Ghana, including Ghana's basic interests. The essentials were broadly Ghana's policy of total liberation of all colonial and trust territories in Africa, African unity, which was later to be adumbrated to mean a continental union government of Africa, and lastly, a policy of non-alignment and positive neutralism. The implementation of the policy of total liberation gained top priority because Dr. Nkrumah had proclaimed to the whole world, on the eve of our independence that "Ghana's independence is meaningless unless it is linked up with the total liberation of Africa." Total liberation was to be achieved within the framework of African Unity. For a start, there should be an economically viable Ghana, which would be friends to all but enemy to none. If Ghana would be free to pursue her national goals, she had to be non-aligned and positively neutral.

Ghana in 1957 was a new nation. It had emerged as a colonial territory into independent nationhood after more than one hundred years of colonial rule. It did not have a previous history of foreign affairs. The various cultures of the various peoples forming the state of Ghana could not admit of having a particular image, as the cultures of the Akans, including the Ashantis, of the Gas, the Ewes, the Mamprusis, the Kusasis, the Dagombas, the Frafras and so on, were different each from the other due to environmental causes. Thus, apart from a common colonial heritage, what, it may be asked, prompted Ghana with its heterogeneous peoples to decide on the kind of foreign policy which I have mentioned? We simply could not have followed the foreign policy of Great Britain, our colonial master, although at independence we inherited whatever treatises or agreements Britain had concluded which affected Ghana whilst a colonial territory. Thus, our foreign policy was adumbrated against the background of what we had learnt about the world, our attitudes towards France whose territories, Togoland, Ivory Coast, and Upper Volta now Burkina Faso, surrounded us, our attitudes towards colonial powers including our own erstwhile master, Britain, our attitudes towards the rest of Africa, our attitudes towards racial discrimination and other racial problems and our attitudes towards existing international organizations particularly the United Nations.

Above all, Ghana was fully conscious of her position within the international society as the first colonial territory in Africa, south of the Sahara to have gained her independence. Her struggles for independent nationhood were part of the total struggles for total liberation by African freedom fighters throughout the continent. Then the participation of her representatives in the Banding Conference[29] held in 1955 must have had tremendous influence on the Government of the Convention Peoples Party (CPP), which led the country into independence with Kwame Nkrumah as the first Prime Minister. Kwame Nkrumah, therefore, became the chief decision-maker, and, like the President of the United States, he made our foreign policy. His official pronouncements on world issues helped in shaping our foreign policy. Therefore, my colleagues and I in the Foreign Service had to articulate this policy and to help formulate attitudes of the Government by the reports which we sent home to the Ministry of External Affairs.

And so, as I soldiered on at the Ghana High Commission, I never lost sight of the basic essentials of my country's foreign policy. I was quick to learn that Ghana needed not to have permanent friends, a fact which we drove home succinctly to the Government. Our supreme objective was to preserve, as far as possible, Ghana's permanent interests, that is, protecting our territorial integrity, building a stable, peaceful, and prosperous nation and giving every Ghanaian the right to education, shelter, food, and clothing. Ghana was not to be embroiled in great power politics, by slamming foreign military bases in our territory, but ought to add her small voice to all those countries advocating peace in our time. In peace, we would be able to develop our resources, reconstruct the colonial economy we had inherited, and promote the well-being of the masses of Ghana.

---

29 Bandung Conference The first large-scale Asian - African or Afro - Asian Conference—also known as the Bandung Conference —was a meeting of Asian and African states, most of which were newly independent, which took place on 18–24 April 1955 in Bandung, Indonesia.

As the premier mission of Ghana overseas, the High Commission in London became a veritable beehive of activities of all kinds in those days. I was conscious of my responsibilities as a trained diplomat and I was determined to work hard to lay a firm foundation for an effective and efficient diplomatic mission in London. In this regard, my High Commissioner was largely helpful and supportive. While the various sections of the High Commission received their basic directives from their home departments or ministries at Accra, they accepted and acknowledged the political head of the Chancery as the chief coordinator of all activities and work at the High Commission and consequently rendered my task of coordination very easy indeed. Of course, each head of section (Mr. E. G. Butterworth – Trade, Mr. J. B. Odunton – Information, Mr. M. A. Ribeiro – Recruitment, Ivor Cummings – Consular, Superintendent of Policy, Panford, and Mr. Ackah – Education and Students Unit) had the right of easy access to the High Commissioner, but I was consulted as Head of Chancery on various matters and, in most cases, the High Commissioner would not meet a sectional head without me. Thus, between 1957 and 1959 when I served under Sir Edward Asafu-Adjaye, the Ghana High Commission worked at its best with every officer contributing his quota effectively. We were running a brand new diplomatic mission which had a definite role to play to put Ghana on the international map during the early years of our independence.

The Ghana Government did indeed look upon the London Mission as vital. In matters of commercial and financial relations, communications and dealings with the foreign media, relations with the British Government, and other foreign governments and in the projection of the African personality, the operations of the Ghana High Commission were regarded as crucial. The Government of Ghana used the High Commission in London as the channel of communication between it and other nations of the world as most of these maintained embassies, High Commissions, Legations, and consular offices in London. For example, it was left to the Ghana High Commission to negotiate the exchange of diplomatic missions between Ghana and the Union of Soviet Socialist Republics (U.S.S.R.). I received specific instructions from the Permanent Secretary of the Ministry of External Affairs at home to negotiate on the basis of reciprocity. For instance, whatever restrictions were imposed on the movement of foreign diplomats in the Soviet Union would be accepted by us on condition that Ghana would impose similar restrictions on Russian diplomats in Ghana. At the time of the negotiations in 1958, my counterpart in the Soviet Embassy was Mr. Semenov, then serving under Mr. Malik, the Ambassador. He was an adroit Russian diplomat who spoke passable English. Years later, in 1978, when I was the Ghanaian Ambassador to the United States, Mr. Semenov was also Ambassador in Washington DC but serving directly as Ambassador Dobrynin's number two.

The High Commission was also called upon constantly to explain the Ghana Government's policies and stands on a number of issues. One such issue, I recall, was the enactment in July 1958 of the controversial Preventive Detention Act and its subsequent application to the case of Major Awhaitey of the Ghana Army who, together with Mr. Reginald R.Amponsah and Mr. Modesto Apaloo, had been arrested in connection with an alleged plot to overthrow the Nkrumah Government by assassinating Prime Minister Nkrumah at the Accra airport on his way to India. The British media particularly the Daily Telegraph, bombarded us with questions as to the propriety of such an Act, whether it was not going to be used capriciously to muzzle opposition to the Government and whether the passing of the Act was not the first step in the path to dictatorship in Ghana. Luckily, the High Commission had received a thorough briefing and background information from the office of the Attorney-General. At that time, the Attorney-General was Mr. Geoffrey Bing, a former British Labor Member of Parliament.

The Preventive Detention Act of 1958 (PDA), we were informed, was passed to deal with tribal conspiracies like the activities of the Ga Shifimo Kpee (i.e., the Ga Standfast Organization) whose avowed aim was to make Accra and the Ga area controlled by the Gas to the exclusion of other tribes and to act as opposition to the CPP Government of Dr. Kwame Nkrumah. The Act provided for detention for up to five years. The detainee had to be served with written details of the grounds of his detention within five days of his arrest and was given an opportunity to appeal against them, but the appeal was to the Cabinet. It was not envisaged that the PDA would be applied against politicians and so when it was used against Amponsah and Apaloo, who had been the General Secretary and Assistant General Secretary respectively of the opposition United Party, it naturally raised alarm. According to the briefing from Accra, Awhaitey, Apaloo and Amponsah had been found by the unanimous report of the Commission, headed by Mr. Justice Granville Sharp and appointed to investigate the activities of those three persons in connection with a reported coup attempt, to have been engaged "since 1958 in a conspiracy to carry out, at some future date in Ghana, an act for unlawful purpose, revolutionary in character." However, the majority of the Commission (Sir Tsibu Darku and Mr. Maurice Charles) found that Awhaitey, Amponsah, and Apaloo "were engaged in a conspiracy to assassinate the Prime Minister, Dr. Kwame Nkrumah, and carry out a coup d'etat." In his minority report, Mr. Gilbert Granville Sharp, the Chairman of the Commission, who had been one of the Commissioners of the Crown Court in Manchester, had found that "there did not exist between Amponsah, Apaloo, and Awhaitey a plot to interfere in any way with the life of the Prime Minister at the airport before his departure for India." Thus, as the Government of Ghana had been impressed that the three persons had been engaged in a conspiracy to perform an act of a revolutionary character, they were sure that it was in the interest of the State to detain them under the Preventive Detention Act.

We went on to explain that the Act had been based on a similar Indian Act and that the British Government had applied a similar Act to Ireland. I must say that we in the High Commission did not impress the media, but I have cited the issue of the Preventive Detention Act to show how we had to be alert to parry the insistent probing of the mass media. It was during such periods when the Press was literally breathing on our necks that J. B. Odunton, head of the Information section, was at his best. An Oxonian himself (he read PPE at University College, Oxford), J. B. became my closest colleague at the Mission. Ever courteous,

149

ever alert, he was a boon to the High Commission for dealing with the mass media. Assisted by a Mr. Saunders, he produced *Ghana Today*, a paper full of current events in Ghana which highlighted Government policies and the activities of Ghanaians in London. It had quite a wide circulation in Britain and elsewhere. I was not at all surprised when news reached me in New York, my second posting, that J. B. had been attached to Buckingham Palace and acted as Equerry to the Queen on Her Majesty's visit to Ghana in 1961.

What was exciting about London then as now was the constant arrivals of Cabinet Ministers and top officials from Ghana. Ministers of State who came to London expected the High Commissioner to meet them at Heathrow Airport to accord them courtesies and welcome. Sometimes, the airplane landed at such ungodly hours as four o'clock in the morning. Not surprising the High Commissioner wisely left this assignment to me. In those days, we did not have a protocol officer as such, but it was arranged that Mr. Anthony W. Ephson, as the Administrative Officer, should also be our protocol officer. He and I would invariably meet the Ministers, get them installed at their hotels or arrange their connecting flights, and then report to the High Commissioner. Mr. Ephson subsequently became our Ambassador to Egypt. With an accounting background, he became extremely useful during the period of my service in London as the Head of Chancery.

London also became a kind of training center for newly recruited foreign service officers like Kwesi Brew and John Sagoe for whom arrangements had to be made in Tours to enable them to study French. Sam Quarm, Aidoo, Kwame Addae, and George Arthur, all came under my tutelage in London. Except for the unfortunate John Sagoe, all the others subsequently became Heads of Diplomatic Missions with the rank of Ambassador, and, from all accounts, they served Ghana creditably. Sagoe was unfortunate in the sense that he did not have a happy married life which militated against his own perspectives. He had been transferred from London to Tunis as Charge d'Affaires sometime in 1961, but for some reason baffling to his colleagues and friends alike, he left Tunis suddenly, returned to London, and tendered his resignation with the ostensible purpose of reading for the Bar at the Middle Temple. What actually transpired was that he had fallen in love with an English typist at the High Commission in London. Thus ended what should have really become a brilliant career. Sagoe later returned to Ghana and passed away.

It was a delightful assignment that I had in London. Chancery was responsible in those days for a multitude of duties, including administration, defense matters, political and economic reporting, the coordination of the various sections of the High Commission, codes, cyphers, and the preparation of bags. In due course, we recruited local staff, mostly Ghanaians who were strictly screened, so that I was able to delegate some routine schedules, not of strictly confidential nature.

In the early days, Sir Edward kept a rather busy schedule. What became his practice was that he would phone me at home early in the morning to give me an indication of the assignments he wanted done as matters of priority. I would in turn brief him before he came to the office. We had a close personal and working relationship and I must say that it was a joy to work under him. He was dignified in every way and his sartorial flair was infectious. He, indeed, urged the staff at the High Commission to be neatly dressed. Nothing slovenly was permitted. Every officer had to work hard, dress well, and show every courtesy to every visitor to the High Commission. A lot of visitors were really Ghanaian students who were expected to take their problems to the Students Unit then situated in Aldwych. But some of the students were politicians who had come to London to further their education and equip themselves for service back in Ghana. Notable among them were Tawia Adamafio, a mature law student who had been an inveterate opponent of the CPP but had converted before arriving in London — he returned to Ghana after having been called to the Bar in 1959 to become the General Secretary of the CPP; Mr. Kwesi Armah, who had been a regional secretary of the CPP was studying to become a lawyer — he indeed became the High Commissioner in London in 1961; and Mr. Ohene Djan, also a law student, who was a really troublesome young man. They regarded the High Commission as the party headquarters and looked upon us diplomats with suspicion. I recall preventing Ohene Djan from placing posters on the Mission wall without permission. He was disarmed by polite firmness.

Frankly, it required tact to deal with these students. I quickly studied the background of a number of them and advised the High Commissioner accordingly. In looking back, I owe my success in London to my ability to get the High Commissioner to identify himself with student causes, which meant that I got involved in handling students without giving cause for rancor and acrimony. Instead of referring them to Mr. Ackah at the Student's Unit, I would treat their insistence on seeing Sir Edward personally with political flair. Invariably they did not have to see the High Commissioner at all.

Of course, the Deputy High Commissioner at the time, Mr. J. E. Jantuah, had natural and amicable links with those student politicians, most of whom had been his colleagues in the CPP. Under normal circumstances, the High Commissioner and his Deputy should have worked together in close collaboration. Not so the two men. It became increasingly embarrassing to work under the two politicians. Both were Ashantis, Kwame Saana Poku having been a CPP activist of no mean stature and Sir Edward having been a traditional politician with deep roots in the Asanteman Council, before opting to become a member of the CPP. The relations between the two were correct. The Deputy could only perform duties assigned to him by the High Commissioner, but since the Deputy regarded himself as a more authentic party man, there was a lot of shadow-boxing. I played the role of an unobtrusive mediator. There was not much delegation to the Deputy who had not, in fact, got his job description or duties clearly spelled out to him. As the official Secretary, I quietly made it known at the Ministry of External Affairs that the way out of the impasse was for Mr. Jantuah to head a mission of his own. Therefore, it was a welcome relief when early in 1959, the Deputy High Commissioner was appointed Ghana's Ambassador to France. He later became Ambassador to Brazil but he resigned afterward to devote himself to the study of the Law. But CPP politicians die hard. He became a Minister of State in the Limann administration, went into exile in Togo when the Government was overthrown by Rawlings, but he subsequently returned to Ghana, and Rawlings appointed him Ambassador to the German Democratic Republic.

It was during my stint at the High Commission in London that I became Joint Secretary with the First Secretary, H. M. Hassan of the Sudan Embassy, to the Committee of African Heads of Missions in London to prepare for the first conference of independent African States which was held in Accra from April 15 to 23, 1958. The conference was the result of consultations which Dr. Kwame Nkrumah had had with representing Heads of African States who had attended the independence celebrations at Accra on March 6, 1957. It was in keeping with Ghana's policy of working towards African unity. Consequently, instructions came from the Ministry of External Affairs that we should contact heads of African missions in London to start working on Ghana's proposed draft agenda for the proposed conference in Accra. For some reason, the Ghana High Commission had become very friendly with the Embassy of Sudan, and so we approached the Ambassador, His Excellency Mr. Sayed Awad Satti who agreed to host the first meeting of Heads of Missions.

Accordingly, the other heads were duly informed. The first meeting took place on August 15, 1957, at the Sudan Embassy. This was the first time ever that representatives of independent African States had met in conclave to discuss African problems. Therefore, I reproduce *in extensor* the minutes of that first meeting as follows:

"Present were Their Excellencies, the Sudanese Ambassador Sayed Awad Satti (Chairman); the Ethiopian Ambassador, Ato Emmanuel Abraham; the Liberian Ambassador, Mr. Clarence Lorenzo Simpson; the Acting High Commissioner, Mr. John E. Jantuah; the Libyan Charge d'Affaires, Mr. Gibril Shallouf; the Tunisian Charge d'Affaires, Mr. Mohammed Esaafi; for the Moroccan Charge d'Affaires, Mr. M. Saadani. The Secretaries were Mr. A. Quaison-Sackey – 2nd Secretary (Ghana), Mr. H.M. Hassan – 1st Secretary (Sudan), and Mr. M. O. Shendi – 3rd Secretary (Sudan)."

1. His Excellency, the Sudanese Ambassador, opened the meeting with a word of welcome and thanks to his colleagues for meeting in his Embassy. He suggested that His Excellency, the Acting High Commissioner for Ghana should preside. His Excellency the Liberian Ambassador supported the move and said that since Ghana initiated the idea of a conference, the Acting High Commissioner should preside over the meeting. But the Acting High Commissioner replied that he was in favour of the Host Ambassador or High Commissioner presiding over the meeting in his Mission, and this was approved.

2. His Excellency, the Sudanese Ambassador invited the Acting High Commissioner to say a few words about the proposed conference. The Acting High Commissioner began by saying that in calling for a Conference of Independent African States, Ghana was not aiming at forming a political or an ideological bloc, but wanted the States in Africa to know themselves, establish personal contacts and exchange political, cultural and social ideas. He invited their excellencies to look upon the conference as a joint effort and not as a Ghanaian affair and stressed the need for mutual coordination of efforts.

3. His Excellency, the Acting High Commissioner proposed a permanent joint secretariat for the meetings in London, and it was agreed that the Ghana Secretary must be one of the two. The Acting High Commissioner proposed that Sudan may provide the other secretary. This was seconded by His Excellency the Ethiopian Ambassador and was unanimously approved.

4. The Acting High Commissioner for Ghana raised a number of points and facts of detail pertinent to the conference in Accra, which were discussed.

a. He mentioned that the Ghana Government had suggested that the date of the conference should be January 20, 1958 and that it should last for a week. Delegates could arrive in Ghana on any date after January 15, and depart at the end of January or the beginning of February. Their Excellencies agreed that the venue of the conference should be Accra, but the Libyan and the Tunisian Charge d'Affaires and the Ethiopian Ambassador said that they would have to refer the date to their respective Governments for approval. The Tunisian Charge d'Affaires informed the meeting that he had no authority from his Government to be present at the meeting, but he hoped that his Government would be in favour of the deliberations. The Libyan Charge d'Affaires also said that he had obtained authority from his Government at the last moment and that he had attended the meeting as an observer. The Sudanese Ambassador said that Sudan would be preparing for General Elections about that time and doubtful whether the date would be convenient to his Government because His Excellency could give no assurance that it would be possible for the Sudanese Prime Minister to lead the delegation. However, he expressed his hope that a Minister might be able to deputize for the Prime Minister if the conference was to be held at the proposed date. It was agreed that the date of January 20 should be referred to Governments for their approval.

b. The Acting High Commissioner said that Ghana had proposed that the conference should be attended by Heads of Governments. His Excellency the Liberian Ambassador said that while he would not stress the point about who must attend the conference, he wondered whether it would not have been better to have started these conferences in Africa at the level of Foreign Ministers, then at the level of Heads of Governments and, lastly, of Heads of States. His Excellency the Ethiopian Ambassador supported the Liberian Ambassador's suggestion since that would make for "a natural growth", the climax of which would be a conference of Heads of States. His Excellency, the

Acting High Commissioner for Ghana favored a conference
of Heads of Governments because that would make a
good impact on the outside world. The Tunisian Charge
d'Affaires supported the Acting High Commissioner and
said that if the conference made a good impact, subsequent
conferences would aim at maintaining the high standard
achieved. It was agreed that the conference should be at the
level of Heads of Governments but that it should be possible
for Ministers to deputize for their Heads of Governments.

c. The Acting High Commissioner for Ghana said that the
Government of Ghana had suggested that the size of the
delegation should be limited to up to five (5) including the
Head of Government, the Ambassador in London, and three
officials including the Delegation Secretary. The Ghana
Government would offer accommodation and hospitality
and would be responsible for the cost of travel in Accra.
Their Excellencies approved of the number but, at the
suggestion of His Excellency the Ethiopian Ambassador, it
was agreed that the attendance at the conference of London
Ambassadors should not be made obligatory, as some of
them might not be able to travel to Accra.

d. The Acting High Commissioner said that the Government of
Ghana was of the opinion that there should be no observers
at the conference from within political organizations
or dependent territories. The reasons were that there
were many political bodies and groups interested in the
conference and it would be difficult to invite all of them;
also, to call for observers from dependent territories would
involve delay and complications, as permission should
be sought from metropolitan powers. His Excellency
the Liberian Ambassador then asked whether the press
would also be excluded. The Acting High Commissioner
replied that it was intended to hold the conference in
private and to issue communiques after each session. The
Ethiopian Ambassador supported the Ghana point and
said that it would be impolite to publicize the haggling and

disagreements at the conference, as that would prejudice the result. This view was supported by the Sudanese Ambassador. The Libyan Ambassador said that while he endorsed the agreement of the meeting that the press should be excluded, he did not agree with the exclusion in principle.

e. His Excellency the Acting High Commissioner in answer to a question said that the participating countries were Egypt, Ethiopia, Ghana, Liberia, Libya, Morocco, Sudan, and Tunisia. He regretted that there was no Egyptian representative at this meeting, but he said that the Egyptian President was in favour of the conference at Accra, and reports of the meetings in London would be sent to the Egyptian Government through the High Commissioner for India in London. As regards South Africa, the Ghana Government had replied that the South African proposal about the inclusion of metropolitan powers in Africa was not acceptable. The South African reaction was being awaited.

f. The meeting agreed to the Ghana proposal that each participating country should nominate an official to be associated with the Secretarial Organization at Accra.

5. The Liberian Ambassador asked whether it would not be a good idea if invitations to the conference were sent out by a group of sponsoring states instead of one country. The Acting High Commissioner said that he would be prepared to refer to Accra to question a group of countries sponsoring the conference. But the Sudanese Ambassador pointed out that Ghana had already sent out the invitations to Their Excellencies' respective Governments, and to think of any change would mean an alteration of the arrangements which had already been accepted. The Liberian Ambassador said that he did not know that the invitations to Governments were the actual ones and added that he accepted what had been done.

157

6. The Liberian Ambassador asked whether Ghana, in fact, consulted other governments before issuing the invitations. The Ethiopian Ambassador replied that during his recent meeting with the Prime Minister of Ghana in London, Dr. Nkrumah had mentioned that consultations had taken place with representatives of independent African states during the Ghana Independence celebrations. The Acting High Commissioner for Ghana then read the following excerpt from the letter dated April 16, 1957, which the Prime Minister of Ghana had sent to Heads of Governments concerned: "You will recall that at the informal consultations which took place at my suggestion in Accra during the Ghana Independence celebrations in March 1957, at which your representative to the celebrations was present, my desire, concurrently published in the World press, to convene a Conference of Independent States in Africa to consider matters of immediate mutual concern, was discussed, and that the general reaction was that such a conference was desirable, if only as a forum for the frank exchange of ideas concerning problems peculiar to Independent African States."

7. Agenda: The Ethiopian Ambassador referred to the provisional Agenda and said that he was not clear about the four points tabulated. He added that he had previously discussed the matter with the Prime Minister of Ghana who promised to send a Memorandum on the Agenda. He went on to say that his Government would like to have a clear elaboration of the points raised so that delegates from Addis Ababa might be well prepared. There should be a solid basis for agreement before the Conference to avoid unnecessary haggling. The Acting High Commissioner for Ghana said that the main objective of the meetings of Heads of Missions in London was to prepare the ground for the Accra Conference by discussing the provisional agenda, expanding it and, possibly, adding to it. Their Excellencies were to clear the ground and put flesh on to the skeleton of the provisional draft Agenda.

The Liberian Ambassador said that Their Excellencies did not want a well-cooked Agenda but they wanted to know "the mind of Ghana." For example, what was meant by the "racial problem" in Point No. 1? Were the Governments going to discuss the "racial problem" in the world or in the United States or in South Africa? The question of views on Foreign Policy alone entails a great deal. In his opinion, an elaboration of the various points raised in the draft provisional Agenda was necessary. His Excellency, the Liberian Ambassador, then suggested, and it was agreed that the Acting High Commissioner should communicate with his Government and ask for an elaboration of the Agenda in the form of a memorandum. The Liberian Ambassador mentioned that he had instructions to add items to the Agenda. He agreed to include a memorandum at the instance of the Acting High Commissioner.

The Chairman said that it was not the intention of the meeting to delete any points from the Agenda, but what was clearly wanted was an elucidation of the Agenda to allow for views from member states.

The Liberian Ambassador moved, and it was agreed that consideration of the Agenda should be deferred until the Acting High Commissioner received the requested memorandum from Accra.

The Chairman thanked Their Excellencies and at the suggestion of His Excellency, the Liberian Ambassador, it was agreed that the next meeting should be held at the Ethiopian Embassy.

The Acting High Commissioner for Ghana thanked the Chairman, Sayed Aswad Sath, on behalf of his colleagues, and the meeting was adjourned at 12:30 p.m."

The preparatory committee of African Heads of Missions in London had four other meetings at the Ethiopian Embassy on November 8, 1957, Tunisian Embassy on December 21, 1957, the Liberian Embassy on February 10, 1958, and finally at the Ghana

High Commission on March 24, 1958, at which the agenda for the Accra Conference was finally approved as follows:

1. Exchange of views on Foreign Policy especially in relation to the African continent, the future of the dependent territories of Africa, the Algerian problem, the racial problem, and the steps to be taken to safeguard the independence, sovereignty, and the territorial integrity of the independent African States.

2. Examination of ways and means of promoting economic cooperation between African States, based on the exchange of technical, scientific, and educational information with special regard to industrial planning and agricultural development.

3. On the cultural level, the formulation of concrete proposals for the exchange of visiting missions between the various countries, both Government and non-Government, which may lead to first-hand knowledge of one country of another, and to a mutual appreciation of their respective cultures.

4. Consideration of the problem of International Peace and conformity with the Charter of the United Nations and the Re-affirmation of the Principles of the Bandung Conference.

5. The setting up of a Permanent Machinery after the Conference. And so, the first-ever Conference of the Independent African States was held from April 15, 1958, to April 23, 1958 at Accra. At that time, there were eight (8) Independent African States, not counting the Republic of South Africa which had been invited but had insisted that the South African Government would only attend if metropolitan powers in Africa would be invited as well. Egypt which had joined Syria to become the United Arab Republic was represented by Dr. Mahmoud Fawzy, the Foreign Minister; Ethiopia by His Imperial Highness Prince Sahle Selassie, son of the Emperor of Ethiopia; Ghana by Dr. Kwame Nkrumah, the Prime Minister; Liberia by President William V. S. Tubman; Libya by Dr. Wahbi al-Bouri, the Foreign Minister; Morocco by Ahmed Balafrej, the Foreign Minister Sudan by Sayed Mohammed Ahmed Mahgoub, the Foreign Minister who later became the President of Sudan;

and Tunisia by Dr. Sadok Mokadem, Secretary of State for Foreign Affairs. Each representative attended the Conference with full plenipotentiary powers so that all the resolutions passed in the agenda, had the full backing of the governments of the Independent African States.

It is of historical importance to underscore the valid point that since the 1st Conference of Independent African States, the whole world sensed what Harold MacMillan, then Prime Minister of the United Kingdom, expressed as "the wind of change" in Africa. There had been an avalanche of independent African States. With the exception of Namibia and the Republic of South Africa where the white minority regimes have clung to political and economic power through the system of apartheid, all Africa is politically independent. Africans have also come to know themselves and realize their common heritage and common destiny. But resolutions on economic cooperation and development notwithstanding, the massive economic and financial problems facing Africa seem to be intractable. The transfer of technology to Africa from the developed world has been niggardly and tardy. What is more, the African conscience has been roused to such a high degree as would pose difficulties in the way of production. We think of free education for all, a national health service, social welfare, good housing, and equitable distribution of wealth before we think of how to produce the wealth. And yet, history informs us that the industrial revolution in Europe, with its incidents of child labor, sordid human habitation, high illiteracy, and shameful health hazards was achieved without the exercise of conscience. Even Japan managed to achieve her industrial and commercial breakthrough at the expense of cheap labor. The story has always been the survival of the fittest, with some benevolent liberal Government interceding to hold the ring. What other path is available for Africa? And so, since 1958, our attempts to establish viable economies and bring prosperity to our peoples have been unsuccessful. Where, like Nigeria, oil was discovered leading to an oil boom in revenue, the breakthrough has not come either. Millions of people are shamefully poor without food, water, clothing, or shelter.

161

One of the resolutions passed was the decision of the representatives of the Accra Conference "to constitute the Permanent Representatives of the Participating Governments at the United Nations as the informal permanent machinery." The African Group at the United Nations was born early in 1959. I shall reserve the functions and effectiveness of the group till later.

Another significant event which occurred soon after the first conference was the independence of the Republic of Guinea in 1958. It was an unexpected event because Guinea as a state in French West Africa had been part of the French political and constitutional system and, indeed a member of the Franco-African community envisaged under the constitution of the Fifth Republic. But something had happened in French-African politics.

As far back as 1946, French-African politicians had wanted the abolition of legal differentiations between Africans and Frenchmen. In October 1946 a Congress was held at Bamako of representatives of the French territories in Africa with the aim of achieving, according to "the RDA claims to Lutte Anti-Imperialist" published later in Paris in 1948, "the realization of political and social democracy in Black Africa." It was at the Bamako Congress that the Rassemblement Democratique Africaine (RDA) was born. Present at that Bamako Congress was Sekou Toure, one of the eleven delegates from Guinea. He became a member of the Coordinating Committee of the RDA and a Vice-President. His rival in Guinea was Yacine Diallo, head of the socialist party in Guinea and a Socialist Deputy. While Yacine Diallo was outside the mainstream of the RDA, Sekou Toure was very much an active member and head of the section in Guinea. The Guinean section of the RDA was reorganized and Sekou Toure became Secretary-General of the Parti Democratique de Guinee (PDG) in 1952. With the support of the organized labor movement, the PDG became a formidable factor to reckon with, and when Yacine Diallo, who had been a leading politician in Guinea, died in 1954, Sekou Toure emerged as the unrivaled political leader.

It was against this political background in Guinea that the Constitution of the Fifth Republic of France became practical politics. Sekou Toure favored a strong federal structure with an elected parliament at the federal level and an executive council, so that there would be two federations, one for French West Africa and another for French Equatorial Africa each working out a relationship with France within the wider community. Most of the leaders of the RDA, like Houphouet Boigny, wanted the French territories to be autonomous entities within the French Community with foreign affairs, defense, and currency matters controlled by the French National Assembly.

General De Gaulle, the President of France, visited Conakry on August 25, 1958. In his speech welcoming de Gaulle, Sekou Toure referred to the proposed referendum in regard to the establishment of the Community and restated his stand in favour of independence and juridical equality within the Community. President de Gaulle replied as follows: "France proposes this Community; nobody is obliged to join it. You have talked of independence. I say here even more loudly than I have elsewhere that independence is up to Guinea. It can have it on September 28 by voting 'No' to the proposal, and I guarantee the Metropole will make no objection. There will, of course, be some consequences for Guinea, but there will be no obstacles in the way. Your country can do what it wants to and can follow any course it likes. If Guinea says 'Yes' – that is, if it freely, spontaneously, of its own accord accepts the constitution – and if France on its side says 'Yes', then the African territories and the Metropole can work together for mutual profit."

The referendum was duly held on September 28, 1958, in France and throughout French-speaking Africa. Only Guinea voted "No". On that day the chief of the French mission in Guinea handed a communique to the leaders of Guinea stating that since Guinea had voted "No" it no longer became, part of French West Africa, that Guinea was no longer represented in any organ of the community and that French administrative and economic assistance was at an end. On October 2, 1958, the Guinean territorial assembly went into special session and proclaimed the independence of Guinea which became the Republic of Guinea, and Sekou Toure was elected the first President by the Assembly. The French Government reacted rather sharply. The majority of the administrative officers left with indecent haste, telephone equipment, and plumbing facilities were destroyed; vital files were taken away. There was, indeed, a concerted effort to sabotage the independence of Guinea. But Ghana and Liberia had recognized the new Republic of Guinea on October 2, 1958. In fact, Ghana rushed to Guinea's aid with 10 million pounds in aid. By October 30, 1958, Great Britain had recognized Guinea.

Sekou Toure sent a special envoy to London in November 1958 and instructions came from Accra to the Ghana High Commission in London to accord all courtesies to that envoy and assist him in his contacts with the British authorities. It was my lot and privilege to meet that special envoy, Diallo Telli, and bring him to the High Commission. He explained the purpose of his mission to the High Commissioner and it was arranged that I took him to the British Foreign Office for a series of discussions. It was at this time that the French media attacked Britain, "the perfidious Albion" for working through Ghana to get Guinea into the Commonwealth. It was altogether a fantastic experience for me to meet Diallo Telli for the first time. He was very articulate and full of energy and conviction, characteristics which became extremely useful at the United Nations. In fact, Guinea was admitted to the United Nations on December 31, 1958, and Diallo Telli became its first Permanent Representative to the UN and Ambassador to the United States.

Ghana was itself admitted to the United Nations on March 10, 1957 and *ipso facto*[30] became a member of the specialized agencies · of the United Nations. The Ghana Government also decided to join the General Agreement on Tariffs and Trade (GATT) in Geneva. The first delegation comprised Franco Ribeiro-Ayeh, then Permanent Secretary, Ministry of Trade, E. Quist-Therson,

---

30 **Ipso facto** is a Latin phrase, directly translated as "by the fact itself", which means that a specific phenomenon is a direct consequence, a resultant effect, of the action in question, instead of being brought about by a previous action. It is a term of art used in philosophy, law, and science.

Permanent Secretary, Ministry of Finance, and myself as the Secretary. Our first act, I recall, was to invoke Article 13 of the General Agreement against Japan and to urge that country to buy more of our cocoa.

I must at this stage state that work at the High Commission was not without its fun and excitement. I relished the Commonwealth nights at the Buckingham Palace which we used to attend with our wives resplendent in Kente cloth. There were also the Queen's tea parties in the summer. Of course, there was a never-ending cycle of receptions, lunches, and dinners organized by other ambassadors, High Commissions, and British friends. The period I spent at the Ghana High Commission was exciting beyond description. Sir Edward's diplomatic parties were really popular and I would be inundated with queries from a Dowager, a certain Marchioness of Winchester, who would express dismay at having not been invited to a particular dinner.

Of course, because of our vigorous foreign policy, Ghana was very much in the news and consequently, the Ghana High Commission was kept extremely busy, especially during the Commonwealth Prime Ministers' Conference held in London in 1958. Dr. Kwame Nkrumah himself attended the Conference and I was detailed to be his Aide-de-Camp[31]. The Permanent Secretary of the Ministry of Foreign Affairs was also in London and, therefore, everybody was on the *qui vive*[32]. Everything went off smoothly to the relief and satisfaction of the High Commissioner.

In March 1959, the new Minister of Foreign Affairs, Dr. Ako Adjei (before this time the Foreign Affairs portfolio had been handled by the Prime Minister himself) arrived in London accompanied by Henry A. H. S. Grant of the Ministry of Foreign Affairs. They then proceeded to New York to attend a special session of the United Nations on the then mandated territory of British and French Cameroons. They returned to Ghana through London.

---

31 An aide-de-camp is a personal assistant or secretary to a person of high rank, usually a senior military, police or government officer, or to a member of a royal family or a head of state. An aide-de-camp may participate at ceremonial functions, and the first aide-de-camp is typically the foremost personal aide.

32 On the alert or lookout.

After their departure, the High Commissioner informed me that the Minister of Foreign Affairs had asked him questions about me and had hinted that he would like to post me from London, but he had convinced the Minister to leave me alone in London as I had been doing a good job. The High Commissioner had impressed upon the Foreign Minister the importance of our London mission and my presence as his official Secretary. If there had to be a transfer, two more years in London would be helpful. I was delighted by my High Commissioner's stand as I had been reading for the Bar at Lincoln's Inn where I had been admitted in 1954.

It was, therefore, a great surprise when on June 26, 1959, a telex message came to my High Commissioner from the Ministry of Foreign Affairs that "it had pleased the Governor-General, Lord Listowel, on the advice of the Prime Minister, Dr. Kwame Nkrumah, to appoint Alex Quaison-Sackey as our Ambassador and Permanent Representative to the United Nations in New York." When Sir Edward relayed this message to me at home early one morning during his normal morning phone calls, I had disbelieved him and had said so. Of course, I promptly apologized. But, frankly, I had not expected to leave London soon after two years' stay, let alone become an Ambassador Extraordinary and Plenipotentiary. Indeed, my relations with the High Commissioner had been very close and happy, and so when Dr. Ako Adjei sought information about my background, Sir Edward Asafu-Adjaye had waxed lyrical about my diplomatic performance and had unwittingly but truthfully told the Foreign Minister that I had been an asset to him. Little did the High Commissioner realize that the Minister was scouting for a young career diplomat to head our United Nations Mission in New York which was going to be a separate entity from our embassy in Washington. At independence, our Mission in New York and the Ghana Embassy in Washington had been run by Daniel Chapman Nyaho, a distinguished educationist who had been the first Secretary to the Ghana Cabinet and had also had a stint of duty at the United Nations Secretariat. The Ambassador himself lived in Washington but came to New York frequently on duty.

My appointment as Ambassador to the United Nations came as a bombshell to the rest of the "faithful nine" and to myself. None of them could, of course, claim seniority over me except by age, because each of us knew very well that the examination which had been planned to grade us after our training never took place and, therefore, we all had to start from scratch, although we had been listed according to age. In any case, no career officer had dreamt that anyone of us would be appointed as Ambassador so soon after independence. In fact, one politician had bragged in the National Assembly (Parliament) that no career officer would ever be appointed an Ambassador so long as the CPP government was in power because we had been pompous and had sounded omniscient. I, therefore, looked upon my appointment at that time as a great challenge to me and my colleagues. Indeed, Sir Charles Tachie-Menson, the then Chairman of the Public Service Commission, had told me in no uncertain terms that the future of my colleagues in the Foreign Service depended upon my success or failure at the national assignment thrust upon me. I was then approaching the age of 35.

The telex which had brought the good news to London had summoned me as well to Accra without delay. The High Commissioner, therefore, dispatched me to Accra where I at once met A. L. Adu, the Permanent Secretary, Dr. Ako Adjei, the Foreign Minister, Sir Charles Tachie-Menson, the Chairman of the Public Service Commission whom I have already mentioned, and then Lord Listowel. It was at the Governor-General's office that I met my old Latin master from Mfantsipim, Michael Dei-Anang, then Secretary to Lord Listowel. The Governor-General congratulated me on my appointment and Dei-Anang expressed joy and stressed that I had to work hard to pave the way for my colleagues.

Later in the afternoon of my arrival, the Foreign Minister took me to the Christiansborg Castle, the seat of Government, and ushered me into the presence of the great man himself, Dr. Kwame Nkrumah, who later became the first President of the First Republic of Ghana. I had been introduced to him in 1949 by my schoolmate and friend, Saki Scheck, just before I had left for the University of Oxford. The second time I met him was in 1958 when he came to London for the Prime Ministers' Conference, and I had to accompany him to Buckingham Palace. I never thought that he would remember me but he did, when he saw me at the Castle. He made me feel at home. He informed me that the Government needed a young man like me at the United Nations, and referred to the same Diallo Telli who was then Sekou Touré's Ambassador to the United Nations. He gave me much encouragement and exhorted me to be fearless and forthright in my work at the United Nations. "But I understand", Dr. Nkrumah said, "you have been educated at Oxford. Do not speak with an Oxford voice. Speak with my voice." It was a moving exhortation and I knew that by the Grace of God, I was going to my new assignment with every support of the Prime Minister and his Government. Dr. Ako Adjei, the Foreign Minister, was visibly pleased that he had discovered me. Little did he know that he had been my political hero and mentor since my Achimota College days!

It was while I was at Accra for briefing and preparation for my new posting that some friends of Kenneth Kweku S. Dadzie, future Secretary-General of UNCTAD[33], talked to me about him. He himself had approached me as a friend and colleague, and expressed a desire to be my second-in-command at the Ghana Mission to the United Nations. Apparently, he had gone against instructions while he was on duty in Paris in 1957 soon after independence to set up the Ghana Embassy in France. Ken had objected to the appointment of A. G. Levantis as Commercial Minister for Ghana for reasons which he had elaborated in a dispatch to Accra. According to the Foreign Ministry, he had gone beyond the bounds of his assigned functions and so had been recalled and put on the carpet. Luckily, Ken had been a college-mate, a colleague, and a friend. He, Justice Patrick Annin, and I had been on the same plane to England in 1959, when Ken and Patrick had gone to Cambridge and I to Oxford. Ken and I had been in close touch when he was a Government Agent at Enchi and I a Labor Officer at Tarkwa. Our paths had crossed

---

33 UNCTAD, United Nations Conference on Trade and Development.

again when both of us had been selected as part of the first eight to train for the Foreign Service of Ghana.

In the circumstances, I considered it a privilege that he had expressed the wish to work under me in New York. I also considered it my duty to help him out of the rut which he had found himself. I succeeded amply in persuading the Foreign Minister and the Permanent Secretary to release Ken for the assignment in New York. Thus it was that from 1960 to 1963 Ken Dadzie worked at the Ghana Mission to the United Nations as my deputy until, at his request, I recommended him for the United Nations Secretariat to work with my friend, Chief Godfrey Kio Jaja Amachree, then Under Secretary-General at the Secretariat.

I returned from Accra to London to organize my family and prepare to leave for New York. My High Commissioner put up a beautiful farewell party for us at which he lauded me to the skies and congratulated me on my new appointment, urging me to continue to work hard for Ghana. I myself had no illusions about the enormity of the task ahead of me and the great challenges it posed, but I was confident that with the guidance of God, I would do my best. I handed over to John Sagoe and Anthony Ephson and on July 13, 1959, I left London in the morning by the British Overseas Airways Corporation's "Comet" jet[34] which had just been introduced into service. I arrived in New York by the afternoon of that day.

Of Sir Edward Asafu-Adjaye I would say that no finer person could have become the first Ghana High Commissioner in London at our independence. He was a man of culture, a true Ashanti nobleman who could hold his own anywhere. After he had won the Profumo Prize in his finals at the English Bar in 1927, he had been called to the Bar at the Middle Temple. He was soft-spoken but witty with a sharp brain. He was a seasoned politician, a Parliamentarian impresario, and a brilliant advocate. He was born an Ashanti chief in his own right. It was with such

---

34 "Comet" jet, The de Havilland DH 106 Comet was the world's first commercial jet airliner. Developed and manufactured by de Havilland at its Hatfield Aerodrome in Hertfordshire, United Kingdom, the Comet 1 prototype first flew in 1949.

a colorful personality with many parts that for two years, I was privileged to work. It was to his eternal credit and a great honor for Ghana that he was chosen as a member of the Commonwealth Constitutional team who went to Guyana, then British Guiana, to make an on the spot study of the constitutional and political situation of that colony and to advise the British Government. The knighthood he received from the Queen in 1961 was given at a time when Ghanaians were forbidden by the Government of Ghana to accept foreign honors, not to mention that Ghana had become a republic. But an exception had been made in his case for his singular service to Ghana and the Commonwealth. I have always counted myself providentially blessed that I had an opportunity of serving under Sir Edward Asafu-Adjaye. May his soul have eternal peace.

CHAPTER 8

GHANA'S AMBASSADOR TO THE UNITED
NATIONS – 1959-1965: PART 1 1959 - 1960

At the Ghana High Commission in London, my duties as Official Secretary to the High Commissioner, Sir Edward Asafu-Adjaye, had included taking care of the work of the Chancery, coordinating the work of the various sections of the High Commission, writing dispatches to the Ministry of Foreign Affairs, liaising with diplomatic missions accredited to the Court of St. James, and dealing with all and sundry who wanted to see the High Commissioner. I also attended conferences and meetings in Britain and in Switzerland where there was as yet no Ghana Mission. My activities in the United Kingdom constituted what can be described as bilateral diplomacy. The main concern of the High Commission in London was to promote healthy diplomatic relations between Ghana and the United Kingdom. However, when I was appointed the Ambassador and Permanent Representative of Ghana to the United Nations, I found myself delving in multilateral diplomacy.

My knowledge of the United Nations and its working prior to my assumption of office as Ghana's Permanent Representative was very dim indeed. What I knew was largely theoretical. As an undergraduate at Oxford, I had been taught international politics and institutions, including the United Nations by H. G. Nicholas, then Fellow of Exeter College, Oxford, and teacher of Politics, who later produced a classic book on the United Nations. Later, at the London School of Economics where I studied International Relations under Professors Manning and Goodwin, I had learned all about the Congress of Vienna, the League of Nations, and the United Nations and its specialized agencies. But studying international institutions was a different thing altogether. It was when I became involved in the actual work of the world organization that I gained an insight into the enormity of the task facing the United Nations as an institution for peace.

It was July 24, 1959, that, accompanied by my colleague, Frederick Arkhurst, then Counsellor at the Ghana Mission, I went to the United Nations Secretariat to present my credentials to the Secretary-General, Mr. Dag Hammarskjold. We were met at the delegates entrance by Mr. Jehan Nous, Chief of UN protocol, and led to the presence of Mr. Hammarskjold. I dutifully presented my Letters of Credence duly signed by Lord Listowel, the then Governor-General of Ghana, representing the Queen. At this time, Ghana had not yet become a Republic. Dag Hammarskjold received my credentials with warm and cordial words of welcome and emphasized the need for close cooperation and collaboration between my Mission and the United Nations Secretariat. He praised the work of my predecessor, Mr. Daniel Chapman (now Chapman-Nyaho) who, though resident in Washington, combining his duties as Ghana's Ambassador to the United States with those of a Permanent Representative at the United Nations, had done a good job. Hammarskjold then wished me well in my new assignment. From the time I first met him to the time he died in a plane crash at Ndola in present-day Zambia in 1961, we worked very closely together indeed.

The period I spent at the United Nations – July 1959 to November 1965 – was extremely busy and eventful. It was in 1960 – 61 that quite a large number of African States became independent and were admitted as sovereign and equal members of the United Nations. This was thus the period when the African voice was loudly and distinctly heard. This was the period when the United Nations itself underwent a major metamorphosis, resulting in the enlargement of the memberships of the Security Council and the Economic and Social Council. The eleven seats of the

Security Council were increased to 15 while the 18 seats of the Economic and Social Council were increased to 27. I was one of the Permanent Representatives who initiated the move to have the increases made and I remember that the delegation of the USSR was opposed to any agreement to increase the seats on the grounds that without the Peoples Republic of China taking its rightful place as a permanent member of the Security Council, no amendment of the Charter should be countenanced. France took a similar stance but when it was found that there was overwhelming support for the increases from African, Asian, and Latin American delegations, the opposition crumbled. The Charter was amended to reflect the increases.

This was also the period of the espousal of the principle of peaceful co-existence by the Soviet Union[35] under Khrushchev and Brezhnev. It was during my years of service at the UN that there took place the Congo (Zaire) crisis[36]; the Cuban missile crisis;[37] the Bay of Pigs[38] (Cuban) fiasco when some American Cuban exiles and mercenaries attempted an invasion of Cuba and failed; the Sharpeville massacre in apartheid South Africa; and this was the time that the Arab-Israeli conflict, nuclear testing and the proliferation of nuclear weapons and non-alignment as foreign policy became momentous and critical issues. This was also the period of the hippies and the beatniks and the Black

---

35 The Soviet Union, officially the Union of Soviet Socialist Republics, was a federal socialist state in Northern Eurasia that existed from 1922 to 1991. Nominally a union of multiple national Soviet republics, in practice its government and economy were highly centralized until its final years.

36 The Congo Crisis was a period of political upheaval and conflict in the Republic of the Congo between 1960 and 1965. The crisis began almost immediately after the Congo became independent from Belgium and ended, unofficially, with the entire country under the rule of Joseph-Désiré Mobutu. By 2008, the war and its aftermath had caused 1.4 million deaths, principally through disease and starvation, making the Second Congo War the deadliest conflict worldwide since World War II. Another 2 million were displaced from their homes or sought asylum in neighboring countries.

37 The Cuban Missile Crisis, also known as the October Crisis of 1962, the Caribbean Crisis, or the Missile Scare, was a 13-day confrontation between the United States and the Soviet Union initiated by Soviet ballistic missile deployment in Cuba

38 The Bay of Pigs invasion (Spanish: invasión de bahía de Cochinos; sometimes called invasión de playa Girón or batalla de Girón, after the Playa Girón) was a failed landing operation on the southwestern coast of Cuba in 1961 by Cuban exiles who opposed Fidel Castro's Cuban Revolution. Covertly financed and directed by the U.S. government, the operation took place at the height of the Cold War and its failure led to major shifts in international relations between Cuba, the United States, and the Soviet Union.

Panthers and the civil rights[39] movement in the United States. This period saw the shameful murder through an air crash of the Secretary-General, Dag Hammarskjold by persons unknown at Ndola in Zambia, and the naked assassination of the President of the United States, John F. Kennedy, whose "ask not what your country can do for you, but what you can do for your country", in his inaugural address in January 1961 had inspired many a patriot of every country in the world. Indeed, this was the period of general commotion in the moral world, when critical and perennial issues of world health, hunger, ignorance, childcare, employment and the worth and dignity of the human person, all cried out for attention and solution.

I had no illusions whatsoever as to the enormity of the task ahead of me as Permanent Representative of a country which prided itself on being the first colonial territory in Africa South of the Sahara to have attained its independence. Ghana's interest was world peace within whose ambit the liberation of colonial and oppressed Africa should have top priority. I realized at once that whatever initiatives Ghana would take must have the backing of the African group as much as possible. With the establishment of the Informal Permanent machinery of the independent African States at the UN, after the 1958 Accra conference, there was indeed a forum to test our foreign policies. The African Group, as this informal machinery was called at the UN, was destined to play a vital role.

It was on May 7, 1958, that my predecessor, Ambassador Daniel Chapman, called a meeting of all African Ambassadors to give

---

39 A hippie is a member of the counterculture of the 1960s, originally a youth movement that began in the United States during the mid-1960s and spread to other countries around the world. It is sometimes spelled Hippy.

The Beatnik was a media stereotype prevalent throughout the late 1940s, 1950s to mid-1960s that displayed the more superficial aspects of the Beat Generation literary movement of the late 1940s and early to mid 1950s.

The Black Panther Party, originally the Black Panther Party for Self-Defense, was a revolutionary socialist political organization founded by Marxist college students Bobby Seale and Huey Newton in October 1966 in Oakland, California.

The civil rights movement in the United States was a decades-long struggle by African Americans to end legalized racial discrimination, disenfranchisement and racial segregation in the United States.

a report of the Accra Conference held the previous month and to explain the mandate given to all African Ambassadors by the Heads of State and Ministers who participated in the Conference, to establish the informal permanent machinery. At the time, the representatives of the Algerian Front of National Liberation (FLN) participated as observers. There was general agreement that the group should meet at least once a month but more often, if need be, especially during the General Assembly sessions.

As soon as I presented my credentials, I called on all my African colleagues and then took my time to call on the Permanent Representatives of the Great Powers, then of India, Iraq, Ceylon[40], Mexico, Brazil, Argentina, and other selected countries. Apart from the African Group, Ghana also belonged to the Commonwealth Group, that is, Britain, Australia, Canada, New Zealand, India, Pakistan, Ceylon, and Ghana. Chairmanship of the British Ambassador, Sir Pierson Dixon with whom I had an instantly warm rapport. I settled down rather quickly.

I vividly recall that at the 14th Session of the General Assembly which was my very first Assembly session, I was accosted in the lobby of the Delegates' Lounge by the famous V. K. Krishna Menon, then the Defense Minister of India, who insisted that a separate African grouping was injurious to the larger interests of the Asian and African Group and that I should use my influence to persuade my African colleagues to desist from pursuing a divisive course of action. "You are trying to kill the Asian and African Group which for a long time had taken the lead in focusing attention on vital world issues like disarmament, colonialism, racism, and apartheid in South Africa", he told me. Of course, I had heard about him before I met him. Krishna Menon was known in UN circles as an eloquent and an outspoken critic of the West, a wise world statesman, albeit disputatious. I explained to him why there was an African Group and I promised that we would work in close cooperation with the larger group and would

---

40 Ceylon was the British Crown colony of present-day Sri Lanka between 1815 and 1948. Initially the area it covered did not include the Kingdom of Kandy, which was a protectorate, but from 1817 to 1948 the British possessions included the whole island of Ceylon, now the nation of Sri Lanka.

even bring certain issues in the first instance to the larger Afro-Asian Group, where necessary. In the event, old Krishna Menon became interested in me and in what I had to say in and out of the United Nations. Throughout my stay, the African Group became stronger and stronger, and our membership increased from 9 to 32 at the time of my departure in 1965. The larger Afro-Asian Group was also stronger as a result of the stronger African group.

I cannot even at this time of my life forget an incident involving Krishna Menon and myself. I recall that when I was the representative of Ghana on the Security Council for two years, from January 1962 to December 1963, one of the big issues affecting international peace and security was the intractable problem of Kashmir, a disputed territory between India and Pakistan. Both India and Pakistan through their High Commissions in Accra sought the support of the Government of Ghana for their case before the Security Council. The Pakistanis were emphatic that the then Prime Minister had categorically stated before the bar of world opinion that when Kashmir had been vacated by the invader, a plebiscite[41] would be organized to ascertain the wishes of the Kashmiri people. The Government of Pakistan had, therefore, insisted that a UN-sponsored plebiscite should be held. India had denied any such promise made by Nehru. After all, the argument went, it had been India which had asked the Security Council in 1948 to demand that Pakistan should refrain from supporting the Pathan tribesmen who had invaded Kashmir from Pakistan's North-West Frontier province. Apart from taking a military situation by sending a five-member commission to mediate and arrange a cease-fire which took effect in January 1949, an attempt was made at the time to find a political settlement. There was agreement that the Kashmiris should be allowed to decide their future by plebiscite but the modalities were never agreed. Although a great effort was again made in 1957 when the Security Council requested its president,

---

41 A referendum is a direct and universal vote in which an entire electorate is invited to vote on a particular proposal and can have nationwide or local forms. This may result in the adoption of a new policy or specific law. In some countries, it is synonymous with a plebiscite or a vote on a ballot question.

Ambassador Gunner Jarring of Sweden, to try and get India and Pakistan to reach a settlement, nothing much was achieved.

But the Security Council had by a resolution reiterated its stand that the way out of the Kashmir problem was to organize a UN-supervised plebiscite. That resolution in January 1957 was supported by 10 of the then 11 members, with the Soviet Union abstaining.

It is against the background of the foregoing, that I made what I considered an impartial intervention at the Security Council in early 1962. The distinguished representative of Ireland, Fred Boland, introduced a resolution asking India and Pakistan to resume negotiations. The Soviet Union vetoed it and the draft resolution was denounced by my friend Krishna Menon as "a hostile act."[42] In my case, after I had delivered my statement before the Council, I received congratulatory handshakes from a number of colleagues, but not from my Indian friends apparently because of my references to a plebiscite.[43] I was then informed that Krishna Menon was heard to have muttered, after my statement, "that black Englishman."[44] I promptly protested to Ambassador Chandra S. Jha, my Indian colleague who in turn promptly reported my protest to Minister of Defense, Krishna Menon. Before long, the old diplomat had come to apologize to me, that he had been misquoted by the pressman who had given me the information, and that he entertained the highest regard for me and for my president, Dr. Kwame Nkrumah who had been his friend many years ago in London. I observed that the old man had been visibly shaken and I helped him out of his embarrassment by stating that I had not believed that he would

---

42 A hostile act is an attack or other use of force by any civilian, paramilitary, or military force or terrorist(s) (with or without national designation) characteristic of an enemy: a hostile nation. opposed in feeling, action, or character; antagonistic.

43 A referendum is a direct and universal vote in which an entire electorate is invited to vote on a particular proposal and can have nationwide or local forms. This may result in the adoption of a new policy or specific law. In some countries, it is synonymous with a plebiscite or a vote on a ballot question. 1956 British Togoland status plebiscite. A referendum on the territory's status was held in British Togoland on 9 May 1956. Since World War I the territory had been a League of Nations mandate, then a United Nations Trust Territory under British control.

44 Black Englishman is a racial and political statement, such partial and unfriendly statement is often made or becomes popular where blacks find themselves among white people.

make the statement attributed to him. Weeks later, my wife received a beautiful gift from V. K. Krishna Menon – an Indian sari. I never saw him again.

Before the 14th Session of the General Assembly came around, I had received instructions to attend a Conference of African Foreign Ministers in Monrovia, Liberia from August 4 to August 8, 1959. The main purpose of the Conference was to enable the representatives of the African States, then only 9 in number, to discuss urgent African problems, notably the independence of Algeria. Present at Monrovia was a strong team sent by the Provisional Government of Algeria formed by the Algerian National Liberation Front (FLN) led by Muhammed Fazid. The resolution on Algeria called for *pourparlers*[45] (negotiations) between France and the Provisional Government of Algeria. It was strongly felt at the Conference that it was impolitic for France to claim that Algeria was part of France, while the FLN had proved that the Arab majority wanted full independence and had demonstrated their preparedness to end the war of liberation and find a political solution through *pourparlers*. French politicians like Jacques Soustelle, who was De Gaulle's Minister of Information had to be convinced that independent Algeria would not be a loss to France. In fact, as it had turned out, General De Gaulle himself was converted to the principle of Algeria for the Algerian but Jacques Soustelle had to resign as Minister of Information to espouse the cause of French Algeria.

On December 3, 1960, it fell to my lot to debate against Soustelle on American TV the cause of an independent Algeria. I remember that he tried to use Communism to convince our American audience that free Algeria would mean Communist Algeria and I had to remind him and convince the same audience that communism was a hobby horse exploited by opponents of African independence to buy American support. I said that great African politicians and leaders like Houphouet Boigny, Gabriel

---

45 Pour Parley is a discussion or conference, especially one between enemies over terms of a truce or other matters. During the 18th and 19th centuries, attacking an enemy during a parley was considered one of the grossest breaches of the rules of war.

D'Arbousier, and Ben Bella were all dubbed as communists and yet their political records did not prove the accusation. I believe I won the day.

In 1960 at the 15th Session, the General Assembly passed a resolution that recognized "the imperative need for adequate and effective guarantees to assure the successful and just implementation of the right of self-determination on the basis of respect for the unity and territorial integrity of Algeria" and recognized "further that the United Nations has a responsibility to contribute towards its successful and just implementation." I can recall that on this resolution, however, African states were divided: several of the French African states took a sympathetic attitude towards France and either opposed the resolution or abstained from voting one way or the other. What was gratifying, in any case, was that France and the then Algerian Provisional Government were able to meet at Evians-Les-Bains[46] on May 18, 1961, to begin serious negotiations. And what was of great importance was that General De Gaulle, one of the greatest leaders France has produced, understood better than perhaps any other French stateman the temper of Africa at the time. And so on July 1, 1962, after a referendum in which the people of Algeria voted in favor of independence and cooperation with France, Algeria became an independent nation. Today, Algeria is very much a free and independent state, and it is a matter of history that it was I who introduced the resolution on the admission of the sovereign and independent Algeria to the UN at the Security Council in 1962. My statement on that occasion so moved the late Presidential candidate, Adlai Stevenson, then the US Permanent Representative that he visited my Mission personally to express his congratulations to me, a rare occasion in those days!

Other issues dealt with by the African Foreign Ministers in Monrovia in August 1959 included the unification of the two commissions under the French and British administrations

---

46 Évian-les-Bains, or simply Évian, is a commune in the northern part of the Haute-Savoie department in the Auvergne-Rhône-Alpes region in south-eastern France.

respectively, apartheid South Africa, South West Africa (Namibia), Nyasaland (Malawi) and the North and Southern Rhodesias.[47]

African Ambassadors were then instructed to mount strong pressure on the British, French, Portuguese, Belgian, and Spanish colonial powers to relinquish their stranglehold on African territories and grant them independence.

The problem of the commissions was that there were some African politicians in West Cameroons, that is, the part administered by the British, who were strongly in favor of unification with their brothers in French-administered Cameroons, and there were others who favored joining the Federation of Nigeria. The first group included Prime Minister Ngu Forocha and S.T. Mina; the other group was led by Endeley, then leader of opposition in the Parliament of British Cameroons. The Foreign Ministers decided that a UN-supervised plebiscite should be organized in the Cameroons to enable the people to decide their own fate. Accordingly, at the 14th Session, African delegations made a common directive at the General Assembly to secure agreement on the holding of a plebiscite.

I must state that I could not have attended a better seminar on the foreign policies of African States than that Conference of Foreign Ministers held in August 1959 in Monrovia. To be exposed to the thinking and maneuvers of plenipotentiaries from Africa and to study them at close range was enough to prepare me for my new assignment at the United Nations. Having rubbed shoulders with Foreign Ministers and Ambassadors in Monrovia, I gained a great deal of confidence and widened my outlook. In a short period, I learnt vital aspects of the foreign policies of the then existing 9 independent African States, namely, the ancient monarchy of Ethiopia, the ancient state of Egypt which had joined Syria to form the United Arab Republic (UAR), the historical but modern

---

47 The territory to the north of the Zambezi was officially designated Northern Rhodesia by the company, and has been Zambia since 1964; that to the south, which the company dubbed Southern Rhodesia, became Zimbabwe in 1980. Northern and Southern Rhodesia were sometimes informally called "the Rhodesias".

States of Libya, Morocco, Tunisia, and Sudan, the oldest African Republic of Liberia, and the so-called new revolutionary states of Ghana and Guinea.

In Liberia, I was also privileged to have come into close contact with the Trinidadian-born George Padmore, a trade unionist, a Marxist revolutionary, and a staunch Pan-Africanist and anti-colonialist. He had been living in Ghana where we met. He had been a close friend and confidant of Kwame Nkrumah, then Prime Minister of Ghana. The record of the two men in the struggle for colonial emancipation was superb and Padmore was in Ghana to help Nkrumah make his Pan-Africanist dreams come true. Padmore advised on the eventual independence and unity of the African continent and establishing links with all black persons in the diaspora. Both Nkrumah and Padmore had been involved in the organization of the Sixth Pan-African Congress in Manchester in 1945, the last in a series of Conferences which focused the attention of the international society on the inequities and injustices of colonialism and imperialism in Africa. Padmore's books are highly political in content and tone. Most of them I had leafed through the *Gold Coast Revolution, Attitude in Africa*, and *Africa, Britain's Third Empire*[48]. They all portray his anti-colonialist posture, but when I met the man in Ghana, I was overwhelmed by his calm and soft manner. There was none of the spitfire and stern posture of a revolutionary. In Monrovia, I asked him many, many questions about his stay in Germany and the Soviet Union and subsequent sojourn in Britain.

George Padmore, it was, who wrote the Constitution of the Convention Peoples Party (CPP) and encouraged party members to meet in a study group which discussed and took decisions on sundry matters affecting the organization of the Party and ancillary bodies like the Young Pioneers and the Builders Brigade. At one of such meetings of the Study Group, there was a hot debate on socialism. Krobo Edusei and Amuah Awuah openly attacked him and asked him why he was living in a posh bungalow and had imported a new car if he, Padmore, was a

---

48 Names of books and write ups by George Padmore which talks about African culture, values and customs, from slavery to freedom.

socialist. Padmore replied that socialism meant prosperity and plenty for everybody, and did not mean poverty and deprivation. He thereupon warned that members of the Party should know how to conduct themselves and be careful lest they be overtaken in a military dictatorship. This was in early 1959. He died in London the same year and his mortal ashes were returned to Ghana and interred at the Christiansborg Castle, the seat of Imperial Power, and the present Ghana Government.

From George Padmore, I learnt a lot about the issues bedeviling the independence struggles in Southern Rhodesia (Zimbabwe), Northern Rhodesia (Zambia), and Nyasaland (Malawi) which in the course of time the British welded together as the Central African Federation, but for whose dissolution Ghana steadfastly worked. There were white settlers in these territories, especially in Southern Rhodesia who were resolute in creating a white enclave in the vain attempt to subjugate the Africans just as Malan, Verwoerd, and Stridjdon, apostles of apartheid, had done in South Africa. I became convinced that independent African states should do all in their power to prevent the creation of another South Africa in Central Africa and it was incumbent on me and my colleagues to watch the maneuvers of the white settlers and to make a constant assessment of British policies towards their territories in Central Africa.

As it turned out, the British Government did not favor any discussion of Southern Rhodesia at the United Nations on the grounds that, that territory was not a non-self-governing territory.

In 1961, as a delegate of Ghana, I challenged the British delegation at the General Assembly in South Rhodesia. I maintained that it was untenable to consider the issue of Southern Rhodesia as falling essentially within the domestic jurisdiction of the United Kingdom in accordance with Article 2 paragraph 7 of the Charter of the United Nations. I argued before the General Assembly that the majority of the population of that territory, who were Africans, had not been consulted on any issue, and that the paramount wishes of the Africans would be that their territory which was not independent should come under the searching light and close scrutiny of the United Nations. The independence of Southern Rhodesia was, therefore, a valid concern of the world organization and members of the General Assembly should be able to discuss the affairs of that territory. My colleague, Sir Patrick Dean, who was then the Permanent Representative of the United Kingdom to the United Nations, vehemently opposed the Ghana move. But I pressed for a vote on the procedural question whether Southern Rhodesia was not a legitimate concern of the General Assembly. The General Assembly voted with a large majority in favor of discussing the issue of Southern Rhodesia because it did not fall within the scope of Article 2 paragraph 7 of the Charter. From then on, the campaign for the independence of that territory intensified and I am proud to maintain that on the instructions of my President, Dr. Kwame Nkrumah, I assisted Joshua Nkomo who was then the undisputed leader of the nationalist front, under the Zimbabwe African Peoples Union (ZAPU), in every way possible.

I had learnt the ropes in a hard way. I believe that it was the hard work I put in during the 14th Session of the General Assembly which prepared me for my subsequent endeavors at the United Nations. In fact, it was during the fourteenth session of the General Assembly which began on September 15, 1959, and ended on December 12, 1959, that I served my apprenticeship at the United Nations.

There were seven main committees of the General Assembly: the first (Political) Committee, the Ad Hoc (Political) Committee; the second (Economic) Committee; the third (Social and Cultural) Committee; the fourth (Colonial-Trusteeship) Committee; the fifth (Administrative and Financial) Committee; and the sixth (Legal) Committee. With the assistance of my staff, I planned to deploy the Ghana delegation in such a way that every committee would be covered. The normal practice was that the Minister of Foreign Affairs of every country would lead the country's delegation to the sessions of the General Assembly. The Ministers would normally stay for a fortnight or so during which time, they delivered an address to the General Assembly outlining and explaining the foreign and other policies of their governments.

Sometimes, these statements were innocuous enough; at other times, they raised fundamental issues impinging upon the policies of other countries. When a delegation felt that they had been attacked in a statement, they would invariably ask to be given the right to reply.

The Ghana delegation in 1959 was led by the Foreign Minister, Dr. Ako Adjei, one of my political mentors, a seasoned and eloquent politician, who had been instrumental in bringing Dr. Kwame Nkrumah into the mainstream of Ghanaian politics. Apart from members of the staff, the delegation comprised three persons from Accra, namely, Teacher Essibrah, a then CPP Member of Parliament, Reverend S. A. Dzirasah, the Ministerial Secretary in the Ministry of Foreign Affairs, and Miss Florence Addison from the Ministry of Education. My staff included Mr. Fred S. Arkhurst who was my deputy but was due to join the staff of the Economic Commission for Africa (ECA) after the session; Mr. Kenneth Kweku S. Dadzie, the replacement for Fred Arkhurst; Dr. Amon Nikoi (Second Secretary); Mr. Yaw Turkson (Second Secretary); Mr. Emmanuel Abdallah (3rd Secretary); and Mr. Hope Yomekpe (3rd Secretary). Mr. Nathan Quao joined the delegation from our embassy in Yugoslavia. We were, therefore, able to service all the committees.

What I did at the 14th Session was to visit all the committees of the General Assembly to acquaint myself with whatever issue was being debated. But before long, I was concentrating my attention on the first and fourth committees. In any case, sometimes when a Ghana delegate at a particular committee felt that my presence at that committee was necessary, he would invite me so as to help resolve an issue. I also evolved the practice of meeting the delegation early in the morning, so that we would brief ourselves and resolve problems encountered during the previous meeting before we parted to our various committees. In this way, I kept track of affairs in all the committees, each of which had a number of items before it to dispose of. On every item, there was a resolution which should be passed by a simple majority. The resolution would then be submitted to the plenary session for consideration before it was accepted by the General Assembly which should pass it by a two-thirds majority, otherwise, the particular resolution would be deemed rejected. Where the Ghana delegation had co-sponsored a resolution, it was necessary that we should stoutly defend the resolution before the plenary session. It was really hard work, and I note from my diary of 1959 the following entry: "On reflection, I can record that I have never worked harder in my life, intellectually and physically, that is, than this session. I put in my energy, my mental prowess, and soul in order to push Ghana and enhance her prestige."

I had successfully gone through my first General Assembly session without blemish. I had taken over as leader of the Ghana delegation because both the Foreign Minister and his deputy had to depart for Ghana after three weeks. At this time, there were only nine African delegations and true to our instructions from our government, there was close consultation and collaboration among us. This meant that I was being sought and consulted constantly and I had to move around quickly and intelligently. Apart from work at the committees, there was a lot of discussion, consultation, and lobbying taking place in the corridors. Frankly, it was in the lobbies and in the delegates lounge that most of the actual work including back-stair intrigues took place. A delegate with instructions from his government to advance an issue or propose a resolution on some vital matter of interest to his government would do so at his peril without a proper strategy of consultation and lobbying. I quickly mastered the art of lobbying which was a *sine qua non* at the United Nations. I also became adept at drafting resolutions and when in my later years at the United Nations, my colleagues were consulting me on draft resolutions and other vital matters, it was principally because of the expertise I had acquired, let alone the strong and positive posture I had taken as Ghana's Ambassador on issues before the world organization.

I cannot discuss the 14th Session of the General Assembly in 1959 without mentioning some experiences I encountered. As my country's representative at the first political committee, I had strong instructions from my government to denounce the attempt by France to carry out nuclear testing in the Sahara. Ghana's stand was consistent with the position of the independent African states at the time. In fact, at the Accra Conference of 1958, the independent African states had declared themselves against the testing and production of nuclear and thermonuclear weapons, and when it became known that the French were preparing to explode a nuclear device in the Sahara, the issue was brought before the meeting of Foreign Ministers at Monrovia in August 1959 for debate and action. A resolution was then passed "denouncing vigorously and with profound indignation, the decision of any government to carry out nuclear tests in the Sahara or in any part of Africa." Thus, at the first Political Committee of the General Assembly, I made a statement detailing the various plans France had made to carry out its plans and informed the Committee of the general indignation felt by the people of Africa against France on the issue of a nuclear test in the Sahara. I then appealed to the Committee to pass a resolution calling on France to stop carrying out any tests in the Sahara.

Subsequently, the General Assembly passed a resolution by a two-thirds majority requesting France "to refrain from conducting such tests in the Sahara". France not only flouted the resolution but conducted four tests on African soil, a flagrant violation which did not help the image of France in Africa. What was of interest was that after I had spoken at the committee, I received congratulatory handshakes from other delegates including three Africans on the French delegation whom I recognized as Dr. Felix Houphouet Boigny, who within a year or so became the Head of State of Cote d'Ivoire, Leopold Senghor, the great African poet, who also became the first President of independent Senegal, and Gabriel D'Arboussier, the French African politician of the Rassemblement Democratique Africain (RDA) fame. I chatted at length with these African political stalwarts whose countries were on the verge of becoming independent African states. I had already met D'Arboussier in 1958 at the Oxford seminar on West Africa, and Houphouet Boigny in Paris in 1956 when as a trainee Foreign Service Officer, I was introduced to him as Minister of State for Health in the French government. I invited them to spend Saturday with me at my residence in New Rochelle. In the event, President Senghor and D'Arboussier turned up for lunch, but the future President of Cote d'Ivoire could not make it and sent me a polite message of apology. I did not realize at that time that some sort of rivalry had already reared its ugly head between my President, Dr. Kwame Nkrumah, and Dr. Felix Houphouet-Boigny whom I also regarded as my President!

The other experience I gained at the 14th Session was how not to use the wrong word at the United Nations at any time. After a brilliant intervention in the debate on disarmament in the first Political committee by the distinguished representative of Sri Lanka, Sir Claude Corea, the French representative on disarmament exercised his right of reply to a statement made by Sir Claude. He referred to Sir Claude as *un homme bien encoute*. Unfortunately, the interpretation sounded that Sir Claude was a man who talked too much. This naturally evoked an immediate protest from the representative of Ceylon much to the chagrin of the distinguished representative of France, who also replied that he had been misinterpreted and that *un homme bien ecoute* was rather complimentary to Sir Claude and meant he was "a man who is listened to with attention." A serious diplomatic incident between Ceylon and France was thus averted!

At another meeting which I attended of the second (economic) committee, there was a seething attack on United Nations experts sent to various developing countries under the Technical Assistance Programme and the Special Fund, now referred to as the United Nations Development Programme (UNDP). A delegate likened a UN expert to a bull who was sent to Sri Lanka to rejuvenate the cattle there, because the cattle population had shown no signs of increase. For some reason, according to this delegate, a whole year passed without a noticeable increase in the cattle population. And so someone who understood the bulls' language was sent to interview the bull and ascertain why the cattle were not breeding. The bull's reply was that it was true that he had been sent by the United Nations to Sri Lanka as a technical expert but that he was in Sri Lanka "in a purely advisory capacity."[49]

---

49 "In a purely advisory capacity" in a chaste or innocent manner.

187

On yet another occasion, the First Political Committee of the General Assembly had been seized of the important issue of the non-proliferation of nuclear weapons which ultimately resulted in the General Assembly approval in 1968 of the non-proliferation treaty. On that occasion, non-aligned states like Ethiopia, Ghana, Egypt (United Arab Republic), India, and Iraq had sponsored a draft resolution to the effect that the proliferation of nuclear weapons in the world should cease. The debate on the issue seemed interminable, necessitating a night session. As Ghana's delegate on this Committee in 1960, I made a pungent statement appealing to the nuclear Great Powers to desist from manufacturing the weapons at all, let alone spreading them. Speaker after speaker made passionate statements some very trenchant. As the sitting went far into the night and there was no sign of abatement of statements and rights of replies, the distinguished representative of Spain was given the floor to speak. In all earnestness, he intoned in impeccable Spanish that he as a person as a devout Roman Catholic. "In the Roman Catholic Church," the Ambassador of Spain went on, "we practice chastity, and the preaching of chastity subsumes virility. I have heard many speeches at the Committee on nuclear chastity. But all those states whose representatives are moralizing on chastity are themselves not atomically virile, how then can they insist on atomic chastity?" Everybody including those who were dozing sat up and applauded. The meeting adjourned until the following afternoon!

So much for the lighter side of the work of the United Nations. There were so many other instances of incidents which broke the tedium at the General Assembly like the time when Premier Khrushchev of the Soviet Union took off his shoe at the General Assembly meeting in September 1960 and began hitting his table as a demonstration of his opposition to the Secretary-General, Dag Hammarskjold, over the Congo (Zaire) issue. There was also the occasion at the Security Council when the distinguished representative of Congo (Leopoldville) vividly and ludicrously described how followers of Prime Minister Patrice Lumumba cut up fellow Congolese (Zaireans) and ate the flesh with blood dripping down their hands in the streets of Stanleyville. All this went to show that the United Nations was a veritable mirror of the world!

I believe that my service at the United Nations for a period of over six years from July 1959 to November 1965 was so eventful that I would do better to sift the events and portray those that I consider would be of interest to the reader than dwell on every event that occurred. What is more, there were certain issues which were considered perennial, that is, they came up for debates every year before the General Assembly without easy resolution. Issues like Disarmament, Palestinian Arab refugees, Apartheid in South Africa, the question of South West Africa (Namibia). Peaceful issues of outer space and economic development were all considered perennial and were debated year after year before the General Assembly.

For Ghana and for me as its Permanent Representative, the preservation of international peace and security was the main concern. Therefore, my mandate was to persuade my colleagues that every issue that militated against the preservation of that peace and security, should be resolved. Colonialism and neo-colonialism must be abolished, apartheid should be dismantled, South West Africa must be independent, there should be comprehensive and complete disarmament in the world, Israeli-Arab conflict should be avoided by finding a just solution to the problem of the Palestinian Arab refugees, there should be a just international economic order such as would enable the underdeveloped countries of the world to make significant gains in economic development. And of course, any world problem which threatened international peace and security should instantly be nipped in the bud, like the Congo crisis in 1960 and the Cuban missile crisis in 1962.

The colonial problem was for Ghana, a priority. When the Charter of the United Nations was signed in June 1945, colonialism was indeed a burning issue. There were statesmen like Herbert Evatt of Australia, Peter Fraser of New Zealand, and Carlos Romulo of the Philippines, later the President of the United Nations General Assembly, who demanded that the Charter should include a

Charter of Colonial Progress, thus internationalizing the colonial problem. But while there was a general acknowledgment that dependent territories should eventually gain independence, no serious attempt was made to formulate any clear-cut political and economic program. Africa was indeed a forgotten continent.

There were only three independent African countries at San Francisco, namely, Ethiopia, Liberia, and South Africa; and apart from Liberia, there was not really an African voice. In the event, Chapter XI was included in the Charter, purporting to set up a statement of principles governing the administration of non-self-governing territories. The fate of these territories was confined to Article 73 in Chapter XI. The pertinent paragraphs read as follows:

"Members of the United Nations which have or assume responsibilities for the administration of territories whose peoples have not yet attained a full measure of self-governance recognize the principle that the interests of the inhabitants of these territories are paramount, and accept as a sacred trust, the obligation to promote to the utmost, within the system of international peace and security established by the present Charter, the well-being of the inhabitants of these territories, and, to this end:

a. To ensure, with due respect for the culture of the peoples concerned, their political, economic, social, and educational advancement, their just treatment, and their protection against abuses;

b. To develop self-government, to take due account of the political aspirations of the peoples, and to assist them in the progressive development of their free political institutions, according to the particular circumstances of each territory and its peoples and their varying stages of advancement;

c. To further international peace and security;

d. To promote constructive measures of development, to encourage research, and to cooperate with one another and, when and where appropriate, with specialized international bodies with a view to the practical achievement of the social, economic, and scientific purposes set forth in this Article; and

e. To transmit regularly to the Secretary-General for information purposes, subject to such limitation as security and constitutional consideration may require, statistical and other information of a technical nature relating to economic, social and educational conditions in the territories for which they are respectively responsible other than those territories to which Chapters XII and XIII apply."

The remainder of the dependent territories, that is, those which had not been colonies of the Allied Powers of the Second World, became known as trust territories. They were, in fact, the former colonies of the defeated Axis powers of Germany, Italy, and Japan. Between the first and second World Wars, they were called mandated territories and had been under the general supervision of the League of Nations. In accordance with Chapter XII of the Charter, the mandated territories were placed under the international trusteeship system of the United Nations, and trusteeship agreements were then signed between the designated administrating authority, on the one hand, and the United Nations, on the other. In this way, various African territories dependent on Germany and Italy, as well as former Japanese territories in the Pacific, were placed under United Nations Trusteeship. As trust territories, there were not only inspected once every three years by visiting missions from the United Nations, but were also given the right to present petitions directly to the United Nations.

Such, in brief, were the two methods by which the architects of the Charter disposed of the colonial problem in 1945. How long it would take for dependent territories to become independent sovereign states was of no particular concern to those who met in San Francisco. However, President Roosevelt is reported in page 573 in "Roosevelt and Hopkins: An Intimate History" by Robert E. Sherwood, to have hinted that the Southeast Asian territories might need twenty years to be ready for independence. In any case, for the trust territories of British Togoland, Western Cameroons and Tanganyika (now Tanzania) under the British; French Togoland and Eastern Cameroons under the French; Rwanda-Burundi under Belgium and SouthWest Africa (Namibia) under Britain and South Africa, it was really a matter of time, when the leaders of the peoples concerned felt they were ready to take over the reins of government. In the case of SouthWest Africa, however, the South African white minority regime has doggedly resisted the United Nations supervision of that territory as a trust territory. The South Africans have argued that the mandate of the League of Nations did not pass to the United Nations as a successor International organization. I shall, therefore, deal with the question of Namibia later on.

In the case of the dependent territories such as the Gold Coast, Nigeria, Sierra Leone, Uganda, Guinea, Senegal and Zaire (Congo Leopoldville) to name only a few, their political future depended partly on the aspirations of the peoples themselves and partly on how the United Nations were convinced by the administering powers of progress being made in the territories.

In 1946, the General Assembly had established the Committee on Information from the Non-Self-Governing Territories to monitor information required from the Administering Authorities of "statistical and other information of a technical nature relating to economic, social, and educational conditions", under Article 73 of Chapter XI of the UN Charter.

It was not simply the enforcement of regulations that made the Committee's work effective and fruitful, rather it was by means of its persuasion, prodding and criticisms that it kept the colonial question alive and continually pricked the consciences of the colonial powers like Great Britain, France, Italy, Belgium, and Portugal. As a result, the first decade of its life saw the number of Non-Self-Governing Territories fall from seventy-five to fifty-five, and the aggregate of their populations fall from about 215 million to about 110 million. Thus, by the end of 1956, Africa had only seven independent states represented at the United Nations. When I arrived at the UN as Permanent Representative of Ghana, there were nine states, Ghana having become independent on March 6, 1957, and Guinea on October 2, 1958. As events turned out, I was elected Chairman of the Committee on Information from Non-Self-Governing Territories at its 11th session in February 1956-57 and this was a great boost in morale for the dependent peoples of Africa, for now, the Committee was presided over by a representative of a country that had itself been until March 1957 a non-self-governing territory. Viewed against what happened when the 15th Session of the General Assembly convened in September 1960, the following comments which I made at the Committee on Information and which were reported in the United Nations Review of May 1960, were prophetic:

"We are no longer dealing (as some people felt at San Francisco that they were) with a semi-permanent state of affairs in which millions of people in Africa, Asia, the Pacific, and the Caribbean have to resign themselves to an indefinite period of tutelage exercised by other countries. The time of colonialism, benevolent or otherwise, is at last really running out.

In my view, therefore, the General Assembly and the Committee on Information will need to give thought to revising their procedures, methods, and specific aims within the broad framework of Chapter XI of the Charter in order to function from now onwards on the assumption that the non-self-governing territories will become independent sooner rather than later. The United Nations must find ways and means to bring all their influence and assistance to bear on the key problems which tend to delay or otherwise interfere with that process and which threaten to weaken independence once it has been attained. This calls for greater concentration on specific problems in certain territories: the problem of race relations, for example in the East and Central African territories, where this is, in fact, the key to the evolution of democratic states; the problem of strong trade union development in territories where indigenous labor forces are growing in size but are at a disadvantage in dealing with non-indigenous management; and the problem, an urgent one almost everywhere, of training local persons for the civil services and for the statutory bodies which are coming to play an increasingly important role in the economic and social advancement of most of these territories."

The comments I made in May 1960, though guarded, were pregnant with strong anti-colonial sentiments which could no longer be ignored by the colonial powers. No longer would they assume that they were the arbiters of elegance to decide the future of their dependent territories and that they would be left alone to use their discretion and their own time in granting independence to all non-self-governing territories of the world.

The revolutionary path to independence of Ghana ran counter to the colonialist notions of discretion and taking their own time. It is true that up to 1948, British colonial policy was still based on the principle of evolution. The events of 1948 in the Gold Coast (Ghana), that is, the boycott of foreign goods, the march to the Christiansborg Castle by the ex-servicemen to present a petition to the Governor which prompted a shooting incident resulting in a number of deaths, the national riots, and the arrest of the "Big Six" (Dr. J. B. Danquah, Dr. Kwame Nkrumah, Akuffo Addo, William Ofori-Atta, Obetsebi-Lamptey, and Ako Adjei) led to the appointment by the British Government of the Watson Commission to investigate the causes of the disturbances, and make recommendations. The foreword to the Watson Report written by the Colonial Office epitomized the British attitude towards their colonies. It reads, "It is an axiom of British colonial policy that progress, whether political, social, or economic, and whether in local affairs or at the center of Government, can be soundly achieved only on two conditions: first, that it rests on the foundations of tradition and social usage which already exist; and second, that changes and developments carry with them the substantial acceptance of the people. It is not impossible, within these limitations, to banish abuses, to adjust anachronisms, and to introduce the framework of modern civilization, but the process must be evolutionary. A European system cannot be imposed arbitrarily on the African society." Frankly, it was anachronistic for the Colonial Office to have written such a foreword in 1948, after more than one hundred years of British rule in Ghana. Events had not stood still, and within nine years, the Convention Peoples Party which was established in 1949 had emerged as the most popular party with Dr. Kwame Nkrumah as its leader ready to take over the reins of power.

As Professor Rupert Emerson of the Center for International Affairs, Harvard, once wrote, "the independence of Ghana in 1957, promptly followed by its UN membership, is usually taken as the watershed which marks Africa's breach with colonialism." And, indeed, as the Permanent Representative of Ghana, I left no stone unturned to bring the colonialism issue forcibly before the UN. I successfully argued that the question of the independence of dependent territories did not fall within the purview of domestic jurisdiction. I could sense the anti-colonial mood of the peoples of the world and what better forum was there to express this international mood than the UN? Thus, simple statistics proved valuable in the fight for African freedom and representation in the UN. Although political considerations were excluded from Article 73(e), yet the very fact that comparisons could be made from year to year on the pace of development in economic, social, and educational spheres had great political significance whose impact were not lost on the colonial powers. Although political progress was not openly discussed at the Committee on Information itself, yet the political content of every statistic discussed at the Committee rang as an obvious question in the ears of the representatives of the colonial powers. At the Fourth (Trusteeship) Committee of the General Assembly and in the General Assembly itself, the colonial powers could not withstand the onslaught of the anti-colonial sentiments. Only Portugal, of all the colonial powers, did not seem to have any conscience at all and seemed impervious to political demands for the grant of independence to Angola, Mozambique, Sao Tome, and Guinea Bissau. Portugal advanced the spurious argument that their territories in Africa were all equal parts of Portugal, an argument which was once maintained by France in her relationship with Algeria.

Thus, as far as the colonial problem was concerned, the anti-colonial delegates to the United Nations were determined to resolve it once and for all. It was in this spirit of confidence that we attended the 15th session of the General Assembly which opened on September 20, 1960.

Family arrives in New York 1959

Nkrumah in New Rochelle, NY at the Ambassador's residence

CHAPTER 9

GHANA'S AMBASSADOR TO THE UNITED NATIONS – 1959-1965: PART 2 1960 – 1964

The 15ᵗʰ Session of the General Assembly proved to be one of the most eventful and exciting sessions during my six and a half years' service as Ghana's Permanent Representative. The colonial issue apart, there were great issues like General and Complete Disarmament, the UN Development Decade, the Congo Crisis, and Apartheid South Africa. To debate these and other matters, Heads of States or Governments or their representative Ministers had descended upon the UN to attend the General Assembly. My own President, Dr. Kwame Nkrumah, arrived in New York on September 21, 1960, and addressed the General Assembly two days later. Other Heads of State and Governments who addressed the General Assembly included King Hussein of Jordan, the King of Nepal, Dr. Marshall Tito of Yugoslavia, President Abdel Nasser of Egypt, President Sukarno of Indonesia, Premier Pandit Nehru of India, Premier Fidel Castro of Cuba, Prime Minister Harold MacMillan of the United Kingdom, Prime Minister Diefenbaker of Canada, President Dwight Eisenhower of the United States, and Premier Nikita Khrushchev of the Union of Soviet Socialist Republics. The United Nations had not witnessed such a powerful and glittering galaxy of world potentates as that attending a General Assembly session.

It was a great moment in my life and career. It was my responsibility to take care of my President while he was in New York. Nothing had to go wrong. I had to make sure that whatever he uttered whether before the General Assembly or before the African Group or before the Secretary-General Hammarskjold's Advisory Committee on the Congo (Zaire), or before the Press was well received. In the event, President Kwame Nkrumah acquitted himself creditably and did Ghana and Africa proud.

I also had to accompany my President on his courtesy calls on other Heads of State and Governments. Dr. Kwame Nkrumah's visits to Nikita Khrushchev, Fidel Castro, Pandit Nehru, and Abdel Nassar were particularly exciting for me. Khrushchev received us at the Soviet country house, Glen Cove, Long Island, New York. He was affable and was keen to show us around the grounds of the beautiful fortress. But I thought he was impulsive and very conscious of the fact that he was the Head of a superpower. He enjoyed gibing at the imperialist powers, especially the United States, which on a previous occasion he had boasted that he would bury. The talks between my President and the Soviet leader ranged between more trade between Ghana and the Soviet Union, and the training of Ghanaian students and personnel in the Soviet Union. President Nkrumah's subsequent trip to the Soviet Union in 1961 was agreed to at the visit in Glen Cove. The luncheon which followed was sumptuous. The best caviar and vodka was served, and there was plenty to go around the Ghanaian entourage of fifteen and the Soviet delegation of twenty.

President Nkrumah's meeting with Fidel Castro in Harlem was a great event. Already there had been a great stir in New York when on his arrival Prime Minister Fidel Castro decided to stay at the Hotel Theresa in Harlem. So Dr. Nkrumah's visit to Harlem added a fillip to the excitement. As the President together with his delegation made his way to Hotel Theresa, hordes and hordes of people crowded the streets to cheer and clap him. They saw in the two leaders, Kwame Nkrumah and Fidel Castro, champions of the anti-imperialist, anti-racist struggle and spokesmen for the "wretched of the earth"[50] (apologies to Fanon).

It was their first meeting ever. They embraced each other very warmly and in doing so took measure of each other. In their discussions, they covered a wide range of subjects – freedom and independence for all colonial peoples, the abolition of poverty and ignorance and disease through revolutionary programs for economic development; apartheid in South Africa; and the need for their countries not to be embroiled in great power conflicts. They also decided to exchange formal diplomatic missions and to harmonize their views on international affairs. This last decision of the two leaders was to be expected. Earlier on February 17 to 20, 1960, the Ghana Government had sent me to Cuba to convey to Fidel Castro and his team of revolutionaries the felicitations and good wishes of the Government and people of Ghana for Dr. Castro's success in overthrowing the Batista regime. In Cuba, I together with my First Secretary at the time, Dr. Amon Nikoi, met President Dorticos (then President of the Republic of Cuba), Prime Minister Castro, Dr. Ernesto Guevara, the famous revolutionary who was then the President of the National Bank of Cuba, Mr. Raul Castro, then the Minister of Defense, and Mr. Raul Roa, the Foreign Minister. There was a thorough exchange of views. Premier Castro asked me many questions about Ghana and Africa and expressed his admiration for Kwame Nkrumah, and we were fully informed and briefed about what was happening in Cuba. Arrangements were made for Dr. Nikoi and me to see something of the country in three days. My report on what I saw and heard in Cuba and my personal assessment of the efforts the Cuban government was making to launch a mass education ("alphabetization of the peasants" it was called) impressed President Nkrumah. Soon after the historic meeting between Castro and my President in Harlem, I was appointed Ambassador of Ghana to Cuba with residence in New York. But

---

50 *The Wretched of the Earth* (French: *Les Damnés de la Terre*) is a 1961 book by the psychiatrist Frantz Fanon, in which the author provides a psychiatric and psychologic analysis of the dehumanizing effects of colonization upon the individual and the nation, and discusses the broader social, cultural, and political implications inherent to establishing a social movement for the decolonization of a person and of a people. The French-language title derives from the opening lyrics of "The Internationale".

we opened a Chancery in Havana with my friend and colleague, H. K. Yomekpe as my Chargé d'Affaires ad interim.

Dr. Kwame Nkrumah's visit to President Nasser was no less exciting. The atmosphere which pervaded the meeting was extremely brotherly and warm. The two leaders had already been collaborating on a number of issues and their revolutionary stance on questions of liberation and independence of colonial territories had been well known. They were true African brothers, especially as Mrs. Fathia Nkrumah was an Egyptian. In their discussions, they went through a whole range of issues, including the problem of the Palestinian Arab refugees, apartheid, African Unity, and the possibility of the organization of a conference of some non-aligned countries. My President had much to explain to President Nasser about Ghana's close relations with Israel, because apart from a thriving diplomatic relationship between Ghana and Israel, there were many Israeli experts in Ghana advising the Government on a number of matters, especially in agriculture and construction. The Ghana State Construction Corporation (SCC) was established with the assistance of Solel Boneh, an Israeli construction company based in Haifa. And it was Israel which helped Ghana to establish our shipping line, the Black Star Line, whose operations were managed with the assistance of the Zion Lines. There was a frank discussion of Ghana and Egyptian foreign policy options, and I could discern that President Nasser had shown a magnanimous appreciation of President Nkrumah's position. After all, the three-year-old independent state of Ghana could not afford not to maintain and promote its own vital interests, relying on the policy of friends to all, enemies to none! Thus, both Nkrumah and Nasser understood each other's position.

It was our meeting with Prime Minister Pandit Nehru of India which provided me with a thorough education in international statesmanship. Nehru's sheer intellectual power was really overwhelming. He had a coolness and a sense of well-being about him, which added to his confidence in himself and in his position as Prime Minister of India, must be the source of his tremendous power. Every word that fell out of his mouth during his discussions with my President was precious and wise. He was at pains to explain to President Kwame Nkrumah India's position vis a vis China, Pakistan, and the Soviet Union. His commitment to a policy of non-alignment, he explained, was mainly due to India's geopolitical situation, but he also felt that, with the polarization of the international society, a non-alignment policy was the only realistic policy to keep the two superpowers at bay. Nehru strongly felt that a non-aligned movement in the world would act as a countervailing balance between the two superpowers. The moral impact of such a movement would be far-reaching. He hinted that he and Marshall Tito of Yugoslavia had discussed a possible summit conference and that President Nkrumah, President Nasser, and President Ahmed Sukarno of Indonesia should meet the two of them to plan such summit.

The Conference of Non-aligned States duly took place in Belgrade, Yugoslavia in 1961 and launched the Non-aligned movement. I was there in Belgrade as a member of the Ghana delegation headed by President Kwame Nkrumah. But more about the Non-aligned Conference later.

I must state that the presence of all these world leaders at the 15th Session of the General Assembly gave the United Nations a great boost and poignantly reminded the citizens of the world that the survival of mankind depended very much on all leaders of all the nations of the world, big or small. Not only that. It dawned on me then that with the presence of all world leaders at the UN, all the foreign ministries of the world had temporarily moved to New York. Every statement from each Head of State and/or Government at that session had an official seal to it. There was hardly any excuse to seek clearance from home!

What I was not sure about was whether the behavior of the leader of the delegation of USSR, Premier Nikita Khrushchev, at the 15th Session of the General Assembly, when he took off his shoes and started pounding the table with it, was official. What happened was that there had been open criticisms against the Secretary-General, Dag Hammarskjold's handling of the Congo Leopoldville's (Zaire's) crisis, and the Soviet delegation's policy statement in regard to the Congo crisis had been particularly virulent. And so on that fateful afternoon, Dag Hammarskjold felt obliged to reply. It was during his intervention that Khrushchev began shouting, "You are not neutral. No man is neutral." And noisily pounded on the table before him with his shoes. He obviously demurred at the Secretary-General's statement that he was Secretary-General for all the members of the United Nations and was prepared to step down if the majority wished him to do so. Shock rippled throughout the General Assembly. I was dumbfounded because I saw Khrushchev actually take off his shoes to do the pounding. For a very long time that dramatic incident lingered in my memory.

One of the most impressive achievements of the 15th Session was the passing of the Declaration on the Granting of Independence to colonial countries and peoples. To the surprise of everybody in the General Assembly, it was Premier Khrushchev in his foreign policy statement who fired the opening salvo by demanding immediate freedom and independence for all non-self-governing countries. He read a draft resolution sponsored by the Soviet Union to that end. This demand was warmly applauded. The Soviet Union had taken the bull by the horns. There was no escape. However, the language was clearly unacceptable to the Imperialists and so after the adjournment for the day, the Afro-Asian Group met to consider the Soviet draft. The feeling was that the Soviet draft was a God-send. So, the Afro-Asian Group should seize the opportunity to prepare a comprehensive and reasoned declaration which could win the unanimous support of all delegations. I was named a member of the drafting committee. It took us hours of hard work of drafting, consulting, and persuading. The final draft we presented to the whole Group for their endorsement was received with acclamation. I remember vividly that every Afro-Asian and later, every Latin American delegation wanted to co-sponsor the draft resolution. The main ingredients were:

1. That there should be an end of colonialism in all its manifestations;

2. That the subjection of peoples to alien subjugation is contrary to the principles and purposes of the Charter;

3. That all peoples have a right to self-determination;

4. That inadequacy of preparation should never be a pretext for delaying independence;

5. That there should be an end to all repressive measures directed against dependent peoples;

6. That immediate steps must be taken to transfer all powers to the people of the territories not yet independent; and

7. That any attempt to disrupt the national unity and territorial integrity of a country is incompatible with the Charter.

43 Afro-Asian states, including Ghana, co-sponsored the draft resolution 1514(xv). It was passed by the General Assembly by an overwhelming majority and acclamation, nine notable abstentions: the United States of America, the United Kingdom, France, Belgium, Spain, Italy, Australia, South Africa, and Portugal. There was great jubilation. The resolution was hailed as an amendment of the Charter, putting an end to all speculation about the colonial problem. Henceforth, no colonial power could withstand the demand for independence. In fact, an enabling resolution was passed to set up a special committee of 24 to oversee the implementation of Resolution 1514 (xv).

The Special Committee on the Situation with Regard to the Implementation of the Declaration on the Granting of Independence to Colonial Countries and Peoples was set up by the General Assembly at its 16th Session by Resolution 1654 (xvi)[51] of November 27, 1961. It consisted of 17 members but was enlarged two years later to 24, and it is still known as the Committee of 24. It was charged "to carry out its task by the employment of all means which it will have at its disposal

---

51 United Nations General Assembly Resolution 1654 of 27 November 1961, titled "The situation with regard to the implementation of the Declaration on the Granting of Independence to Colonial Countries and Peoples" was a resolution of the United Nations General Assembly during its sixteenth ... that affirmed the resolution also provided for immediate

within the framework of the procedures and facilities which it shall adopt for the proper discharge of its functions." It became necessary to set up this implementation committee because the colonial powers, notably Portugal, were shuffling their feet. They gave all kinds of reasons why they should not relinquish imperial power. For example, Portugal had always insisted that her overseas territories like Angola, Mozambique, Guinea Bissau, Principe, and Sao Tome were part of metropolitan Portugal. Admittedly, there were many Portuguese citizens residing in those territories who enjoyed the comforts and privileges in a colonial territory and did not contemplate returning to Europe. Besides, the exercise of imperial power afforded these settlers all the protection they needed to safeguard their investments. However, I could not fathom how any of these African territories could be part of Portugal. I conducted interminable arguments with my friend, Signor Noguerra, the then Portuguese delegate, and then the Foreign Minister of Portugal. He did appreciate the logic of my contentions but never yielded ground.

Britain, on the other hand, did not argue that Southern Rhodesia (Zimbabwe) was part of Great Britain. But the British would not accept the fact that it was a colony. My colleagues and I had argued in the Fourth Committee of the General Assembly that Southern Rhodesia was not independent, that it was a colony. The majority of the population who were Africans had not voted for the white-settler minority who were ruling the territory, and therefore it was incumbent upon the British Government to consider the wishes of the African majority as had been enunciated in the Devonshire Declaration of 1923. In spite of our arguments, the British maintained that the issue of Southern Rhodesia came under Article 2(7) of the Charter, that it was a matter which was essentially within the domestic jurisdiction of Southern Rhodesia. The fallacy of that position was obvious as it was the British delegation that always spoke on behalf of Southern Rhodesia.

It was because of the recalcitrant attitude of the British colonial power towards this issue that compelled me to challenge my good friend, Sir Patrick Dean, the then Permanent Representative of the United Kingdom to the UN during the General Assembly debate. The Special Committee for the Implementation of the Independence Declaration had included Southern Rhodesia on their list of colonies yet to achieve independence, but Britain opposed the inclusion. Therefore, at the General Assembly, I argued on behalf of the African States that Southern Rhodesia was not independent whether it was self-governing or not. Besides, the term "self-governing" could not properly be applied to that territory as only the white minority were self-governing themselves and lording it over the African majority. I called upon the General Assembly to pronounce on the issue of whether Southern Rhodesia fell within Article 2 paragraph 7. The General Assembly voted with an overwhelming majority to support my contention that Southern Rhodesia did not fall within the purview of Article 2 paragraph 7. That territory was, therefore, included on the list of countries that had not yet attained independence. Southern Rhodesia had to be dealt with by the Implementation Committee.

With all these developments, the Fourth Committee had to decide the fate of the Trusteeship Council and the Committee on Information from non-governing territories. There was definitely the need for one committee to coordinate all the work done by the various organs dealing with the question of self-government and independence. So the General Assembly passed Resolution 1970 (xviii) on December 16, 1963, at the 18th session that "all United Nations activities concerning the self-governing territories should now be coordinated and consolidated, with a view to the immediate ending of colonialism." So it was that the colonial incubus was effectually laid to rest. It was only a matter of time when all the British "dependencies", so called, in East and Southern and Central Africa, including Zimbabwe where the white minority settlers, had a stranglehold on the African majority, became independent and sovereign nations.

The Portuguese territories in Africa and elsewhere remained part of metropolitan Portugal in spite of internal strife and international opposition. But then the inevitable occurred when President Salazar, the dictator of Portugal, was overthrown, and

Angola, Mozambique and other Portuguese territories in Africa attained independent nationhood. As I write, there are now fifty-one independent African states. When apartheid is finally dismantled in South Africa, giving way to a truly multiracial majority rule in that unhappy country, and when the South African Government vacates its illegal occupation of South West Africa (Namibia), with the full implementation of the Security Council Resolution 435, the Organization of African Unity would welcome into their fold Azania (as South Africa is called) and Namibia. The United Nations had thus played a vital role in the process of decolonization.

I had myself entertained a strong belief that the United Nations could be an effective and a decisive instrument for peace if Permanent Representatives representing our different Governments worked hard to remove all the causes which militated against the preservation of peace. It is true that foreign policies of countries are in the main formulated by our different Governments. But in quite a number of cases, it is a small committee of Government or the Head of State or Government himself/herself who decides what should be done in the field of international relations. And since the United Nations is the only medium where such policies can be enunciated barring press conferences and communiques at home, the Permanent Representatives can play a decisive role even in the formulation and of course in the promotion of the policy. During the Congo crisis, for example, the President of Ghana, Dr. Kwame Nkrumah, was constantly on the phone to me at my residence instructing me what to do. On a number of occasions, I expressed certain views which he accepted and encouraged me to propagate. However, I made sure that I sought the views and counsel of close associates like Ambassador Omar Lourfi, later Mamoud Riad of Egypt, Omar Adeel of Sudan, Adnan Pachachi of Iraq, Simeon Adebo of Nigeria, Diallo Telli of Guinea, Hans Tabor of Denmark, Tesfaye Gebre Edjy of Ethiopia, Chandra Jha of India, Manji Stiva of Tunisia, Ahmed Ben Hima of Morocco, Assuan Usher of Cote d'Ivoire, Mr. Zenon Rossides of Cyprus and Gershon Collier of Sierra Leone, to name a few. Those were great diplomats whose opinions and views were highly respected. I was also in close touch with Lord Caradon (Sir Hugh Fost) of the United Kingdom, who always maintained that I was too extreme in my contentions; Governor Adlai Stevenson of the United States who was an extraordinary politician and adapted easily to the diplomacy at the United Nations; Ambassador Federenko of the USSR (Zorim, his predecessor in office used to consult me on a number of issues but he was not as open as Federenko with whom I shared the habit of wearing bow ties and smoking Cuban cigars); Armand Berard of France and Astrom of Sweden. We took quite a lot of initiatives sometimes conferring with the Secretary-General and the members of the Secretariat like the indomitable Dr. Ralph Bunche and Proteitch of Yugoslavia, and Alexander McFarquar of the United Kingdom, Brian Urquhart of the United Kingdom, and Philippe de Seynes of France.

I never for once underrated the Security Council with its limited but powerful membership, for I understood the important role it had to play in all matters affecting international peace and security. Nevertheless, I always gave the pride of place to the General Assembly where almost every independent nation of the world was a member and had a say. In my view, it was an important assembly of sovereign and equal nations and it truly mirrored the world as it was. There, every sovereign nation was a nation, whether a dwarf or a giant and the moral authority of the world could only be evinced in the General Assembly. True, the resolutions of the General Assembly were not mandatory in the sense that they were enforceable under Chapter 12 of the United Nations Charter, but they had such a persuasive force as commanded the attention of the peoples and Governments of the world.

The Uniting for Peace resolution of the General Assembly in 1950 over the Korean issue had often been cited as an example of how powerful the General Assembly could be when there had been a stalemate in the Security Council. However, during the period of my service at the UN, the General Assembly became a factor to reckon with, not only in terms of increased membership with the accretion of newly independent African, Caribbean, and Asian nations but also in terms of the high quality of the representation.

There was no doubt that countries vied with each other to send effective diplomats to the UN to represent them. Then, every potentate, every President, every Prime Minister, and Minister of State relished addressing the august Assembly.

Each session of the General Assembly had its own problems to grapple with and was no less eventful than its predecessor. Usually, three weeks were devoted to the General Debate, so-called, where every Foreign Minister or leader of the delegation held forth at the rostrum to explain his country's policies on various issues of the world. Each session was also obliged to tackle and find solutions for the *soi-disant* perennial problems of the world like disarmament, the proliferation of nuclear weapons, outer space, global economic developmental problems, the Palestinian Arab refugees, apartheid South Africa and Namibia, to mention a few. But then apart from the settled agenda approved by the General Committee, the General Assembly or the Security Council could at any time be seized of an issue which in the opinion of the membership after proper consultations merited attention and consideration, like the Congo (Zaire) crisis, the Sharpeville massacre or the Cuban missile crisis.

The General Assembly declared the 1960s as the United Nations Development Decade by its resolution 1710 (XVI) passed during the 16th session in December 1961. The President of the General Assembly was Ambassador Mongi Shim of Tunisia who had had his candidature sponsored by the Middle East and Asian countries at that time. He was an adroit diplomatist and politician who, together with a powerful band of Tunisian nationalists led by Habib Bourguiba led the struggle for Tunisia's independence. Mongi Shim was a short man, rather Turkish in appearance. He was affable, intelligent, and kind, and given to deep reflections. He remained a confirmed bachelor. I was one of the Vice Presidents elected to assist him, and I, therefore, served on the General Committee which was responsible for the agenda of the General Assembly and the procedural problems and interpretation of the Rules of Procedure.

The mood of the delegations at the UN at this time was that having successfully tackled and resolved the colonial problem, the time had come to tackle the whole problem of the economic development of developing nations and to promote international cooperation, particularly in the economic and financial fields. The battle cry was TRADE not AID!![52] It was true that there were several bilateral agreements between nations by which financial and technical assistance had been given by developed industrial nations to the less developed, mainly agricultural countries. However, the prevalent feeling was that financial aid and technical assistance should be multilateral and that the whole international economic order needed overhauling.

Article 55 of the UN Charter enjoins that the United Nations shall promote higher standards of living, full employment, and conditions of economic and social progress and development." But the UN was not doing all the things that the Charter stipulated. The vital freedoms from hunger, ignorance, disease, and exposure were still far from realization. Developing countries containing the bulk of the world's population were beset with chronic social and economic problems. Their economic and financial structures were weak. Terms of trade were against them as primary producing countries. Each developing nation by itself was helpless within the milieu of the international economic order. Concerted action by all nations, developed and developing was called for to address the gross inequities and injustices suffered by the majority of the peoples of the world.

Long before I became my nation's Permanent Representative to New York, the United Nations had adopted in 1950 the Expanded Programme of Technical Assistance (EPTA) to enable developing countries to receive the much-needed assistance in the planning of their economies. The funds for the program were to be supplied to the United Nations by voluntary contributions. There was set up the Technical Assistance Board (TAB) consisting of representatives elected by the UN General

---

52 The trade-not-aid strategy is based on the idea that if developing countries were able to trade more freely with wealthy countries, they would have more reliable incomes and they would be much less dependent on external aid to carry out development projects.

Assembly and representatives of the participating specialized agencies. Technical assistance was only given to a country when such assistance was requested. It was confined to the supply of experts in technical fields, for example, to advise and train local personnel in land, monetary and taxation matters or to advise the requesting government on how to develop their fishing, mineral, and forest resources or public works. But the success of the EPTA depended upon the size of contributions and yet the larger donors like the United States, Britain, and France at this time believed strongly in bilateral programs which were immeasurably bigger than EPTA.

In 1959, the United Nations Special Fund was also set up. The purpose was to harness funds for pre-investment works in receiving countries. The fund was to assist in the formulation of material development plans, the setting up of financial and development institutions for economic and social planning on a regional basis. I served on the Governing Council as a representative of Ghana and I had the good fortune of working closely with Paul Hoffman, an indefatigable Managing Director of the Special Fund. The Fund, like its predecessors, was financed by voluntary contributions and in 1959 the General Assembly decided on a yearly target of $150 million. The Fund carried out surveys on national resources, research in feasibility projects, and the training of manpower for development. The regional institutes were sited in Santiago, Chile in 1962, Dakar, Senegal in 1964, and Bangkok, Thailand in 1964. They were set to give courses in economic development, carry on research, and help countries in a particular region with their economic and social planning.

I must say that Paul G. Hoffman was a devoted UN man with a strong international flair. He believed strongly in multilateral aid systems and he was at pains to cajole the 26 identified developed countries to channel their aid through the United Nations. He bemoaned the fact that in 1957 and 1958, out of $3.0 billion in grants and net loans, $2.6 billion were bilateral and only $0.4 billion was multilateral. The explanation for this penchant for bilateralism by developed countries was given by Richard

N. Gardner who in 1964 was the US Deputy Assistant Secretary for International Organization Affairs when he said that if grants and aid are passed through the UN "large amounts of capital aid would be dispersed under circumstances that would not assure the promotion of US foreign policy objectives." (Gardner's *In Pursuit of World Order*, Praeger, New York, 1964)

However, the Special Fund proved to be a success and it was eventually transformed into the United Nations Development Program (UNDP) and headed by the same Paul Hoffman. Thus, for technical assistance, development, and international economic cooperation.

Efforts in the United Nations both within the General Assembly and in the United Nations Secretariat to promote economic development in less-developed countries were relentless. All the various economic and social programs by the UN were coordinated by the Under-Secretary-General for Economic and Social Affairs, who in my time was Philippe de Seynes of France. He was a pragmatic economist who believed that new technologies should be tailored to serve the special conditions of particular regions. He said in his report in 1963 that the United Nations was responsible for "facilitating the birth and development of an indigenous technology with which to correct or compensate for accidents of geology or climate, of helping countries which still lack them, to obtain minimum scientific facilities ..., of encouraging the modern spirit of science and technology and of preparing the institutional changes which this development requires." The task of economic development in developing countries has become stupendous and has always been linked indissolubly with the volume of earnings and the availability of the requisite foreign exchange.

A list of all this question of economic development cannot, therefore, be divorced from trade. When the developing countries were crying in the 1960s "Trade Not Aid", they were merely emphasizing the fact that it was they who possessed most of the raw materials and primary products needed by the 26 developed countries and that if they received an equitable and fair price for their products, they could do without aid. Ever since the establishment of the United Nations, the developing countries had been asking that their products be allowed to enter the developed countries without the imposition of customs duties and other penalties, that developed countries should remove restrictions on imports from developing countries and that foreign exchange earnings of developing countries needed to be boosted to enable them to purchase capital equipment. It was patently clear that the developing countries needed to coordinate their efforts if the much-desired goals would be achieved. The developed or industrialized were dictating pace. The price for capital equipment is set by them and the price for primary products from developing countries is also set by the same industrialized countries. A desperate situation, that was. Therefore, the developing countries looked upon the United Nations as the instrument to redress the imbalance and injustice.

A number of developing countries joined the General Agreement on Tariffs and Trade (GATT) which had been set up in 1947 in Geneva. Ghana joined GATT in 1958 and I was lucky to be a member of the first Ghanaian delegation of three, the 2 others being the Permanent Secretary of the Ministry of Trade, Mr. M. F. Ribeiro-Ayeh and the Permanent Secretary of the Ministry of Finance, Mr. E. Quist-Therson. I was then the Head of Chancery of the Ghana High Commission in London. I remember that in our maiden intervention, Mr. Quist-Therson caviled at the trade restrictions imposed by Japan who did not buy our cocoa but were selling electronic products and textiles to us. Though Japan was the worst offender, developed countries were too restrictive in their trade practices, erecting high tariff walls, and indulging in quantitative restrictions. But GATT proved unsatisfactory to the developing countries and the call for a world trade conference became incessant. Even the Soviet Union joined in the chorus. The pressure became so strong that in 1962 the General Assembly in Resolution 1785 passed at the 17th Session agreed to hold the United Nations Conference on Trade and Development (UNCTAD) in 1964.

Nkrumah and his Cabinet Ministers at New Rochelle, 1960

213

Kwame Nkrumah and Fidel Castro

Nkrumah and Krushchev

Kwame Nkrumah addresses the United Nations General Assembly

Kwame Nkrumah and AQS with Ghanaian entourage and embassy staff, after arriving in New York for the 19th General Assembly

Kwame Nkrumah poses with other Heads of State in New York for the 19th General Assembly

AQS, Ghana's ambassador to Cuba with Castro and staffers

CHAPTER 10

GHANA'S AMBASSADOR TO THE UNITED NATIONS – 1959-1965: PART 3 1964 – 1965

The UNCTAD was convened in March 1964 under the Secretary-Generalship of Dr. Raul Prebisch of Argentina. He had been previously the Executive Secretary of the Economic Commission for Latin America (ECLA) and was found in him a great advocate for the developing countries. Ghana sent a strong delegation under the able leadership of the then Foreign Minister, Mr. Kojo Botsio. I was the deputy leader at Geneva for Ghana and had the good fortune of chairing the Group of 77 consisting of developing countries from Africa, Asia, Latin America, and the Caribbean. In all, there were 2,000 delegates from 119 countries and our conference lasted until June 1964.

Dr. Prebisch himself set the tone of the Conference. The United Nations had set a target of 5% minimal growth during the United Nations Development Decade declared in 1961 by the General Assembly at the 16th Session (Resolution 1710 (XVI), December 19, 1961). Dr. Prebisch argued that if this target should be reached, "there would be an estimated gap in the foreign exchange requirements of the developing countries amounting to $20 billion a year, and that even with as much as a $10 billion inflow of foreign public and private capital, an increase of $10 billion in net exports by the developing countries would be necessary."

The Conference itself was divided into a number of committees which dealt with tariff preferences, quantitative restrictions, shipping and insurance, commodity agreements, and purchase of primary products and quite a host of other trade and tariffs issues. It is pertinent to observe that while UNCTAD was in process, there was a meeting of GATT as well. Geneva became a veritable beehive of activity. It was a mini-General Assembly session and I was up to my neck in a bog of work, shuttling from the Group of 77 to This vs. That committee, lobbying, and drafting. I must say here that although the developed countries, including the Soviet bloc, were there in Geneva, yet I did not notice much enthusiasm on their part. They evinced some sympathy for our plight and our desire to close the trade gap, but the burden of the Conference fell on the Group of 77. We dictated the pace.

The main conclusions of the Conference included the elimination of all protective and other restrictions on the importation of primary products by developed/industrialized countries; tariff preferences for the manufacturers and semi-manufacturers of the developing countries; permission for developing countries to subsidize their exports; commodity agreements to regulate prices and the setting up of buffer stocks; compensatory financing in years when foreign exchange earnings were low; reduction in the cost of shipping and insurance; easing of the servicing charges on foreign debts; agreement on special regional trade arrangements among the developing countries; the establishment of a new trade organization to be called UNCTAD with a 55-member Trade and Development Board which would meet between regular sessions of the UN. It was to be serviced by a Secretariat. As could be expected, the General Assembly agreed to the appointment of Dr. Raul Prebisch as the first Secretary-General of UNCTAD with the Secretariat established in Geneva.

All issues affecting international peace and security are first handled by the Security Council on which the Charter had endowed a primary responsibility. Unlike the General Assembly, the Security Council in practice meets once a month, even if to eat lunch. When I served on the Security Council for two years from January 1, 1962, until December 31, 1963, the practice was that delegations took turns to provide lunches once a month. But the

Council could be called into session at any time, and if you were the President for a particular (the Presidency was by a monthly rotation according to the English alphabetical order), you could not leave New York without informing the Secretariat of where they could reach you in case of a crisis.

It was to the Security Council then that the Congo crisis was brought. Congo (Leopoldville) as Zaire was then called was suddenly granted independence by Belgium on June 30, 1960. I use the term "sudden" because the second conference of the Independent African States was being held at Addis Ababa, Ethiopia from June 15 to June 24, 1960, when we received reports of Rhodesian troop movements along the frontiers of the Congo. I was then serving on the Steering Committee of the Conference as the representative of Ghana. I took part in drafting the following telegram which was sent to the Belgian Foreign Minister by the Chairman of the Conference, Yilma Deressa of Ethiopia.

"The Second Conference of Independent African States is deeply concerned at certain news reports referring to large-scale movements of troops from neighboring countries at the frontiers of the Belgian Congo. The Conference wishes to remind your Government that such troop movements can constitute a threat to the territorial integrity of the Congo, for whose defense your Government is still fully responsible. The Conference would like to be informed of the veracity of this news and to receive an assurance from the Belgian Government that all necessary steps have been taken to consider this threat."

Thus, the Belgian Government was left in no doubt that the Independent African States at the time were watching events in Africa as they unfolded and that they would not in any way tolerate any obstacles put in the way of Congolese independence by the European settlers in Central Africa, especially in Rhodesia. The Belgian Government in a rather curt reply accepted their responsibility of defending the Congo until after June 30, 1960, which was the date that had been set for the independence of the Congo.

Consequently, there had been a Round Table Conference where there had been an agreement between the Belgian Government and the representatives of various parties in existence in the Congo, including traditional rulers, on the "Loi Fundamentals"[53] for an independent Congo. Elections were duly held on May 11, 1960, and the Mouvement National Congolais (MNC) led by Patrice Lumumba won the majority as one single party. Patrice Lumumba, therefore, became the Prime Minister and with the help of MNC-Lumumba, Mr. Joseph Kasa-Vubu, leader of the Abako Party, a vociferous group from the Bakongo tribe, became the President of the Republic. It must here be explained that Congo (Leopoldville) had adopted the Belgian system of constitutional government where the Prime Minister is the Head of Government, and King Bandonin of the Belgians, the Head of State in a purely ceremonial capacity. Mr. Kasa-Vubu as President was like the King of Belgium.

Soon after independence, the Congolese Cabinet decided that change should be made in the Civil Service and in the Army to promote deserving Africans to more responsible positions. To that end, the Commander of the Congolese "Force Publique", a Belgian by the name of Gen. Emile Janssen, was requested to consider promoting soldiers like Sergeant -Major Victor Lundula to officer rank. General Janssen was reported to have rebuffed Lumumba, whereupon the Prime Minister dismissed the General and ordered him to leave the Congo forthwith. Meanwhile, white officers were telling their African subordinates that they should not expect any promotions and that, independence or not, the Belgians would control the Force Publique. There was a mutiny and the African soldiers were on the rampage. Hell broke loose! Then, the Belgian Government on the pretext that they had the right to protect Belgian nationals in an independent Congo (Leopoldville) sent in Belgian troops. This triggered the Congo crisis and prompted the urgent appeal by Prime Minister Patrice Lumumba and President Joseph Kasa-Vubu to the Security Council of the UN on July 12, 1960, requesting military aid against

---

53 A letter of intent (LOI) is a document declaring the preliminary commitment of one party to do business with another. The letter outlines the chief terms of a prospective deal. Commonly used in major business transactions, LOIs are similar in content to term sheets

the Belgian "act of aggression." I was a keen observer of events which unfolded in the Congo (Leopoldville) and I wondered whether the whole Congo episode could not have been handled in another way. In my view there was a complete lack of trust between the new Congolese Government and their people on the one hand, and the Belgians on the other.

The underlying cause was not difficult to discern. For far too long the Congolese people had chafed under Belgian colonialist oppression and brutalities. Frankly, Belgian colonial rule had not been as enlightened as that of the British or the French or the Portuguese. Unlike the French or the Portuguese, for example, who intermarried freely and respected the African and his culture, the Belgians had practiced racial discrimination, bordering on blatant apartheid in Zaire. There was deep resentment felt by the Congolese against the Belgians. What was more, memories of the atrocities perpetrated against the Congolese in the so-called Congo Free States under King Leopold II of Belgium[54] had died hard. It was a matter of historical significance that Edward Dene Morel in his book *Red Rubber* published in 1906 portrayed a picture of human barbarity, thus evoking an international outcry against Leopold II and all his works. The *London Daily Mail*, for example, came out that *"Red Rubber* is the most appalling indictment of personal rapacity, cruelty, expropriation of life and labor, maladministration and tyrannical atrocity ever recorded in irrefutable proof against any one man in any country or age. The horror of it stands out naked." Then the British politician and statesman, Ramsay MacDonald was reported to have said that "nothing tells the horrible way in which the Congo has been governed by King Leopold II of Belgium so effectively as *Red Rubber*." And the prestigious *London Times* reported "Morel,

---

54 In the period from 1885 to 1908, many well-documented atrocities were perpetrated in the Congo Free State (today the Democratic Republic of the Congo) which, at the time, was a colony under the personal rule of King Leopold II of the Belgians. These atrocities were particularly associated with the labour policies used to collect natural rubber for export. Together with epidemic disease, famine, and a falling birth rate caused by these disruptions, the atrocities contributed to a sharp decline in the Congolese population. The magnitude of the population fall over the period is disputed, but it is thought to be between one and fifteen million.

Other inhuman treatment were, mutilation and brutality, prisons and hostage taking, wars and rebellions, child labour, etc.

unlike the Congo Free State Government, publishes not only the conclusions to which his inquiry leads him, but also the evidence upon which they are based. He quotes all his authorities, gives chapter and verse for all his statements."

It was against that background that the feeling of Prime Minister Lumumba and his people, must be viewed. Independence had come and the Congolese people who had not taken kindly to the Belgian administration which their forebears had described as *bula matadi* (breaker of men) were to become masters of their own country. But this was not to be. They had been taunted by Belgian officers of the Force Publique. They had naturally reacted. But then they saw their hard-won independence threatened by the intervention troops sent in by their erstwhile colonial masters. The natural thing to do was to appeal to the world body for immediate assistance.

However, I must say that Ghana was the first country to which the Congolese Government had turned for direct military assistance. But Dr. Kwame Nkrumah, then President of Ghana, advised Lumumba to appeal to the Secretary-General of the United Nations for immediate multilateral assistance. As soon as the Congolese appeal was received on July 12, 1960, the Security Council was promptly convened to consider the appeal. On July 14, 1960, the Security Council passed its first resolution on the Congo (Leopoldville) that authorized the Secretary-General "to take the necessary steps in consultation with the Government of the Republic of the Congo, to provide the Government with such military assistance as may be necessary until, through the efforts of the Congolese Government with the technical assistance of the United Nations, the national security forces may be able, in the opinion of the Government, to meet their tasks."

In the very midst of settling the issue of Belgian intervention, Moise Tshombe of Katanga, on July 14, 1960, announced the independence of Katanga. The reaction of Ghana's President Kwame Nkrumah was that. "In Katanga, regrettable and most vicious attempts are being made by vested interests to bolster up a puppet regime ... by using poor Moise Tshombe against his own government to break up the Congo Republic by secessionist activities. The Congo is one and indivisible." Then Albert Kalonji announced the secession of South Kasai and made himself King. Both these areas contain some of the Congo's richest deposits of minerals, especially copper, diamonds, and cobalt, and the country's enormous natural resources have always attracted heavy capitalistic investments.

With the passing of the Security Council resolution, the Secretary-General, Dag Hammarskjold, was left with the awesome responsibility of mounting peace-keeping operations in the Congo (Leopoldville). Thus, into Leopoldville, now Kinshasa, poured troops and military and civilian personnel from Canada, Ethiopia, Ghana, Liberia, Morocco, Nigeria, Ireland, India, Malaysia, Pakistan, and Sudan all under the auspices of the UN and in no time wearing the famous UN blue beret. Such military assistance provided by the UN was meant, in my opinion, to enable the Congolese Government "to meet their tasks" which included the restoration of law and order and the maintenance of the territorial integrity of the Congo.

Therefore, it was natural that Patrice Lumumba and his Government should have expected the UN troops to get rid of the Belgian soldiers who had committed "acts of aggression" and to assist it to crush the secessionists Moise Tshombe of Katanga and Albert Kalonji of South Kasai. It was because Secretary-General Dag Hammarskjold disagreed with Patrice Lumumba on the modalities of carrying out the spirit and letter of the Security Council Resolution of July 14, 1960, that Dag Hammarskjold had difficulties with some African countries like Ghana, Guinea and Morocco, and the Soviet Union. At the time of the Congo crisis, Tunisia, which had secured a sear in the Security Council by the Middle East seat (there was not yet an African seat), took an active part in the debates through her Ambassador and Permanent Representative, Mongi Shim, who became President of the General Assembly in 1961 by dint of the Middle East allocation. Ambassador Shim said that the UN intervention in the Congo was "to prevent a continuation of what is considered to be a violation of Congo's sovereignty and independence."

225

This was during another debate at the Security Council on July 22, 1960. The Secretary-General himself who had had experience in peace-keeping operations in the Middle East (UNEF – United National Emergency Force) must have regarded the United Nations Operations in the Congo (UNOC) as *sui generis*[55].

In fact, it did appear during the whole Congo debacle that something had gone wrong somewhere. There was a strong feeling that the Katanga secession had been allowed to survive for too long and that the UN troops should have moved in to crush it. On the other hand, the Secretary-General Hammarskjold thought otherwise. In the Congo, Dag Hammarskjold had ordered, through Dr. Ralph Bunche, Under-Secretary-General, who was then the UN Administrator overseeing the Congo operations, the disarming of the Congolese troops. Dag, during the Security Council debate on July 22, 1960, had said that "the difficulties which have developed in the Congo are connected with the maintenance of order in the country and the protection of life." But then the disarming of Congolese troops as such became a moot point. The difficulty was to countenance the secession of Katanga backed by Belgium and mercenary troops and arms, while the Congolese Government which was not given such military assistance "until the national security forces may be able, in the opinion of the Government, to meet their task", were leaving their loyal troops disarmed. It was not surprising, therefore, that Antoine Gizenga who was Lumumba's Deputy told Hammarskjold, "we do not understand why we, victims of aggression who are at home here, are being systematically disarmed, while the aggressors, the Belgians, who are conquerors here, are permitted to keep their weapons and their means of inflicting death." However, Dag Hammarskjold stuck to his guns and maintained that the UN troops "would not be authorized to action beyond self-defense" and "they may not take any action which would make them a party to internal conflicts in the country."

---

55 Sui generis is a Latin phrase that means "of its/his/her/their own kind, in a class by itself", therefore "unique". A number of disciplines use the term to refer to unique entities.

Ghana's role in the Congo was stupendous but delicate. President Kwame Nkrumah himself took an active interest in the events of the Congo. He had met Patrice Lumumba at the All-African People's Conference in 1958 at Accra and had taken a liking for him. Lumumba was dynamic and fearless and was an orator who could move the masses. When the crisis broke out after the coming of independence in June 30. 1960, Prime Minister Lumumba had turned to Osagyefo Dr. Kwame Nkrumah for military help. Ghana was, therefore, one of the first countries to have sent troops to the Congo. Ghanaian troops consequently became very popular, but because of the UN Secretariat's orders that Congolese troops should be disarmed whenever possible, Ghanaian troops found themselves in a delicate situation. They were intrinsically effective and carried out their UN duties assiduously. In New York, my Mission received all the instructions regarding what our people must do in the Congo. The telexes were pouring in all the time, some coded or in cipher, and my staff and I were stretched to the limit. One of my Third Secretaries, Mr. Ketosugbor, broke his back through sitting before the telex for days. I also used to receive direct phone calls from President Nkrumah himself either congratulating me on some effective intervention I had made or giving me direct instructions on what to say or do. At one time, I recall that my President told me by phone that he was going to withdraw Ghanaian troops from the Congo because the UN was not carrying out its own mandate. As soon as I arrived at the Ghana Mission on 144 East 44th Street, I received a message that Secretary-General Dag Hammarskjold wanted to see me immediately. He had not sought me out so early in the morning before and although I was an Ambassador Extraordinary and Plenipotentiary, it was with a sense of awe that I went up to the 39th floor to see Dag. His eyes were red. He was in an open-necked shirt without a tie, pacing up and down, smoking his cheroots! "Mr. Ambassador, look at this." He showed me a telex from Accra in which the President of Ghana had threatened to withdraw our troops. I told him not to worry and that I would be in touch with my President. Dag looked at me and smiled and confessed that Ghanaian troops were doing a good job and if we withdrew, others would follow

227

suit. He praised Brig. J. A. Ankrah (as the General was then known) and his troops in Leopoldville and Port Franqui. In any event, Ghana did not withdraw the troops.

Meantime, there were incessant criticisms from the Soviet Union, France, and some African and Eastern European countries about Hammarskjold's handling of the Congo crisis. The Soviet Union and France, for different reasons, threatened not to pay those portions of their assessments relating to the peace-keeping operations in the Congo. However, Hammarskjold was undaunted and he set up the Congo Advisory Committee, consisting of Permanent Representatives, mainly of the African States, who had contributed contingents to the UN force in the Congo. It was an effective safety valve for the Secretary-General, and it enabled him to know and understand how Africans felt about the operations in the Congo. I was an active member of that Committee, and I belonged to an inner core of Ambassadors whose views Dag Hammarskjold constantly sought.

The Congo crisis proved a veritable albatross around Hammarskjold's neck. At the 15th Session of the General Assembly, Premier Nikita Khrushchev bitterly attacked Hammarskjold on his handling of the peace-keeping operations, calling on him to resign and accusing him of pandering to the imperialists instead of implementing the resolutions of the Security Council. I have already narrated the story of Khrushchev's taking off and pounding his shoes at the General Assembly. But Hammarskjold kept his cool and maintained his ground that he did not have to resign because of one great power's insistence. After all, all the other member states mattered. Hammarskjold was given a spontaneous ovation as a mark of the confidence we all had in him as Secretary-General.

The really difficult moment of the 15th Session of the General Assembly was the seating of the Congolese delegation, because although Congo (Leopoldville) had been admitted to the UN as a member state, I had not forgotten the words uttered by the President of the General Assembly, Mr. Frederick Boland, and then the Permanent Representative of Ireland. He made the following suggestion: As members of the Assembly are aware, the situation in the Congo has been the subject of much discussion in the United Nations within recent weeks and even within the past few days, and the constitutional and political position in that country still remains, unhappily, far from clear. In these circumstances, we are faced with a difficulty as regards the implementation of the resolution we just adopted. The difficulty is one for the Assembly itself, and I would suggest to the Assembly that the best solution of this would be to refer it to the Credentials Committee. As I hear no objection to this suggestion, it will be considered as adopted."

The Assembly President's suggestion was both practical and intelligent. There had been no opposition either in the Security Council or the General Assembly to the Congo's admission to the UN as a member. The General Assembly had adopted a resolution to that effect. What was at issue was whether to seat the delegation whose names had been submitted by the Prime Minister of the Congo, Patrice Lumumba, or whether to accept those submitted by President Joseph Kasa-Vubu as Head of State. There had been a sharp disagreement between Lumumba and Kasa-Vubu about the governance of the Congo. Lumumba had always favored a strong centralized government while Kasa-Vubu supported a federation. Therefore, apart from the problem of law and order and the protection of life, there did not seem to be concord at the helm of affairs. To compound the problem, Joseph Mobutu, a young Congolese whom Lumumba had appointed as Chief of Staff of the Congolese Army announced that he had dismissed both the President and the Prime Minister. The General Assembly was bound to resolve the issue of seating the Congolese delegation at one time or the other.

Then to confuse the issue further, the President of the United States, General Dwight Eisenhower, decided out of the blue in November 1960 to invite President Kasa-Vubu to come to New York to present a delegation to the United Nations. On President Eisenhower's instructions, the United States delegation insisted upon a meeting of the Credentials Committee, where it held an automatic majority. The Committee approved of the list of Congolese delegates submitted by President Kasa-Vubu. Of course, I fought hard in the General Assembly against this obvious maneuver. I did so because of strong personal convictions – Kasa-Vubu was not an Executive President while Lumumba was Prime Minister and Head of the Congolese Government by dint of his party MNC – Lumumba having won a majority of seats during the general elections. When I attended the Conference of Foreign Ministers of the Independent Africa States in Leopoldville called by Prime Minister Lumumba from August 25 to August 29, 1960, it was evident that the generality of the Congolese supported their Prime Minister. Also, among other clauses, the independent African States "reaffirmed full support and backing to the Central Government of the Republic of the Congo, which is the only legitimate and lawful authority, in entrenching and strengthening the independence, unity and territorial integrity of the Republic of the Congo." In the face of the facts and whatever way, you interpreted the Constitution of the Congo, the legitimate authority in the Congo was the Central Government headed by Lumumba which had invited the UN in the first place to the Congo.

I doubt whether the United Nations had ever before heard such bitter debate or witnessed such crass pressure politics as it did during the month of November, or at least until November 22, 1960, when the credentials of the Kasa-Vubu delegation were finally accepted. So strong were the railroading tactics, so furious the charges and counter-charges and ·so thick the suspicions that all delegations, including the African delegations, seemed divided solely along the lines of Cold War allegiances, for or against the United States or the Soviet Union. This should not have been so since the Congo issue was an African issue. However, because Russia supported Ghana's stand on the Congolese issue, Foreign Minister Charles Okala of Cameroun coined the phrase "Quaison-Sackey – Zorin Incorporated", accusing the Ambassador of Ghana of toeing the line of Valarin Zorin, the USSR Ambassador to the United Nations.

What became clear even after seating the Kasa-Vubu delegation in November 1960 was that the Congo crisis could not be effectively resolved without reckoning with Lumumba and the Central Government he headed. It was true that there was a semblance of a coup d'etat by Mobutu but Prime Minister Lumumba was a veritable factor not to be avoided. Hammarskjold himself was aware of this, and in that there had to be an attempt at reconciling Patrice Lumumba, Kasa-Vubu, Mobutu, Tshombe, and other leaders of the Congo (Leopoldville). Accordingly, a UN Reconciliation Committee of eight persons was dispatched to the Congo in early 1961 to perform the task of reconciliation. I was a member of that Committee under the chairmanship of Jaifa Wachuku, then the Foreign Minister of the Federal Republic of Nigeria.

We had a series of meetings with leaders in Leopoldville and met Joseph Kasa-Vubu, the President. He was not exactly forthcoming and we all called him "the Sphinx". He had the capacity of sitting quietly and calmly without batting an eye. When we asked about the whereabouts of Lumumba, we were informed by Kasa-Vubu that he was in prison in Stanleyville. Actually, news of Lumumba's arrest at Port Franquin had been received while we were in New York in December 1960. We proceeded to Stanleyville and met Antoine Gizenga, who at first refused to talk to the Committee unless we had produced Lumumba. He attacked the UN bitterly. In the end, we had a fruitful discussion with Gizenga and we got to know that Lumumba had been transferred as prisoner to Elizabethville in Katanga. So to Katanga, we flew. That flight from Stanleyville to Elizabethville was the most dangerous I had experienced. It was a military plane without seats but with seat belts in the floor. That was the only means of transport available at that moment of time. We took a risk and we nearly perished. On our way, the plane hit a tropical storm: the turbulence was so great that any drop of the plane in altitude felt like a crash. Any time we dropped in altitude, the stomach sank and each of us shouted for "God", "Allah", "my God", "Me Nyame" (I heard myself shout). It was a desperate and terrible experience. As things calmed down, the pilot confirmed that we had been saved by a miracle. The plane had no radar, and we had been lucky to reach Elizabethville. We duly found our way to one hotel in Elizabethville. An appointment was arranged with Moise

Tshombe. He confirmed to us in our discussions that Lumumba was in his custody. But then Tshombe was at pains to point out all the atrocities Lumumba and his followers had perpetrated on the Congolese. He continued in the same vein at dinner that evening. However, he promised me an interview with Lumumba the following day.

On the following day, we heard that Patrice Lumumba had been murdered, that in fact he had died on the very day we had arrived at Elizabethville. I was shocked but not at all surprised. Indeed, a week before this murder, I had been asked in Leopoldville by the US Ambassador to the Congo (Timberlake, I think) what I thought would happen in the Congo if Lumumba were not alive. He, for his part, was convinced that the Congo would be more stable, and as Andrew Tully printed in his book *CIA: The Inside Story* (New York, William Morrow &Co., 1962), page 226, "Brutal as it was, however, there was no denying that Lumumba's death had cleared the air and contributed to an atmosphere where steps could be taken towards the unifying of the Congo." When the United Nations Command in the Congo finally acted to expel the Belgian soldiers and foreign military adventurers and mercenaries from Katanga and to ensure the territorial integrity of the Congo, the UN had to fight a war in Katanga not against the Congolese as such, but against mercenaries backed by the gigantic Union Lumiere de Haut Katanga and the financial interests of Belgium and South Africa. Such were the high points in a very confused, often chaotic international situation.

Poor Lumumba! He was my guest at my official residence in New Rochelle. He and Mpolo and Bomboko and other members of his cabinet had come to the US in August 1960 to solicit bilateral financial assistance from the US and Canada, and, if possible, the Soviet Union through the Soviet ambassador. On the night of Lumumba's arrival in New Rochelle, I received a report that there was a prowler in my garden. I went out and saw Mr. Vasily Kuznetsov, the Deputy Foreign Minister of the USSR who had been sent to the UN to handle the Congolese problems before the UN. I arranged for him to meet Lumumba. From New York, Lumumba went to Washington and then to Ottawa.

I joined him and his delegation in Ottawa. My instructions from Ghana before he arrived in the US was to make sure that he did not entangle himself in any financial deals. Reports had been received at Accra about Mr. Detweiler's multi-million financial agreement with Lumumba. My task was to extricate him from it, which I did. He returned to the Congo without any conclusive agreements. The task was to bring peace and order in the Congo.

I feel proud that I had an opportunity of serving Ghana during the Congo crisis. Ghana was strongly in favor of respect and support for constitutionalism in the Congo. I had prophetically mentioned Cyrille Adonla, a trade unionist and independent politician as a compromise Prime Minister after Lumumba's death. Adonla was indeed elected Prime Minister by the Congolese Parliament, the majority of which were Lumumbists. Ghana had been vindicated.

I must say that Dag Hammarskjold was completely unprepared for the Congo situation. The crisis broke suddenly and unexpectedly for the UN. The Security Council had passed the resolution of July 14, 1960, requesting, in fine, that a United Nations Peace- keeping operation had to be mounted in the Congo to assist the Central Government of the Congo to keep law and order, vacate the Belgian intervention, and to preserve its territorial integrity until such time that the Congolese Government itself could do all these things themselves. It was like the UN being asked to keep a truce or protect some national borders. Dag Hammarskjold had able lieutenants in Dr. Ralph Bunche who had represented the UN during Congo's independence celebrations but had had to stay on at the request of Dag when the crisis broke out, Dr. Robert Gardiner of Ghana who succeeded Dr. Bunche, Ambassador Dayal of India, and General Van Horn of Sweden.

To me, Dag Hammarskjold was a great international statesman who was fast becoming the very embodiment of the UN itself. I had worked closely with him on the re-organization of the UN Secretariat and on the Congo crisis, and had liked him for his quick grasp of issues. I had the utmost respect for him for his wit, courtesy, culture, and scholarship. I recall that during the

Security Council debate on the Congo situation on September 16, 1960, I had received instructions from President Dr. Kwame Nkrumah of Ghana to make an intervention and point out that Ghana "had not been very happy over certain matters in connection with the application of the resolution." (July 14); but then he had asked me to appeal to Council members "to refrain from all personal attacks on Mr. Hammarskjold." I remember quoting some parts of words used by Edmund Burke in 1774 in his tribute to the Earl of Chatham. I said that the clear vision of this man "has merited rank, his superior eloquence, his splendid qualities, his eminent services, the vast space he fills in the eyes of mankind" must embolden us to pay tribute to him (Dag) for his great services in the cause of peace." As I spoke these famous words, Dag Hammarskjold blushed, but he must have known that I had recognized him as a very great man indeed. I am also convinced that he knew that Ghana's policy and contribution towards the Congo were basically sound. Unfortunately, he was a year too late in recognizing it, and then he died in a plane crash in N'dola in September 1961 in the cause of the peace of the Congo, of Africa, and of the world.

Yet another major African issue which was of great concern was the whole question of Apartheid in South Africa and the independence of Southwest Africa (Namibia). As far as the independence of Namibia was concerned, I know that it was a matter of time when South Africa would have to let go its stranglehold on a territory which was the proper and legitimate concern of the UN. After all, Namibia was a mandated territory under the League of Nations and South Africa had neither the moral right nor the legal capacity to occupy it. As for apartheid, it is a stated racial policy of the white-dominated South African regime and some other action than debates at the UN was required to combat. I remember raising the issue of sanctions during the debate on the Sharpeville massacres in 1960.

The Security Council of the UN was seized of the critical issue of repression and senseless killing of unarmed Africans in Sharpeville by the apartheid regime of South Africa. I received instructions from my government to intervene in the debate at the Security Council, and forcibly call the attention of the international community to the horrors of apartheid. The Sharpeville massacre took place on March 21, 1960, when South African police shot and killed a number of Africans in Sharpeville township for refusing to carry their "passbooks"[56] and burning them openly in protest against apartheid and all the "pass laws.[57]" It was a senseless massacre and international opinion was outraged.

I spoke before the Security Council on March 31, 1960, when Mr. Cabot Lodge, the US Ambassador to the UN was the President of the Council for the month of March. I concluded my statement as follows: "It must be said that in South Africa, there are two main races warring in a single bosom. For a long time, the two and a half million whites in South Africa have been the "spoiled darlings" of the Great Powers and through the long silence and sometimes the backing of these powers, the Boers and the British people who by the grace of God found a haven in Africa, have been emboldened to hold to ransom the eleven and a half million Africans in that territory. That is why my delegation feels that this grave situation can be remedied by the Great Powers themselves, notably the United Kingdom and the United States.

While my delegation is only a petitioner and therefore cannot prescribe what remedy this august body should adopt, we would today on behalf of our suffering compatriots in the Union of South Africa, appeal to the Security Council to take an action which will make the Union Government overhaul its apartheid policy. The people of Africa and Asia demand an atonement. They feel that this Council must assert its moral authority by deploring the incidents of March 21, by recognizing clearly the danger it constitutes to international peace and appealing to the Union Government to abandon its policy of apartheid. Perhaps, this Council may see its way clear to delegating the representatives of the United Kingdom and the United States to convey your

---

56 A passbook or bankbook is a paper book used to record bank or building society transactions on a deposit account. Traditionally, a passbook is used for accounts with a low transaction volume, such as savings accounts.

57 In South Africa, pass laws were a form of internal passport system designed to segregate the population, manage urbanization, and allocate migrant labour.

appeal directly to the Union Government, requesting it to come to terms with the African leaders. If the Union Government fails to respond to the appeals of the Security Council, the government and people of Ghana would urge the Council to take economic or diplomatic sanctions against the Union Government. Mr. President, you are on a conspicuous state and millions in Africa, Asia, America, and Europe watch your demeanor."

My statement was given wide coverage in the New York communications media, notably the New York Times of April 1, 1960. Calls for sanctions in those days against South Africa for its apartheid policies were rare. The trading partners of South Africa and powerful financial interests continued to invest in that country, giving a boost to its obnoxious and inhuman policies. But the writing has been on the wall and the white South Africans would have to come to terms with the African National Congress which since about 1909 has been fighting for majority rule in South Africa.

At the 16th Session of the General Assembly, Ghana was elected to the Security Council to serve for two years, starting from January 1962. The seat available was the so-called Commonwealth seat being vacated by Ceylon (Sri Lanka). I had lobbied my Commonwealth colleagues and there had been a tacit agreement because of the active role I was playing at that time at the UN. Thus, I became the representative of Ghana on the Council in my own right and not as a petitioner seeking permission to speak on a matter which affected Ghana or Africa as a whole.

According to the Charter of the UN, the Security Council is deemed to be in permanent session. In my time, it could be convened at any time. Therefore, the representative of a country serving on the Security Council had to make himself always available. You could be summoned by day or night, at any time there was a crisis. In any case, whether there was a meeting or no, the Council met every month for lunch, given by each member by rotation. The presidency of the Security Council was by rotation in alphabetical order and so I was the Council President twice.

During my tenure at the Security Council, there were some tricky issues which bedeviled international peace and security. Notable among these were the Kashmir question between India and Pakistan about which I have already written earlier in these memoirs, Arab-Israeli conflicts, and the Cuban Missile Crisis of 1962.

The Arab-Israeli conflicts hinged on the Palestine Refugee problem. Before the 1978 Arab-Israeli war, there were skirmishes from both sides, and the Council would be called upon to condemn this or that raid on some Arab settlements or an Israeli *kibbutz*[58]. Invariably, the Council called on both sides to desist from acts of aggression and preserve the peace.

But by far the most serious issue that came before us in my time was the Cuban crisis. The General Assembly was in session and I was as usual very busy, drafting resolutions, writing statements or going over them, and moving from committee to committee. Suddenly, one evening about 9 o'clock, I received a message from the Russian Mission that the Council would be meeting the following day on October 23, 1962. I had indeed heard in the corridors of the UN that an American U-2 aircraft was supposed to have detected that some nuclear missiles had been installed in the island of Cuba. As Cuba is about 90 miles from the United States, I was not surprised when I got to know later that the meeting had been called by the United States delegation. Ambassador Valerian Zorin of the Soviet Union happened to be the President of the Security Council for October 1962.

On the morrow of October 23, the UN was agog with activities. There was news that the US had mounted a naval blockade around Cuba. The papers that morning carried a statement broadcast by President John Kennedy of the United States that the American Navy would turn back any ships bound for Cuba, carrying "offensive weapons", and that Premier Khrushchev of the USSR had "to move the world back from the abyss of

---

58 A kibbutz is a collective community in Israel that was traditionally based on agriculture. The first kibbutz, established in 1909, was Degania. Today, farming has been partly supplanted by other economic branches, including industrial plants and high-tech enterprises.

destruction" by removing the missiles which had been trained on the United States from Cuba.

When the Council was called to order, the agenda had been circulated and there was a request from the representative of Cuba, Ambassador Mario-Garcia Inchaustegui to take part in the debate. Cuba was then not a member of the Security Council. The representative of the US, Ambassador Adlai Stevenson presented a draft resolution pointing out that the Russians had stealthily installed nuclear missiles in Cuba, thus endangering international peace and security, that UN observers should be sent to Cuba to see to the dismantling of the missiles and that the US was prepared to negotiate with Russia on "measures to remove the existing threat." The Russians also presented a draft resolution. Both Adlai Stevenson of the US and Valerian Zorin of the Soviet Union presented their sides of the issue. I still remember that the Security Council Chamber was packed full of delegates and visitors. Security was tight. We had to be protected from cranks!

Ambassador Garcia spoke for Cuba. His was a powerful attack on the United States and imperialism in general. Cuba, he said, had the sovereign right to order its international relations as was befitting a sovereign and independent nation. Therefore, the United States had no right to blockade a small and powerless nation like Cuba. His statement was naturally emotional, but whether or not he had sought instructions from Havana on what to say about the US draft resolution is/was difficult to know but the Permanent Representative of Cuba hysterically declared that Cuba would never admit any UN observers to Cuba as requested by Ambassador Stevenson's draft resolution. Ambassador Mario-Garcia Inchanstegui was soon after the Security Council debate removed from the UN. He had been a great friend and colleague, as I was also the Ambassador of Ghana to Cuba at the time with residence in New York.

Ambassador Mahmoud Riad and I, who were the two African representatives on the Security Council took advantage of the adjournment to meet a large number of representatives from non-aligned countries to discuss what should be done. This was a veritable crisis which could engulf the world in a nuclear holocaust. The two of us were, to quote a world statesman, "on the world stage and people all over the world were watching our demeanor." It was decided at the meeting that we should present our draft resolution as coming from the non-aligned nations of the world and that the two of us together with Ambassador Rossides of Cyprus who had chaired the meeting, should see the Secretary-General of the UN. We had a full discussion with U Thant who felt strengthened by the fact that the non-aligned nations were acting in concert with him. We then advised him to contact Washington, Moscow, and Havana, and convey the anxieties of the world about the grave situation. He should prevail upon Kennedy and Khrushchev to desist from any further acts that would result in war. We were on the brink of a holocaust and so the two Heads of States should try and disengage themselves from their stated stands. U Thant went along with us all the way.

The Secretary-General accordingly sent messages to President Kennedy and Premier Khrushchev saying that "representatives of a large number of member governments" had requested him to appeal to them to refrain from aggravating the situation and to give time for negotiations. There should be "the voluntary suspension of all arms shipments to Cuba and also the voluntary suspension of the quarantine measures for a period of two to three weeks". Mahmoud Riad and I had before then put in our draft resolution as a riposte to the two drafts from the United States and the Soviet Union. The draft resolution sponsored by Egypt and Ghana had requested the Secretary-General "to confer promptly with the parties directly concerned" about the means of removing the threat and normalizing the situation. It then called upon the parties, the Soviet Union, the United States, and Cuba, to refrain from any actions that might aggravate matters.

What must be emphasized is that in the Cuban missile crisis there was, to use UN parlance, "eye-ball to eye-ball confrontation" between the Soviet Union and the United States. The non-aligned nations, therefore, felt called upon by the dictates of international conscience to intervene through the Secretary-General to avert

239

a colossal catastrophe. In the event, Khrushchev sent a message to U Thant that "I agree with your proposals" while Kennedy responded that the threat was not of the making of the United States but had been created by "the secret introduction of offensive missiles into Cuba, and the answer lies in the removal of such weapons." But Kennedy expressed support for U Thant's moves. There was also great pressure on Fidel Castro to halt work on the installations in Cuba.

Whilst the various moves were being made to save the world from the brink of disaster, the Security Council had met on October 25, 1962, to continue its debate on the crisis. Unfortunately, Ambassador Zorin challenged Ambassador Adlai Stevenson to produce what real evidence there had been that Russia had placed missiles in Cuba. Frankly, it was difficult to understand why the Permanent Representative of the Soviet Union sought refuge in that way. He had spoken as if he had received no firm instructions from his government. Adlai Stevenson on the other hand had come to the Security Council Chamber armed with firm instructions and aerial photographs, perhaps unknown to Zorin. Ambassador Adlai Stevenson firmly replied that "We do have the evidence ... Mr. Zorin, I remind you that the other day you did not deny the existence of these weapons. But today, if I heard you correctly, you now say that they do not exist ... Let me ask you one simple question. Do you, Ambassador Zorin, deny that the Soviet Union has placed and is placing medium- and intermediate-range missiles on sites in Cuba? Yes or no?" It was at this momentous moment that Stevenson said that he was prepared to wait for an answer until "hell freezes over." The Security Council Chamber filled to maximum capacity, was agog with muted excitement but with great foreboding. Was there going to be a third world war, a nuclear holocaust?

Then Ambassador Zorin retorted in his own inimitable way: "I am not in an American courtroom, Sir, and therefore I do not wish to answer a question that is put to me in the way a prosecutor puts questions. You will have your answer in due course ... continue with your statement. You will have your answer in due course."

240

Of course, Stevenson proceeded to present the evidence. On his instructions, one of his aides mounted aerial photographs in an enlarged form of Soviet missile sites in Cuba. The evidence was overwhelming. There was no doubt. The real problem for the Security Council was to act quickly to ease the situation by removing the threat to international peace and security. And as I have already narrated a lot of hard work had gone on behind the scenes.

My own statement on presenting the third draft resolution before the Security Council on October 24, 1962, was well-received as an effective non-aligned statement. I ended by saying that "the responsibility of the Security Council is overwhelming. What is urgently needed is negotiation between the parties concerned to resolve the present crisis on the basis of mutual respect for each other's sovereign rights, and my delegation would urge that this Council authorize the Acting Secretary-General (at this time, U Thant was still acting in the aftermath of Dag Hammarskjold's death by air crash) to confer with them immediately with a view to facilitating such negotiations." I then presented the non- aligned draft resolution to that effect, co-sponsored by Egypt and Ghana.

U Thant traveled to Cuba to have serious talks with Fidel Castro and his government. He also maintained close contact with Moscow and Washington. On October 28, 1962, the Soviet Union announced to the relief of an anxious world that the missiles and launching bases in Cuba would be dismantled, and they were dismantled. The United States, on the other hand, having satisfied itself by air reconnaissance that the launching bases had been dismantled and that the 42 missiles had been removed, lifted the blockade by January 7, 1963. It was reported that Fidel Castro sent back to the Soviet Union 28 Ilyushin bombers which the Russians had brought to Cuba along with the missiles.

And so, ended a crisis which had begun on October 14, 1962, with the American U-2 aircraft having detected the installation of Russian nuclear missiles that had been trained on the United States in San Cristobal, Cuba. But the sequel to all was that the Russians were not pleased with the performance of their

Ambassador, Valerian Zorin during the Security Council debates. They had him replaced by the *bon vivant*, Ambassador Nikolai Federenko, who immediately became my close colleague and friend. Then the Cubans, as I have already narrated, removed their Ambassador Mario Garcia-Inchanstegui, for blowing his top and for committing his government in Havana without proper consultations. I was sorry to see him go.

I have so far given the readers of these memoirs a bird's eye view of my activities at the United Nations during my tenure of office as Permanent Representative of Ghana to the UN. I have already stated that there were a number of issues which, however portentous they might have been before, became perennial to be debated every year. Examples of such were Disarmament, the Palestine Refugee Problem, Apartheid in South Africa, Southwest Africa, Arab-Israeli conflicts, the Cyprus question, the problem of Racism, and the whole question of the international economic order.

On the Arab-Israeli conflicts, I must mention that during my time in the Security Council, I had proposed the setting up of an Arab state to absorb all the Arab refugees. This was before the 1967 Arab-Israeli war. I had made the proposal on the instructions of my President, Dr. Kwame Nkrumah, but it was muted and was not considered as practical politics, though some of my Arab colleagues quietly expressed support for the idea in the corridors.

Indeed, quite a lot of the work at the UN took place in the corridors and in the committee rooms where various groups – African Group, Afro-Asian Group, the Latin American Group, the Commonwealth Group – held consultations and conferences. Also, incessant visits to the Delegates' Lounge often yielded rewards. Some draft resolutions would be shown to you or you would be whisked away to some conclave or two or more delegates where some important international problem would be thrashed out, or some idea of the Secretary-General's would percolate through the Secretariat to be considered by a few delegates. The UN did indeed mirror the world.

242

Like most governments of the world, the Government of Ghana looked upon its Permanent Mission to the UN as a key mission. Therefore, the Permanent Representative had no respite. In fact, in my time, I was called upon by my government to perform, apart from work at the UN, special duties in certain parts of the world. Early in 1960, I was sent to Cuba to meet Fidel Castro and Ernesto Che Guevara and to assure the government and people of Cuba the support of the government and people of Ghana for the ongoing revolution in Cuba, after the overthrow of the Batista regime. Later, I became the first Ghana Ambassador to Cuba with residence in New York. In 1960, I was appointed the Special Representative of the Ghana Government to Argentina to participate in the celebrations of the 150th anniversary of the Mayo revolution. In 1961, I joined my President, Dr. Kwame Nkrumah in Belgrade, Yugoslavia, to attend the first Conference of the Non-Aligned countries. From the UN, I attended all the conferences of African Foreign Ministers in Liberia (1959), Ethiopia (1960), Cairo (1961), and Congo (Leopoldville). And then in May 1963, I was a delegate to the Conference of All African States at Addis Ababa where a supreme effort was made to merge all the various groupings in Africa – the Brazzaville Group, the Casablanca Group, and the Monrovia Group[59]. There in Ethiopia, I served as a member of the Drafting Committee to draw up a charter, which resulted in the formation of the Organization of African Unity (OAU). And in early 1964, I was sent to Guyana (then called

---

59 A linguistic divide was manifest through the three emerging groups dominating the continent's geopolitical scene at the time.

The Brazzaville Group comprised of twelve countries – Cameroon, Congo-Brazzaville, Côte d'Ivoire, Dahomey (Benin), Gabon, Upper Volta (Burkina Faso), Madagascar, Mauritania, Niger, the Central African Republic.

The Casablanca Group, sometimes known as the 'Casablanca bloc', was a short-lived, informal association of African states with a shared vision of the future of Africa and of Pan-Africanism in the early 1960s.[1] The group was composed of seven states led by radical, left-wing leaders — Algeria, Egypt, Ghana, Tanzania, Guinea, Libya, Mali, and Morocco.[2] The conflict and eventual compromise between the Casablanca Group and the Monrovia Group led to the establishment of the Organisation of African Unity.

The Monrovia Group, sometimes known as the Monrovia bloc, officially the Conference of Independent African States, was a short-lived, informal association of African states with a shared vision of the future of Africa and of Pan-Africanism in the early 1960s. The Monrovia Group comprised the twelve countries of the Brazzaville Group as well as Ethiopia, Liberia, Nigeria, Sierra Leone, Somalia, Togo, Tunisia and Congo (Kinshasa).

British Guiana[60]) to prepare the ground for a Ghanaian Mission which would attempt to bring about reconciliation between Premier Chaddi Jagan and Mr. Forbes Burnham (later President Burnham) in order that Guyana might achieve independence in unity and peace.

By 1963, I had become a veteran delegate to the United Nations, heavily involved in all its activities. Of the African Group, I was the doyen. It was for that reason that when the African Group decided that it was high time the United Nations had an African presidency in the General Assembly in rotation with other geographical areas, I presented my candidature for the post of President of the General Assembly. It was true that Ambassador Mongi Shin of Tunisia had been President in 1961 but he had done so by dint of being an Arab from Tunisia which was considered as being entitled to the Middle East privilege of nominating a President.

The African Group made it known to the European, Asian, Latin American, North American, and Middle Eastern delegations that 1964 should be the year when Africa would present a candidate as President of the General Assembly. It must be explained that there is nothing in the Charter which would support the African claim except that the principle of geographical distribution is implicit within the principles and purposes of the Charter.

Soon after I had presented my candidature which I announced to the African Group at a meeting on August 9, 1963, my colleagues and friends, Ambassadors Omar Adeel of Sudan and Nathan Barnes of Liberia also put in their candidatures on the instructions of their governments or so they claimed and explained to me. The African Group was thus faced with three candidates. A lot of lobbying took place. In fact, my colleague, Ambassador Omar Adeel toured Latin America and obtained the implicit support of Latin American delegates. My own strategy was to emphasize

---

60 The Guianas, sometimes called by the Spanish loan-word Guayanas, are a region in north-eastern South America which includes the following three territories: French Guiana, an overseas department and a region of France.

to UN colleagues the fact of my having stayed at the UN longer than any other African Ambassador at the time.

But the response would always be that the choice of the Africans would be the Assembly's choice. Of course, I knew that voting for the President of the General Assembly was by secret ballot and that in 1962 there were two Asian candidates to be voted upon by the General Assembly. There was Ambassador Zafrulla Khan, Permanent Representative of Pakistan, and Ambassador Malalasekera of Ceylon (Sri Lanka). Ambassador Zafrulla Khan won the election to become the President of the 17th Session of the General Assembly in 1962. It was after becoming the President of the General Assembly that he was elected a member of the International Court of Justice.

The African Group discussed the issue of three candidates, but as we took decisions by consensus, voting to select one of the three was completely out of the question. As September 1964 drew near it had become embarrassing for African delegates not having been able to select one candidate. The only solution would have been for any two of us stepping down and leave one candidate. Luckily for the African Group, the United States Government at this time expressed their intention of invoking Article 19 against the Soviet Union, France, and other eastern European governments to prevent them from voting in the General Assembly. Therefore, the opening of the 19th Session was postponed from the normal date of the second Tuesday of September to December 1, 1964, to allow consultations to take place. This gave the African Group some time to decide.

It was expected that the African Heads of State who met at the Organization of African Unity (OAU) conference in October 1964 in Cairo, Egypt, would take a decision on an African candidate. I myself attended the Conference as a delegate and was elected Chairman of the Political Drafting Committee of the Conference, but no decision was taken by our Heads of States. This was a wise step. All three candidates were supported to be able Ambassadors. Therefore, at the African Group meeting in early November, it was decided that every African Mission to the UN would seek instructions from its government as to which of the three candidates the particular government would support for the Presidency. The Chairman of the Group, Chief Simeon Adebo, Ambassador of the Federal Republic of Nigeria, with the unanimous approval of the Group, tasked the Ambassador of Cote d'Ivoire, Assuan Ussher, to go to every African Mission to find out which of the three candidates was the choice of the particular Permanent Mission. After Ambassador Assuan Ussher had obtained the choices of all the thirty-two African Missions, he had to inform the Chairman of the African Group so that a special meeting of the Group would be convened to receive the report of the Ambassador.

The African group was accordingly called into session on Thursday, November 26, 1964, to receive and consider the report. On that afternoon, all the African Permanent Representatives attended the meeting. News had already spread that the African Group would meet on that day to choose their candidate for the Presidency of the General Assembly. It was the first time in the history of the United Nations that the African Group had met to choose their own candidate for the Presidency.

Thus, outside the meeting room there had assembled reporters, pressmen, and cameramen all agog to honor the decision of the African Group. I still recall the atmosphere prevailing in our meeting room on that afternoon. No news had leaked out and it was clear from the manner of the normally-reticent Ambassador Usher of the Cote d'Ivoire that he alone knew the fate of the three contestants. The moments of waiting were really anxious.

Then Ambassador of Nigeria, Chief Simeon Adebo, Chairman of the African Group, gaveled the meeting to attention. He explained the meeting as a special one to enable the African Group to receive the report of Ambassador Usher of Cote d'Ivoire. The Chairman called upon the Ivorian Ambassador. He in turn reported that true to his mandate he had visited every African Permanent Mission to the United Nations and had obtained the name of the candidate the particular Mission favored. He reported that each Mission had informed him that the Permanent Representative had received definite instructions from their Government as to their support.

Ambassador Usher's findings were that 4 Missions supported His Excellency Mr. Nathan Barnes of Liberia; 8 Missions supported His Excellency Mr. Omar Adeel of Sudan, and 20 Missions supported His Excellency Mr. Alex Quaison-Sackey of Ghana. At that point of the deliberations both the Ambassadors of Liberia and Sudan informed the Group that on instructions from their governments, they were withdrawing from the contest. There was spontaneous clapping. The Chairman of the Group then announced that the African candidate to be President of the 19th regular session of the General Assembly was Ambassador Alex Quaison-Sackey. The reaction to Chief Adebo's announcement was electrical. I received a standing ovation. I wept unashamedly. The Chairman then expressed the gratitude of the African Group to Ambassador Assuan Usher and dilated on the virtues of African Unity. For my part, I thanked the other candidates for their magnanimity and praised the African Group for the happy resolution of the question of the African candidacy. My colleagues vied with each other to shake hands with me, congratulating me on my success and wishing me well in what was going to prove a difficult session of the General Assembly.

Alex with Major-General Stephen J. A. Out

Dr. Evans-Anfom and family

Malcolm X at Ambassador's residence in New Rochelle
with Alex and Nathan Quao

CHAPTER 11

OPENING OF THE 19TH SESSION OF
THE GENERAL ASSEMBLY

The opening of the 19th regular Session of the General Assembly had been scheduled for Tuesday, December 1, 1964, at 3 p.m. With the unanimous nomination of my candidature as President, the stage was set and I had to prepare to assume my duties.

Long before the opening of the 19th Session, the United States delegation headed by Governor Adlai Stevenson, had made it known that they would invoke Article 19 of the Charter of the United Nations against those members of the organization who had failed or refused to pay their arrears. Those members included two permanent members of the Security Council, namely France and the Union of Soviet Socialist Republics.

According to Article 19, "A member of the United Nations which is in arrears in the payment of its financial contribution to the Organization should have NO VOTE (my emphasis) in the General Assembly if the amount of its arrears equals or exceeds the amount of the contribution due from it for the preceding two full years. The General Assembly may, nevertheless, permit such a Member to vote if it is satisfied that the failure to pay is due to conditions beyond the control of the Member."

It was in the light of Article 19 and its invocation by the US and other western countries that frantic efforts had been made by the Secretary-General and some members of the Non-

Aligned delegations to persuade France and the Soviet Union and its satellites in Eastern Europe to pay some "substantial" contributions in order to avert a crisis. Their efforts were in vain. France argued that the expenses incurred by the United Nations Operations in the Congo (now Zaire) in 1960-1963 should not be deemed as expenses of the Organization and therefore could not be part of the financial contributions France should make. On the other hand, the Soviet Union and the delegation from Eastern Europe had criticized the UN's handling of the Operations in the Congo insisting that the mandate of the Security Council was not properly carried out by the Security Council. The Soviet Union, therefore, insisted that Article 19 was irrelevant in the issue. The majority of the UN membership, however, believed that the US delegation's threat was not a bluff and that the Soviet Union and France should make some contribution to help the situation. No compromise was forthcoming.

Therefore, the 19th Session was opened without the crisis having been resolved.

According to Article 20 of the United Nations Charter, "The General Assembly shall meet in regular annual sessions and in such special sessions as occasion may require." The General Assembly's rules of procedure require that the regular annual sessions should open on the second Tuesday of every September. But the opening can be postponed if circumstances demand a postponement, as in fact occurred in 1964.

It had become increasingly clear by the middle of 1964 that member states were not paying their contributions towards the expenses of the organization. There were large arrears to be made good by the Soviet Union and other Eastern European countries and France. The financial situation, therefore, gave cause for anxiety and the then Secretary-General, U Thant, began to confer with a number of countries including the Permanent Members of the Security Council about the resolution of the financial problem. As the months passed, the Secretary-General found himself in a quandary.

The financial situation as the Secretary-General reported and repeated in January 1965 to the Assembly was that total net cash resources in respect of the regular budget, the UN General Account, the United Nations Emergency Force (UNEF) and the United Nations Operations in the Congo (ONUC) special accounts, amounted to the equivalent of $14.6 million. Of this amount, $9.3 million represented collections of contributions from members during a period of two weeks. A cash reserve of $14.2 million, moreover, was little more than the amount required to maintain minimum bank balances throughout the world for the purpose of meeting day-to-day expenditures at the levels currently authorized.

The Secretary-General pointed out that the accounts showed $136 million as the total amount of assessed contributions outstanding, and past experience provided no grounds for anticipating payment of more than $6 or $7 million of this amount within the next several weeks. In the meantime, the organization's current payroll and other normal expenses on all accounts might be estimated as requiring average monthly cash disbursements of not less than $9 million. These requirements took into account any growth of the organization's responsibilities, notably in connection with trade and international development.

The Working Capital Fund to which recourse would otherwise be had pending receipt of assessed contributions had been virtually depleted because of the Fund's providing advances of almost $40 million; $39.7 million had been expended to finance past budgetary appropriations. Therefore, the Working Capital Fund needed to be quickly and adequately replenished.

What was more, the United Nation's indebtedness to Governments mainly in goods and services previously supplied amounted to an estimated total of $45 million. This was exclusive of indebtedness to Governments in respect of the amortized principal of outstanding UN bonds amounting to $154 million Thus, the financial picture of the United Nations was clear to all member states. The Secretary-General approached the United States, the Soviet Union, and representative groups of member states to make contributions to ease the financial situation, all to no avail. The Soviet Union through the Permanent Representative, Ambassador Nicolai Federenko, maintained that "we shall not participate in the financing of such organs of the UN as the United Nations Convention for the Unification and Rehabilitation of Korea, the UN Truce Supervision Organization in Palestine, and of certain other measures and organs which were established in violation of the UN Charter." The Soviet Union also refused to participate in defraying the expenses involved in the special expenditures for the peacekeeping operations in the Congo (Zaire), and for the maintenance of the Emergency Force of the UN in the Near East. The same attitude was taken by all the Eastern European countries. France, on its part, refused to pay for the peacekeeping operations in the Congo.

With such blatant refusal on the part of the Soviet Union, France, and a number of countries to pay their contributions, a critical issue emerged. Were these countries bound to pay their assessments in accordance with Article 17 of the Charter of the United Nations? The Soviet Union and the others refusing to pay maintained that expenditures involved in peacekeeping operations were NOT expenses of the organization under Article 17. On the other hand, the United States of America and the majority of the membership of the United Nations considered that every authorized expenditure of the United Nations formed part of the expenses of the organization.

It was during the dissension and lobbying in the corridors of the UN that it became clear that unless substantial payments were received from those members in arrears, there would be a postponement to December 1964 of the opening of the General Assembly. Meantime, the Heads of States of the Organization of African Unity (OAU) were due to meet in October 1964. Secretary-General U Thant, therefore took advantage of his address to the OAU Summit to impress upon the Heads of States the need for taking appropriate measures to appeal to all member states of the United Nations to make substantial financial contributions to ease the situation and avoid a crisis. The OAU was disturbed by the situation and passed a resolution appealing to all peace-loving governments and peoples to save the United Nations from disaster.

Before December 1, 1964, the financial situation was still critical. The Soviet Union, the Eastern European countries, and France were not budging. The United States delegation headed by Governor Adlai Stevenson took a positive stand. They made it known that they would invoke Article 19 of the Charter of the United Nations against all those Member States of the organization who had failed or refused to pay their arrears by the time of the opening of the General Assembly. There was much concern in the United Nations' lobbies. Those members in arrears included two Permanent members of the Security Council, that is the Union of Soviet Socialist Republics and France. Therein lay the basis of a terrible conflict which must be avoided at all costs.

According to Article 19, "A member of the United Nations which is in arrears in the payment of the financial contributions to the Organization shall have NO VOTE (my emphasis) in the General Assembly if the amount of its arrears equals or exceeds the amount of the contributions due from it for the preceding two full years. The General Assembly may, nevertheless, permit such a Member to vote if it is satisfied that the failure to pay is due to conditions beyond the control of the Member." Clearly, in the case of the Soviet Union, there was a palpable refusal to pay. It was not like Member States like Libya which had no ability to pay in those days.

Frantic efforts were made all round to avoid a confrontation. The Secretary-General held consultations with the Permanent Members of the Security Council and other delegations to thwart off a crisis which would bedevil the organization. The time for opening the General Assembly was fast approaching. With the threat of the invocation of Article 19 hanging like a Sword of Damocles[61], it was impossible to open the General Assembly without a confrontation. It would be impossible even to elect the President of the General Assembly. Most delegations hold the view that Article 17(2) which reads "The expenses of the

---

61 A situation in which something very bad could happen to someone at any time.

organization shall be borne by the Members as apportioned by the General Assembly" applied to <u>all</u> expenses of the organization and that the Soviet Union's position was motivated by "Cold War" considerations.

Such was the situation when the opening day of the General Assembly arrived. There was general consensus through consultations that since Africa had nominated a candidate as the President of the General Assembly, no voting would basically alter anything. The President should, therefore, be elected by acclamation. The President would then preside on the basis of consensus and during the General Debate, he and the Secretary- General would intensify their consultations to find a solution for the impasse.

The Chairman of the delegation of Venezuela, His Excellency Mr. Carlos Sosa Rodriguez, who was the President of the 18th Regular Session of the General Assembly, opened the session as Temporary President. He called for a minute of silent prayer or meditation as follows, "I request representatives to stand and observe one minute of silent prayer or meditation." After the representatives had stood in silence for a minute, he gaveled and requested them to take their seats.

The Temporary President then spoke as follows: "At the beginning of the 19th Regular Session of the General Assembly, it falls to me to welcome all the representatives present in this hall. I wish to express my heartfelt hope that at this 19th Session of the General Assembly there will prevail the same spirit of harmony which characterized the last regular session of the General Assembly over which I had the honor to preside."

"Today, more than ever, it is imperative that our debates should take place in an atmosphere of understanding and mutual respect because the problems that will have to be faced in the course of this session are many and serious. Today, more than ever, we must realize the need to preserve this organization and to enable it to achieve its objectives of peace and harmony among nations.

To that end, we must be ready to make sacrifices, convinced that the sacrifices we make will not be in vain, because the cause of the United Nations is a just one."

"I express my deepest hope that the work of this 19th Session of the General Assembly will be crowned with success and that at the end of the session our organization will emerge strengthened and that we will have made one more step towards the effective achievement of the concepts of the Charter."

Ambassador Rodriguez then called on the Secretary-General of the United Nations U Thant, to make a statement, which he did as follows: "In view of the differences of opinion which have arisen among Member States regarding the conduct of the 19th Session of the General Assembly, I have been in consultation with several delegations for the past week with the sole purpose of avoiding a confrontation. In this connection, I may mention that there is understanding to the effect that issues other than those that can be disposed of without objection will not be raised while the General Debate proceeds."

"I hope that all delegations will agree with this procedure. As far as today's meeting is concerned, there is general agreement, I believe, that on the above basis, we may proceed with the following items of business: 1. Appointment of the Credentials Committee; 2. Election of the President; 3. Admission of new Members to the United Nations. I would recommend that the General Assembly proceed accordingly."

The Temporary President then drew the attention of the General Assembly to the Secretary-General's statement and said that if there was no objection "we shall follow the procedure he has outlined". It was so decided. On that basis, the Temporary President proposed the following nine members to constitute the Credentials Committee for the 19th Session: Australia, Cambodia, Costa Rica, the United States of America, Guatemala, Ireland, Madagascar, the United Arab Republic (Egypt and Syria), and the Union of Soviet Socialist Republics. There was no objection and it was so decided.

Then came the moment everybody had been waiting for: the election of the President. I had come to the opening of the General Assembly in my kente[62] cloth, the resplendent national dress[63] of Ghana which had been worn by all members of the Ghana delegation including the then Foreign Minister of Ghana, His Excellency Mr. Kojo Botsio. The General Assembly hall was filled to capacity, everybody agog with anxiety.

The Temporary President continued as follows: "The Assembly will now proceed to the consideration of the next item, the election of the President of the 19th Regular Session of the General Assembly. I have been given to understand that there is only one candidate for this post, His Excellency Ambassador Alex Quaison-Sackey of Ghana. In accordance with the procedure to which the General Assembly has already given its assent, I would propose that His Excellency Ambassador Alex Quaison-Sackey be declared elected by acclamation President of the 19th Regular Session of the General Assembly."

The acclamation was demonstrated by delegates standing and clapping. It was, for me, a moving and unforgettable moment in my life. Ambassador Sosa Rodriguez then said in Spanish, "Expressing my most sincere congratulations to His Excellency Ambassador Alex Quaison-Sackey, I take great pleasure in handing over to his capable hands the responsibilities of the high post of President of the General Assembly and I invite him to come to the rostrum and take the Chair." The Protocol Officers accordingly came to the Ghana delegation seats to collect me and I was led to the rostrum amidst deafening cheers and jubilation.

As the newly elected President of the General Assembly, tradition demanded I make an opening and acceptance address. I wish to produce verbatim my address to the General Assembly on December 1, 1964, as the Presidency was the highlight of diplomatic careers.

---

62 Kente, known as *nwentoma* in Akan or *kete* in Ewe, is an indigenous Ghanaian textile, made of interwoven cloth strips of silk and cotton.

63 A folk costume expresses an identity through costume, which is usually associated with a geographic area or a period of time in history. It can also indicate social, marital or religious status.

"It is with a profound sense of gratitude and humility that I take this chair to serve you as President of the 19th Session of the General Assembly. By your unanimous decision, you have bestowed on me an honor which goes far beyond my humble person, for this is a tribute to Africa and to Ghana in particular, and above all to millions of people of African descent everywhere."

There was at this point a standing ovation led by African-Americans who had filled the gallery to full capacity.

"It is my earnest prayer that with your ready cooperation I shall carry out the onerous burden which devolves upon me at this session and thus requite the confidence which you have so ungrudgingly placed in me."

"I came from a young but dynamic country in Africa. For centuries and centuries, it smarted under the exploitation of European adventurers who called it the "Gold Coast." Then for more than one hundred years, it was under British rule. It was not until March 6, 1957, that the Gold Coast became a free and independent Ghana and was admitted to the United Nations as a Member State. Since then Ghana has played an active role in international affairs by throwing its weight solidly on the side of peace. Ghana has an unshakable faith in the United Nations and has consistently supported the purposes and principles of the Charter."

"In Africa, Ghana has bent all its energies, in concert with other sister African States, to the building of a united Africa in the cause of peace. At the very start of Ghana's independence, the President of Ghana told the world that "Ghana's independence is meaningless unless it is linked with the total liberation of the African continent." It can be said that since 1957 Africa has not been the same again. It is a measure of the strides Africa has made that within seven years the number of independent African States increased from eight to thirty-six. Today, we have witnessed the renaissance of the African Personality here, in this very Assembly. Indeed, who would have thought in 1945 that a representative of *Afrique Noire* would today be presiding over the General Assembly of the United Nations?"

"Yes, nineteen years ago the voice of Africa was frail and hardly audible. For centuries the personality of Africa was truncated by dint of foreign domination, exploitation, and oppression. For centuries Africa suffered the indignity of slavery and spoliation unparalleled in the history of mankind. African humanity suffered the worst form of degradation and devaluation, and yet Africans are not bitter. Was it Sayed Ahmed Mahgoud, then Foreign Minister of Sudan, who once said that "the African is naturally tolerant; we are prepared to forgive, for ours is not a creed of hate."

"There was an international conspiracy to obliterate Africa's glorious past. When vision was short and knowledge scant, men called Africa the "Dark Continent"[64], and some historians even made futile attempts to denigrate African's contribution to world civilization. To them, the exploits and grandeur of the great empires of ancient Ghana, Mali, Songhai, the powerful kingdoms of Ashanti, Buganda, Ife, and Benin, belonged to the realms of mythology. To them, before the advent of Europeans, all was darkness and void.

"But we who believe in the African personality are conscious of our ancient roots. We draw strength and inspiration from our glorious past, from the efflorescence of the powerful and enlightened civilization along the banks of the life-giving Nile, from the famous institutions of advanced studies in Timbuktu and from the glorious existence of Ethiopia."

"Today divided and mutilated, Africa is regaining its dignity and independence and is steadily moving towards its determined goal of continental unity and total liberation. The Organization of African Unity, in spite of severe handicaps, is tackling African problems with vigor and imagination. Africa is discovering its ancient glory and pride in a brave new world. Its future is now indissolubly linked up with the destiny of Asia, Latin America, and the rest of the world. Africans are resolved to play an effective

---

64 The Dark Continent is a place that stretches beyond the Known World which is nested inside the gigantic Lake Mobius. The ancestors of the human race apparently migrated from there to the Known World, as the deciphering of myths and the study of ancient ruins seem to testify.

role in world affairs. Indeed, they have already begun to make fruitful contributions toward the solutions of many difficult problems facing the United Nations. And why not? After all, the famous dictum of the Roman thinker, Seneca, has never lost its relevance that *Ex Africa semper aliquid novi* – out of Africa always something new.

"The United Nations, conceived in the sweat, tears, and blood of a world conflagration, has been buffeted by both extremes of fortune for nineteen years, but it has shown a wonderful resilience in the face of crises which have threatened its very existence. The opening session of each General Assembly should, therefore, serve as an occasion to reaffirm our faith in the United Nations and to rededicate ourselves to its purposes, ideals, and principles."

"Sometimes we tend to become disheartened when we consider the long list of problems confronting the world. We have tough problems such as the present financial and constitutional crisis due to peacekeeping operations, Korea, Vietnam, Germany, general and complete disarmament, decolonization, apartheid, refugees, human rights, and economic development. Some of these problems have been tackled with vigor by the United Nations. Others, like divided Germany, have not been properly discussed at this Assembly. But it is my conviction that, given a large fund of goodwill and a spirit of tolerance and compromise, we can grasp the nettle and take the sting out of these seemingly intractable problems."

"There are a few bright spots in the history of our organization when these qualities have saved the day and dissipated the specter of failure. It is my belief that this spirit of tolerance and compromise will once again prevail in the search for a firm solution to the financial crisis resulting from peacekeeping operations."

"This should give us hope that in the fire and crucible of crisis and danger we shall forge an organization which will fulfill its primary role of saving "succeeding generations from the scourge of war.""

"This is the greatest challenge of our time. There is a great commotion in our moral world. We have witnessed during the life of the United Nations conflicts in various parts of the world. It is true that no single power would be foolhardy enough to start a war, but there are rumblings beneath the surface of the world situation and, as the late Dag Hammarskjold once said, 'politically, the world situation represents a picture of interlocking stalemates.' Is it impossible for us to take another look at these stalemates and make fresh attempts to solve them? Perhaps we may give thought to the setting up of some ad hoc committees to study critical questions and endeavor to find solutions for them".

"Let us do some heart-searching. Does the peace of the world depend upon the United Nations or does the United Nations depend upon peace between the Great Powers? I must say here that it lies within your power, all of you representatives from Member States to make the United Nations a strong organization, a bastion for peace and security. We should not be hemmed in by age-old ideas of power politics. We should make full use of the Charter of the United Nations, which is a living and dynamic document. It is essential for us to maintain inviolate the courage of our convictions. We should place great premium on spiritual values which alone have sustained mankind in times of triumphs and tribulation up to the present day. We must all gird our loins to raise high the standard of freedom, justice, and peace."

"One of the tragedies of our world today is the scorn with which some view the whole question of international morality. To them it is anathema. Problems can only be solved in terms of power politics and rigid legality or political expediency. What they fail to realize, however, is that our civilization, if it must survive, should be humanistic and not purely technical. I am not advocating the wanton sacrifice of principles we hold so dear, but where some measure of accommodation can pave the way toward the solution of a problem, we must not lack the courage to do so. We must not be afraid to reconsider our position, to re-examine our attitude when changing circumstances make that inevitable. It is in this spirit that all of us who have pledged ourselves to observe the aims and purposes of the Charter should approach our responsibility."

"It is in this spirit also that I approach the task entrusted to me as President of this General Assembly. I am confident that with your support and cooperation I will live up to your expectations. It gives me great courage to face my onerous responsibilities when I look back over the impressive succession of distinguished and dedicated former Presidents who have left their imprint on the work of the General Assembly. Their records will serve as a guide and inspiration to me."

"But now, I deem it a great pleasure to pay special tribute to my immediate predecessor, my friend, and colleague, Dr. Carlos Sosa Rodriguez, whose efficient, dignified, and impartial conduct of the 18th Session of the General Assembly has won him universal applause and admiration. I shall endeavor, with your help, to follow his footsteps and draw inspiration from his impressive record".

"I also know that in all my endeavors I can count on the wisdom, knowledge, and the assistance of our Secretary-General. Let me here thank him for the significant work he is doing. He is in firm control at the head of the Secretariat, where his able lieutenants are giving of their best."

"We have on the agenda of the 19th Session many burning questions which call for our urgent and dedicated attention. Let us approach these problems in a sober and earnest mood devoid of rancor. Our debates should reflect a genuine desire to seek solutions and to reach decisions. I am confident that the worthy precedents set by previous sessions will be scrupulously observed, so that we may effectively complete the various items within the time available to us."

"It will also be my special privilege and pleasure to preside over the admission of the new member states of Malawi, Zambia, and Malta. The birth of every new state is for us an occasion of great rejoicing, for it signifies the progressive eradication of the cancer of colonialism."

"Furthermore, the injection of new blood into our Organization will assure it a vigorous and fruitful existence and a realization of its goal of universality."

"Let us all hope that in our lifetime it will be possible for us to see the complete eradication of domination and racialism. Let us attack the ramparts of oppression, ignorance, disease, and poverty and fulfill man's yearning for universal prosperity and progress. Let us continue to work for peace. It is to this end that we should bend all our energies. This session of the General Assembly should take a step nearer our objective."

"I implore you to approach the work of this session in a spirit of frankness, courage, and dedication, and with a singleness of purpose, strive to bequeath to succeeding generations an effective world organization, capable of ensuring the peace, happiness, and well-being of mankind. The United Nations is our international ship of state. It should cut through the icebergs and weather every storm. It must sail on. As the poet Longfellow put it:" "... sail on, O ship of State! Sail on, O Union strong and great! Humanity with all its fears, With all the hopes of future years, Is hanging breathless on thy fate!"

"What has begun as an Assembly of crisis should end as an Assembly of harmony and peace. May Divine Providence guide our deliberations."

I have reproduced my address to the 19th Regular Session of the General Assembly on December 1, 1964, for its historical significance. I was the first black African and the youngest to be president of the General Assembly and I was presiding at a critical period. The cold war was raging and I believed that my address would set the tone and bring about a harmonious resolution of the differences which divided the United States on the one part and the Soviet Union and the Eastern European bloc on the other part. France had happened to be on the Eastern

264

European side because the Government of France had also refused to pay its assessment of the peace-keeping operations in the Congo (United Nations Operations in the Congo) now Zaire. Thus, the General Assembly over which I was presiding had faced a crisis engendered by certain members refusing to pay their contributions of the UN assessment.

AQS takes over as the President of the UN General Assembly

Alex with Secretary-General U Thant

265

Alex with Secretary-General U Thant

CHAPTER 12

THE 19TH SESSION OF THE GENERAL ASSEMBLY

OTHER ASPECTS OF DIPLOMATIC LIFE

It will be unfair to give the impression that my six and a half years in New Rochelle, New York was all work and no play. That I took my work as Ambassador seriously, there was no doubt. My record spoke for itself. But I took my extra-U.N. activities rather seriously as well. I played golf all over New York State, although I was an honorary member of the Mamaroneck Country Club. I played to an eleven handicap. My wife and I attended concerts and operas. Our friends, Lester and Joan Avnet made sure that we attended all the premier performances. We were seen a lot at the Lincoln Center. And of course, we traveled throughout the length and breadth of the United States giving lectures not only about Ghana and Africa but also about the United Nations and its peace-keeping endeavors. My family and I mixed freely. Our parties and New Rochelle and our receptions at the United Nations were popular throughout our stay in New York. My own view then was that the Ghana Ambassador was popular because Ghana was the first African country south of the Sahara to gain its independence. But years later in 1978 when I became Ghana's Ambassador to the United States, our parties and receptions were equally popular, and very often, people sought to be invited. I cannot explain this one.

In the United States, I was in tune with the events that were galvanizing American society. Our sojourn coincided with the wind of change that gained momentum in the 1960s with the added impetus of the civil rights movements. I knew personally most of the Civil Rights leaders – Whitney Young of the Urban League, Franklin Williams, Elliot Skinner, Ralph Bunche, and Ambassador Dudley through whose instrumentality I became a Life Member of the National Association for the Advancement of Colored People (NAACP)[65], Reverend Abernathy and Reverend Dr. Martin Luther King, Jr. of the Southern Leadership. On the day of his departure to Stockholm to receive his Nobel Peace Prize, I had the rare privilege of having lunch with Martin Luther King Jr. at the United Nations Secretariat together with U Thant, the Secretary-General, Adlai Stevenson, and Ralph Bunche. My friend, Malcolm X came to most of my parties at New Rochelle. Paul Robeson and his wife spent a day with us in New Rochelle and it was a great delight to tell his own story of the gigantic struggles he had gone through. The great William DuBois and Shirley I knew. Our friends like Arthur Krim, Jonathan and June Bingham, the Avnets, drew us into the center of occurrences and events as they unfolded.

I became a close observer of the American, whether black or white. I knew the Jewish Americans and their sensibilities. They were a fantastically intelligent and able group, very sensitive to what was going on around all of us. The black American felt very American and I wondered why their white counterparts were wary of accepting them as equals. For my part, it was in the United States and indeed in Brazil and the Caribbean that I became alive to the uniqueness of our African culture. In spite of living in countries of advanced technology, the African-Americans, the African-Brazilians, the African-West Indians, and other Africans in the diaspora I thought had kept their 'Africanness'.

To my mind, the uniqueness of our African culture is only appreciated against the background of competing cultures in countries like the United States of America, Brazil, and the Caribbean. Our music, our art, our attitude to life, our reaction to injustices, to name a few attributes, stand out in bold relief in

---

65 About the NAACP. Founded in 1909 in response to the ongoing violence against Black people around the country, the NAACP (National Association for the Advancement of Colored People) is the largest and most pre-eminent civil rights organization in the nation.

the countries I have mentioned. I say this because when you visit Africa, the culture you see around you has in many ways been adulterated by invading influences, Moslem and Western. It is like visiting Virginia or the Carolinas in the United States and listening to 17th or 18th century English spoken which you would never hear in the England of today. Go to Provo near Tuscaloosa in Alabama to see authentic African culture!

All that I am saying is that my wife, children, and I were very much at home in the United States. We felt part of the struggles that were raging. We were prepared to suffer discrimination because of our color rather than make out that we were diplomats from Ghana. I had a number of experiences, but I could talk about two or so.

There was the morning we got up from bed in New Rochelle to find that some loads of rubbish had been piled under our flagpole standing in the middle of our front lawn. Then on one cold and chilly day when there was snow everywhere, we saw that someone had put a clay figure of a black man with deep red lips holding a lamp in the middle of our driveway. We reported both incidents to the police, but we never bothered to find out which of our neighbors had perpetrated these deeds. Round about the same time in 1961 I received an anonymous letter in which I was addressed as "Dear Head Nigger"[66]. The contents were that I had never had it so good and that I should return with all my black colleagues to Africa where we belonged. I read that letter in the General Assembly and Ambassador Adlai Stevenson, the poor man, had to go up to the rostrum to render a public apology.

The last incident I want to mention was when I was traveling on a Pullman from Alabama to Florida. I was traveling with my colleagues, J. B. Phillips and Richard Harlley, the UN security man attached to me when I was President of the General Assembly. When we decided to have a meal on the train, we found all the tables taken up except one where there was one solitary lady with three places available. The porter directed us

---

66 **niggerhead** or **nigger head** is a former name for several things thought to resemble the head of a black person

to that table. Just when we were settling down to our meals, the lady feigned illness, as if she was going to faint. She promptly got up without touching her soup which was in front of her and left. I was watching the scene with sincere amusement. As she was going to her cabin, the porter followed her. Unfortunately, the porter knew my identity as the current President of the UN General Assembly because Mr. Harlley had told him so. He imparted this information to the lady when he followed her to the cabin because as a black porter, he had instantly sensed that it was because of our presence that the middle-aged lady had vacated her seat. The porter told us so. As we were about to finish our meal, the lady returned to the table and began "I understand one of you is an Ambassador and President." The three of us got up instantly as if we had planned this course of action and left the table without a word. The porter came to my cabin with apologies from the lady!

And so, we spent nearly seven glorious and fantastic years in the United Nations in the service of Ghana. I was the chief spokesman at the UN for Dr. Kwame Nkrumah, the 1st President of Ghana, and was articulating Ghana's foreign policy in international forums everywhere. It was from New York that I served as Ambassador of Ghana to Cuba (1961 - 1963) and Mexico (1961 – 1963). These two Central American countries afforded us great opportunities of understanding the Latin character and appreciating and enjoying the warmth of the Cuban and Mexican populations. Mexico, I found a rather fascinating country. It was my first time of meeting Indians and Spaniards mixed together in such a fantastic fashion. The pyramids outside Mexico City were as imposing as any high-rise building. I remember climbing one of them with my son K.B. to the very top. The copper and silver works of the Mexican were really impressive. The diet was quite near African food, except that the Mexicans added lime to every food. The altitude was about 5,000 feet and so oxygen was thin and I found myself panting for breath in Mexico City. Therefore, at the least opportunity I traveled to Acapulco, a most dazzling Pacific city, quite a playground, I thought.

Ghana's relations with Mexico were good and warm, and I was accorded every courtesy when I came there on duty. We developed our relations to the extent of deciding to have a resident Ambassador. I was having a Charge d'Affaires in Mexico City with an efficient office. I still recall my work with K. P. Odum, Wallace, and Bosom, good and cooperative colleagues. As responsibilities grew, I had to concentrate on my work at the UN. In fact, about the same time resident Ambassadors were appointed by the Ghana Government for both Mexico and Havana.

I have already written a bit about Ghana's relations with Cuba and how I was appointed non-resident Ambassador to Cuba. One of my very able lieutenants in our New York Mission, Mr. Hope K. Yomekpe, was sent to Havana as my Charge d'Affaires. He held that position with great credit to himself but I lost him a year after, as the President wanted him to work at the African Affairs department attached to the President's Office. He was succeeded by an equally able officer, Ebenezer Akuete, an extremely shy but effective diplomatist. The Ghana Embassy in Cuba was popular and we lived next to the Guinea Embassy which had been given one of Upman's giant mansions in Havana.

My greatest recollection was my friendship with Castro and Che Guevara. I basked in Ghana's popularity. The two great men were always ready to hear about Nkrumah and Ghana. I felt at home in Cuba, not because of many people of African descent in that country but because there was so much positive thinking and action there. The Cuban Revolution was a real revolution and I felt part of it. I had been there to witness the great alphabetization programs being implemented with peasants from the rural areas coming to live in the posh hotels where they were taught to be literate. It was a fantastic experience. The peasant in Ghana owned his own plot or plots of land and if he worked really hard could become opulent. Not so his counterpart in Cuba who was invariably a wage earner working for some absentee landlord. Thus, the revolution in Cuba had galvanized the peasants into action and they could see a national leader, Fidel, who shared their aspirations and battled along with them to overcome their

271

deprivation and correct all the injustices of the past. There too they were not as endowed with many natural resources as Ghana. But they had sugar cane and the best tobacco produced anywhere. Of course, the Cuban cigar has always been famous. There can really be no substitute. It was a joy after the hard toil at the UN to spend the less busy months of June, July, and August in Havana on comparatively easy assignments. After multilateral diplomacy at the UN, it was refreshing to be in Havana interacting with Foreign Minister Raul Roa who was imbued with revolutionary zeal and fervor in spite of his advanced age. On looking back, it was my periodic sojourns in Cuba and Mexico which made me appreciate the problems of Latin America and helped to consolidate the relations of the African and Latin American groups at the United Nations.

CHAPTER 13

CLOSING OF THE 19TH SESSION OF THE GENERAL ASSEMBLY

S ecretary-General U Thant's statement before the 19th Session of the General Assembly comes to a close on September 1, 1965:

"Before the 19th Session of the General Assembly comes to a close, I wish to make a brief statement. I believe there will be general agreement that the 19th Session which began in an atmosphere of crisis is ending on an encouraging and hopeful note. So much of the credit for this change of atmosphere is due to the leadership of the President of the 19th Session of the General Assembly, His Excellency Dr. Alex Quaison-Sackey, Foreign Minister of Ghana, to the patient and constructive work of the Special Committee on Peace-Keeping Operations, and to the cooperation of all delegates. I wish to take this opportunity to pay my respects to you, Mr. President, and to the representatives of Member States gathered here today."

This was followed by a minute of silent prayer or meditation.

"I now invite the representatives to stand and observe one minute of silence dedicated to prayer or meditation. I declare closed the 19th Session of the General Assembly."

Closing Remarks of the President of the General Assembly,

"It is in a spirit of humility that I would like to respond to the kind tributes which have just been paid to me. There is no doubt that never in the annals of the United Nations has the existence of the Organization been so threatened. We also know the legal, political, and financial problems arising out of the issue of Article 19 whose applicability in regard to the United Nations operations in the Congo and the UN Emergency Force became a bone of contention at this 19th Session. In fact, as Cicero would put it, "things reached such a state of debility that things were well-nigh extinction."

"But then the Assembly itself acted to avoid such a catastrophe. It managed to move along gingerly and delicately dealing only with essential matters, allowing its President to guide it in a spirit of compromise and cooperation. The patience and forbearance shown by the Members of the Organization have now borne fruit. Thus, though the 19th Session began, as the Secretary has just pointed out, in a mood of despondency, we now wind up fortified in our beliefs that the UN is here to stay and it is bound to grow from strength to strength. This transformation has been brought about mainly by the goodwill and understanding which member states have shown in order that the UN may be strengthened and made an effective instrument for the attainment of the high purposes of the Charter."

"On this occasion, may I say how sorely we miss our departed colleague who was beloved by all sides of this house, Ambassador Adlai E. Stevenson. In this very hall, tributes have already been paid to his memory and I would like to join my voice with those tributes."

"The 19th Session will certainly be remembered for the many novel procedures it had to adopt in order to be able to function without resorting to voting on substantial issues. Even so, it has some accomplishments to its credit. To begin with, it welcomed three new Member States, two from Africa and one from Mediterranean Europe: namely Malawi, Zambia, and Malta. Then the vacant seats on the Councils were filled and the Councils were enabled to function as usual. The mandate of the UN Relief and Works Agency (UNRWA) for the Near East was extended. The United Nations Conference on Trade and Development was established as an organ of the General Assembly and the Trade and Development Board set up. The Assembly also approved the Secretariat of the Conference and confirmed the appointment of the Secretary-General of the Conference by the Secretary-General of the UN."

"However, I believe it will be generally agreed that the most important decision taken by the 19th Session was the establishment of the Special Committee on Peace-Keeping Operations. As a result of the Committee having to meet under the Chairmanship of the President of the General Assembly, my responsibilities have continued through all these months. I am happy with the outcome of the work of the Special Committee, and now men everywhere can heave a sigh of relief that the 20th Session of the General Assembly will work normally and try to resolve the many vital problems which today bedevil the peace of the world. I wish to take this opportunity to express my deep appreciation to the members of the Special Committee whose constructive efforts have produced a consensus which has been embodied in its reports and have been adopted just now by the Assembly. It has by no means completed its work, but the progress it has already made deserves our warmest praise. I would like to wish the Committee continued success in its comprehensive review of the whole question of peace-keeping operations in all their aspects."

"Yesterday, the Secretary-General announced that the amendments of the Charter had come into force which increase the membership of the Security Council and of the Economic and Social Council. As the members of the Assembly will remember, General Assembly Resolution December 17, 1963 (XVIII) which embodied these amendments called for Member States to ratify them by September 1, 1965. That proviso has been met and, as President of the Assembly, I wish to thank Member States for their cooperation in making this possible."

"I would also like to take advantage of this opportunity to make a brief reference to the 20th Anniversary of the founding of the United Nations, which was celebrated in San Francisco in the last days of June of this year. Our special gratitude is due to Mayor Shelley of the City of San Francisco, to the Chairman of the Citizens Committee of the City of San Francisco, Mr. Mortimer Fleishhacker Jr., and to the Chairman of the Executive Committee, Mr. Robert Gross, for their great and successful efforts to celebrate the 20th Anniversary in a fitting manner."

"And now, I wish to pay tribute also to the Secretary-General, a man who is the very embodiment of the UN, through whose assistance and wise guidance all my efforts would have been to no avail. I would also like to extend my thanks to the Under-Secretary for General Assembly Affairs, Mr. C.V. Massimiliano, who has quietly but effectively been my sheet anchor, and to all the members of the Secretariat who have assisted me in the conduct of the 19th Session. Their task was made more difficult by the fact that the normal rules of procedure could not be followed by the Assembly. Their assistance and advice was available to me freely at all times, and for that, I am very grateful. There are many of my UN colleagues whom we do not even see in this hall whose work is an important element in the successful functioning of the Assembly. I refer here to the Conference officers, interpreters, verbatim reporters, translators, typists, and reproduction personnel, as well as the public information staff, my own immediate staff and countless others who have to work long hours when the Assembly is in session in order that our work may proceed expediently and smoothly. I thank them."

"Let me again express my gratitude and appreciation to Lord Caradon of the UK, H.E. Kurt Waldheim of Austria, H.E. Mr. Gershon Collier of Sierra Leone, H.E. Mr. Justice Arthur Goldberg of the US, H.E. Mr. Silva of Brazil, the Honorable Mr. J. Kamachi of Kuwait, H.E. Mr. Malacela of Tanzania who have spoken at this meeting. I believe that they have spoken out of the kindness of their hearts and their friendship for me. I look forward to working with all my friends in continued cooperation and harmony.

Thank You.

CHAPTER 14

FROM PEKING TO USSHER FORT
FEBRUARY, 24 –26 1966

It was a cool morning when I woke up on Thursday February 24, 1966, in Rangoon, the capital city of Burma. My sleep had been interrupted several times that night of February 23, 1966, by weird cries of what I thought was a bird, but which I learnt afterwards was some kind of alligator common in those parts. I reflected then that those cries were ominous and that our journey to Peking the following morning was going to be eventful.

I got my luggage ready and called in my personal assistant to clear the room before we joined the President, Osagyefo Dr. Kwame Nkrumah at the Presidential Lodge. A security man suddenly appeared and insisted on searching my luggage for fear that some enemy might have planted an explosive which would blow up the Ilyushin 18 that the Chinese had brought to collect the President and his entourage to Peking en route to Hanoi. I did not like this search, but, then, I remembered that on leaving Accra, I had had to send my luggage the afternoon previous to our departure, and I learnt afterwards that this kind of search had become a routine when Osagyefo was traveling ever since the Kulungugu incident[67] in 1962 when an attempt was made on the President's life.

---

67 Kulungugu is a small town in the Upper East Region of Ghana and a minor entry point at the border of Burkina Faso and the Bawku Municipal District of Ghana.
Kulungugu is noted as the site of the Kulungugu Bomb Attack, a failed attempt at the assassination of Ghana's first president, Dr. Kwame Nkrumah.

The morning newspapers did not help matters much. The late Dr. M. F. Dei-Anang, the late Mr. Enoch Okoh, Mr. Kwesi Armah, then Minister of Trade and myself were reading and found that there had been upheavals in Syria, Iraq, and changes in government in Morocco and Mauritania and problems in Milton Obote of Uganda's government. I remarked rather drily that Africa and the Middle East seemed to be in ferment. Osagyefo retorted that the only way to prevent these upheavals in Africa, like the problem faced by President Obote, was to have a Union Government of Africa because there would be trouble for most heads of state in Africa if they did not respond to the yearning of their people for economic and social emancipation and prosperity.

It was against this background that we left Rangoon for Peking on that special Ilyushin 18 plane sent by the Chinese Government. We were seen off by General Ne Win, President of Burma.

General Ne Win had impressed me by his toughness. At a private dinner, he gave in honor of Osagyefo Dr. Kwame Nkrumah, I had been privileged to sit at his left hand side as Foreign Minister and, therefore, I plied him with questions about Burma and his relations with U Thant, then Secretary-General of the United Nations. He felt strongly that Burmese politicians did not do much for the Burmese people and allowed Burma to suffer economically. About U Thant he said little. But he spoke about the late Prime Minister Aung Sang and his cabinet with great reverence. He was convinced that the murder in cold blood of Aung Sang and his cabinet hampered the progress of Burma to a great extent. Ne Win was determined to keep Burma on a straight and narrow path without involvement in the Cold War. What fascinated me about General Ne Win was his passion for golf which he confessed helped him to relax after his onerous State duties.

Therefore, I left Rangoon with a determination that on our return from Hanoi I would put forward suggestions to improve the work of the Cabinet and bring about a liberalization of ideas and action which I found lacking in Ghana on my return from the

United States, after eleven years absence abroad. One of these suggestions I in fact broached to Osagyefo the President in the airplane. I told him that my short experience with the work of the Cabinet had left me with the impression that only routine matters from Ministries had come up for discussion and support. No policy matters, e.g., affecting the economic situation, had been advanced for consideration. I therefore suggested that if one Tuesday Cabinet meeting was devoted to routine matters, the next Tuesday should be set aside mainly for policy matters. In this way, new Ministers like me would have an opportunity of advancing ideas and proposals affecting every aspect of Government. Osagyefo Dr. Kwame Nkrumah was quite impressed with our discussion. He said that some years ago there used to be two Cabinet meetings a week, on Tuesdays and Fridays, but he did not know why the practice was discontinued. He thought we should discuss this matter again on our return. He himself felt that Cabinet meetings were to be used not solely for routine matters.

The voyage to Peking was quite smooth. We played cards while Osagyefo played chess with Sam Morris, a member of the Publicity Secretariat at the Flagstaff House, the office of Osagyefo the President.

When the stewardess announced that we were about to land, I looked out of the window. There was snow everywhere and it was still snowing when we came out of the plane. Chou En-Lai, the Prime Minister of China, and Liu Shao-chi, Vice Chairman, met Osagyefo at the airport.

The reception was tremendous. Drumming, clapping of hands, waving of flags, and shouting greeted us. The diplomatic corps was out in full and I believe every important official in the Government of Peking was here. But I did not see Chairman Mao Tse-Tung and Chen Fe. I learnt afterwards that Mao was out of Peking in a retreat. We shook hands and made our way to the official guest house, about an hour's drive away from the airport. The time was about four o'clock in the afternoon in Peking which would be about 12 midnight in Ghana.

The arrangement was that the official delegation should assemble at Osagyefo's suite as soon as we had washed and unpacked, to discuss our meetings with the Chinese government officials and the banquet in the evening. No sooner had we assembled than the security officer, announced that the Chinese Ambassador to Ghana, Mr. Hua wanted to see Osagyefo Dr. Kwame Nkrumah. At first, we were hesitant to open the door as we did not want the Chinese to prevent us, by an argument, from going to Hanoi. But on second thoughts, the President asked that the Ambassador be ushered in. With a shaky hand and a quivering voice, Ambassador Hua read from a piece of paper which contained a monitored message from the Chinese Embassy in Accra. The message read that "a section of the police and a section of the army are attempting to seize power in Ghana. There is fighting going on around Flagstaff House. The leader of the coup-makers is Colonel Kotoka."

Those of us present – Messrs. Dei-Anang, Okoh, Kwesi Armah, F. S. Arkhurst, Yaw Eduful, and myself – all showed surprise. But Osagyefo put up a bold front and said that this was nothing, it would fizzle out. The Chinese Ambassador withdrew but returned soon after with another message which confirmed that there had been a coup d'etat in Ghana and that Major-General Charles Barwah had been killed. There were demonstrations before the Chinese Embassy while there was still shooting at Flagstaff House.

The rest of our delegation was waiting at the hall but, from their faces, it was evident that they had heard about the coup. Osagyefo told the group that "they say some people are trying to take our power in Ghana. Let them try." There was a discussion about whether we should go to the banquet that night. I had earlier suggested that we should get the Chinese government to give us a special plane so that we might proceed at once to Cairo and, if possible, from Cairo to Accra. I insisted that we should cancel our plans for Hanoi. Osagyefo pounced on me and said, "What do you mean? As for you, Quaison-Sackey, if I follow you I will get nowhere." He said this in the Fante language. Anyway, we went to the banquet at about 8 p.m. Chinese security was on tenterhooks. Our own security man had been put in another house. I must say that it was the most painful banquet I had ever attended. The atmosphere was friendly but charged. Everybody by then had heard of the coup d'etat in Ghana and it must have been embarrassing to the diplomatic corps, but everybody behaved correctly. Osagyefo Dr. Kwame Nkrumah gave a most moving speech, a powerful tirade against the Imperialists and neo-colonialists.

Sleep did not come readily that Thursday night of February 24, 1966. On our return from the banquet, there were more telegrams informing us that there had actually been a coup d'etat, that some Ministers had been killed, and that there were demonstrations in Accra. Although we had heard rumors upon rumors of attempted coups, this was a surprise. It was clear on my return from the United Nations in November 1965 that there was discontent throughout the country and that Osagyefo the President was isolated from the people, a fact which Professor William Abraham, Vice-Chancellor of the University of Ghana and Special Adviser to the President made bold to point out in a series of articles published in the Ghana dailies. All these thoughts flashed through my mind. It was an agonizing experience – we were too far away and felt marooned.

On the following day, February 25, 1966, we had a long meeting with Osagyefo about what to do in the circumstances. More reports had poured in. Telephone calls and cables and telexes had been received through the Chinese government. We were informed that some activists of the Convention Peoples Party (C.P.P.) had been killed, including Kofi Baako, then Minister of Defense, Kweku Akwei, Party Education Secretary, Kofi Batsa, Editor of *Spark* a weekly periodical by the Bureau of Hate. We learnt that there was fierce fighting in the regions, especially in the Central Region, but that the Presidential guard had surrendered. It was not clear from the reports whether the whole Armed Forces were involved and what were the genuine feelings of the masses. Osagyefo joked with us by appointing some of us Generals, Colonels and Majors, e.g., Dr. E. A. Baiddoe the President's physician was appointed a Brigadier whereupon he

281

shouted back that he was a simple medical doctor – "As for me I am a doctor; I am not a freedom fighter."

Osagyefo Dr. Kwame Nkrumah went into conference with Premier Chou en Lai and most of us retired to our rooms. After what appeared a long time, I was called to see the President. I was wearing a morning gown and I was just putting my hands into my pocket to retrieve a nail clipper when the Chinese security man drew his pistol. I put up my arms and hurriedly explained in English that I was the Minister of Foreign Affairs. Of course, I was visibly shaken when I appeared before the President to whom I complained about the behavior of the security man. Present with Osagyefo were Messrs. Dei-Anang, Kwesi Armah, Enoch Okoh, and Fred Arkhurst. Osagyefo told me that it would be good if I went to Addis Ababa to attend the O.A.U. Ministerial Council Meeting scheduled for February 28, 1966, so that a resolution would be passed to support "the Constitutional Government of Ghana headed by Dr. Kwame Nkrumah." Without hesitation, I argued that what was likely to happen would be a procedural wrangle over credentials. In that case, most delegations would be guided by the instructions of their governments and their attitudes towards the *de facto* or *de jure* situation in Ghana. After some discussion, I agreed to go so long as there was some resistance in the Central Region and the situation was still undecided. By this time, a report had reached us that a National Liberation Council had been formed with General J. A. Ankrah as Chairman and Police Commissioner J. W. Harlley as Deputy Chairman. Osagyefo's countenance changed rather visibly at the mention of Harlley's name. Apparently, Osagyefo had placed infinite confidence in Harlley and the police and must have felt betrayed. I later held a meeting with Osagyefo and Premier Chou En-Lai. Chou En-Lai told me point blank that the mission with which I had been entrusted was a dangerous one – a cloak and dagger mission – and so I should be careful. Unfortunately, I had to go by commercial flight from Peking to Shangai to Canton and take a train to Hong Kong. He also advised that I should read the message to the Ghana Armed Forces which Osagyefo the President was supposed to read before the World Press in Peking. I did not understand why the Chinese government did not want President Nkrumah to speak from China, appealing to the soldiers and the police to lay down their arms and return to the barracks. Was it because the Chinese believed that "power must flow out of the barrel of a gun"? Be that as it might, I went to the Ghana Embassy with my officials and read before the World Press, Osagyefo Dr. Kwame Nkrumah's message appealing to the soldiers and the police to return to the barracks, and to the Ghana populace to remain calm. From all accounts, I read the message well. As the President himself was not around, the Press did not ask any questions.

On the morning of my departure from Peking, that was, Saturday February 26, 1966, I was summoned at dawn to Osagyefo's bedroom. He was still lying in bed, his eyes very red, holding a white handkerchief. We discussed my trip which was going to be a long one and tricky. He made me kneel before him and he placed his right palm on my head and said "My spirit go with you." Thus, on Saturday February 26, 1966, I set out on a very important mission on behalf of Osagyefo Dr. Kwame Nkrumah, to Addis Ababa in Ethiopia to fight for the "constitutional and legal government of which Dr. Kwame Nkrumah is the head" against the National Liberation Council which had sent a delegation from Accra to Addis Ababa. It was with great anxiety that I took a plane from Peking to Shanghai and another one from Shanghai to Canton, but I missed the train which was to take me and my entourage from Canton to Hong Kong. Those accompanying me were Dr. J. E. Bossman, then High Commissioner of Ghana in London who was to proceed to London from Frankfurt "to man" our London Mission; Mr. J. H. Sackey, then Director of the Eastern European and China desk who was going with me to Addis Ababa; and Mr. Albert K. Haynes, my personal assistant, who was proceeding to Ghana to report my movements to my family.

Whilst we were in China, we felt that we were under surveillance. At Shanghai, while waiting for our plane to Canton, we were royally treated to a sumptuous Chinese lunch of twelve courses! I had an inward presentiment that we were being watched, and indeed my traveling companions told me afterwards that their feelings were the same as mine. The plane to Canton delayed and we missed our train to Hong Kong and so we had to spend a night in Canton, a factor which was bound to affect my movement towards Addis Ababa.

We spent the afternoon sampling the commercial and cultural life of Canton. We visited the Trade Fair Center and the Cultural Park in Canton, and I was pleasantly surprised to see goods being advertised and general commercial activity going on as you would see in London or in New York. We also visited the famous mausoleum in Canton built in commemoration of the heroes who had died in the fight against the Kuomintang and the warlords before Mao Tse Tung won the day. We were told that in Canton, Mao himself taught the peasants how to improve their lot and to appreciate the virtues of Marxism/Communism.

Frankly, I have never seen so many people herded together as I saw in Canton. Everywhere, in every nook and cranny I saw men and women and children in such large numbers that I was tempted to feel that should there be a stampede, there would be a disaster!

The guest house in Canton was comfortable, though cold. My room was so chilly that I was compelled to request a heater. I managed to steal a wink but I was rudely awoken from sleep by someone whistling behind my window the popular song of the Convention Peoples Party "There is victory for us." I thought I was in a nightmare, but when I woke up, I could hear the whistling tailing off.

The following day was Sunday February 27, 1966. We had lost the better part of a day because by then we should have been in Hong Kong making our way towards Frankfurt in Germany where Joe Sackey and I would connect a plane for Addis Ababa. I was in an expectant mood, almost in a reverie, when Dr. Bossman asked whether we had heard someone whistling "There is victory for us" the previous night. Everybody had heard it. Was that an omen? The song itself ran as follows:

There is victory for us

There is victory for us

In the struggle of Africa

There is victory for us

Forward Ever

Backward Never

In the name of great Africa

There is victory

It must have been whistled to spur us on. We could not tell who had done the whistling, but we were fortified in our belief that we were involved in some cloak and dagger diplomacy.

It was thus a great relief to leave Canton by the morning train for Tsientsien on February 27, 1966. The train journey was delightful; there was an opportunity to see the terrain of China. Every inch of land was under cultivation. I saw women and girls working on the land. The irrigation system must have been superb because I saw canals or trenches full of water everywhere. It was a moving sight and my mind went back to my native Ghana where large tracts of land remain untouched and untilled. Soon we were in Tsientsien. All formalities over, we crossed over to the British side to take the train to Hong Kong. When we arrived in Hong Kong, the train station was really full of pressmen, cameramen, and journalists. I was not sure who had tipped the press that I would arrive at the station in Hong Kong at that precise hour. But they were there and as soon as we disembarked there was "click, click, click, click." Questions followed us "Where is Nkrumah? What is the Ogyesafo doing (they could not pronounce Osagyefo)? Who is Mr. Quaison-Sackey? Is the Foreign Minister going to Addis Ababa?" For some time, the press followed us, not knowing who Quaison-Sackey was. I tried to dodge the flashes until we got to the offices of the Chinese Travel Agency. My car door was forced open – someone had recognized me as Quaison-Sackey.

At that point, I let them take all the photographs they wanted to their hearts' content. But the press would not let me alone. They followed me to my hotel – Hotel Miramar. Some journalists who had known me at the United Nations greeted me and wanted a word with me. Meantime, newspapers were shoved into my room and I quickly read that there was a *de facto* situation in Ghana and that there had been a proclamation obviously drafted by the law officers in the Attorney General's Department, establishing the National Liberation Council as the Government of Ghana.

When the pressmen came to my rooms in Hotel Miramar, I made a short statement that I was on my way to Addis Ababa, where I had instructions from Dr. Kwame Nkrumah to oppose the delegation sent by the military regime to the meeting of the Council of Ministers of the Organization of African Unity; that from Addis Ababa I would go to Ghana and submit myself to the new regime.

From Hong Kong, we boarded a British Overseas Airways Corporation (BOAC) plane to Bangkok, New Delhi, Teheran, and Frankfurt. At each stop, the press came on board and pressed me for an interview which I never gave. We arrived in Frankfurt at about 3 in the morning on Monday, 28th February, 1966. An official of the BOAC came on board and informed me that the arrivals terminal was full of cameramen and journalists who had congregated to mob me. He could not guarantee my safety or security. And so while the other passengers remained on board, my colleague Joe Sackey and I were taken by special car first to the BOAC office away from the terminal and then to a small pension in Bad Soden near Frankfurt.

At this point, I was really tired and I was determined to have some rest until my plane was ready to take me on the last leg of my trip to Addis Ababa. However, at Bad Soden a number of things happened, whether by design or not, I could not fathom. The press I was supposed to elude at Frankfurt airport came to Bad Soden. All the Western newspapers were in my room and reading them convinced me of the hopelessness of my mission to the O.A.U. The situation in Ghana was *de facto*; there were still demonstrations against the Government of which I was Foreign Minister; C.P.P. Ministers had streamed to report at police stations, some wearing white, and there was Osagyefo's statue before Parliament broken and lying down with children playing on it. It was at this point that I became definite in my own mind that I should return to Ghana. I felt instinctively that I should not go to Addis Ababa. After all, there was no fighting in the regions and no Minister had been killed as we had heard in Peking. No proper arrangements had been made for my security and safe-conduct, and I was at the mercy of International Intelligence. I remembered what Chou en Lai had told me about cloak and dagger diplomacy. I had to face reality. From the newspapers, I read the coup d'etat in Ghana was popular and hoping that the new regime would usher in a new era of freedom and liberalism. I decided against going to Addis Ababa and then into exile. Joe Sackey shared my feelings.

Therefore, I rang Mr. Richard J. Blankson, my wife's cousin, in London and requested that he reserve seats for me and Joe Sackey on the Ghana Airways flight going to Accra on that day. We went to London by an Australian plane. Scotland Yard was at the airport to meet me. I was exhaustively interrogated by Scotland Yard. They wanted to know whether I would seek asylum in Britain, and what were my intentions. I was given an escort when I decided to take some rest at the house of my wife's cousin, Mr. Richard Blankson, then a Recruitment Officer at the Ghana High Commission, while I was waiting to emplane.

The Ghana Airways VC10 plane took off at 10 p.m. on February 28, 1966, and we arrived at Accra about 6 in the morning on Tuesday, March 1, 1966. The plane was immediately surrounded by armed soldiers, as it taxied to a stop. An army officer came on board the plane and called me by name. He requested me to take off my coat and follow him while all the other passengers waited on board. Frankly, I began to shiver in my bones, especially as the stewardesses on looking through the windows saw the armed soldiers ready for action. But as if the officer had sensed my trepidation, he whispered into my ear that I should not be frightened because it was all routine. It was a comfortable assurance but I could not contain my anxiety as I saw the guns trained on me and moving when I was descending the gangway. On reaching terra firma (the ground), I felt a sensation. There was a whiff of fresh air. This sensation stayed with me as I drove under police escort to my residence (which is now the Indian High Commission) to be searched.

My residence at the airport was a shambles. The place had been ransacked, and I saw broken furniture, my papers strewn all over the place, my mattresses cut open and my personal belonging looted. An eyewitness account was that a band of soldiers on the rampage had forcibly demanded the keys to my house from Mrs. B. A. Mensah, my landlady next door, who informed them that I was on a mission abroad. My family had fortunately gone to Winneba a day previously and so these soldiers had a field day. Our food, drinks, clothes, china, cutlery, money, and precious documents had been taken. The soldiers helped themselves liberally to whatever they could get hold of. The scene was so appalling that the soldiers and police who had brought me from the airport muttered sympathies and the women among them wept openly.

From the residence, I was taken to the Accra police station where my personal particulars were taken prior to my going into protective custody at Ussher Fort prison in Jamestown, Accra. From the police station, I was taken to the Police Headquarters where all members of the "National Liberation Council" had assembled to meet me.

General J. A. Ankrah was the Chairman of the National Liberation Council (N.L.C.) – the name given to the new military regime. I knew most of the nine members by name but I was introduced to all of them including Colonel Kotoka and Major Afrifa who were supposed to be the coup leaders. I knew General Ankrah and his deputy, Police Commissioner John Harlley very well. They had been my friends for a number of years, and the two were at pains to assure me that the whole exercise was not against the Convention Peoples Party government as such, but against

Osagyefo Dr. Kwame Nkrumah personally, who had "become too much of a dictator".

I informed the NLC of my movement from Peking and gave reasons why I had decided to return home instead of going into exile. I told them not to lose sight of the great contribution Osagyefo Dr. Kwame Nkrumah had made to Africa whatever his failings. I was informed that I had to go into protective custody as all former Ministers and Members of Parliament were either in Ussher Fort Prison or Nsawam Prison, but that the Council was not insensitive to my good work at the United Nations, especially as a former President of the UN General Assembly.

From the Council chambers, I was led like a lamb under heavy army escort to a big hall where there had assembled the police, soldiers, civilians in every walk of life, cameramen, journalists, and the press. The lights were focused on me. I must have looked troubled. The fact was that I had traveled for four days, without change of clothes, in a heavy three-piece suit and I was in a veritable state of fatigue and agitation. I narrated at the press conference my movement from Peking to Accra. I answered a barrage of questions. All this was published by the NLC because I believe, my views favored the new regime, but, in reality, the love of my country was a motivating factor. Not that I loved Dr. Nkrumah less, but I loved Ghana more.

From the press conference I went to Ussher Fort prison, having taken a short rest, under military escort and police guard, at the bungalow of my uncle Dr. Ebenezer A. Sackey, then Chief Executive of the Volta River Authority.

Of my treatment in Ussher Fort Prison, I will say little. It was not a happy place to be held in protective custody. We were eight in the same cell: Colonel David Zamlebigu, Commander of the President's own guard; Brigadier Hassan, Head of Military Intelligence; Lt. Col. Sampson-Acquah, Military Secretary to the President; Mr. Kojo Botsio, Chairman of the Planning Commission; Mr. L. Abavana, Minister of Interior; Mr. M. F. Dei-Anang, Ambassador at Large at the President's office, and Mr.

Ayeh Kumi, Financial Adviser to the President. Our cell was called by the wardens and prisoners, the United Nations because of my long association with the world body. Our loo, our drinking water, and food were in the same room. Today, the authorities would give us newspapers to read, tomorrow they would tell us we were not supposed to read the papers. Everything was like a dream. After two weeks or so in "protective custody", I was released with Mr. Kojo Botsio and Mr. Dei-Anang. Four days later, I was re-arrested at my home and returned to Ussher Fort Prison. Mr. Botsio and Mr. Dei-Anang were also back. No reasons were given. For me what was painful was that I did not see the sun during the day. We were led to the communal bathroom at 5 a.m. and at night and, therefore, those in my cell, except Mr. Ayeh-Kumi who was taken to a commission of inquiry every morning, did not see the sun. It was only when you felt ill that you went to the dispensary and enjoyed the sun.

Throughout my stay in Ussher Fort, I was besieged by pressmen and journalists wanting to know my views on this or that. It was gruesome, especially as one did not move without a guard. After nearly five months, I was released only to fall seriously ill to be admitted at the hospital. I had edema. My blood pressure was very high and the doctors said I was psychosomatic. I was in and out of the hospital for about a year until I regained good health, but the high blood pressure stayed with me and has had to be controlled.

It was clear to me even when I was in protective custody in Ussher Fort Prison where my journey from Peking ended, that I was a marked man not only by the NLC but also by my former President, Dr. Kwame Nkrumah. Whilst in prison, I was taken out three times to see M. A. K. Deku, a member of the NLC who was in charge of criminal investigation and police intelligence. On my first appearance before me, he grilled me about Dr. Nkrumah and wandered whether the Chinese Government would do anything untoward against Ghana. On my second visit, Mr. Deku wanted to know all about my accounts abroad, how much money I had, and whether I had properties in England or the United States. I had been away from Ghana solidly from 1955 to 1965. He was kind to confide in me that the NLC had received information that I ran a fleet of taxicabs in New York. There were other fantastic allegations, e.g., that I used my residence as "a gambling den". On my third visit, he merely ordered the armed policemen guarding me to take me around Accra for a breather. Once in the car, I directed him to drive me by the Achimota Golf Club through the University of Ghana, Legon, and back to Ussher Fort. It was in June and the greens and flowers were so beautiful and tantalizing that I wanted my freedom there and then. I was moved. I adopted my mother's eyes.

From all these visits, I gathered that the NLC was wondering what to do with me. A great debate was going on. Some members felt that my international standing should be utilized, that I should lead a goodwill mission to Europe and the United States. It was also felt that I should become Commissioner of Foreign Affairs or Prime Minister. The late A. L. Adu of blessed memory was the father of Ghana's Foreign Service and was responsible for the recruitment of eight of us as pioneer diplomats ("the faithful eight") told me that when he was consulted on these matters, he advised that I should be left alone. Later on, when I was released and called to the Osu Castle the following day (Osu Castle has been the seat of government from colonial days), General J. A. Ankrah, then Chairman of the NLC, told me "Alex, you have been on my conscience" and informed me that the NLC wanted to make use of me. I informed him at once that I was anxious to proceed to England to read for the Bar as I had been admitted to Lincoln's Inn, London in 1954 but had not taken my examinations although I had eaten my dinners. I implored him not to embarrass me by offering me any appointment because having served under Dr. Kwame Nkrumah, I could not possibly serve under the NLC. He understood. He informed me that Commissions of Enquiry were going to be set up to go into the assets of Ministers, Members of Parliament and certain specified persons of the Convention People's Party (CPP) and that as soon as I was cleared by an assets commission I would be permitted to leave Ghana. Soon after General Ankrah's promise, I received assets and liabilities forms from the Attorney General's department.

291

I completed these forms in due course. In them, I had to state my name and address, my education, all my earnings and expenditures since I started to work in 1948; all the properties I had acquired since then and the sources of income. It was an ordeal to remember everything, especially as I had undergone a traumatic experience staying in Ussher Fort Prison and with all my personal items looted including vital documents. Eventually, in 1965, I appeared before the Annie Jiagge Assets Commission. Justice S.S. Okunnor was the prosecuting counsel who examined me in chief. I did not find it necessary to engage a defense counsel. Then individual members of the Commission asked me questions. I appeared a second time when the Commission examined me on certain electricity bills on my house at Kanda Estate in Accra. Members were extremely courteous to me and I left them with the impression that there was nothing more to account for. I, therefore, applied formally to the Ghana Government for permission to proceed to England to pursue my legal studies. During that period in 1967, Mr. Victor Owusu, a barrister of great repute in Ghana, was my golfing partner every Wednesday afternoon. He was then the Attorney-General of the Republic. I talked to him about my application and he also assured me that if I was "cleared" by the Jiagge Assets Commission the Government would permit me to leave. Meantime, he advised me to seek an interview with Brigadier Afrifa as he then was.

I had an interesting interview with Brigadier Akwasi Afrifa. He apologized to me for having placed me under protective custody, asserting that I had brought great honor to Ghana and Africa by my work at the United Nations where I had risen to become President of the 19th Session of the United Nations General Assembly. But then I was one of those who had enhanced the international image of the former President, Dr. Kwame Nkrumah, and helped sustain the Nkrumah regime. He was rather forthright. He informed me that he had opposed other members of the National Liberation Council who were inclined to grant me permission to proceed overseas. His reason was that I was an important member of Dr. Nkrumah's Cabinet and there was no telling what I would do when I left Ghana. I assured him that the only purpose for going to England was to complete my Bar studies. As I was talking to Afrifa, I took in my surroundings very quickly and tried to make a quick appraisal of the man's personality, his motivations, and fears. He considered me dangerous and felt that I was in a position to thwart his ambitions, whatever they were. But then, he came out to say that he admired me and had looked upon me as an inspirer of the youth. He himself would like to go to Oxford eventually to read Philosophy, Politics, and Economics (PPE), which was what I read for my degree at Oxford, and then become a barrister. He finally said that as soon as they heard from the Annie Jiagge Commission favorably about me, I would be given permission to leave Ghana.

Eventually, I received a letter from Mr. L. K. Apaloo who was then Secretary to the NLC conveying the Council's permission to leave Ghana. I left Takoradi by the mail M.V. boat Apapa in September for Liverpool.

Throughout this period, I never sought for office under the NLC, nor was I offered any. Indeed, I did not proceed to Ghana after the coup to seek for any favors. I did not go to Addis Ababa as I had intended to partly because the basis for attending the OAU Conference of Foreign Ministers did not exist and there were no constitutional forces fighting for the CPP government and Kwame Nkrumah, as we had been made to understand in Peking, and partly because my personal security was not guaranteed. I was not properly prepared for cloak-and-dagger diplomacy. My failure to continue my journey to Addis Ababa was described by Dr. Nkrumah as a betrayal in his book *Dark Days in Ghana*. His book was clearly charged with emotion. He wrote that I went to the toilet more than twenty times, implying that I was afraid about the coup. That was an unfortunate gibe because it was not true. I remember that it was Kwame Nkrumah who broke down, so much so that he could not face the World Press to make his statement urging the Ghana Armed Forces and the police to return to the barracks. I had to read that statement, having taken along Mr. Yaw Eduful, who was then in charge of the President's Publicity Secretariat, Mr. H. V. Sekyi, the then acting Permanent Secretary of the Ministry of Foreign Affairs and other officers.

That press conference was indeed my last formal service to Dr. Kwame Nkrumah as President of Ghana....perhaps it did not represent the acme of political perfection but in an imperfect society ...

And this is all he wrote.

POSTLUDE

On 4th July, 2018, President Nana Addo Dankwa Akufo-Addo, President of the Republic presented posthumously during the 58th Anniversary of the Republic a citation to Ambassador Alexander Quaison-Sackey in recognition of, and gratitude for, your pioneering and distinguished service to the Republic of Ghana in the conduct of her diplomacy and foreign policy. Your invaluable contribution is appreciated by a grateful country. The Award Ceremony held at Jubilee House in Accra was to honor the 10 pioneers of the Ghana Foreign Service.

He was not there to receive the honor, having died in December, 1992. The notice in the New York Times said as follows:

Alex Quaison-Sackey, Ghanaian Official, 68.

Alex Quaison-Sackey, the first diplomat from a black African nation to serve as President of the General Assembly of the United Nations, died Monday at Korle Bu Hospital in Accra, Ghana. He was 68 and lived in Accra.

Mr. Quaison-Sackey died of a pulmonary embolism, said a son, Dr. Egya Quaison-Sackey of Baltimore.

Alex Quaison-Sackey was a diplomatic troubleshooter for Kwame Nkrumah, Ghana's first President, from the moment of Ghana's independence in 1957. He was First Secretary at the Ghana High Commission from 1957 to 1959 and served as the country's representative at the United Nations from 1959 to 1965.

Born in a family active in politics in the coastal town of Winneba, Mr. Quaison-Sackey was politically active as an undergraduate in Achimota College, near Accra, from which he graduated in 1948, and while earning an honor's degree at Oxford University in 1952.

Mr. Quaison-Sackey was elected President of the General Assembly in 1964 and served until 1965.

Mr. Quaison-Sackey remained close to President Nkrumah and was with him on a peace mission in Vietnam in February 1966, when the Nkrumah Government was overthrown by the army.

From 1978 to 1980, Mr. Quaison-Sackey served as the country's Ambassador to the United States.

In addition to his son, Egya, Mr. Quaison-Sackey is survived by his wife, Elsie; two daughters, Awo, of Cheshire, Conn., and Yaaba, of Accra; his two sons, Kweku Bondzie of Philadelphia, and Nii, of San Diego, and three grandchildren.

THE LIFE AND TIMES OF
DR. ALEX QUAISON-SACKEY

MR. K. B. AYENSU

On the 9th of August 1924, under the zodiac sign of Leo, a man destined to be immortalized burst upon the earth like a luminous phenomenon from celestial space. Upon impact at a certain spot at Winneba, that phenomenon began to glow like a raging, if benign, fire. Presented with John Oxenham's choice of ways, Alex Quaison-Sackey opted to be a high soul. And so he climbed the highway and did transcendental things. Even at the risk of sounding rather hackneyed, I have to recall *Julius Caesar* in order that I may hold up our hero as a man whose life was gentle, and in whom the elements so mixed that nature might stand up and say, THIS WAS THE MAN.

In his long quest for spirituality, Alex sought and gained three important dimensions. One, he learnt to bend with humility and resignation to the will of God. Two, he acknowledged that death holds no terrors equal to the stain of personal dishonour. Three, he completed his instruction on how to die.

The twilight between life and death is often plagued with morbid fear and mental pain. It is good to know that when Alex arrived in his twilight zone, he suffered neither of these. Weak but still resilient, he made cheerful conversation, even joked, a few hours before he died. He saw death coming but, like John Donne the poet and divine, he pooh-poohed death's claim to pride, might and dread. The peace which attended his closing hours may be captured in the words of a lovely hymn attributed to Ambrose of Milan:

Grant to life's day a calm unclouded ending,
An eve untouched by shadows of decay,
The brightness of a holy death-bed blending
With dawning glories of the eternal day.

Some say there is something in a name; at least there could be. Five popes took the name Alexander, and the first of them was canonised. Three Russian czars were Alexanders. Earl Alexander of Tunis of Second World War fame was a great military strategist. One of the kings of Yugoslavia was called Alexander. Prince Alexander of Battenberg, also Prince of Bulgaria, became British and took the name Alexander. From him is descended the Duke of Edinburgh, Queen Elizabeth's consort. Bestraddling all the Alexanders mentioned is Alexander the Great (356-323 B.C.), general, king, conqueror, who made the spread of Christianity possible 400 years after his own time.

In his own quiet way, our Alex too was great. He derived his strength from his uninhibited delight in the truth as revealed in God's Word. It worked for him like an enabling Act of Parliament which gave him the authority, and even the audacity, to say, to do, and to achieve.

Alex's father, Alexander Emmanuel Sackey of Winneba, well known as Kweku Sekyi, and his mother, Alberta Ekua Kwesiwa Quaison of the royal house of Ewusiedwo in the Ahanta District of the Western Region, were keen followers of the Methodist Tradition. Alex was of the lineage of Nana Acquah I and his father's brother was Nana Ayirebi Acquah III, both Amanhene of the Effutu Traditional Area. At his outdooring Alex was named in honour of his grandfather, Kodwo Sei (he himself was born on a Saturday). His parents and he were registered singers in this Church.

Alex left the Winneba Methodist School in 1940 with a distinction to his name. He went to Mfantsipim Secondary School in the following year. He joined the Mfantsipim Evangelical Group (M.E.G.) and preached at Antem and Ekon, villages near Cape Coast. At his last Speech and Founder's Day in 1945 his eloquence and voice tone as Senior Prefect so impressed the Headmaster that he set about persuading him to train at Wesley College, with the Ministry in view. He left the School with exemptions from London Matriculation and Oxford Re-sponsions.

Between 1946 and 1948 he was at Achimota, studying for the intermediate examinations for the Bachelor of Arts degree of London University. While at Achimota he intensified his Christian endeavours and was made President of the Student Christian Movement (S.C.M.).

Alex was admitted to Exeter College, Oxford in October 1949 on a Gold Coast Government scholarship. In the usual time he was matriculated into the university. At Oxford he kept up his membership of the S.C.M. and joined the Oxford Inter-Collegiate Christian Union (O.I.C.C.U.). In 1952 he graduated from the Honour School of Politics, Philosophy and Economics (P.P.E.) which Oxonians call Modern Greats (as distinct from Ancient Greats which is based on the humane subjects). His Bachelor's degree was subsequently advanced to the Master's in the Oxford tradition.

Soon after going down, he returned home and joined the Gold Coast Civil Service in the Labour Department. His career as a Labour Officer was rather short-lived.

In 1955 a new circumstance arose which set his mariner's compass in the direction of diplomacy. His achievements as a diplomat were acknowledged by American universities with the award of the honorary degrees of Doctor of Laws and Doctor of Letters. His diplomatic career itself will shortly be articulated by an official of the Ministry of Foreign Affairs. His career as Minister of Foreign Affairs will also be mentioned.

After the 1966 coup d'etat which toppled Kwame Nkrumah's government, Alex was detained. When he was freed the following

299

year, he went to London and continued the Law Studies he had begun when he was with the Ghana High Commission. While in London he worshipped regularly at the Methodist Church at Golders Green where he lived. In July 1969 he was called to the Bar by the Honourable Society of Lincoln's Inn.

He returned to Ghana in the same year and registered as a Barrister and Solicitor of the Superior Court of Judicature. After practising briefly from the Chambers of Lynes Quashie-Idun and Company in Accra, he set up Sackandah Chambers in the same city with his close friend, E. B. Okai Anderson, in October 1970. The name of the Chambers reflects the names Sackey and Anderson who did not only study together at the Inns but also wrote their final examinations at the same time.

When Alex returned home in 1980 from his diplomatic position in Washington, D.C., he engaged himself in various private consultancies in Ghana and Nigeria. In 1988 he joined the executive staff of Japan Motors Trading Company in Accra. The company will soon pay him a tribute.

In January 1991 Alex and four other Ghanaians were appointed 'Goodwill Ambassadors' by the Ghana Red Cross Society to support the World Campaign for the Protection of Victims of War. The Red Cross received the support of the Red Crescent Movement. The 'Goodwill Ambassadors' were to create a public awareness of the plight of refugees and victims of war who had taken up residence in Ghana. For many years Alex was President of the Ghana United Nations Association.

A careful analysis of Alex Quaison-Sackey will reveal that the consuming passion of his adult life was diplomacy rather than politics. Politics is noisy and could easily create the impression of ascendancy over diplomacy. Alex was cast in the mould of a diplomat, and when one looked at him in full panoply one saw a diplomat *par excellence*. Consider his elegance, poise and suavity; his disposition, unobtrusiveness and *sangfroid*; his apparel, circumspection and language.

300

In the centre of Alex's being stood Christ with all the paraphernalia of full occupation. He realised that Christianity, far from being a routine subscription to a fashionable creed, really consisted in a loving and serious attachment to Christ. As a pupil and as a student, he was proud to witness Christ in any circumstance. He touched the lives of many people by building his life into their lives. Of his work for the Church, the Methodist Church of Ghana will presently give testimony. The Leaders' Meeting of this Church has also recorded his activities in a tribute published in the brochure.

In the early 1950s a lady from this town was studying in Norwich, England, for the Cambridge Diploma in Education. She was called Elsie Blankson, daughter of the celebrated Church organist and composer, Oman Blankson of Winneba. In 1951, while he was still an undergraduate at Oxford, Alex married this lady. The marriage was not the fruitage of a ship-board romance but that of a romance budded in Ghana and delicately transplanted in British soil.

Alex and Elsie had six children: Egya Akumbia, Nana Bordoh, Awo Aferba,Kweku Bondzi Asiedu (popular as K.B.), Nenyi Embir and Yaaba. There are three grandchildren. Alex was a fine family man whose leadership was very much in evidence. His attainment of full parental stature was rewarded by the conferment, by the Congregation of Elsie and Children, of the style and title, 'M'paa'(My father).

Elsie knows the 900-odd hymns in the Methodist Hymn Book. If Alex did not enjoy that facility he certainly sang many of them with heart and soul, including No.832 which his Alma Mater, thinking ahead, chose as its school song. His patronage of choral groups was tremendous, and he gave them moral and other forms of support.

The sound of 'asafo' drums moved Alex very deeply. He belonged to the 'dentsefo'(the second battalion at Winneba). As a young man he 'must have yearned to be one of the cracks who guard the flag. They are known as 'asakanmbafo'. As a reward for merit,

301

he was installed 'Oman Supi'. He was later elected Gyasehene, and the Traditional Council will this morning tell you about it.

Alex was a very conscientious Freemason. He was initiated in a Lodge under the Grand Lodge of England which was founded over 275 years ago. That was at Tarkwa when he was a Labour Officer. He later joined the English Lodge at Winneba. At the level of the District Grand Lodge, he rose to the high office of Past District Senior Grand Warden. He was mindful of his mother Lodge at Tarkwa and maintained his support of it. When he died he was the Master of a Lodge in Accra. He ranks among the few Freemasons who have taken the mastership into the grave. He was well enough to attend a Lodge committee meeting the day before he was admitted to hospital.

Alex was gregarious by nature and, understandably, a club man. Himself a great raconteur, he enjoyed being regaled with stories by his friends. On hearing a good one, he would exclaim, 'Fantastic' and when he was more animated, 'Fantastico'. His sense of humour was quite boundless, his smile ever present, his laughter always catching. Full of the joy of living, he was all the time on the move. In a manner of speaking, he tended to "fill the unforgiving minute with sixty seconds' worth of distance run". That distance run included the publication of a book entitled *Africa Unbound* (Praeger, 1963).

Alex was an epicure (or was he a gourmet?). He set store by acculturation, and despite his exposure to exotic cuisine, that of his own private choosing was topped by Effutu dishes. He felt that when one was eating well one should not be disturbed. He regarded distractions as vexatious and depreciative. He was a man of vast concerns: spirituality, peace, justice, culture, human well-being and many more, as well as mundanities like food and drink and raiment.

The saga of Alex Quaison-Sackey or Kodwo Sei or M'paa may be told endlessly. It will be sufficient to end by stressing that he was a soldier of Christ who, in full gospel armour, was on a perpetual crusade. I am persuaded that when he was dying he

302

was privileged to whisper some of the words of Emily Elliott's hymn, "Thou didst leave Thy throne and Thy kingly crown," -

When the heavens shall ring

and the angels sing,

At Thy coming to victory,

Let Thy voice call me home saying," yet there is room,

There is room at my side for thee."

May my wish for Alex find acceptance with God and redound to his prosperity in the place where he is gone. Hallelujah, Amen.

AUTOGRAPH BOOK

Alexander Quaison-Sackey Sekondi
18 August, 1949
People asked to write "YOUR FAVOURITE LINES AND
SIGNATURE, PLEASE"

Alexander Quaison-Sackey
"I rejoice in Christ Jesus and I have no confidence in the flesh."

Gandhi
"The worst domestic oppression is better than any form of
generous and paternal imperialism."

What does the Christian say about this?

E. F. Bine
Beulah Lane, Cape Coast
"He prayeth but who lovest best. All things both great and small."

B. K. Bondzi-Simpson
"The great men of the world are those that soon or late challenge
everything. They challenge life itself. They say 'I have obeyed
enough. I shall now command.'"

Paul Brako
Social Welfare & Housing, Accra
"May the God guide you through all your days in your new
destination."

Francis Obeng Asante
Presbyterian Church, Asiakwa, Akim Abuakwa
"For the testimony of the Lord is pure, making the wise simple."

Unknown
19 July 1948
"Keep always with you wherever your course may be, the company of great thoughts, the inspiration of great ideals, the example of great achievements and the consolation of great failures. So equipped you can face without perturbation the pursuit of fortune, the buffet of circumstances and the inscrutable vicissitudes of life."

Alex Nii Blebo Andrews
Betmo House, Accra
"Go forth to life O child of Earth. Still mindful if they heavenly birth Thou art not here for ease or sin
But manhood's noble crown to win."

Unknown
"Nor when our days are done
And the last utterance of doom must fall
Is the doom anything memorable for its appareling The being of man facing it is all." *John Drinkwater*
19 July, 1948

K. K. Asamoah
Methodist School, Koforidua
"One must make of life a dream and out of that dream a reality."

J. K. Okine
Accra Academy, Accra
"Trust no <u>future</u> however pleasant Let the dead <u>past</u> bury its dead Act, act in the living <u>present</u> Hearts within and God overhead."

Kwame Bosque-Hamilton 18 July 1948, Gold Coast
"A gown that fits everybody, fits nobody: stick to your honest opinion and give in only to reason."

E. Oforo Bah
Achimota College, Achimota 19th July, 1948
"Life consists of two parts,
The first part and the second part,
The second part, like X'mas comes last
And it is the happier."

J.H. Stoove Duncan-Neizer
Jukwa Road, Cape Coast
"Without great men there can be no history; and without history a country remains perpetually pigeon-holed on the shelf of progress." Dr. J. B. Danquah

J. B. Danquah
July 21, 1948
Autograph only

Your dear friend,
Kofi Amos Coleman *("Aborigines")*
"One begins with fire and ends in smoke. Another with smoke, and, without raising expectations high, surprises us with dazzling miracles." — Roscommon

J. A. Apeakorang Nyakrom
"Man is a man not according to his external form but according to the nature and degree of his love and wisdom.".

Letitia Dua
Presbyterian Church, Suhum
"As for me and my house, we will serve the Lord."

J. K. Fierabor
c/o Mr. J. K. Monnie
U. A. C. Accra
Nil sine numina "(Nothing without God.) It is better to be sure than be sorry."

Annie R. Agyei-Mante
Accra
"Love one another"

E. B. Pupulampu
Akropong, Akuapem
"Abide in me, and I in you …". John 15:4

G. A. Odonkor
"In all thy ways acknowledge Him and He shall direct thy paths."

W. L. Tsitsinam
Alavanyo Kpeman via Kpandu
"There is a tide in the affairs of man which, taken at the flood, leads on to fortune; omitted, all the voyage of their life is bound up in shallows and in miseries. On such a full sea are we now afloat. And we must take the current when it serves or lose our ventures." — "Shakespeare: Julius Caesar"

"'Lines by great men all remind us that:
The heights by great men reached and kept
Were not attained by a sudden flight.
But they while their companions slept,
Were toiling upward in the night.' — Longfellow"
F. Addae Achimota

"Life is not all a bed of roses – nor is it a crown of thorns. The more mature you become, the less childish you tend to be. But always remember that the child is the father of man" *Anonymous*

"God be with you till we meet again." *Anonymous*

"This life is but a pilgrimage. We are not here to stay." *AA*

1. "A contribution is the property of the people and not any class of …
2. 'Individuality is the only quality of real progress.' — J. S. Mill

3. Self-government is an indestructible and inalienable right of man.
4. The power of the government is delegated power, that of the people is the real and supreme power.
5. Politics is not metaphysics or geometry but a moving area of moral ...
6. A foreign government is an evil and corrupt caricature." — *K. A. Annan*

E. Gyekye
Education Department, Accra
"The best is yet to be."

Irene M. Lilley
"With my best wishes to you and with pleasant memories of the class of '48."

David ?????
"If you can dream and not make dreams your master If you can think and not make thoughts your aim You will be a man .... My Son."

E. K. Newman
1. "The only man who is fully conscious of his ignorance is the man who has learned a good deal."
2. "A man is more than half successful if he knows when and where to give the right information."

J. M. Archie-Ocran, Accra
"Keep pushing the wiser than sitting aside
And dreaming and sighing and waiting the time
In life's earnest battle, they only prevail
Who daily march onward and never say, 'Fail'"

Wilmot
"Turn your eyes upon Jesus Look full in his wonderful face
And the things of earth will grow strangely dim In the light of His glory and grace."

Eve Wilmot
"Trust in the Lord with all thine heart, and lean not to thine own understanding; in all they ways acknowledge Him and He shall direct thy paths." Proverbs 3:5b

C. Anang
"Let prayers be your morning hymn and evening hymn. For through prayers everything will be answered by God."

J. Morgan ????
"Smiling Through."

Odonkor Azu-Mate
"It is not wisdom to be only wise
And on the inward vision close the eyes
But it is wisdom to believe the heart
To trust the soul's invisible surmise
Let this be your skill,
Your only out."

Emmanuel A. Ghan
"Trust in the Lord, in Him alone there is strength.
Success comes to those who always put their trust in Him.
Whilst you are away from here, remember this."

S. E. Sagoe
"Go out and put your hand into the hand of God and that should be to you better than light and safer than knowing the way."

??Acquah
"Humility is the avenue to Glory."

????
"Always remember that only the best is good for Africa."

Maggie Q. Sackey
"Surely goodness and mercy shall follow me all the days of my life and I will dwell in the house of the Lord forever."

"'We are such stuff as dreams are made on,
And our little life is rounded with a sleep.' — Shakespeare"
P. K. Abbam
Winneba

A. K. Ghanney
"The spirit of Self help is the root of all genuine growth in the individual, and exhibited in the life of many."

B. A. Forson
"Prove all things but hold fast that which is good."

K. O. Sackey Accra
1. "Opportunities are not playthings. The young man's progress in the business world and his early success depends upon his ability to see, appreciate and act upon the opportunities that arise in his particular sphere of action."

2. "It is a common plea of the faint-hearted that success depends mainly on luck. I do not believe at all in luck, and the man who is content to wait for a stroke of good fortune will probably wait until he has a stroke of paralysis"

3. "Be content with your lot; but always be fitting yourself for something better and something higher. Do not despise what you are. Be satisfied for the time, and not grumbling and finding fault."

K. A. Ghanney
"Be still and know that I am God. I will be exalted among all the earth. The Lord of hosts is with us. The Lord of Jacob is our refuge. The Lord of Jacob will guide you through your journey."

A. K. Ghanney
"He that is down needs fear no fall, he that is low, no pride. He that is humble ever shall have God to be his guide."

Clement Tagoe
On board R. M. A. Manton
"For your motto take these three words: Faith, Hope and Determination."

Anthony G. Sarilla (ADO Nigeria)
On R. M. A. Manton
"Ubi magnitudo; ibi veritas"

P. E. Anin Trans-Sahara
On R. M. A. Maonton
"Fiat institia; ruat caelum"

S. A. Boaitey
"Strive hard for there is yet hope in the future."

A. H. Osei
"Oh! Motherland 'tis for thee that we labour."

K. Haizel
Over the Sahara
"Help Us in Our Thirst for Light
We live not for ourselves but for others."

R. A. H. Blankson
"The rare action is in virtue than in vengeance."

Annan
"May our purpose be achieved on this trip."

A. P. Hammond
"Honour and shame from no condition rise
Act well thy part, then all the honour his." Anonymous

H. Jones
"Wishing you a happy stay in England."

K. K. Dadzie
"Gee, its wonderful, isn't it? We'd better make the best out of our chances!"

Anonymus
"Life is what you make it."

"AQS in
France; on flight to London on the R. M. A. Manton 5:40 GMT 30
August, 1949
'My country 'tis of thee,
Sweet land of liberty,
Of thee I sing.—Samuel Francis Smith" [then, in italics:]

Elsie A. Blankson
"Talents differ
All is well and wisely put ..."

Anonymous
"To see the vision of excellence so far as our limitations allow;
to get at least a glimpse of the unchanging values of the eternal
world as they are revealed in whatever is beautiful and good in
the material world of earth; to attempt to make one infinitesimal
contribution towards a society which will embody them
more fully than does our own – to do that is to take seriously
the tremendous words of Christ 'Be ye therefore perfect.'" Sir
Richard Livingstone

Amonoo
"Arise or be forever fallen."

Alex Quaison-Sackey
"Radical politicians based themselves on the frustrated. West
Africa is full of disaffected young people. Small African traders
who find the competition with Lebanese or with Africans from
other areas hard going; primary school graduates pouring out of
the schools at accelerating pace, and looking for clerical jobs which
do not exist; primary school teachers who, like school teachers
everywhere, consider themselves underpaid; wage earners who
have learnt to expect an annual increase of wages irrespective
of what happens to productivity; farmers who want higher
prices; men who resent chiefly authority; unsuccessful claimants
to chieftaincy; groups who wish to leave one chieftaincy and

313

come under another – this is the stuff of West African radicalism. Unemployment, due to young people leaving the land for the towns faster than the towns can provide jobs, supplies the radical politicians with a solid core of devoted party workers." *Politics in West Africa* by Prof Arthur Lewis

NOTE: "Modern democracy, with mass parties tolerating each other's opposition, is a very recent phenomenon in the world's history, so recent that it would perhaps be more surprising if West African politicians had decided to work this system than that they should have decided against it."

"For a principle to find a great leader who is himself a man of principle is almost a happy accident, and is not very likely except in a political framework which imposes high standards of political behavior. The history of democracy is a history of the efforts good men make to hold bad men in check; and this is a process which West Africa will have "just as much difficulty in learning as men in any other part of the world."

BIOGRAPHY FROM THE UN ARCHIVES

From UN.org

Elected President of the Nineteenth Session of the General Assembly

Alex Quaison-Sackey, who today was elected President of the nineteenth session, of the General Assembly has been the permanent Representative of Ghana at the United Nations and Ambassador Extraordinary and Plenipotentiary since 30 June 1959.

He headed the Ghana delegation to the fourteenth., thirteenth, sixteenth, seventeenth and, eighteenth sessions of the General Assembly. He was elected as one of the 13 Vice-Presidents of the sixteen session in 1961.

While Ghana's Representative on the Security Council, Mr. Quaison-Sackey, served as its President in June 1962 and again in July 1963.

He was elected as Chairman of the United Nations Committee on Information in -Non-Self-Governing Territories in 1960, and as second Vice-Chairman of the Governing Council of the United Nations Special Fund in 1961.

In 1961, he also was a member of the United Nations Congo Conciliation Commission.

Born in Winneba, Ghana (then the Gold Coast) on the 9th of August 1924, Mr. Quaison-Sackey attended the Mfantsipim School at Cape Coast and continued his studies at Achimota College.

In 1948, He was President of the Political Youth Organization in Winneba in the struggle for the Independence of Ghana.

In England, he studied for an honours Degree in Philosophy, Politics and Economics at Exeter College, Oxford, from 1949 to 1952.

On his return from England, he was appointed Labour Officer in Ghana, 1952-54, and during this period, he lectured in Economics and Government for the Ghana People's Education association.

In 1954, he entered Lincoln's Inn and during that year he also represented his Government at the Cambridge Conference on-African Administration.

Mr. Quaison-Sackey was one of the first Foreign Service Officers appointed before his country's independence, and undertook studies in international relations and in international law at the London School of Economics.

In 1957, he was a member of the first Ghana delegation to the session of the Contracting Parties to the General Agreement on Tariffs and Trade (GATT) in Geneva. Subsequently, he served as Head of Chancery and Official Secretary in the Ghana High Commissioner's Office in London until 1959.

He attended the Monrovia Foreign Ministers Conference of Independent African States in 1959. During the same year, he was appointed Ambassador Extraordinary and Plenipotentiary and Permanent Representative of Ghana to the United Nations.

In 1960, he attended the Second Regular Conference of Independent African States, held in Addis Ababa in June, as well as the Leopoldville Conference of Foreign Ministers in August.

Mr. Quaison-Sackey was a member of the Ghana delegation to the Belgrade Conference of Non-Aligned Countries in 1961; to the Conferences of Heads of African States in Addis Ababa in 1963 and in Cairo in July 1964; and to the Cairo Conference of Non-Aligned Countries in October 1964. During the Cairo Conference of Non-Aligned Countries, he was Chairman of the Political Drafting Committee.

He served as acting Chairman of the Ghana delegation to the United Nations on Trade and Development held in Geneva in 1964, and was for one week Chairman of the Co-ordinating Committee of the Group of African, Asian and Latin American countries at that Conference.

In November 1964, he headed Ghana's delegation to the Conference on Peace-Keeping Forces, held in Ottawa, Canada.

At United Nations Headquarters, he has served as Chairman of the African and the Asian-African Groups for several terms.

He is married and has five children. He is author of *Africa Unbound*, a book published in May 1963.

He has been Ghana's Ambassador to Cuba since 1961, and to Mexico from 1962 to March 1964.

COLLECTION OF ARTICLES ABOUT ALEX DURING THE TIME HE WAS AT THE UNITED NATIONS

Ghana's Voice at U.N.

Alex Quaison-Sackey

UNITED NATIONS, N.Y., Nov. 8 – In the short span of sixteen months Alex Quaison-Sackey has managed to make Ghana's voice heard frequently in United Nations meeting rooms. Many diplomats agree he made it heard forcefully.

Man In The News: Those who have watched his political fortunes prosper maintain that his success was entirely predictable. Even as an Oxford undergraduate, he displayed an aggressiveness of purpose that could not be overlooked.

As Ghana's chief spokesman, Mr. Quaison-Sackey must speak in many voices, On some occasions it is as a member of the Commonwealth in partnership with Britain, Canada and others. But more often it is as spokesman for one of the leading new African countries.

Since the onset of the Congo crisis in July, Ghana has been in the forefront of those African states that have upheld the legal right of Patrice Lumumba, the deposed Premier, to head the Congo Government.

Again today Mr. Quaison-Sackey, in Ghana's name, circulated a cabled protest from the Congo disavowing the right of President Joseph Kasa-Vubu to speak in the name of the Congolese people.

Ghana's position — repeatedly argued by Mr. Quaison-Sackey – has been that Mr. Lumumba's Government is the only legally constituted Government since it alone is an elected authority.

A Young U.N. Envoy: The Ghanaian diplomat, who is 36 years old, is one of the youngest to attain the rank of chief permanent delegate here.

This achievement was noted, somewhat wryly, by a lower-ranking Asian delegate who was at Oxford when Mr. Quaison-Sackey turned up to begin his studies in philosophy, politics and economics.

Outwardly, the Ghanaian delegate is a man of easy-going temperament who smiles often, enjoys his own jokes enormously and is fond of jazz.

He startled more staid diplomats last summer by becoming the patron of a jazz festival in Central Park and inviting fellow diplomats to pass up "cold war" talk to attend what he promised would be a "cool, cool war."

In a more serious vein, he explained that he felt music might be more of a harmonizing instrument than diplomatic speeches.

The Ghanaian representative has a collection of brightly colored Western weskits. But he also delights in Ghanaian dress and seems perfectly at ease in the colorful robes of his county.

Born in the fishing town of Winneba, he was educated at Mfantsipim, a Methodist mission school.

He grew up in the British colony of the Gold Coast – it did not become the independent state of Ghana until 1957 – and spent many hours at the palace of his uncle, who was an important chief. There he learned to play the *boma*, a wide drum, and the smaller *mpintsi*. He still enjoys a session with the drums.

Student of Law: After studying international law and government at the London School of Economics, he was appointed in 1952 as a labor officer and was one of the first to enter Ghana's foreign service. He came to the United Nations in July of 1959.

His wife, the former Elsie Blankson, came from the same seacoast town. They met when they sought roles in a student performance of *Romeo and Juliet*. They won the two main roles and were married later in Britain. They have three sons and a daughter.

The Quaison-Sackey family lives in an imposing English stone home in New Rochelle that has been decorated with Ghanaian art, paintings, sculpture and cloth hangings.

Published: November 9, 1960
Copyright The New York Times

1963 GHANA ASKS UN TO SUSPEND PORTUGAL

UNITED NATIONS, N.Y. – Ghana today [July 24] called for the "suspension" of Portugal from the United Nations if it has not freed its African territories by the start of the General Assembly session. Ghana Ambassador Alex Quaison-Sackey also demanded an embargo on the supply to Portugal of all arms and equipment likely to be used in pursuing its colonial policy and said the colonies were a threat to peace. "All the African states call on this Council to take firm action against Portugal's policy of oppression," he told the UN Security Council debate on Portuguese colonial policy.

U.N. ASSEMBLY AVOIDING AN ELECTION

Special to The New York Times

UNITED NATIONS, N. Y., Nov. 27 – The presidency of the 19th session of the General Assembly opening Tuesday, was assured today to Alex Quaison-Sackey of Ghana.

Some observers believed this might it possible to elect Mr. Quaison-Sackey, a 37-year-old, Oxford graduate, by acclamation and avoid the awkward question of whether the Soviet Union should be allowed to vote without paying its debts.

Because of refusal to pay assessments for United Nations peace-keeping operations, the Soviet Union is in arrears the equivalent of two years' dues, which, under Article 19 of the Charter, would mean the forfeiting of Moscow's Assembly vote.

Chief S. O. Adebo of Nigeria as spokesman for the 33-natino African group, announced that the two other candidates, Omar A. H. Adeel of the Sudan and Nathan Barnes of Liberia, had withdrawn in favor of Mr. Quaison-Sackey. The retiring president is Dr. Carlos Sosa Rodriguez of Venezuela.

Published: November 28, 1964
Copyright The New York Times

GHANA DELEGATE ASSAILS AIRDROP

He Calls Operation in Congo 'Affront' to Africans

By Farnswoth Fowle, Special to The New York Times

UNITED NATIONS, N.Y., Nov. 29 – Alex Quaison-Sackey, delegate of Ghana, criticized today the United States-Belgian action in the Congo as "an affront" to the Organization for African Unity.

He did not object to the "rescue operation as such," but said "there are political implications."

Mr. Quaison-Sackey said a committee of the African organization had been meeting in Nairobi on the fighting between Congolese Government forces and rebels "to bring off a cease-fire and a disengagement" just at the time the Belgian paratroopers were dropped in Stanleyville.

The Ghanaian delegate, who is expected to be named President of the General Assembly when it convenes Tuesday was interviewed on the Columbia Broadcasting System television program "Face the Nation." He did not dispute a suggestion that President Kwame Nkrumah of Ghana was showing reticence on the Congo issue by not denouncing the United States and Belgium.

"We are playing our cards," he said, adding that "my President views with concern" what has happened. He added it was "the thinking" of the Asian and African countries that the rescue of white hostages from rebel hands would be taken up by the Organization for African Unity Dec. 18.

"We all want an active United Nations," Mr. Quaison-Sackey said. He declared the 1946 Charter was "nebulous in parts" and reflected the view at the time that the great powers would finance peace-keeping operations and provide any troops the organization might need.

"There was no thinking that small countries would take part in such operations," he said.

He differed with the Soviet view that the Security Council was the only United Nations body with jurisdiction over peace-keeping operations.

"The entire Assembly has collective responsibility," the Ghanaian delegate asserted. Speaking as a member of the African-Asian bloc, he said, "We think that if an operation is initiated in the Security Council and fails, it should go to the General Assembly for some kind of resolution."

He proposed that if action in the Security Council was vetoed the Assembly should be able by a two-thirds vote to send it back to the Council. Then, he said, if on reconsideration there was a second veto in the Security Council, the Assembly could by a second two-thirds vote be allowed to take appropriate action.

The proposal would amplify the Uniting for Peace resolution of Nov. 3, 1950, which provides that when the Security Council cannot act because of a veto, the Assembly may make recommendations for collective action. The resolution has been opposed by the Soviet bloc.

Published: November 30 1964
Copyright The New York Times

DEBONAIR DIPLOMAT

Alex Quaison-Sackey

Special to The New York Times

UNITED NATIONS, N.Y., Nov.30 – In the nineteen-thirties, when Ghana was the Gold Coast and self-government and independence seemed remote for most of Africa, the late Sir Alfred Zimmern, a professor of international relations at Oxford, remarked that young Africans were not content to limit their studies to the practical arts of agriculture and technology. One such young man was Alex Quaison-Sackey, the unopposed candidate for President of the General Assembly.

Young Africans were well aware, Sir Alfred said, that the senior Colonial Service officers sent from Britain to rule them had studied Latin. So they, too, wanted to study Latin.

Latin as a status symbol may have seemed medieval to progressive educators in the West. The fact remains that the young Quaison- Sackey, born in the West African colony Aug. 9, 1924, did learn enough Latin to teach the subject. He also went on to Oxford to study philosophy, politics and economics.

At the age of 40, he would be the youngest President of the Assembly in its 19-year history.

For the last five years Mr. Quaison-Sackey (the first part of the name is pronounced KWAY-sun) has been Ghana's chief delegate here. He has not lost the breezy charm that he brought with him to the post. Tall, debonair, convivial, he is popular among his fellow-delegates.

He has the knack of being noticed, even when wearing Western dress, as is his custom, rather than the green-and-gold gowns that Ghanaians sometimes wear on ceremonial occasions. Often it is a flamboyant waistcoat; almost always it is an eye-catching walking stick, decorated with colored beads – a symbol of authority.

He Favors 'Cool' Jazz

Mr. Quaison-Sackey is an occasional jazz musician and identifies himself publicly with the "cool" school. He learned to play the drums from his uncle, Nana Ayirebi-Acquah, an elected chief, and he insists that West Africa is the "old country" for the jazz that evolved in the United States.

In the summer of 1960 he was chairman of a jazz festival in Central Park and announced it was to be a "cool" war to provide a diversion from the cold war.

That summer, when the Congo's internal and international disputes first became a matter of major United Nations concern, he was host at his residence in New Rochelle to the Congolese Premier, the late Patrice Lumumba.

In his early years here Mr. Quaison-Sackey's chief role was as orator and spokesman for the outspoken anticolonial and pan-African aims of his Government and his President, Kwame Nkrumah.

Two Rivals Withdraw

His candidacy in recent months for the General Assembly presidency has brought no slackening; in fact, this year, with the tacit understanding that an African would be elected, the question turned more on the enthusiasm of the other new African countries than on the opinions of other governments.

Until last week there were two rivals for the presidency, Omar Adeel of the Sudan and Nathan Barnes of Liberia, but Mr. Adeel, who is 41, and Mr. Barnes, 50, withdrew and the African states agreed on Mr. Quaison-Sackey.

Several months ago, when he began sporting a goatee, he told an acquaintance who was joking about it that he would shave it off if he won the General Assembly presidency.

Mr. Quaison-Sackey's wife is the former Miss Elsie Blankson, whom he met at school in Ghana. They have five children. The three eldest, who helped integrate the Roosevelt School serving their well-to-do New Rochelle neighborhood, are continuing their studies in Ghana. Two are still with their parents – one is in kindergarten in New Rochelle and the youngest is not yet of school age.

In addition to his excellent English and school Latin, Mr. Quaison-Sackey speaks two Ghanaian languages, Fante and Twi, as well as French and a little Spanish.

Published: December 1, 1964
Copyright The New York Times

EXCERPTS FROM QUAISON-SACKEY'S ADDRESS AT U.N.

UNITED NATIONS, N.Y., Dec. 1 – *Following are excerpts from the speech by Alex Quaison-Sackey of Ghana upon his selection today as President of the 19th General Assembly:*

It is with a profound sense of gratitude and humility that I take this chair to serve you as President of the 19th session of the General Assembly. By your unanimous decision you have today bestowed on me an honor which goes far beyond my humble person, for this is a tribute to Africa and to Ghana, in particular, and above all to millions of people of African descent everywhere.

It can be said that since 1957 Africa has not been the same again. It is a measure of the strides Africa has made that within seven years the number of independent African states increased from 8 to 36. Today, we have witnessed the renaissance of the African personality here, in this very Assembly. Indeed, who would have thought in 1945 that a representative of *Afrique Noire* would today be presiding over the General Assembly of the United Nations.

Yes, 19 years ago the voice of Africa was frail and hardly audible. For centuries the personality of Africa was truncated by dint of sovereign domination, exploitation and oppression. For centuries Africa suffered the indignity of slavery and spoliation unparalleled in the history of mankind.

We who believe in the African personality are conscious of our ancient roots. We draw strength and inspiration from our glorious past.

Ancient Glory and Pride

Today divided and mutilated, Africa is regaining her dignity and independence and is steadily toward her determined goal of continental unity and total liberation. The Organization of African Unity, in spite of severe handicaps, is tackling African problems with vigor and imagination.

Africa is discovering its ancient glory and pride in a brave new world. Its future is now indissolubly linked up with the destiny of Asia, Latin America and the rest of the world. Africans are resolved to play an effective role in world affairs. Indeed, they have already begun to make fruitful contributions toward the solutions of many difficult problems facing the United Nations. And why not? After all, the famous dictum of the Roman thinker Seneca has never lost its relevance that *Ex Africa semper aliquid novi* ("Out of Africa always something new").

The United Nations conceive in the sweat, tears and blood of a world conflagration, has been buffered by both extremes of fortune for 19 years, but it has shown a wonderful resilience in the face of crises, which have threatened its very existence. The opening session of each General Assembly should, therefore, serve as an occasion to reaffirm our faith in the United Nations and to rededicate ourselves to its purposes, ideals and principles.

Sometimes we tend to become disheartened when we consider the long list of problems confronting the world. We have tough problems such as the present financial and constitutional crisis due to peacekeeping operations, Korea, Vietnam, Germany, general and complete disarmament, decolonization, apartheid, refugees, human rights and economic development.

Some of these problems have been tackled with vigor in the United Nations. Others like divided Germany have not even been properly discussed at the United Nations. But it is my conviction that given a large fund of goodwill and a spirit of tolerance and compromise we can grapple the nettle and take the sting out of these seemingly intractable problems.

Let us do some heart-searching. Does the peace of the world depend upon the United Nations or does the United Nations depend upon peace between the great powers? I must say here that it lies within your power, all of you delegates from member states, to make the United Nations a strong organization, a bastion for peace and security.

International Morality

One of the tragedies of our world today is the scorn with which some view the whole question of international morality. To them it is anathema. Problems can only be solved in terms of power politics and rigid legality or political expediency. What they fail to realize, however, is that our civilization if it must survive should be humanistic and not purely technical.

I am not advocating the wanton sacrifice of principles we hold so dear, but where some measure of accommodation can pave the way toward the solution of a problem, we must not lack the courage to do so. We must not be afraid to reconsider our position, to re-examine our attitudes when changing circumstances make that inevitable. It is in this spirit that all of us who have pledged ourselves to observe the aims and purposes of the Charter should approach our responsibility.

We have on the agenda of this 19th session many burning questions which call for our urgent and dedicated attention. Let us approach these problems in a sober and earnest mood devoid of all rancor. Our debates should reflect a genuine desire to seek solutions and to reach decisions.

It will also be my special privilege and pleasure to preside over the admission of the new member states of Malawi, Zambia and Malta. The birth of every new state is for us an occasion of great rejoicing, for it signifies the progressive eradication of the cancer of colonialism. Furthermore, the injection of new blood into our organization will assure it a vigorous and fruitful existence and a realization of its goal of universality.

Let us all hope that in our lifetime it will be possible for us to see the complete eradication of domination and racialism. Let us attack the ramparts of oppression, ignorance, disease and poverty and fulfill man's yearning for universal prosperity and progress.

Let us work for humanity, not merely for nationality. Let us continue to work for peace. It is to this end that we should bend all our energies. This session of the General Assembly should take us a step nearer our objective.

Published December 2, 1964
Copyright The New York Times

U.N. DELEGATES EXPECT NO SEAT FOR RED CHINA THIS SESSION

By Sam Pope Brewer, Special to The New York Times

UNITED NATIONS, N.Y., Dec. 1 – The new President of the General Assembly, Alex Quaison-Sackey of Ghana, and many delegates believe that Communist China will fail again this session to gain membership in the United Nations but probably will win a seat next session.

The consensus is that Peking will have more support than last year, but not yet a two-thirds majority.

The question is among the most controversial that will arise when the Assembly gets to voting on resolutions. Eight countries so far have asked for debate on the item: "Restoration of the lawful rights of the People's Republic of China in the United Nations."

Communists have consistently contended that Nationalist China (Taiwan) illegally occupies seats in the General Assembly and the Security Council that belong to the Communist Government on the mainland.

Potential new votes favoring Communist China would arise from the recognition of the Peking Government by Paris in January. France voted against admission last year. So did 19 former French colonies.

These would produce a majority but not the two-thirds vote needed. By a 1961 resolution of the General Assembly, change in representation is classified as an important item, and requires a two-thirds vote.

Some delegates have argued that that vote applied only to the 1961 session and that the question of a simple or two-thirds majority must be reviewed each year.

They were overruled in 1962 and last year, but if the argument were accepted this session, a simple majority would be enough to remove the question from the "important" category. If this were done, another simple majority would be enough to seat Communist China.

Published: December 2, 1964
Copyright The New York Times

WELL, AS SOMEONE SAID, HUMANUM EST ERRARE*

Special to The New York Times

UNITED NATIONS, N.Y., Dec. 2 – Alex Quaison-Sackey of Ghana, the new president of the General Assembly and a onetime Latin Scholar, aroused classicists on his first day in office.

In his inaugural speech yesterday, Mr. Quaison-Sackey said, "The famous dictum of the Roman thinker Seneca has never lost its relevance that *Ex Africa semper aliquid novi*" – "Out of Africa, always something new."

331

Classicists were quick to point out that the source was not Seneca but Pliny the Elder, whose Latin was a translation of the Greek of Aristotle.

Piero Vinci, the delegate of Italy, appeared unaware of the slip; he said in the Assembly today that he was proud Seneca had been quoted, because this great Roman "knew how much his country owed to Africa"

* Seneca

Published: December 3, 1964
Copyright The New York Times

U.N. ARREARS PLAN IS MODIFIED TO MEET OBJECTIONS BY SOVIET

By Thomas J. Hamilton, Special to The New York Times

UNITED NATIONS, N.Y. – Dec. 21 – A 12-man African and Asian committee gave approval tonight to major changes in a plan drawn up by Alex Quaison-Sackey, President of the General Assembly, intended to settle the crisis over unpaid Soviet assessments.

Members of the committee said that the changes had been made in accordance with amendments submitted by the Secretary General U Thant, and that they were intended to make the plan acceptable to the Soviet Union.

One of the two principal changes proposed today by Mr. Thant, and accepted by the African and Asian committee, would eliminate the requirement that "substantial and adequate" voluntary contributions be made by all 115 members of the United Nations to solve the financial crisis.

The revised plan gives no indication of the amount expected from the Soviet Union, which owes $52.6 million in assessments for the United Nations peace-keeping missions in the Congo and the Middle East.

The other main change would include a reference to Article 19 of the Charter, which stipulates that nations more than two years in arrears on overall assessments are to lose their votes in the Assembly.

Members of the African and Asian committee said the inserted provision had the same meaning as the clause in their previous proposal. This stated that "to avoid a confrontation at the present session of the General Assembly, the question of applicability of Article 19 should not be raised.

Mr. Quaison-Sackey's plan, like the original plan for a "rescue fund" drawn up by Dr. Carlos Sosa Rodriguez of Venezuela, made no reference to Article 19.

Under both plans voluntary contributions from all members would be accepted as the immediate solution of the crisis. Since Article 19 was not mentioned, it might remain applicable if the contributions were not sufficient, or if another crisis arose over unpaid assessments.

The African and Asian committee included the mention of Article 19 to meet objections of the Soviet Union. Moscow rejected the first plan for a "rescue fund" because it would not agree to an arrangement under which it would appear to be making a contribution under the threat of losing its Assembly vote, as demanded by Washington.

Members of the committee said the revised plan – attributed to Mr. Thant rather than to Mr. Quaison-Sackey – would be admitted tomorrow to the Soviet Union and the United States.

Committee members expressed confidence that, if it was approved by Moscow and Washington, the Assembly would be able to adopt it in the form of a resolution tomorrow and the crisis would be ended by tomorrow night without a delay envisaged by Mr. Quaison-Sackey.

Under the Quaison-Sackey plan, Mr. Thant would announce to the Assembly about Jan. 15 whether the pledge for voluntary contributions were adequate. The Soviet Union agreed last week to make a commitment to Mr. Thant – and only to Mr. Thant – on the size of its contribution to the proposed "rescue fund" and on when it would be paid.

Published: December 22, 1964
Copyright The New York Times

U.N. FUND ACCORD IS BELIEVED NEAR

Assembly to Meet Today on "Unfinished Business"

By Thomas J. Hamilton, Special to The New York Times

UNITED NATIONS, N.Y., Dec. 22 – Alex Quaison-Sackey, president of the General Assembly, called today for an Assembly session tomorrow on "unfinished business." He thus encouraged the belief among many delegates that a provisional settlement of the United Nations financial crisis was at hand.

During the day Mr. Quaison-Sackey distributed to delegates copies of a resolution that he intends to introduce tomorrow. It would have the Assembly request all members to make voluntary contributions to the hard-pressed United Nations treasure.

However, Mr. Quaison-Sackey did not deliver the final text, which he had promised to leading delegations at 4 P.M. A reliable source said the delay had resulted from questions directed to Mr. Quaison-Sackey by the Soviet delegation on the meaning of his plan.

It was said the Assembly President had submitted amended provisions.

Quaison-Sackey Visits Thant

The developments prompted Mr. Quaison-Sackey to pay a surprise call late this afternoon on the Secretary-General, U. Thant, who is recuperating from a peptic ulcer at his home in Riverdale.

One well-informed delegate said that if any changes of consequence were made in the proposal tonight or tomorrow morning, there would not be time to get instructions from governments for a decision tomorrow.

In that case, he said, the proposal would probably be postponed until Money.

Well-informed sources predicted that unless the situation improved tomorrow, Mr. Thant would come to the United Nations late in the afternoon to take personal charge of the efforts to work out an agreement. They said this was the more likely because the Russians asserted tonight that they had no instructions and would receive none in time to permit the Assembly to take action tomorrow.

Speeches scheduled for tomorrow in the Assembly's general debate were canceled to permit immediate consideration of Mr. Quaison-Sackey's proposal.

Also scheduled for adoption tomorrow is a resolution under which the Assembly would authorize the Secretary-General, U Thant, to meet the expenses of the organization until the 1965 budget is adopted next year. Delegates have agreed to a procedure under which no votes are to be taken while the crucial finance issue remains unsettled.

After Mr. Quaison-Sackey's announcement a number of delegates and members of the Secretariat expressed the belief that the Assembly would recess tomorrow afternoon for Christmas and reconvene around Jan. 11. Mr. Quaison-Sackey's proposal provides that the no-voting procedure continue until Jan. 15 or whenever Mr. Thant can report to the Assembly that contributions are satisfactory.

Tewfik Bouattoura of Algeria, chairman of the African-Asian group in United Nations, indicated at a news conference that he believed the United States and the Soviet Union were near agreement on Mr. Quaison-Sackey's proposal.

By nightfall, however, this optimism had turned to uncertainty, and some delegates said that the situation was as critical as on the opening day of the session. At that time, the Assembly avoided a confrontation between the United States and the Soviet Union on unpaid Soviet assessments by adopting the no-vote procedure.

According to reliable sources, the Soviet Union is adhering to its commitment to inform Mr. Thant – and nobody else – of the size of the contribution it intends to make against the $52.4 million Russian arrears for the United Nations Congo and Middle Eastern peace-keeping operations.

Under United Nations financial regulations, the Soviet Union would have to pay about $17 million on these arrears, plus its assessments on the 1964 regular budget, to escape application of Article 19 of the Charter. It is subject to loss of vote in the Assembly under this article.

Published December 23, 1964
Copyright The New York Times

GLUM HOLIDAY AT U.N.

Work Impeded and Vacations Short Because of Impasse Over Arrears

By Tania Long, Special to The New York Times

UNITED NATIONS, N.Y., Dec. 25 – Little Christmas spirit was evident in the closed-in world of the United Nations as the delegates began their brief holiday recess.

For a number of reasons, irritation and frustration the halls and lounges. Many delegates had to scrap elaborate plans to get away from New York with friends or families. The vexations issue arising out of the Soviet Union's arrears in its share of United Nations peace-keeping costs was unresolved, despite last-ditch efforts by the Secretary General, U Thant, and by Alex Quaison-Sackey of Ghana, President of the General Assembly.

To many delegates of small nations, the cost of remaining in New York through the search for a solution became an unexpected burden. It led to angry protests against the protracted wrangle over whether the Soviet Union is to lose its vote, as the United Sates insists, because of the arrears.

There were also delegates who hoped to be reunited with their families in their homelands by now. AS far as anyone could remember, never before had the United Nations worked Christmas Eve, as it did when the Security Council met yesterday. And it was highly unusual for the Assembly to have so short a recess; it reconvenes Monday.

On Dec. 1, when the General Assembly opened, it planned to recess at noon Wednesday, Dec. 23, and to resume in the middle of February or early in March.

But as the holidays approached without an agreement, the foreign diplomats began rearranging their plans from day to day. In the end, the Assembly was recessed for five days and the Security Council for three.

The edginess in the mood of the delegates was reflected in sardonic banter in their lounge on Christmas Eve. At the bar, delegates compared notes on what they might be doing if things had only gone according to plan. As the diplomats tried to top one another's woes, the conversation sounded like a competition among the extravagant literary fictions of Baron Munchausen.

At one of the many round tables, there were gloomy prognostications about the United Nations.

With a wry smile, one senior delegate said he hoped to heaven that "they" would go quickly about building the United Nations School at the north end of United Nations Plaza, to face the United Nations Library at the south end.

"Then," he said, "we'd at least have the library and the school, even if nothing is left in between." Ground for the school is scheduled to be broken next year.

337

Other delegates could be heard muttering about the gifts that they had bought and could not take home in time.

Before returning home in the past, delegates – especially some from Communist countries – went on huge shopping sprees, buying all the latest gadgets unavailable in their own countries and taking home all the latest objects of feminine fads.

This has been a peculiar Assembly session in more ways than one. Because the dispute between the Soviet Union and the United States has prevented balloting so far, the Assembly has been operating without the customary vice presidents.

Since a vote is needed to elect vice presidents – there were 17 during the previous Assembly – the President, who was chosen by acclamation, has no one to help him. If he leaves the podium, he must adjourn the session. So far, Mr. Quaison-Sackey has gamely stuck to his seat throughout the morning and afternoon meetings, which generally last three hours apiece.

Because there is no voting, there have been no meetings of the committees in which much of the work of the United Nations is done; a vote is required to elect committee chairmen.

Published: December 26, 1964
Copyright The New York Times

Quaison-Sackey Arrested

ACCRA, March 2 (Reuters) – Ghana's former Foreign Minister, Alex Quaison-Sackey, declared his support of the country's new leaders when he returned to Ghana today, but he was placed in protective custody.

He said at a news conference that Mr. Nkrumah had asked Soviet and Chinese help to return to power. But Mr. Quaison-Sackey added he did not think the overthrown President would get aid.

He added: "I do not think Nkrumah will let this revolution go by without challenging it. That is something to watch."

The former Foreign Minister said he was going to prison after the news conference.

Published: March 3, 1966
Copyright The New York Times

Quaison-Sackey Waits in Accra Prison

By Lloyd Garrison, Special to The New York Times

ACCRA, GHANA, March 8 – Ghana's old prisons have remained the same over the years, but in the last 12 days the inmates have changed radically.

In the wake of the army's revolution Feb. 24, more than 1,100 political prisoners who were jailed without trial under Kwame Nkrumah has been released.

Now their cells hold roughly 500 of Mr. Nkrumah's apologists – his ministers, members of his Parliament, districtcommissioners and leaders of his Convention People's party, Ghana's only party.

Of the total, 361 are in Ussher Fort prison, the former Dutch slave fortress whose cell windows are too high for prisoners to enjoy the splendid view of Accra Harbor.

The yard is swept immaculately clean. There are flower beds along the narrow walkways. The only sign of Ussher Fort's age is the corrosion on the bars in the cells, developed in more than two centuries of exposure to the Ala's breezes.

None of the prisoners is favored more than another, but one who is likely to be released soon is a man almost as well known outside Ghana as Mr. Nkrumah himself. He is Alex Quaison-Sackey, Ghana's former Foreign Minister, who last year served as President of the United Nations General Assembly.

The 41-year-old Oxford-educated diplomat was with Mr. Nkrumah in Peking at the time of the coup, on a mission to seek a compromise formula to end the war in Vietnam. He voluntarily returned to Ghana knowing that he would be detained along with the rest of Mr. Nkrumah's ministers.

Jokes About the Future

Today he sat in the prison superintendent's outer office and joked about his future.

"I don't know how soon I'll get out," he said. "But I get food brought in. I've seen my wife three times, and I've got enough pencil and paper to write a new book. I think I'll call it *From Peking to Ussher Fort.*"

Mr. Quaison-Sackey has long been associated with Mr. Nkrumah's campaign for an African union government. But until early last year he had been abroad for almost 11 years and was never associated with Mr. Nkrumah personally.

In fact, informed observers here say that the only reason Mr. Nkrumah made him Foreign Minister was to get him out of the world limelight.

In Peking, Mr. Nkrumah received the new of the coup with no emotion; according to Mr. Quaison-Sackey he immediately concluded that the uprising was the work of a few traitorous officers.

"He may still believe it," Mr. Quaison-Sackey said. "He is a deluded man. I can't understand why Sekou Toure made him Co-President of Guinea. I have great respect for Toure – but he never even consulted his people. He's foolish. What he did was unconstitutional."

After the Guinean's designation it was explained that the title was honorary.

The former Foreign Minister said he expected that neither Moscow nor Peking would stick by Mr. Nkrumah even though all their technicians had been expelled from Ghana by the new regime, the National Liberation Council.

340

"The Soviets are duty-bound to recognize us," he said, " and as for China, all they have to do is to abide by Mao's saying: Power flows out of the barrel of a gun. Well, the military is in charge here and its popular backing is visible for everybody to see."

As he spoke, the sound of drumming and singing welled up from the street outside the superintendent's office. It is almost two weeks since the day of the coup but hundreds of people in Accra are still demonstrating in favor of the new regime.

"You know," Mr. Quaison-Sackey said, "I sat for years at the U.N. defending Ghana against attacks that Nkrumah was conducting subversion. And now that he's gone we know of the guerrilla training camps here and we know the accusations from brother African states were true. But now the climate has changed. There is so much we can do now that that man is gone."

He rose to return to his cell. "I'm reading a good book," he said, "it's John Oliver Killens's *Black Man's Burden*. And I've just finished *the life of Ali Khan* by Slater. Now that's very good prison reading, don't you think?"

Published: March 9, 1966
Copyright The New York Times

341

FROM THE US DEPARTMENT OF STATE ARCHIVES – JOHNSON ADMINISTRATION

Foreign Relations, 1964-1968, Volume XXXIII, Organization and Management of Foreign Policy; United Nations

Released by the Office of the Historian Documents 317-341.

Memorandum From Samuel Belk of the National Security Council Staff to the President's Special Assistant for National Security Affairs (Bundy)/1/

Washington, December 1, 1964.

/1/Source: Johnson Library, National Security File, Country File, United Nations, Memos, Vol. 1. Confidential.

SUBJECT

THE 19TH GENERAL ASSEMBLY OPENS

The SYG's language as he opened the GA is interesting:

"In view of the differences of opinion which have arisen among Member States regarding the conduct of the Nineteenth Session I have been in consultation with several delegations for the past week with the sole purpose of avoiding a confrontation. In this connection I may mention that *there is an understanding to the effect that issues other than those that can be disposed of without objection will not be raised while the General Debate proceeds.* [Italics mine]/2/ I hope all delegations will agree with this procedure. As far as today›s meeting is concerned there is general agreement that on the above basis we may proceed with the following items of business:

/2/Brackets in the source text.

1. Appointment of the Credentials Committee.

2. Election of the President.

3. Admission of new members.

I would recommend that the Assembly may proceed accordingly." Following this, a highly nervous Sosa Rodriques managed to get the Credentials Committee appointed by the Assembly "without objection" (interpretation: "I don't care"). Next, Alex Quaison-Sackey of Ghana became President of the 19th GA "without objection" because (1) the other two candidates withdrew and left him as the only candidate, and (2) Quaison-Sackey reportedly had $150,000.00 to spend on behalf of his candidacy from the coffers of Accra. This is not a happy choice for us, but what can you do when it was already agreed that an African would be the GA President for this session, and the other two African candidates withdrew.

Quaison-Sackey, as a first order of business made a sharp, anti-colonial speech that might have been drafted by Nkrumah himself.

He then proceeded to get three new members admitted (Zambia, Malawi and Malta) "without objection". Quaison-Sackey then adjourned the Assembly until 10:30 tomorrow. At that time representatives of the new member states will speak and most likely a number of other welcoming speeches will follow. That should occupy the day.

Next, the Assembly will go into the general debate which could easily occupy the time between now and Christmas recess. So much for the non-voting General Assembly for the time being.

The important work now at hand is what the Secretary can accomplish with the Russians beginning with another lunch with Gromyko tomorrow. There are four items — requiring no vote — on which there could be forward movement and, as of now, it is the Secretary's plan to propose them to Gromyko:

1. The establishment of a voluntary fund into which the Russians can make a contribution and take care of their debt to the Organization. The Russians have agreed to this in principle, but the terms of reference have not yet been worked out.

2. The creation of a Committee to take a new look at long — range — financing or, alternatively, refer the matter to the already existing Committee of 21 (Finances).

3. An agreement with regard to the membership of councils- the membership of the Security Council and ECOSOC will change at the end of the year and this should not be delayed.

4. A means whereby the SYG can continue to expend funds at the current rate until a new budget can be agreed upon.

This is where we now stand. The key to where we emerge is in the Secretary's pocket.

A mildly humorous sidelight on the afternoon's procedures was the dropping of the language "by acclamation" for "without objection" because it was argued that the former could be interpreted as a unanimous affirmative vote. Therefore, the business accomplished was "without objection", but with applause. One purist in Harlan's office yelled: "Oh no! They can't applaud! They're voting!" End of report.

SEB

318. Telegram From the Mission to the United Nations to the Department of State/1/

New York, December 1, 1964, 8 p.m.

/1/Source: National Archives and Records Administration, RG 59, Central Files 1964-66, UN 10-4. Confidential. Drafted by Richard Pedersen on December 1.

1937. Re: Article 19.

1. Early this morning Stevenson called SYG to suggest that SYG have meeting today in his office including US, USSR, UK, France, Sosa (Venezuela) and Quaison-Sackey (Ghana) to try to reach final agreement before GA opened. SYG agreed and called meeting at noon, SYG adding chairmen LA and Afro-Asian Groups.

2. Prior to meeting we drafted statements for possible use by SYG and Pres in which SYG would refer to consultations he had undertaken on crisis and their continuation and Sosa would then suggest GA start its work "on such basis that no voting would be involved."

3. When meeting convened SYG noted he had been consulting members with "sole motive" of avoiding confrontation and asked for this meeting to discuss conduct of opening session. Stated that USSR yesterday had proposed fol procedures to avoid confrontation and facilitate negots outside chamber: GA would meet as scheduled, Pres would be elected and new members admitted by acclamation or without opposition; General Debate would subsequently proceed as scheduled; USSR would then discuss future business with colleagues, including Vice-Preses, chairmen of Comites, elections to Councils, and budget.

4. Stevenson then said that as presented by SYG Sov position was not satisfactory. There must be no voting until such time as agreement was worked out. Otherwise Art 19 could arise at any minute. If there were agreement on no voting and SYG

346

said so something along suggested lines might be all right. But it would have to be explicitly clear there would be no other business and no votes taken.

5. Caradon (UK) said purpose of meeting was to avoid confrontation and we must not fail. As he understood position shared objective of those in room was that we go through period of no vote so we could find solution. Issue was how this was to be stated. Public impression was very important and we must act openly and not risk dangers of misunderstanding.

6. SYG then said he thought positions were very close. It was now question of formulations and procedures. With spirit of give and take he thought we could reach agreement.

7. Stevenson then read draft statements he thought SYG and Pres might make, which would refer to continuation of consultations and to GA proceeding on such basis that no voting would be involved.

8. SYG said that in principle he was prepared to make such statement if it acceptable to all. He had had impression Gromyko would prefer that Pres make any statement.

9. Sosa noted proposal on no voting meant waiving of rules. Believed this should be raised by SYG, not by outgoing Pres. He would then put issue to Assembly to obtain Assembly's concurrence.

10. Fedorenko (USSR) said SYG had expressed main Sov points in clear terms. He wished to stress that USSR's only idea was and is to have clear understanding among ourselves. It would then be satisfactory to open session as described by SYG and elect Pres by acclamation; then to admit new members in same way. If some states wished to make statements there would be no objection but there would be no controversial aspects for today's work of GA. GA would then proceed with General Debate. No other steps would be taken until consultations were completed. He noted Gromyko and Rusk intended to

have further talks. Beyond this there was no necessity to take up other aspects now, especially those of interest to one side. When meeting was ended we should tell other members of GA what we have agreed. No special statement by SYG was needed. This would be one-sided. We should simply go ahead with this understanding as there was no real problem now involved. Statement would be a "precondition" to further work of session, and this would not be right.

11. Seydoux (France) said it would be difficult to postpone opening of GA further. GA would lose prestige and it would be shock to public opinion. He thought confrontation should be avoided. But election of new Pres and admission of new members could be accomplished today. Position of future would be reserved. Perhaps a suspension of GA should follow this afternoon's session for several days during which consultations would continue.

12. Sosa said if no agreement reached on procedure it might be wise to adjourn as Seydoux had suggested. GA could be adjourned either after election of Pres and admission new members or before these two items.

13. Stevenson said he understood Fedorenko as suggesting we go ahead with General Debate, while Seydoux suggested recess. Noted GA rules required election of new Pres to be without nomination and by secret ballot. Election without objection would therefore require waiving of rules. If there was agreement, we could proceed on all these items without voting we could agree, but there needed to be explicit understanding on basis of which we could proceed. He failed to understand Fedorenko's view that statement on non-voting would complicate matters. We needed to have precise understanding on procedure under which controversial business would be avoided and we would proceed without objection. On Seydoux's suggestion of recess US had no firm views.

14. Quaison-Sackey (Ghana) said he wished make appeal. There was nothing fundamentally different between views of US and USSR. One wanted statement; one did not. He stated everyone knew about discussions which had taken place and about today's meeting. He therefore thought some kind of statement was called for so that GA would know we were not following normal procedure. Statement of SYG might avoid word voting but get same meaning with other suitable language. He did not favor further suspension of GA procedures.

15. Vidaurre (Dominican Republic) stated LA group would have no objection to SYG's proposal and appealed to all to agree to it.

16. Bouattoura (Algeria) agreed with Quaison-Sackey that we were close to agreement. Question was how to express this to membership. Quaison-Sackey's proposal was a good way and he was sure SYG could do this. Problem was how to proceed with GA work without disturbing consultations going on outside. We should go ahead into General Debate with understanding no voting should take place. Consultations would continue with parties concerned, following which GA could follow its normal procedure. But GA should be convened. Two postponements had already been a blow and further postponement would be another.

17. Fedorenko then asked questions about Credentials Comite, to which we had referred in our statement. Stated he understood this was appointed by Pres. Sosa said Credentials Comite in fact had to be confirmed by GA but that there had never been vote on confirmation.

18. SYG said that it might be useful for him to make short statement as suggested by Quaison-Sackey, avoiding contentious phraseology, to explain why new procedure adopted.

19. Fedorenko stated he wished members to understand that anything beyond what SYG had suggested at start of meeting must be studied by his Del. He must see text of any statement that SYG would make and decision on it would be "in competence of Chief of our Del."

20. SYG then produced one-sentence statement to effect that there was "an understanding" that controversial issues would be avoided while consultations were taking place. Plimpton suggested this might be modified to add something like "issues other than those which can be unanimously agreed upon."

21. Fedorenko stressed again that USSR had to study anything new. SYG said he could have draft available by 2:30 PM. Fedorenko said the sooner the better. SYG then said he would have revised sentence available in five minutes. Short discussion on scenario of opening moments of GA followed, after which Narasimhan (UN) distributed revised text as fols: "There is an understanding to the effect that issues other than those that can be disposed of without objection will not be raised while the General Debate proceeds." SYG suggested meeting reconvene at 2:45 for 15 minutes. In meantime he would draft rest of statement.

22. Stevenson asked whether SYG's sentence was intended to be applied to procedural questions as well as to substantive items on agenda. Noted procedural question might arise at any time without notice and precipitate issue in spite of intention of agreement. He assumed Chair could handle such issues without vote. SYG said his statement was definitely applicable to procedural problems as well and Quaison-Sackey indicated he would handle them in accordance with the statement. Fedorenko added that if anyone who did not understand situation should try to raise such problem he was sure Chair could handle it.

23. Meeting reconvened at 2:45 at which time SYG distributed full statement contained USUN 1938./2/ Only change in key

sentence, as Dept will note, is substitution of «while General Debate going on» for «while consultations take place».

Fedorenko had draft copy of SYG›s full draft statement when he walked into room with several ink changes on it. When meeting started SYG said last minute corrections had been made and statement would be distributed shortly. Thus it appeared Fedorenko had already seen and agreed to full statement. *Comment:* It was interesting that Shukodrov (Gromyko›s interpreter) joined Fedorenko, Morozov and Fedoseev in afternoon meeting, while only latter three were present in morning.

/2/Not printed. (Department of State, U.S. Mission to the United Nations, Subject Files, Reel 142, Frame 9)

24. In response SYG's request for views Fedorenko promptly said Sov position was that it would be best if there were no statement. If there had to be one USSR had "no objection to this text."

25. Stevenson said he understood opening day procedure under statement would be on these lines: After SYG's statement Sosa would say, "I assume there is no objection and we can proceed on these lines; there being no objection it is so decided." Appointment Credentials Comite, election of Pres, and admission of new members would then be accomplished on no objection basis. On this understanding he agreed to draft statement. SYG and Sosa both said this was correct understanding of procedure. SYG then distributed short statement for Sosa under which he would say if there were no objections it was so decided. Fedorenko said that if others agreed to this statement USSR had no objections.

26. Seydoux said that if understanding involved budget and elections to Councils he would have reservations, but if statement was agreed around table he would be reluctant to oppose it for today's procedures. SYG said he took it from Seydoux's comments that he had reservations but was not objecting. Meeting then adjourned.

27. US participants in meetings were Stevenson, Plimpton, Yost and Pedersen.

Stevenson

319. Memorandum of Conversation/1/

SecDel/MC/7

New York, December 2, 1964, 1 p.m.

/1/Source: Johnson Library, National Security File, Country File, United Nations, Memoranda of Conversation, Vol. 1. Confidential. Drafted by Akalovsky on December 7. The memorandum is Part V of V. The meeting was held at the Soviet Mission.

SECRETARY'S DELEGATION TO THE NINETEENTH SESSION OF THE UNITED NATIONS GENERAL ASSEMBLY

New York, December 1964

SUBJECT
Article 19

PARTICIPANTS
U.S.

The Secretary Ambassador Stevenson Mr. Cleveland Ambassador Yost Ambassador Kohler Mr. Tyler
Mr. Akalovsky
U.S.S.R.
Foreign Minister Gromyko
Deputy Foreign Minister Semenov Ambassador Dobrynin Ambassador Fedorenko
Mr. Smirnovskiy Mr. Sukhodrev
The Secretary wondered whether Mr. Gromyko had any views on how we should proceed with respect to the UN problem. He

believed, and he thought Mr. Gromyko was of a similar opinion, that the Secretary should take considerable part in discussions of problems related to peacekeeping operations, both past and future. We were interested in both those aspects and we would like to know what Mr. Gromyko's views were on them.

Mr. Gromyko thought that there was agreement to continue consultations and inquired whether Ambassador Stevenson had any comments to make.

The Secretary commented that, as a general observation, he believed we would need quite detailed consultations in New York and that the Secretary General should be involved in them. As to the aspects of the problem relating to the future, we were interested in the Charter's provision for "primary responsibility" of the Security Council for the maintenance of peace and international security. However, the Charter did not state that the Security Council had exclusive responsibility and we believed that the General Assembly had important powers in this respect. Those powers were perhaps residual inasmuch as they resulted from a situation where the Security Council may be unable to act. In any event, we believed that the Security Council was important and the United States and the Soviet Union, as members of the Security Council, were interested in its having primary responsibility for the maintenance of peace and international security.

The Secretary then noted that the membership of the United Nations had considerably changed over the past years. For example, there were some members today who contributed as little as .04% of the total UN budget. Indeed, one could construct a hypothetical two-thirds majority in the General Assembly whose total contribution to the UN budget would amount to something like 5%. For these reasons, we believed that those who carried a larger financial burden should have a greater voice in financial decisions. Thus, there were two points of interest to us: (a) the Security Council's primary, but not exclusive, responsibility for the maintenance of peace and international security, and (b) that those who carry a heavier financial burden should have a greater voice in financial decisions.

Mr. Gromyko asserted that the question was not as the Secretary had formulated it. The question was not of the Security Council's having primary and the General Assembly a non-primary responsibility. This was a quantitative rather than a qualitative approach, i.e. it was placing the question on the basis of the degree of responsibility. In fact, the point was that under the Charter the Security Council had authority to pass binding decisions whereas the General Assembly had no such authority. The General Assembly could take only consultative decisions, in other words, make recommendations. Thus, the question should not be turned upside down. There was no point in breaking into an open door. The Soviet Union knew, and had so stated, that the General Assembly could discuss matters relating to the maintenance of peace and international security. No one had any objection to that. But the General Assembly could not take binding decisions whereas the Security Council could both discuss problems relating to the maintenance of peace and international security and take binding decisions on them. The Soviet Union had itself participated in the drafting of the relevant provisions of the Charter. Mr. Gromyko suggested that actions and decisions be based on the Charter and that everything be kept in perspective in the process of analyzing the situation.

Ambassador Stevenson recalled that, as Ambassador Fedorenko would probably remember, way back in March it had been agreed to discuss all questions arising from the past and also those related to new arrangements for the future. The question now was how, where, and with whom we should discuss peace-keeping operations and finances. As far as we were concerned, we were prepared to start from either end, from the past or from the future. As to the past, he understood that the Soviet Union was willing to make a voluntary contribution to some rescue fund. He wondered whether we should discuss that first or whether future arrangements should be taken up as a first order of business. He reiterated that the U.S. was willing to proceed either way. He noted that the duration of Mr. Gromyko's stay in

New York might be a factor in this respect. Regarding substance, Ambassador Stevenson said it was hard for him to say anything now and he thought that perhaps it would be better to settle procedure first.

Mr. Gromyko said there were two ways of proceeding: a) to discuss the past, which would be simpler, or b) to discuss the past, the present, and the future, i.e., all questions relating to peace-keeping, including finances. Obviously, the latter was a much more complex problem and apparently the range of differences in the positions on it was much greater. The Soviet Union was prepared to proceed either way, but the two of us and others as well should keep in mind that one method is simpler and the other more complex.

Regarding the question of contribution, the U.S. side had already been informed that the Soviet Union would be willing to discuss this matter either in a committee set up for the purpose of discussing all questions relating to peace-keeping, or on the basis of the Afghan proposal. The latter covered only the past and consequently it involved a narrower range of problems. The Soviet Union accepted the language of the Afghan proposal as a whole. That proposal stated that all UN members would voluntarily contribute to a fund, and obviously the Soviet Union was not excluded. As to the amount, the Soviet Union understood the term "voluntary contribution" to mean only one thing, namely, that the Soviet Union itself would determine the amount of its contribution, without anybody else's diktat or even advice, to which the Soviet Union would never agree. If the Afghan proposal was accepted by common agreement, the Soviet Union would take part in such an arrangement. However, in such an event, it would be the Soviet Union's understanding that the entire question of the Soviet contribution would be disposed of and no one would have any more claims in the future. He also noted that the question of the form of a contribution would have to be settled.

Governor Stevenson wondered whether we should discuss bilaterally the question of a voluntary contribution or the broader complex of questions, or whether those questions should be taken up with the Secretary General and other powers. In addition, of course, there was the Committee of 21 where these matters could be discussed. This was a procedural question, but he thought its solution would accelerate our work.

Mr. Gromyko said he did not exclude bilateral discussions like the current one. Neither did he exclude discussions with the Secretary General; indeed, such discussions were desirable. Discussions could also be held in the various groups which had been formed recently, and all these discussions could proceed in parallel. Perhaps some special committee could be formed. Thus there was a whole series of fora, but he wished to point out that in those groups already in existence no socialist states were represented. Those groups included mostly representatives of the various blocs. Therefore, perhaps it would be better if a special, more representative committee were created. However, the Secretary General would be consulted in any event, and of course nothing ruled out U.S.-Soviet bilateral consultations. It went without saying that, whatever the forum, decisions would not be taken by a vote, but only on the basis of agreement.

The Secretary commented that the question of a fund was not a very suitable subject for bilateral discussions. The Soviet Union had never asked the U.S. for money, and the U.S. had never asked for money from the Soviet Union. On the other hand, the Secretary General asked both the U.S. and the U.S.S.R. for money. Therefore, perhaps the Secretary General should take a more active role in this matter. He would surely want to consult the major powers — the U.S., the U.S.S.R., the U.K., and France — both as regards the fund and the problems of the future as related to the Charter. The Secretary said he wished to point out that the reason he had not mentioned China in this connection should in no way be interpreted as an indication of a change in the U.S. position.

Governor Stevenson also said the Secretary General should be in charge of the rescue operation. However, he believed that the U.S. and U.S.S.R. should inform the SYG of their bilateral discussions and of their intention to discuss the problems relating to the future.

Mr. Gromyko then raised the General Assembly's order of business. He said the Soviet Union was firmly opposed to any indefinite postponement of the major political issues before the Assembly. He wanted to make clear that consultations should move promptly. Perhaps it would be simpler to take up the past first, because discussion of the broader range of questions might take more time and might go even into the next GA. As far as the Soviet Union was concerned, it hoped this would not be the case, and it wished agreement on all these questions as soon as possible. In any event, the broader complex of problems could be discussed in parallel with the discussion of the past.

Ambassador Stevenson noted there was an understanding not to have any voting until the general debate ended. If the fund question was resolved, the General Assembly would proceed with its normal business. The procedure suggested by the Secretary would take care of that. Governor Stevenson then summed up the suggested procedure, saying that the Secretary General would chair the discussions on the voluntary fund, for which there had been several proposals, including one by the four and another by the Afro-Asians — the so-called Pazhwak proposal./2/ Thus, the Secretary General could convene a meeting with the U.S., the U.S.S.R., and with any other party as he deemed necessary. Meanwhile, whenever useful, bilateral discussions could take place regarding the future. Those discussions would cover such questions as the primacy of the Security Council, limitation on the General Assembly, etc.

/2/A non-aligned nations draft proposal being circulated by the representative from Afghanistan.

Mr. Gromyko said we should not impede the work of the non-aligned delegations, because they wanted to help. Therefore, we should ask the Secretary General to consult with any delegations he wanted to invite, and he probably would not exclude the U.S. and the U.S.S.R. Then, in a couple of days, the U.S. and U.S.S.R. could meet to review the situation.

Ambassador Fedorenko wondered whether there was any point in going far into the history of the various proposals. He thought it more useful to concentrate on what was before us today: (a) the Soviet suggestion for a committee to discuss all peace-keeping questions, and (b) the Pazhwak proposal. He said the Soviet Union had nothing to do with the Pazhwak proposal. It has been developed by twelve Afro-Asian delegations and advanced by Ambassador Pazhwak. The Soviet Union accepted the proposal in an effort to meet the U.S. halfway. It regarded the proposal as a mutually acceptable compromise solution of the UN's financial difficulties. The proposal certainly did not reflect the Soviet position as it had been stated both in New York and Washington. Ambassador Fedorenko did not see any point in taking up those proposals which were already dead and which had never deserved serious consideration, let alone implementation. He would, therefore, wish to see the U.S. concentrate on the Pazhwak proposal, which he believed was feasible and which had been made in an effort to help out of the situation. He thought the U.S. and U.S.S.R. should be able to get together on its basis.

Ambassador Stevenson thought it was now agreed that the Secretary General should be informed that the two sides had had bilateral discussions and that they believed, subject to his approval, that he should take up with whoever he wanted the question of a fund.

Mr. Gromyko suggested that the two sides review the situation in a couple of days. Meanwhile, the Secretary General would consult with the various delegations, but not necessarily with all of them at the same time. We should not prescribe any procedure for the Secretary General.

Ambassador Stevenson agreed and then asked whether Mr. Gromyko could help him understand the proposal which the Soviet Union said it was willing to accept. Mr. Gromyko had said that the Soviet Union was prepared to agree to the creation of a fund. It would be very helpful if he could describe his conception of such a fund, the form of the contribution, and the purpose for which the money would be used.

Mr. Gromyko said the UN would be saved by contributions from all, not just the Soviet Union. The Soviet Union would not contribute for the operations in the Congo or in the Middle East, but rather to the UN as a whole. As to the size of the contribution, he reiterated that it would be strictly up to the Soviet Union to determine. The Soviet Union would contribute as much as it believed to be necessary. This was a matter of policy rather than money.

Ambassador Stevenson commented that since the contributions would be voluntary, somebody might not wish to contribute.

Ambassador Fedorenko quoted from the text of the Pazhwak proposal that contributions would be made by the entire UN membership. Ambassador Stevenson remarked that the more members contributed, the better.

The conversation ended at about 4:30 p.m.

320. Memorandum of Conversation/1/

Washington, December 17, 1964.

/1/Source: **Johnson Library, Administrative Histories, Department of State During the Presidency of Lyndon B. Johnson, Vol. 2, Part 5. Confidential. Drafted by Hartley (IO/ UNP).**

SUBJECT
Charter Amendment

PARTICIPANTS

Mr. Michael N.F. Stewart,
Minister,
British Embassy
Mr. John K.E. Broadley, Second Secretary, British Embassy
Mr. Joseph J. Sisco, Deputy Assistant Secretary
Mrs. V.F. Hartley

The Minister called at his request to discuss ratification of the pending Charter amendments. He referred to an earlier conversation last May when we had indicated that we had no intention of proceeding with ratification at this time since this was likely to trigger an across-the-board review of the UN and all its works. The UK had accepted this position. However, the UK now saw no advantage in further delay and its UN delegation saw certain positive advantages in an early announcement of the UK's intention to ratify, particularly before the USSR had acted. The inclusion of such an announcement in the British general debate speech at the General Assembly was therefore being considered. However, the British wished to know the US view before making a final decision. The Minister noted that if the general debate speech is in January, it will probably be made by the Prime Minister and will be a major foreign policy statement. He also recalled that the new Government has repeatedly indicated that it considers the UN of primary importance.

Mr. Sisco pointed out that the situation is still unclear with respect to the Article 19 problem and that while the Rescue Fund idea would probably be pushed ahead, details with respect to it were likely to remain unclear for some time. If the Article 19 problem has been resolved when the British make their general debate speech, then an announcement of their intention to ratify would create no problems. If the situation is still uncertain, however, such an announcement would create certain difficulties for us. We simply cannot proceed toward ratification so long as the Article 19 problem is with us and British ratification is almost certain to increase pressure on us to act. Moreover, it is likely to create the impression that there is a split between the US and the UK over Article 19.

321. Memorandum of Conversation/1/

SecDel/MC/45

New York, December 19, 1964, 1 p.m.

/1/Source: National Archives and Records Administration, RG 59, Conference Files, CF 2449. Confidential. Drafted by Akalovsky on December 21 and approved in S on December

30. The memorandum is Part V of VI. The meeting was held at a luncheon in the Secretary's Suite at the Waldorf Towers.

SECRETARY'S DELEGATION TO THE NINETEENTH SESSION OF THE UNITED NATIONS GENERAL ASSEMBLY

New York, December 1964

SUBJECT

Article 19

PARTICIPANTS

U.S.
The Secretary
Ambassador Stevenson
Ambassador Thompson
Mr. Akalovsky
U.S.S.R.
Foreign Minister Gromyko
Deputy Foreign Minister Semenov
Ambassador Dobrynin
Ambassador Fedorenko
Mr. Sukhodrev

Mr. Gromyko wondered how long the GA recess for the holidays should be. He asked whether it should be three or four days.

Governor Stevenson commented that if the financial situation were resolved, it had been suggested that the recess be from

December 23 to January 11. As far as we were concerned, we had no particular views on this point.

Mr. Gromyko wondered why the recess could not end earlier.

Governor Stevenson said there was no particular reason except that a longer recess would give more time to the Secretary General to do his work. There would be no difficulty from us on the recess if the financial problem were resolved. However, it would be quite difficult to resume before January.

Mr. Gromyko said the Soviet Union did not like the draft resolution prepared by Quaison-Sackey and publicized in the press./2/ He did not know whose initiative this was, but the Soviet Union did not like it.

/2/The General Assembly president had been circulating various informal proposals for settlement of the Article 19 controversy.

The Secretary observed that the Soviet Union had suggested certain amendments to that resolution, some of which we accepted.

Mr. Gromyko asserted that no formal amendments but rather only a few suggestions had been put forward by the Soviet Delegation.

Governor Stevenson said we had told Quaison-Sackey that some of the Soviet suggestions were acceptable; for our part, we had also given him some suggestions. Thus Quaison-Sackey now had both Soviet and U.S. views. He wondered whether the Soviet Delegation had been in touch with Quaison-Sackey today.

Mr. Gromyko replied in the negative. He said that in any event the Soviet Delegation did not like Quaison-Sackey's draft and was not optimistic about it.

Governor Stevenson inquired what the problem was.

Mr. Gromyko replied that Quaison-Sackey's draft was different from the non-aligned draft,/3/ which the Soviet Union accepted. If we were to work on the basis of Quaison-Sackey›s draft, the Soviet Delegation would have to keep amending it until it was brought back to the non-aligned draft. He did not see any point in following such a procedure. The Quaison-Sackey draft as a whole was not acceptable to the Soviet Union, whereas the non-aligned draft, which provided for voluntary contributions, was acceptable.

/3/Reference is to one of a series of drafts being circulated by a group of states led by Afghanistan. The Mission to the United Nations had forwarded the latest version in telegram 1722 from New York, November 18. (Department of State, Mission to the United Nations, Subject Files, Reel 141, Frames 161-163)

Governor Stevenson commented the Soviet Union apparently did not like the idea of a fund. We did not particularly care about this point; nor did we care about the provision regarding the future. The main point now was to avoid a confrontation.

Mr. Gromyko stated the easiest way to proceed was to accept the Pazhwak draft.

Governor Stevenson said the Pazhwak draft would make us buy a pig in a poke. He wondered whether Mr. Gromyko could explain his understanding of it.

Mr. Gromyko said that when the General Assembly started working normally, all parties would make their contributions. However, the Soviet Union could not make any commitment because this would be contrary to the concept of voluntary contributions. The Soviet Union believed it had made a step of good will by accepting the idea of voluntary contributions, and he hoped that step would be appreciated. He reiterated that Quaison-Sackey's draft was not acceptable, even though some of its provisions seemed to be all right. For example, the Soviet Union would not object to having a report by the Secretary

General, even though it was not quite clear why such a provision was necessary since the Secretary General was free to report at any time.

The Secretary suggested that the Soviet Delegation discuss the matter with Quaison-Sackey, who might have some further ideas.

Ambassador Fedorenko noted the U.S. had suggested a different wording for the reference to Article 19. He wondered what the point was.

Governor Stevenson said there was a difference between saying that Article 19 would not be raised and a wording merely referring to our desire to avoid confrontation. We did not see how one could state that a provision of the Charter should be ignored.

The Secretary pointed out it would be risky business if the Assembly were to be allowed to amend the Charter by a resolution of this kind.

Mr. Gromyko said he did not attach particular importance to phraseology, but he did wish to repeat that Quaison-Sackey's draft was unacceptable.

Governor Stevenson asked again what the Soviet Union's difficulty was with the draft which we believed met the points made by the Soviet side.

Mr. Gromyko said that as far as the Pazhwak draft was concerned, he did not wish to create constitutional difficulties and now saw the point raised by the U.S. regarding reference to Article 19. He said he would consider the U.S. suggested wording on this point. As to a report by the Secretary General, he reiterated he did not see why such a report was needed but was not strongly opposed to it. He thought perhaps provision for such a report might be included in the Pazhwak draft. He suggested that the Pazhwak draft be adopted as the basis for proceeding further and repeated that the Quaison-Sackey draft was not acceptable.

The Secretary said his impression was that Quaison-Sackey's draft included a great deal of what was in the Pazhwak draft. Perhaps with amendments both sides had suggested the Quaison-Sackey draft would not create difficulties.

Mr. Gromyko reiterated the Quaison-Sackey draft was not acceptable. However, he did now understand the U.S. point regarding reference to Article 19. We should take the Pazhwak draft and perhaps change the language of the reference to Article 19 if the U.S. attached importance to that point. Moreover, if the U.S. believed it was important to have a report from the Secretary General, that could be considered too. The U.S. should think this over. As far as the Soviet Union was concerned, it had understood long ago the difficulties the U.S. had and this was why it had made this step of good will.

The Secretary pointed out we had also made a step to meet the Soviet Union in moving from compulsory to voluntary contributions.

Mr. Gromyko argued that the Soviet step was greater because the Soviet Union now agreed to make a voluntary contribution.

The discussion then turned to Europe (see separate memorandum of conversation)./4/

/4/A copy of this memorandum of conversation is in the National Archives and Records Administration, RG 59, Conference Files, CF 2449.

322. Telegram From the Department of State to the Mission to the United Nations/1/

Washington, December 24, 1964, 7 p.m.

/1/Source: National Archives and Records Administration, RG 59, Central Files 1964-66, UN 10-4. Confidential.

1632. Subject: Article 19.

On basis of most recent developments, situation can now be summed up as follows:

Over past two weeks UN has been engaged in exercise to find formula under which Soviets could make early payment without loss of face and without sacrifice their publicly announced position of principle.

This effort has now broken down because Soviets apparently insist that whole Article 19 question be dismissed from consideration, and that Assembly decide to take up business as usual, before sufficient payments are made by delinquents to avoid application of Article 19. US and others, on other hand, have been unable to agree that Article 19 has no application, until sufficient payments have been made to bring about this result under terms of article itself.

In light of foregoing, Department believes we should defer any further US initiatives on planting shrubbery to serve as face-saving rationale for action by USSR and other delinquents. We should now concentrate on adopting US position most likely to produce necessary payments to avoid application of Article

19. In next few days mission should reiterate our fundamental view in corridor discussions: We wish GA to get on with normal business as soon as possible, but this can only be done — without Article 19 confrontation — if sufficient amounts forthcoming from delinquents to remove loss-of-vote issue. Perhaps Soviets could now be persuaded to concentrate on private commitments which might be given either to SYG or GA President.

We have no need at all for statement by GA President re contributions, so any further initiative on this score should come from USSR or others. But in all discussions we must make clear no statement will be acceptable to us which tends load scales in favor of conducting GA business by voting prior to satisfactory resolution of Article 19 problem. While we do not insist on statement by GA President affirming our position and indeed question need for any statement, we can not accept one which prejudices it. Accordingly, most realistic course would seem to have statement which is totally neutral on the point, if in fact Soviets wish any such statement at all.

Suggest you inform Quaison-Sackey we do not consider any statement necessary but if he believes otherwise, suggest you tell him that statement next Tuesday/2/ should be brief and comprise two simple elements: (1) an appeal for voluntary contributions, and (2) announcement of Assembly recess until January 11 (or 18). Following is what we have in mind for content of such statement.

/2/December 29.

"Since the opening of the 19th Session of the General Assembly on December 1, members of the Assembly have engaged in useful discussion of ways to meet the present financial difficulties of the United Nations.

As the Assembly now recesses the 1964 part of its 19th Session, I am addressing an appeal, as President of the General Assembly, to all member states to make voluntary contributions to the United Nations in a cooperative effort aimed at bringing the financial situation of the organization to solvency, with the clear understanding that such contributions would not be construed as changing the basic position of principle of any individual member.

Having made this appeal, which I commend to the most earnest consideration of all member states, I declare the 19th session of the General Assembly recessed until January 11 (or 18)."

As part of closing statement, we assume Quaison-Sackey would read to GA appropriate language of authorization of continuing expenditures by SYG.

While it is possible that another delegation (such as Sweden) might usefully discuss above course of action with Quaison-Sackey, we inclined to think it desirable for mission to take this matter up with him direct. In any event, it is most important to discuss on basis of precise text for presidential statement, our suggestion for this is given above.

Rusk

323. Memorandum From Samuel Belk of the National Security Council Staff to the President's Special Assistant for National Security Affairs (Bundy)/1/

Washington, December 28, 1964.

/1/Source: Johnson Library, National Security File, Country File, United Nations, Memos, Vol. 1. Confidential.

SUBJECT

Developments at the UN

Stevenson returned from Libertyville this afternoon (I think at the Secretary's insistence) in order to attend a meeting with Quaison-Sackey at 3:45. Quaison-Sackey had met with Fedorenko earlier.

At the 3:45 meeting, it appeared that the Russians had become more reasonable on several counts:

1. They now are willing to have Quaison-Sackey take informal soundings from the members in order to ascertain whether Mali or Jordan have a majority for a contested Security Council seat. Earlier it had seemed the Russians might be willing to risk a vote. (There is a widespread feeling among the members that new Council members should take their seats before the end of the year on a "no objection" procedure. Actually, the Charter does not require this.)

2. The Russians are willing for the SYG to make a simple appeal to the GA for funds, but they are attempting, at the same time, to get the SYG to say that, when the GA reconvenes, business will proceed normally. This we cannot buy and we have said so--firmly. We would have to know that the Russians had paid--not merely pledged--enough to accept such language in the SYG's appeal.

3. The Russians also have agreed to allow the SYG to continue spending at the present level, on a "no objection" procedure, until the new budg-et can be voted on. They have said, however, that they will wish to record a reservation following the "no objection" procedure. This reservation presumably would have to do with expenditures for UNEF.

Quaison-Sackey now plans to convene the GA on Wednesday/2/ afternoon for the above activities and then adjourn until January 11. This, of course, could easily change.

/2/December 30.

If you fly down with the Secretary, and should this subject arise, you might express strong suspicions about accepting pledges instead of cash from the Russians. I mention this because no one has been able to find out just where the Secretary stands and we are afraid he might be a bit soft on this one point.

In direct answer to your question about a head-count on the Article 19 matter, should it come to a vote within the next day or two, both the Department and New York believe we are still safe in getting an easy simple majority, but are increasingly less sure that we could get an easy 2/3 vote to support enforcement of Article 19. It is unclear just how much erosion there has been among the African states because of the Congo affair. The Department has asked New York today for a hard count and we should have their reply tomorrow.

SEB

324. Memorandum of Conversation/1/

Washington, December 28, 1964, 3:40 p.m.

/1/Source: Johnson Library, National Security File, Country File, United Nations, Memoranda of Conversation, Vol. 1. Confidential. Drafted by Judd. The memorandum is Part I of II. The meeting was held in the Secretary's office.

SUBJECT
Article 19

PARTICIPANTS
U.S.
The Secretary
Thomas M. Judd, EUR/BNA
UK
The Lord Harlech, British Ambassador Michael Stewart, British Minister

Lord Harlech said he had had a call from London. The British Government would like to know before tomorrow's discussion what the current attitude of the U.S. was on the Article 19 question. It seemed to HMG that if the Soviets maintained their present position of saying they would pay but not how much or when, this would be unsatisfactory from the British point of view. The problem would be holding the waverers in line.

The Secretary said that we had made major concessions to the Soviets. There had been some slight movement on their part as well. The major problem was how to get more time, perhaps two or three weeks, to try to get things settled. A plan was currently being discussed for an adjournment, perhaps combined with an appeal for voluntary contributions. The trouble was that a resolution was needed to provide funds for continuing operations, including UNEF. The Soviets might not let a "no-opposition" resolution go through. If not, we would have a nasty row on our hands.

Lord Harlech said he had the impression that the Soviets have been losing ground with the neutrals. Secretary Rusk replied that it did look that way but we would still prefer that Article 19 not come to a vote. However, we were not sure that the Nineteenth General Assembly could continue if the problem were not settled.

Lord Harlech asked if he was correct in assuming that the U.S. position was that ordinary business within the Assembly should not go on unless the Soviets made a payment of $17 million or more. The Secretary affirmed that this was our position. Lord Harlech then asked if the UN authorities were aware of how much the U.S. thought the Soviets should pay. The Secretary answered that neither Quaison-Sackey nor U Thant had mentioned to us any figure less than $17 million.

325. Memorandum From Samuel Belk of the National Security Council Staff to the President's Special Assistant for National Security Affairs (Bundy)/1/

Washington, January 5, 1965.

/1/Source: Johnson Library, National Security File, Country File, United Nations, Article 19, Vol. 2. Confidential.

SUBJECT

Situation Report on the UN Financial Crisis

Harlan Cleveland spent the day with the Mission in New York yesterday drawing up plans for the period between now and January 18 when the GA is scheduled to reopen. With U Thant in the Virgin Islands and Quaison-Sackey in Palm Beach, it was agreed that we should begin this week to work hard bilaterally with the Russians in both Washington and New York. Stevenson and Plimpton have been in town today working out further details with the Department. The following views will be taken to the Secretary this afternoon:

It was agreed that we should begin immediately to destroy any hope on the part of the Afro-Asians that the Pazhwak Plan (which would set aside Article 19) will be acceptable to us.

In addition, it was agreed that a Department Circular/2/ or a message from the Secretary should be sent out within the next day or so making it fully clear that there will be a confrontation when the GA reconvenes unless an adequate payment has been made. The circular also would say that if there is a confrontation and Article 19 is not upheld--i.e., if we lose--then we will be compelled to make a reassessment of our entire financial relationship to the UN; but avoid getting into details because Congress would have to be consulted.

/2/Circular telegram 1225, January 7. (National Archives and Records Administration, RG 59, Central Files 1964-66, UN 10-4)

Foy Kohler and Stevenson dined with Dobrynin last evening when the whole matter of Article 19 was discussed. According to Stevenson, the pitch he and Kohler took was to impress upon Dobrynin that the time had come, during the GA recess, to solve the problem if a confrontation was to be avoided. Dobrynin listened and said he would report their views to Moscow. (Kohler returns to Moscow later this week and hopes to see Gromyko next Tuesday.)/3/

/3/January 13; see Document 328.

There also has been some discussion of requesting the President to intervene by sending a message to Kosygin. I have discouraged this, for the time being, on two counts: (1) the Department must once again, here and in posts abroad, make our position clear to the members of the Organization; (2) January 18, when the GA is scheduled to reconvene, is on the eve of the Inauguration and this is scarcely the time to involve the President personally in a confrontation with Russians.

On the assumption that the Russians do not pay up by January 18, my prediction is that the Afro-Asians again will find a way to avoid a confrontation with the Russians. This they could do either by postponing the opening of the GA until later (March 1 already has been mentioned) or by continuing to do what business they can do on a "no objection" basis. Neither course embues the Organization with very much nobility, but short of adequate Soviet payment, this is probably what will happen.

I also should add an encouraging note from the French Delegation (the Financial Counselor) who has said that the French intend to pay up. However, whether this intention is shared by De Gaulle remains a crucial unknown.

Samuel E. Belk/4/

/4/Printed from a copy that bears this typed signature.

326. Memorandum From Samuel Belk of the National Security Council Staff to the President's Special Assistant for National Security Affairs (Bundy)/1/

Washington, January 7, 1965.

/1/Source: Johnson Library, National Security File, Country File, United Nations, Article 19, Vol. 2. Confidential.

SUBJECT

UN Miscellany

Article 19: As you probably know from the press, the Committee of 12 (Afro-Asians) have called on the U. S. and the USSR to get together and solve the problem bilaterally. This is typical of this group who seem to become more and more uninformed on what is going on. U.S.-USSR bilaterals have been going on for the past ten months and are continuing still.

When Stevenson met with the Secretary on Tuesday,/2/ the latter was very bearish about pursuing the bilateral angle in New York until we get a response from Moscow either as a result of Dobrynin›s dinner/3/ or a meeting between Kohler and Gromyko.

/2/January 5; no record of the meeting was found.

/3/See Document 325.

Both in New York and in a circular to all posts, we already are making a strong effort to knock down the Pazhwak Plan (the Afro-Asian formula for side-stepping Article 19). Another circular is being prepared instructing Ambassadors to make another démarche to foreign ministers emphasizing our determination to apply Article 19 if adequate payments have not been made.

The Secretary apparently had a very easy time with the Foreign Relations Committee on this problem./4/ He told Stevenson that the Committee was quite satisfied as long as it was understood that those countries in arrears would either pay enough money or lose their vote. The Committee members apparently alluded on several occasions to the joint resolution on the matter. The Secretary seemed unworried about getting the necessary funds from the Congress for UN activities as long as we held firm on Article 19.

/4/For text of the briefing, see *Executive Session of the Senate Foreign Relations Committee Together with Joint Sessions with the Senate Armed Services Committee (Historical Series), vol. XVII, Eighty-ninth Congress, First Session, 1965.* (Washington, GPO, 1990), pp. 1-34. According to *The New York Times,* January 7, Senator Fulbright, upon exiting the meeting, told reporters that Rusk had not been hopeful of resolving the Article 19 impasse.

There is no further word from the French.

Stevenson: Those who know him well were worried about what they described as his «rather bad performance» in the Department. In a word, he does not want to face up to a confrontation. The short time I saw him he certainly did not look at all well. As you know, he saw the President for about forty-five minutes at the end of the day./5/ The short press statement from the *Star* (attached)/6/ is the extent of my information on that meeting. Thank the Lord it didn't get any greater play than it did. Actually, his remarks to the press were very much in the same mood of his pitch in the Department.

/5/January 5; Stevenson's notes of the meeting are in Papers of Adlai E. Stevenson, vol. 8, pp. 667-668.

/6/Not attached. Replying to reporters questions following his meeting with the President, Stevenson commented that he intended to stay on at the United Nations through the end of the current General Assembly session and had not discussed his future with Johnson. On the Article 19 issue, he commented: "I think it would be well to avoid a confrontation on this, win or lose," adding that the U.S. position would win the support needed to prevail but its victory might not be as conclusive or unanimous as the United States would like. (*Washington Star,* January 6, 1965)

Stevenson is still determined to give a speech during the remaining part-about one week-of the general debate. The Department quite correctly is holding him off for now. This is a statement we will wish to examine closely if and when it is made.

SEB

327. Telegram From the Mission to the United Nations to the Department of State/1/

New York, January 13, 1965, 8:35 p.m.

/1/Source: Johnson Library, National Security File, Country File, United Nations, Article 19, Vol. 2. Confidential; Priority.

2647. Article 19 — Conversation with SYG. Stevenson, Plimpton and Noyes called on SYG, Bunche was present.

1. SYG said Amb Bouattoura (Algeria), on Dec 30, had presented him with text of draft statement which he said had been unanimously agreed to by AA group,/2/ and suggested that SYG, if such a statement could be agreed on, should make it to the Assembly on Jan 18. If there were no agreement on this statement, AA group would table a reso along same lines. SYG had received a different story from Amb Barrington (Burma) who told him AA group had not agreed that it would table any reso and that many delegations had indicated they needed instructions. In any case SYG had circulated this paper and was awaiting reactions.

/2/The informal proposal was being circulated by the African-Asian group.

2. SYG understood US did not agree to second para of statement and Russians did not like last para. There were 21 speakers remaining in general debate which should take up first week of resumed session. This would allow time for further discussions if necessary. SYG understood from Suslov (UN) there was no change in Soviet position, but was seeing Fedorenko in few minutes and would then find out./3/

/3/In a handwritten note on the telegram, Belk commented, "Still no report of this meeting. SB"

3. SYG understood US position to be if Fedorenko would pledge privately to SYG the payment of sufficient amount to clear Art 19, and SYG would pass this privately to US, we might be able to get over present difficulties. Stevenson responded that it was not necessary for SYG to pass details of Soviet position to us but only to advise us that he personally was satisfied that amount was sufficient and there were no unacceptable conditions attached to the pledge. Stevenson said we could find way to resume voting as soon as USSR gave him private pledge in satisfactory amount and form./4/

/4/In an attached January 14 memorandum to Bundy, Belk commented: "The critical paragraph is number 3 where Stevenson badly erred. The Department (Sisco) quite rightly has told him that we cannot buy his position as stated for all the obvious reasons. The Department's position has been and continues to be that the amount contributed by each country must be made public."

4. SYG said his hunch was USSR would pledge less than $25.2 mil which was necessary. He didn't know how much less. Stevenson said if SYG was not satisfied, there would then be no bais for settlement, to which the SYG agreed.

5. Stevenson indicated our view that a simple appeal by the SYG would be a better procedure than a statement based on Algerian text. He thought SYG was probably right in estimating that USSR was not prepared to contribute enough to satisfy Art 19. SYG indicated there was also the problem of the French. In this connection he said they had instructions not to participate in any discussions or negotiations. If there were a system for whispering pledges, he felt it would have to apply to all the states subject to Art 19, since they would all have to be treated alike, to which Stevenson agreed.

6. Stevenson asked what we could do in present situation if there were no agreement. SYG replied that we would presumably have a showdown although there was talk of a postponement. Quaison-Sackey (GA Pres) was strongly opposed to postponement because it gave a picture of UN as a paralyzed, futile organization in the jaws of death. As a practical matter SYG thought there were many difficulties in working out a postponement until the next session on a no objection basis, and said there were ten important items which had to be dealt with, including assessments to the regular budget and UNEF, UN Institute, International School, ECOSOC elections, UNCTAD and UNWRA. SYG also pointed out a single state could destroy the whole plan by objecting to one or more of these actions being taken.

7. Stevenson said that postponement was not a wise course. We felt it would discredit the UN by indicating that it was unwilling to face the issue and to apply the Charter. It could also mean that we would have to get along without the Assembly in case of an emergency requiring UN peacekeeping activities. We had deferred confrontation since Dec 1 and now were in the same situation we were in then. We did not see any point to further delay. He understood full well that a confrontation was serious and might do damage to UN but we felt that postponement would also damage UN. Bunche interjected it seemed to be six of one and half dozen of another.

8. There was discussion of motives for USSR position. Stevenson indicated we thought their face could be saved by going along with any one of the proposed plans which had been put forward. Bunche expressed the view that issue was fundamental and was the same one that arose in the troika fight, i.e., whether the UN should be an action organization or not. Stevenson agreed and speculated that the USSR preferred to fight not on the question of future procedures where they were opposed by the majority, rather than on the question of Art 19 where they had some support from the AAs. Those AAs who supported the Pazhwak plan did not understand what was at stake. If Art 19 were not applied, all assessments would be put on a voluntary basis where everyone would pick and choose what he wished to support. Peacekeeping of UN would be seriously diminished, the organization would be discredited, and the implications were very serious.

9. Stevenson asked SYG his personal views as to what course should be followed. SYG said if arrangements could be made to dispose of the 10 essential items of business, he would personally prefer a postponement to a confrontation. He did not plan to press this position on others, however. There was a discussion whether a postponement to June 1 or to the fall would be preferable from this point of view. He agreed that the June 1 date would enable GA to proceed without a new budget, ECOSOC elections, UNWRA and perhaps other items. Stevenson said that while some might favor postponement to one of the other dates and it was arguable that smaller countries needed time to realize the full implications of the issue we faced, we felt it was better to go to a confrontation which we expected to win.

10. SYG indicated he preferred to talk to Fedorenko before recommending a course of action. He said the Russians had paid $3.5 mil more towards their 1964 regular budget assessments. It was agreed that this left about $21.7 mil which needed to be paid to satisfy Art 19. SYG said Turner (UN Controller) had asked him whether he would accept

a pledge of payment over a two-year period if the amount was satisfactory. Stevenson said Soviet credit was good and if the payment was to be made in days or weeks this would be one thing if over a period of years, it would be more difficult. He thought it would be for SYG to decide. Plimpton pointed out that this would involve next year's assessment and that in interim before payment by SYG's books would show arrears beyond Art 19. It would take a GA decision to get any assessments off the books.

11. Stevenson said he was concerned that the USSR really wanted a showdown rather than that they were simply trying to save their face. He thought they hoped they might win on the issue and having won would produce a situation in which all assessments were voluntary and peacekeeping activities would have been eliminated except for those approved by the SC. They had been talking about voluntary contributions primarily to minimize AA reaction. SYG felt this was possible. Stevenson said if this was true state of affairs we faced a major crisis in which further documents and paper work would be useless. We had to face this crisis and we thought we could get a two-thirds vote. If we won, we would have saved the structure of the organization. We could then be magnanimous about reaching a solution. If we lost the confrontation, the structure of the UN would be undermined. We had recognized in our proposal to the Russians that we needed new procedures for the future which did not involve enforcing peacekeeping assessments against major powers. We ought to be able to solve these problems if we could get over the immediate issue. He thought the AAs would also be willing to negotiate new arrangements for the future along the same lines.

12. Discussion returned to the Pazhwak plan. Plimpton indicated that we had been told that there was a firm understanding that contributions would be substantial. He had also been told by some members of the Committee of 12 it was part of their plan that private assurances would be given to the SYG as to the amounts and nature of the payments to be made

by the states in arrears. SYG indicated he had never been informed of this fact.

13. Plimpton suggested that if no agreement could be reached on the Pazhwak plan, the SYG should make an appeal anyway on 18th. SYG said Fedorenko had earlier objected to his making an appeal unless it was in same terms as Pazhwak plan. Stevenson said he thought it would be difficult for USSR to disregard an honest plea from SYG. SYG did not commit himself but said he would get in touch after his discussion with Fedorenko.

Stevenson

328. Telegram From the Embassy in the Soviet Union to the Department of State/1/

Moscow, January 15, 1965, 9 p.m.

/1/Source: National Archives and Records Administration, RG 59, Central Files 1964-66, UN 10-4. Secret; Limdis. Repeated to USUN.

2052. In accordance instructions Deptel 1931/2/ I raised Article 19 question with Gromyko in my meeting with him this afternoon, noting initially that Secretary somewhat discouraged at the lack of progress resolution impasse.

/2/Dated January 2, it reported on the contents of a 25-page letter from Khrushchev to President Johnson, December 31, 1964, regarding the use of force in the settlement of disputes. The letter was delivered on the morning of January 2 by Dobrynin to Rusk. The telegram summarized Rusk's initial response. (Ibid., POL 32-1) No instructions were transmitted in this telegram. Subsequently, circular telegram 1255, January 14, transmitted the draft text of a Johnson response and circular telegram 1254, January 14, provided instructions for its presentation. (Both ibid.)

Gromyko said he failed understand why Secretary should be disappointed since Sovs have accepted proposal of non-aligned nations which he felt was in line with Secretary's suggestion as to how problem might be solved made to Dobrynin before beginning GA. Sovs were prepared to make voluntary contribution but insisted that this should be purely voluntary and no one should tell the Sovs how much they should pay or purposes for which their contribution should be spent. Sovs felt strongly these matters their own business. Gromyko felt suggestions as to size of Sov contribution were both "unrealistic and ridiculous" and in any case represented wrong approach to problem. He felt US should recognize that the Soviet agreement non-aligned nations proposal represented major concession and hoped it could form basis for realistic solution of problem to permit us get on with discussion more important questions.

I said we recognized that both we and Sovs have made moves to reconcile strongly held positions of principle and each should recognize these as concessions by other side. This problem is to agree on a compromise solution which would permit both sides maintain substance their positions — i.e. Sovs position would be met by voluntary payment agreement and our position to be met by assurance that payment was sufficiently large obviate Article 19 application. Briefly our position is that the Sovs are entitled to decide the form they prepared to pay and objectives for which contribution should be spent but such sum must be large enough to meet arrearages problem.

Gromyko said obviously we in best position to know how our requirements can be met but equally the Sovs in best position to know how their requirements can be met. One thing is clear: "We know what we can do and what we can't do; we have made concession and we cannot go further." He admitted that the latest version of non-aligned nations proposal was not completely satisfactory to Sovs. They objected particularly to clause calling for "substantial" payment and provision that contribution would result in solvency of organization. Amended to meet these points the proposal would be acceptable. Gromyko felt US should stop raising impossible demands, agree to the substance

381

of proposal and help to remove problem from agenda in order to permit us tackle really important questions either under UN aegis or in other channels. He would note that while President and Secretary speak of need to improve relations situation in UN is becoming aggravated and this somewhat inconsistent with professed aims US leadership. I noted that the latest version non-aligned resolution was not totally acceptable to US, particularly clause providing for suspension of Article 19. To US basic problem is to discover solution which would not violate position of principle either side. UN was drowning man but no use throwing preserver only half way.

Gromyko ended conversation by noting that it was Sovs who had life preserver and pointing out that he felt not much purpose carry on conversation since both sides could only repeat initial positions.

Kohler

329. Memorandum of Conversation/1/

Washington, January 18, 1965, 11 a.m.

/1/Source: Johnson Library, National Security File, Country File, United Nations, Memoranda of Conversation, Vol. 1. Secret. Drafted by Spiers and approved in S on January 28. The meeting was held in the Secretary's office. The memorandum is Part I of III.

SUBJECT

Article 19

PARTICIPANTS

The Secretary
The Undersecretary
William R. Tyler, Assistant Secretary, EUR
Ronald I. Spiers, EUR:RPM

Joseph Luns, Foreign Minister of The Netherlands
Ambassador Carl W.A. Schurmann, Dutch Ambassador to the U.S.

Foreign Minister Luns alluded to a New York Times report of this morning that U Thant intended today to issue an appeal for funds, propose that normal procedures (including voting) be reinstituted and that the subject be considered further in the light of the amount of money received./2/

/2/The text of U Thant's statement in the UN General Assembly, January 18, is in *Public Papers of the Secretaries General of the United Nations, U Thant, 1965-1967,* **pp. 27-29.**

The Secretary said that we would be disappointed if this report were correct. Our position on this issue has not changed. Essentially, we believe that the Soviets should come up with enough money by one means or another to avoid the voting problem. We do not see the outcome very clearly, and we do not know whether the Soviets, if they are outvoted, will stage a walkout. We do not believe; however, they would withdraw from UN membership.

Luns said that since his last talk with the Secretary the Dutch position had hardened. The Netherlands would not pay one dollar under any voluntary contribution's formula. This would only serve to bail the Soviets out.

The Secretary noted that we and the Dutch had different assessments as to the outcome of a vote, and the Dutch and US delegations in New York were now comparing notes. He recalled that the US judgment was that the vote would be approximately 58-28-28. The Dutch estimate was less favorable.

Luns asked what the US position would be if a 2/3 vote were not achieved. The Secretary said that a severe view is taken of this issue, and at minimum support for the UN would become "voluntary" for everybody, including us. The General Assembly might be confronted with an amendment to the Charter explicitly removing the obligation in Article 17 and making an appropriate change in Article 19 in the event this question is unfavorably resolved.

Luns said that he had been giving this matter careful thought. He thought it would now be better for the UN to face a real test and that the Afro-Asians should feel the heat of this problem. This would be healthy for the organization in the long run. The Netherlands might elect, without reducing the amount it spends for technical assistance, to pay the same sums it now channels through the UN through other bodies. He asked what the US position would be if the Soviets, after winning a vote, paid their contribution voluntarily. The Secretary said the US would probably find some way to put proportionate amounts into a general fund, provided the Soviets "pay enough." This might be accomplished in part by canceling some bills due. Luns said that the Netherlands would not follow this course. The Secretary said this was a very disagreeable problem. If the UN's financial base is changed from a mandatory to a voluntary one, the result is certain to be resentment and uncertainty. Mr. Ball noted that the UN would have to be sustained by a succession of charity drives.

Luns noted that he disagreed with the point made by the Italian representative in the Western European group discussion in New York to the effect that a firm position could not be taken because of the French. The Secretary noted that the problem for France was only a matter of a million dollars, when possible refunds and reductions were considered.

330. Memorandum From the Assistant Secretary of State for International Organization Affairs (Sisco) to Secretary of State Rusk/1/

Washington, January 18, 1965.

/1/Source: Department of State, U.S. Mission to the United Nations, Subject Files, Reel 142, Frames 506-509. Confidential. Drafted by Sisco on January 18.

SUBJECT

Session with Ambassador Stevenson on Article 19, 3:00 p.m. January 19th

We are in a difficult bind. If we press the confrontation and succeed in denying the vote to the Soviets, this would satisfy American public opinion. Moreover, perhaps this sort of a defeat of the Soviets might force them to make a contribution of a more substantial character than presently seems contemplated. The Moroccan Foreign Minister, for example, said to me yesterday that the Indonesian withdrawal/2/ has placed the USSR in a much more vulnerable position regarding the UN in relationship to Communist China. He contends that there is now more pressure on the Soviets to accommodate itself to the UN and to stay within it rather than to find itself ostracized and thereby give added ammunition to the Chinese Communist vilification of the UN and possible future moves to set up some rival mechanism.

/2/On January 2 President Sukarno announced in a speech that his nation was withdrawing from the United Nations.

On the other hand, the more likely situation is that once the Soviets have been denied the vote, the Assembly will be paralyzed by at least a walk-out, there will probably be appeals for the Soviets to return, there would probably not be any kind of a Soviet contribution, and the onus and the pressure will in considerable measure be on us. Of equal importance, Article 19 and the principle of collective financial responsibility will have been confirmed but without making progress on future arrangements to increase the role of the Security Council in peacekeeping and to set into train procedures designed not to deny the residual power of the Assembly but to promote the more responsible exercise of that power.

If we press the confrontation and lose the vote, in the words of Senator Frank Church, we will have the worst of both worlds and there will be a sharp diminution of support in this country for the UN. More important, the Johnson Administration will

385

have taken a licking on a fundamental foreign policy issue just a few days after the Inaugural.

Our tentative voting estimate is 58 in favor of application of Article 19, 28 against, and 28 abstaining. USUN is making a final check of the accuracy of this estimate. This is too close and uncertain for us to be confident of winning the vote. Equally relevant is the question of whether we have the simple majority required to insist that a vote on the application of Article 19 be taken, even if we wanted confrontation now. USUN is not sure we have this simple majority, believing the pressure will be strong for postponement.

In these circumstances, I believe we should:

a. Continue to maintain the posture in favor of applying Article 19; and

b. Be prepared to acquiesce in an unprejudicial postponement, preferably until June, if a majority desires.

During the period of postponement, we would then have to make a major effort in linking the past debts with future arrangements, even though prospects for an Agreement are admittedly very slim.

If it is agreed that we should proceed along the above lines, we should give advance notice to key members of the Senate Foreign Relations and House Foreign Affairs Committees.

Before arriving at the above judgment, we have explored the following other options singly or in combination and found them wanting one way or another.

1. Future Peacekeeping Operations by Voluntary Payments.

Ambassador Thompson has suggested we might promote or sponsor a General Assembly consensus or resolution which would declare that any future peacekeeping operations to which the major powers have not given their assent or acquiescence would be financed by voluntary means. Such a proposal could be given quietly to the Secretary General for negotiation or announced by Ambassador Stevenson in a general debate speech. This would get the Assembly as well as the American people focusing on future arrangements and help to get us away from the present "no-pay no-vote" straight-jacket we are in. Such an Assembly decision has the obvious advantage that we would be in no danger in the future of being assessed for a UN Force in the South Africa, the Portuguese Territories, or Cuba if established by a 2/3rds GA vote contrary to our wishes.

The difficulty is that this proposal is unlikely to work. It meets the Soviets only part way and therefore is not likely to result in a contribution to meet the Article 19 minimal limit. More important, it might well cause a crisis of confidence among our closest European and Latin American allies who, while not precluding such a proposal as the ultimate outcome of negotiations, would see this as a sharp reversal of our position in favor of Articles 19, 17 and collective financial responsibility and a move of weakness. Finally, it is unlikely that the Assembly would be willing to adopt this proposal, since a good many small countries would not distinguish between this proposal (which seeks to separate out the financial aspects) from the kind of proposals the Soviets have made intended to negate entirely the future power of the General Assembly in the peacekeeping field.

2. Amendments to the UN Charter.

If the Assembly gives us the wrong answer on Article 19 we could submit an amendment to the Charter designed to formalize the result-ant reinterpretation of Articles 19 and 17. A discussion of the pros and cons of this proposal as well as the form such amendments might take are attached (Tab A)./3/ In short, we feel that if the Assembly has failed to sustain Article 19, a preferable alternative would be for the United States to announce we would no longer consider Article 17 binding and that no Charter amendment would be necessary to make this position stick. It is doubtful whether such Charter amendments would in fact be approved by enough UN members to enter into force. Finally, the adoption of such Charter amendments would remove an element of flexibility for the future which it might not be in our interest to discard.

/3/None of the tabs is printed.

3. Provisional Voting.

I have previously sent you a brief memorandum regarding this possibility (Tab B). While some awkward circumstances would result, it is technically feasible. Its weakness is that it would be a further retrogression from the position we have taken on Article 19 without any real prospect that this would in fact bring forward the required financial contribution from the USSR.

4. Substantial Soviet Payment Combined with Reduction in Soviet Arrears.

In order to avoid Article 19, the amount of payment required from the USSR was $26.5 million--$17 million for peacekeeping expenses and $9.5 million on the regular budget. In the last two weeks, the USSR has paid $4.9 million on the regular budget, which leaves a required payment of $21.6 million in order to escape Article 19. The UN Comptroller has been examining the availability of ONUC and UNEF surpluses, made up of the excess of these assessments over the actual obligations incurred, with the thought that the surpluses might be applied in some form to all UN members. Our estimate is that this could reduce the overall Soviet arrearage by a minimum of $2.2 million. If the Soviets were willing to make a substantial payment of about $20 million (which is still below the minimal figure it now owes in order to escape Article 19) it could contend that its contribution was not related to the removal in principle of the application of Article 19. The $2.2 million reduction could them be applied subsequently and thereby eliminate the Article 19 problem without the Soviets having made the minimal payment directly. While I see no objection to having the Secretariat explore this proposal, provided it is clearly understood it is not a US suggestion, my judgment is that it is unlikely the Soviets would be willing to make such a substantial contribution and lend itself to this kind of a bookkeeping device.

331. Memorandum From Samuel Belk of the National Security Council Staff to the President's Special Assistant for National Security Affairs (Bundy)/1/

Washington, January 25, 1965.

/1/Source: Johnson Library, National Security File, Country File, United Nations, Memos, Vol. 1. No classification marking.

SUBJECT

Developments at the UN

A member of Stevenson's staff has telephoned to say that the SYG had met with Fedorenko and subsequently called Stevenson to report that the Soviet position was so vague and ambiguous that he (the SYG) had no idea how much or when the Russians would pay, even if voting were allowed before the payment was made./2/ (In other words, it sounds as though the GA would have no greater assurance from the Russians if the Pazhwak Plan were adopted than it has now.) The SYG felt that the GA was headed for a confrontation on Wednesday if not sooner. When the SYG questioned Fedorenko about a possible postponement, he said they would want to know more about it and that they would have to talk to the Afro-Asians about it.

/2/Reported in telegram 2876 from New York, January 25. (Ibid.)

The Assembly did not meet this morning as a tribute to Churchill,/3/ and this has set the agenda back. Because of this, Stevenson probably will speak tomorrow morning instead of this afternoon. The text of his speech is attached./4/ It is interesting that the Secretary re-wrote parts of the Stevenson-Sisco draft (see marked portions) in order to retain, as he put it, «a maximum of flexibility.» The real meat of the speech begins on page 12. Other than the fact that, it seems to me, it is a bit wordy, I have no trouble with it. If you do, please let me know.

/3/Churchill died January 24.

/4/Not found.

SEB

332. Memorandum by Ralph Bunche of the United Nations Secretariat/1/

New York, February 2, 1965.

/1/Source: Johnson Library, National Security File, Country File, United Nations, Article 19, Vol. 2. No classification marking. The memorandum was given to Bill Moyers of the White House staff who forwarded it to President Johnson on February 5. (Memorandum from Moyers to Johnson, February 5; ibid.) The President passed the memorandum to Bundy. In a March 2 memorandum to the President, Bundy commented, "I don't think there is anything for us to do on this one right now." (Ibid.)

This a purely personal statement. The viewpoints are my own. U Thant has not been consulted about it, nor is he aware of it. The same applies to Adlai Stevenson.

The plight of the United Nations today is desperate; its future is gravely threatened. Never in its history has the Organization been in such dire trouble, the representatives of its Member States so frustrated or its effectiveness so diminished. This critical situation must be weighed against the indispensability of the United Nations if peace is to be saved and the world is to survive in civilized form.

The salient facts of the deep United Nations crisis over the arrears in payments and Article 19 of the Charter are the following:

1. The General Assembly has been in session for two months but has been unable to take up any of the urgent work on

its agenda. Consequently, the United Nations has already suffered a severe loss in both effectiveness and prestige throughout the world; and it could be reduced before long, if the present impasse continues, to a completely ineffectual body which would sooner or later wither away.

2. The conviction is growing, I believe rapidly, amongst the Members of the United Nations that there is very little basis for hope that an accommodation can be achieved on the issue of the arrears and the application of Article 19 through negotiations at the ambassadorial level here at the United Nations. This unavoidably leads to the conclusion that only the President of the United States and the leaders of the Soviet Union, acting either separately or in direct communication as in the case of the Cuban crisis, can resolve the difficulty and thereby save the United Nations.

3. Although the problem itself is important in terms of principle and morality, of Charter interpretation and application, it does not affect directly any vital security, political or economic interest of the United States as, for example, Cuba, nuclear testing or Panama would and did, or of France and the Soviet Union.

4. After prolonged negotiation, the specific issue on which the future of the United Nations now depends is the following:

The Russians, although refusing to admit any legal obligation to pay the special assessments for the United Nations peace-keeping operation in the Congo and in Gaza-Sinai, have stated a willingness to make a substantial voluntary contribution of an unspecified amount which, however, would not be pledged or paid until the General Assembly actually resumes its "usual procedure" (meaning voting) and until assurance is given that the question of the applicability of Article 19 will not be raised during the current session of the General Assembly. But they flatly refuse to disclose to anyone beforehand the amount they intend to contribute. They say to do so would be submitting to unacceptable "pressure".

The United States, on its part, refuses to accept as good enough the Soviet promise of a contribution, even though publicly declared, since no indication is given of the amount to be contributed and no assurance is provided as to when anything will be paid. The United States insists that at least the Secretary- General and/ or the President of the General Assembly must be informed of the amount which the Soviet Union intends to pay and must determine this to be satisfactory in the context of Article 19 *before* any voting can take place in the General Assembly without Article 19 being invoked. The United States, as Adlai has put it, doesn›t take to the idea of buying a «pig in a poke.»

Almost everyone at the United Nations, Delegates and Secretariat officials alike, has been seeking intensively to find a way out of this dilemma with, regretfully, no success.

I have not the slightest doubt in my own mind about the soundness, legal and moral, of the United States position on Article 19. I have great doubts, however, that the United States position can attract enough votes in the General Assembly to sustain it conclusively. This is because it is almost certain that many member states will abstain on a show-down vote, even though they accept the United States interpretation of Article 19 and are sympathetic to the American position. They would be motivated, I believe, not by lack of courage or principle, but by a conviction that if France and the USSR and other financial delinquents should be actually deprived of their vote under Article 19, they would walk out of the Assembly if not the entire Organization, rather than pay up their delinquencies under what they would consider to be conditions of duress and humiliation. This would reduce the General Assembly, and possibly the whole Organization, to futility, since it would no longer be representative of the main groups of powers in the world.

The membership of the United Nations, of course, is sharply divided over the proper interpretation of Article 19, with a significant number, including France and the Soviet Union, vigorously opposing the American interpretation of the Article. It is not, therefore, an open and shut case.

392

The United States has made important concessions on the issue. It has gone along with two postponements of the Assembly. It did not force the issue at the outset of the Assembly's session and permitted it to get partially organized and under way through actions by consensus, acclamation and informal procedure. The United States does not demand actual Soviet payment in advance of the resumption of the formal voting, if a formal pledge of an adequate size is made. It is not insisting that the Soviet Union pay up to the very last cent of its arrears. The United States has also declared its wish to avoid a confrontation on this issue.

The Soviet Union contends that it also has made important concessions, but can go no further. Soviet spokesmen assert that the original Soviet position, as stated emphatically to U Thant by Mr. Khrushchev himself last August, was that the Soviet Union would pay "not one kopek" to the United Nations for the "illegal" United Nations peace-keeping operations. Subsequently, the Soviet Union agreed to make a voluntary contribution for an amount which would not be disclosed until the Assembly resumed its normal procedure. Later still, the Soviet Representative indicated that this would be a substantial contribution; and then announced it publicly. A Soviet contribution of any amount in this context does, it would appear, compromise the original Soviet position. He also agreed to the postponements of the Assembly and he claims to wish to avoid a confrontation on the issue.

There are not a few at the United Nations who reason that the present paralysis of the General Assembly suits quite well the inner policies of the Soviets in that they have always favored the Security Council with its veto over the Assembly, and therefore they could be only happy at seeing the United States at least sharing the blame for the Assembly's plight, if not taking the major part of it.

Contrary to popular notion, no formidable sums of money are involved. The United Nations indebtedness to Governments and for replenishing the Working Capital Fund, other than the unamortized principal of the United Nations Bonds, amounts to

86.7 million. Of this amount, $6,642,000 is owed to the United States, principally for the Congo operation. A contribution of $21.7 million from the Soviet Union would meet the existing requirements of Article 19. This is not primarily a financial problem, therefore, although because of the impasse over this issue of Article 19 the United Nations is in most serious financial shape.

It is tragic that the bright future of the United Nations should thus be darkened by an issue that derives from its past. The arrears relate primarily to the huge Congo operation, which is over, since the United Nations Force left the Congo at the end of last June. The Gaza-Sinai Force remains, but is not very costly. There is ample reason to believe that agreement between the United States and the USSR on future peace-keeping operations and their financing could be reached in time once the issue of the arrears on past operations would be settled. France, presumably, would then come along, albeit reluctantly.

In the prevailing circumstances, there would seem, on this issue to be mainly the following courses of action open to the United States Government:

a. To proceed to a direct confrontation on the issue in the Assembly, bearing in mind, however, that any clear-cut "show-down" on this issue is unlikely since it is certain to become enmeshed in an endless and acrimonious procedural wrangle, with confusion compounded by the injection into the debate of a multitude of inefficacious proposals for solution of which there is already a profusion. Moreover, the voting, when ultimately reached, would almost certainly be inconclusive in resolving the issue, whichever way it went and it might well go against the United States because of the necessity of mustering a two-thirds vote.

b. To accept, although not initiate, another extended postponement which, however, may not hold much promise while holding the United Nations up to ridicule, unless the purpose would be to afford an opportunity for a direct appeal to the President of the United States and to the leaders of the Soviet Union to collaborate in finding a solution.

c. To adopt a possible "summit" approach to the Soviet Union, with a view to a dialogue between the President and the Soviet leaders, as there was between Kennedy and Khrushchev in the Cuban crisis.

d. To test the good faith of the Soviet Union on its promise of a substantial contribution by announcing a willingness, in the interest of preserving the United Nations and reviving the General Assembly, to accept the Soviet announcement of their intention at its face value and act accordingly. This would mean agreeing, *before* the Soviet contribution is actually made or formally pledged, *not* to invoke Article 19 for the rest of the nineteenth session of the General Assembly. There would, naturally, be those who would decry such a course as a *surrender* to the Soviet Union, particularly if the Soviet contribution should then turn out to be not substantial enough to be satisfactory in the context of Article 19. But there would be many others, including, I believe, the overwhelming majority of the Members of the Organization, who would consider this to be an act fully justified by its purpose of salvaging the international organization, and who would see it as a gesture of magnanimity and statesmanship worthy of the richest and most powerful country in the world. There can also be little doubt that the Soviet Union would be the target of severe disfavor from the overwhelming majority of the Members of the United Nations should it not then live up to the expectations aroused by its promise to contribute.

In taking such a step, the United States could, in fact, largely cover and safeguard its position on Article 19 by an explanatory statement which could include all necessary reservations and which could emphasize that from the beginning the sole purpose of the United States in raising the issue of Article 19 has been to protect the Charter and the strength of the Organization in its peace-keeping role, and that its present step is a continuation of this policy. At the worst, the United States would be holding up on Article 19 only until September, when the next session of the General Assembly convenes. The principle of collective financial responsibility should, naturally, be strongly reasserted. The supporters of the United States position would need to be consulted so as to avoid any feeling by them that they were being "let down".

Fully recognizing the risks in pursuing this latter course, I would nevertheless, think it worthy of serious consideration.

The United Nations unquestionably has been, and will be further, weakened because some of its members fail to meet their Charter obligations by refusing to pay some of the assessments due. But the very nature and existence of the United Nations is rooted in the fact that some states, members as well as non-members, cannot always be relied upon for good and honorable conduct. The "good guys" seem always to carry more than their share in any organization or institution, domestic and international alike. Moreover, it is only realism to face the fact that a United Nations, even with some delinquent members, particularly if these should be France and the Soviet Union, is still preferable by far to no United Nations at all, or to an ineffective one, as it would surely be without those two countries.

The domestic political repercussions to the suggested course would probably be strong, at least for a while. For even in the United States today, magnanimity can be mistaken for weakness and statesmanship for lack of nerve. In this case, however, so much is at stake that risks of some kind are not only inescapable but justifiable. After all, twenty years of achievement and advance in international organization and order, as well as the future effectiveness of the United Nations, are in serious jeopardy over an issue which does not directly affect the vital interests of any of the countries mainly concerned.

It would not avail very much to save the Charter and lose the Organization.

Ralph J. Bunche

333. Memorandum From William Buffum of the Bureau of International Organization Affairs to the Assistant Secretary of State for International Organization Affairs (Cleveland)/1/

Washington, February 5, 1965.

/1/Source: Johnson Library, National Security File, Country File, United Nations, Article 19, Vol. 2. Confidential. Drafted by Virginia Hartley (IO/UNP) on February 5. Handwritten annotations on the memorandum read: "Very interesting JJ [Sisco]" and "Might be useful to have this document translated into form usable for educating Hill and public. But it raises question —'How and when did we get into our extreme position?'"

SUBJECT

Background on the Financing of UN Operations

We have recently made a new search of our early files to see if there is any additional light that can be thrown on the thinking with respect to the financing of UN operations in the peace and security field at the time the Charter was drafted.

We have found nothing that would in any way tend to invalidate the Court's Advisory Opinion or acceptance of this opinion by the Assembly (with U.S. concurrence). Neither, however, have we found anything indicating that the "Founding Fathers" actually contemplated the financing of such operations through the budgetary powers of the Assembly. Rather, it appears, there was not any real consideration of this question. In connection with the Article 19 impasse and your interest in how we handle forthcoming Congressional consultations on the subject, the following analysis of early Charter developments relating to this question may be helpful.

Strangely enough, at no time were the budgetary arrangements for the future organization a matter of serious controversy or lengthy consideration by the Department, by the U.S. Delegation to the San Francisco Conference, or in connection with ratification. Discussion in the Department prior to Dumbarton Oaks revolved almost entirely around whether the League precedent should be followed and all budgetary powers vested in the Assembly or whether these powers should be shared with the Council. This question was resolved by providing, in the U.S. Proposals at Dumbarton Oaks, for a system of weighted voting in the Assembly on budgetary matters. However, we did not press this proposal at Dumbarton Oaks, and the question of budgetary arrangements presented no problem there. Similarly, there appears to have been practically no discussion at all of budgetary matters by the U.S. Delegation to the San Francisco Conference, despite the fact that two members of the House of Representatives (and two Senators) were on the Delegation. Nor did the question of the Assembly's budgetary power arise in the Big Five consultations during the Conference. In the Department's testimony before the Senate Foreign Relations Committee in connection with ratification, the Assembly's powers under Article 17 are noted but not elaborated on and gave rise to no questions from the Committee members.

Budgetary discussions at the San Francisco Conference itself centered around whether the method of apportionment should be specified in the Charter, whether the method of preparing and examining the budget should be specified in the Charter, and whether a penalty should be provided for members that failed to meet their financial obligations, (which the League Covenant had not done). Given the fact that any operation involving substantial numbers of troops is bound to be costly, this general lack of concern on the part of the U.S. and others with the financing of such operations can only be explained in terms of the difference between the powers of the Assembly and of the Security Council and in the context of Article 43.

The only discussion of use by the Organization of armed force was in connection with preventive and enforcement measures undertaken by decision of the Security Council. While the Assembly was given residual powers of a recommendatory nature in the peace and security field, on which it was later possible to build the Uniting for Peace procedure, *there is nothing in the early record to indicate that it was ever contemplated that the Assembly would undertake, on a recommendatory basis, actual military operations even of a peacekeeping character. Therefore, we can only conclude that the possibility was not foreseen that Assembly recommendations involving costly operations might be given a mandatory character so far as their financing involved the Assembly's power to assess. So long as the use of armed force was thought of solely in the context of Security Council action, where the veto applied, the United States and the other great powers had no reason to be concerned about the financial implications for them of such action.*

This safeguard was reinforced for the great powers and extended to other members by Article 43 of the Charter which made the actual provision of "armed forces, assistance, and facilities" to the Council contingent upon the subsequent conclusion of "a special agreement or agreements" between the Council and Members or groups of Members subject to ratification by the signatory states. The legislative history of this article seems to indicate that the question of the financing of any military operation by the Security Council was also deferred pending the conclusions of these agreements.

The US Proposals at Dumbarton dealing with the provision of forces stated that the Council "should be empowered to call upon the member states for economic, financial, and commercial and other assistance necessary to support and to supplement international action involving the use of armed force", and that member states should undertake to give such assistance, "the terms to be determined in consultation between the executive council and member states." This provision is dropped in the Proposals as agreed to at Dumbarton Oaks but the paragraph dealing with the special agreement or agreements, which in the original US proposal referred only to "forces and facilities" now refers to "forces, facilities and assistance" as it does in Article 43 of the Charter.

The original US proposals also stated that members should agree "to join in mutual efforts to afford relief and aid to states assuming undue burdens through participation in security measures involving the use of armed force instituted by the executive council." This provision is broadened in the Dumbarton Oaks Proposals and in the Charter (Article 49) to declare the members should (shall in the Charter) "join in affording mutual assistance in carrying out measures decided upon by the Security Council". *Thus, while the principle of common responsibility for collective action was recognized, there appears to have been no effort made to spell out exactly how the burden of such action was to be shared.* The only amendment offered at San Francisco was South Africa›s unsuccessful proposal to put the burden on the aggressor state.

An interpretative statement by a Canadian Delegate at San Francisco declares that in his opinion it was not possible to draft a text on the payment of the costs of enforcement action that could lay down definite rules for application in all types of cases that might arise. He thought Article 49 quoted above and Article 50 (providing for recourse to the Council in the event of "special economic problems arising from the carrying out of preventive or enforcement measures") "taken together would permit arrangements to be made for sharing the costs of enforcement action among the members if this proved desirable. Otherwise an inequitable financial burden might be placed on certain members who were acting on behalf of the Organization."

In reading this statement it must be borne in mind that when the Charter was drafted it was thought that the principal burden of any enforcement action would fall on the five permanent members of the Security Council. Moreover, under the Charter, decisions of the Security Council are to be carried out by all members or only some members as the Council may decide and carried out by the members "directly."

The contemplated Article 43 agreements have never been concluded but the UN action in Korea, of all UN actions to date, seems most closely to approach the type of enforcement action contemplated in the drafting of the Charter. Here the United States controlled the action and paid the lion's share of the costs. *The idea of trying to assess the UN membership generally for the costs of the Korean operation was never contemplated, since members participating in the action were doing so on the basis of a recommendation of the Security Council, not a decision* (in the absence of Article 43 agreements). Had the Assembly's budgetary powers been generally recognized as clearly extending to the costs of the Korea action, it seems unlikely that the US would have willingly assumed such a large share of the costs or that John Foster Dulles, who played an active role at San Francisco, in answering criticism of the Korea action in the Foreign Relations Committee, would have said:

". . . If, for instance, the expense of that could be spread over the United Nations in the same way that the budget is met, or something of that sort, some formula might be found so that if an emergency came, nations could act knowing that that would not necessarily involve them in an expense which they could not foresee, or perhaps could not bear if they did foresee it."

From the above it seems clear (1) that, as originally contemplated, preventive or enforcement action under a Security Council decision was not to be financed through the Assembly's power of assessment, and (2) that preventive (peacekeeping) or enforcement action under an Assembly recommendation was not contemplated at all and that therefore no thought was given to the financing of such action. On this basis, it might be argued that although the Assembly does have the power to assess under Article 17, to consider this power mandatory in the case of the costs of operations undertaken on the basis of an Assembly recommendation is within the letter but goes beyond the original intent of the Charter. This would apply in the economic and social as well as the peace and security fields.

334. Telephone Conversation Between President Johnson and the Representative to the United Nations (Steven- son)/1/

February 6, 1965.

/1/Source: Johnson Library, Recordings and Transcripts, Recording of Telephone Conversation between President Johnson and Ambassador Stevenson, Tape 65.06, Side A, PNO 1. No classification marking. The President was in Washington; Stevenson was in New York City. There is no indication of the time of the conversation. This transcript was prepared in the Office of the Historian specifically for this volume.

LBJ: Yeah.

AES: Hello?

LBJ: Yeah, yeah.

AES: and we're not going to have to ask you whether-to take any political heat because there isn't any. . . .

LBJ: I got a very distressing memo from Bunche./2/ I wish you›d talk to him. Tell him that you have thoroughly gone over this with me and that I shared your view that we ought to go just as far as we could with any self-respect to find an area of agreement, and you had done that. And you›d touch base with Fulbright ahead of time and . . .

/2/Document 332.

AES: Well, the trouble with that is . . .

LBJ: . . .tell him I'm just as distressed as he is.

AES: I would have gone further, as you know, as I told you yesterday/3/ that the State Department was ready to go and anxious to do that, uh, what, just ten days ago and I talked to Mac Bundy about it. You were ill at the time. And he didn›t take it up with you. I would have gone further and accepted the $15(?) million payment and made a big play to the General Assembly that while we were, ah, while we were, ah, conceding[?]/4/ this point, for the present[?], at least until next September, we were doing so in order to preserve the organization without prejudice to our position, but I could never get any support for that at the State Department, and I also rather have the feeling that they wanted me to take the preliminary measures, the preliminary proposals first. Having made them, I don›t think now I can well go back and capitulate further.

/3/No record of a February 5 telephone call or meeting was found. However, according to the President's Daily Diary, Stevenson and Johnson met on February 4 at the White House between 12:19 and 12:24 p.m. "The President and Mrs. Johnson presented him a small cake, decorated with one candle, reading, 'Happy Birthday Adlai.'" (Johnson Library) No further record of this meeting was found.

/4/All brackets in the source text.

LBJ: Well, you know the situation there better than I do. Let me transfer you and you dictate this memo. I've got a group here . . .

AES: I will, I will, Mr. President.

335. Telegram From the Embassy in the Soviet Union to the Department of State/1/

Moscow, February 6, 1965, 7 p.m.

/1/Source: National Archives and Records Administration, RG 59, Central Files 1964-66, UN 10-4. Confidential; Priority; Limdis. Repeated to New York and passed to the White House.

2270. Embtel 2270./2/

/2/Dated February 6, it read: "I agree with Ambassador Stevenson conclusion no point pursuing UN finance

question further with Gromyko here. Personally feel forward prospects for agreed solution negative and showdown in UNGA better now than after adjournment present session without settlement this question." (Johnson Library, National Security File, Country File, United Nations, Article 19, Vol. 2)

On further reflection and after rereading entire file recent messages on Article 19 exercise, I have come to conclusion that perhaps we should make final high-level approach to Sovs before showdown in GA, not in Moscow but in Washington. I continue to believe, as indicated reftel, that postponement is not in our interest and obviously in putting suggestion outlined below I assume we are both willing and able block any GA ground swell in favor of postponement.

As Amb Stevenson points out in USUN 3107,/3/ Fedorenko›s unyielding posture would seem rule out any change in Sov position. Same was certainly my conclusion after my last discussion of subject with Gromyko Jan 15. However, seems possible Soviets may still not be persuaded we prepared to face showdown or that we could bring UNGA around to this if we wished. In this light, recent lower-level approaches (reminiscent of Soviet behavior at time Cuban crisis) and hints by Sov spokesmen from time to time that we should bypass Fedorenko may have been feelers, indicative what Soviets might be prepared to do if question really came to crunch.

/3/Dated February 5; it reported on Stevenson's discussions with Fedorenko regarding a compromise on the Article 19 issue. (Ibid.)

I suggest, therefore, that Secretary may wish to summon Dobrynin in final effort break log-jam. At such meeting, I would think it essential that Dobrynin be told unequivocally that Sovs have choice between fair settlement (on terms put by Stevenson) or showdown with inevitable implications for our bilateral relations and that they must make up minds without delay. Posing problem in this way could not be read by Sovs as weakness and while approach may net us nothing it may conceivably smoke out ultimate Sov position.

Kohler

336. Memorandum From Gordon Chase of the National Security Council Staff to the President's Special Assistant for National Security Affairs (Bundy)/1/

Washington, February 8, 1965.

/1/Source: Johnson Library, National Security File, Country File, United Nations, Article 19, Vol. 2. Secret. Bundy wrote "Good work" at the top of the memorandum.

SUBJECT

Article 19

The following reports on Article 19 events over the past few days and indicates where we now seem to be heading:

1. On Wednesday,/2/ there was a bit of a flurry in the U.S. Government when the Russians in New York seemed interested in finding solution to the Article 19 controversy. Tab 1/3/ reflects the apparent Russian interest./4/ (Stevenson saw the President alone at noon on Thursday and, reportedly, the Article 19 situation was reviewed.)/5/

/2/February 3.

/3/None of the tabs was found attached.

/4/Reported in telegram 3059 from New York, February 3. (Johnson Library, National Security File, Country File, United Nations, Article 19, Vol. 2)

/5/See footnote 3, Document 334.

2. With a break in the dispute seemingly a possibility, *on Thursday evening,* the Department instructed USUN to approach the Russians/6/ (to be followed by an approach in Moscow) to see whether, in fact, the Soviets were seriously interested in any of three possible solutions. The Department›s instruction are attached at *Tab 2.*

/6/Telegram 1945 to New York, February 4. (Johnson Library, National Security File, Country File, United Nations, Article 19, Vol. 2)

3. *On Friday,* Stevenson talked to Fedorenko and proposed the three possible solutions. The upshot of the talks was a cold shower for our side; Fedorenko knocked down immediately and forcefully all three solutions and ruled out a possible change in the Soviet position. In its report of the Stevenson/Fedorenko conversation (at *Tab 3*),/7/ USUN went on to recommend that Ambassador Kohler not take this matter up with Gromyko since such a step would be interpreted as a sign of weakness.

/7/See footnote 3, Document 335.

4. *On Saturday,* Ambassador Kohler reported (*Tab 4*)/8/ his agreement with the USUN view that he should not take the matter up with Gromyko. On the same day, Kohler had second thoughts (*Tab 5*)/9/ and suggested that Rusk talk to Dobrynin in Washington. (As of this writing, State was still considering this possibility.)

/8/See footnote 2, Document 335.

/9/Document 335.

5. As of noon on Saturday (before the second cable from Kohler), State's rough guess for the future scenario was as follows:

   a. *On Monday* (February 8), the Assembly will convene at 3:00 P.M. The Secretary General will recommend that the General

Assembly take action, by the «no objection» procedure, on 4 or 5 items (e.g., elections to fill 6 vacancies in ECOSOC; appeals for payments towards the 1965 budget).

b. The Assembly will then probably recess for a few days. During this period 2 items will be thrashed out: *First,* the General Assembly will have to decide on how long the adjournment should be. If there must be an adjournment, we, the Latinos, and West Europeans are generally in favor of a short adjournment with a specific end in sight (May 1); we want to keep pressure on the Russians. U Thant seems to prefer to not set a date. The Africans, who once seemed to want a short adjournment, now seem to be favoring a longer adjournment; they feel that it will cost too much money to meet in May, go home, and then come back again for the fall session. The Russians probably don›t care as between May or September; their primary concern (as is ours) is to not get tagged with the blame for causing the adjournment. *Second,* the group will have to decide on the type of forum to be used to carry on the talks about Article 19. The Western group prefers that the Committee of 21 take on the Article 19 problem--because the membership could simply not be better from our point of view. For roughly the same reasons, the Soviets prefer to have Article 19 discussions held in a smaller group.

The General Assembly will probably meet on Friday and decide to adjourn until May or September./10/

/10/The General Assembly adjourned its work on February 18 and set September 1 for renewal of its discussions. No agreement had been reached on the Article 19 dispute.

GC

337. Memorandum From Gordon Chase of the National Security Council Staff to the President's Special Assistant for National Security Affairs (Bundy)/1/

Washington, February 12, 1965.

/1/Source: Johnson Library, National Security File, Agency File, United Nations, Vol. 1. Confidential; Eyes Only. Pages 2 and 3 of the memorandum are dated February 13.

SUBJECT

Article 19, Harlan Cleveland, and Meeting with President

Early this week I went over to State to meet Harlan Cleveland. We talked at some length about Article 19. I think the following represents the bare-bones of his present thinking on the subject, which, in general, still seems to be quite fluid.

1. If there were a confrontation at the UN, we could get our 2/3 majority and win it. It is, of course, debatable whether we "win" if we take away the Soviet Union's vote.

2. The important point, however, is that a confrontation will never take place. The GA will simply not give us the majority of votes we need to get to the point of having one. (Dick Gardner, to whom I spoke later in the week, disagrees. He feels that, by September, the Afro-Asians will see that the GA is being hamstrung indefinitely, and will probably be willing to face a confrontation.)

3. Interminable postponements suit the Russians just fine. In effect, it makes the General Assembly a "no power" unit and leaves all the power with the Security Council; this, of course, is what the Russians have wanted all along. On the other hand, interminable postponements don't suit us--we want the GA to have a peace-keeping function.

4. How do we get out of our dilemma? One possibility-- we let the present impasse continue for a while and then make a unilateral statement to the effect that if the GA is not willing to enforce compulsory contributions from its reluctant members, then we, too, will have to work on a voluntary contribution basis. While we would say this in sadness, in

fact, this voluntary system, once achieved, has a distinct silver lining. *First,* a voluntary system will make it easier for international development and international peace-keeping operations to be undertaken; put another way, getting everybody to participate in UN operations is possible only at the costs of drastically limiting the size and scope of UN operations and of limiting such operations to those which the Soviets are prepared to back. *Second,* a voluntary system will allow us to avoid paying for a UN operation to which we fundamentally object.

5. If we decide to go ahead on this tack, we are faced with some tactical problems. For example:

    a. Won't the Hill say that we've caved to the Russians? Probably — but there would be several mitigating factors. *First,* there is a strong feeling on the Hill that no one wants to see the UN bust up for *a lousy $20 million bucks. Second,* a system of voluntary contributions will be very appealing to some. Senator Lauche, for instance, is always throwing up the bugaboo that the UN, some fine day, is going to force us into some peace-keeping venture to which we fundamentally object.

        These built-in mitigating factors plus a series of strong consultations with appropriate Congressmen to argue the logic of points 1-4 above could make the Hill problem a tolerable one.

    b. What about the American public? We would probably have to begin quietly playing a somewhat different tune than we have been playing (no mor — "put the Russians' feet to the fire"). It is pertinent to note that the same built-in factors which will tend to mitigate Congressional reaction against a caving on Article 19 and a system of voluntary contributions will also mitigate the public's reaction to it.

6. In closing, Harlan indicated that a meeting with the President on this subject and on other basic UN subjects might be useful. For one thing, it might be good to expose the President

to some of the above-type argumentation; this has not yet been done. For another thing, with his long parliamentary experience, the President might have a real contribution to make on this problem, which involves a parliament in New York and a parliament on the Hill.

7. *My view*--From a couple talks that I have had in IO, I get the sense that the people there feel that the UN is at an important crossroads (e.g. power of the GA vis-à-vis the SC; the balance of power in the UN between little and big nations); that the President is not entirely up on these issues; and that, in general, he is not being exposed enough to non-Adlai-type UN thinking.

While I have no real way of knowing the state of the President's UN education, I am persuaded that there are in the air some important basic UN issues and that it might be well for the President to put aside an hour, sometime during the next couple weeks, to hear about these issues and the possible U.S. options for dealing with them. If you agree, I think the first step is to get informally from State a clear idea of exactly what the substance of such a meeting with the President would be. We can then decide whether or not we want to go through with it.

GC

Talk to Cleveland informally about exact nature of possible meeting with President but, at this point, making no firm commitment on such a meeting./2/

/2/Bundy checked this option.

Let's leave it alone for now.

338. Editorial Note

Ambassador Stevenson and Secretary General U Thant discussed the possibility of a Security Council meeting on the Vietnam issue on February 16. The U.S. Permanent Representative sought to discourage the idea of a public discussion at that point. In a

February 17 memorandum to the President, Stevenson outlined his talks with U Thant and suggested alternative means to utilize the United Nations to advance the search for a peaceful resolution of the Vietnam crisis. The Stevenson-U Thant memorandum of conversation and the Stevenson memorandum to the President are printed in the *Papers of Adlai E. Stevenson,* vol. 8, pages 700-704. Additional documentation relating to the Secretary General›s role in the Vietnam crisis is in *Foreign Relations,* 1964-1968, volume I, Document 427, and ibid., volume II, Documents 161 and 164.

339. Memorandum From Secretary of State Rusk to President Johnson/1/
Washington, February 25, 1965.

/1/Source: Johnson Library, National Security File, Agency File, United Nations, Vol. 1. No classification marking.

SUBJECT

U.S. Pledge to the UN Expanded Program of Technical Assistance and the Special Fund

Recommendation:
With the recent recess of the General Assembly until September, I recommend that we proceed to make our pledge for calendar year 1965 to two related UN development programs--the Expanded Program of Technical Assistance and the Special Fund./2/

/2/President Johnson checked the approve option.
Background:

While most other countries previously contributing to these programs have announced their pledges for 1965, the U.S. deferred making its pledge, pending developments with respect to the resolution of the UN constitutional and financial crisis. Now that the General Assembly has recessed without prejudice to the application of Article 19, I believe that we should go ahead with our pledge of up to $60 million. These funds are available

411

within the FY 1965 appropriation in the A.I.D. program for voluntary contributions to international organizations.

Any further delay in the pledge is likely to produce a considerable amount of disorder in the implementation of technical assistance projects already underway. It will likewise inhibit the program planning process of the Special Fund. I believe that the point has been made that the United States should not be taken for granted. I feel that any further delay will only complicate our position rather than helping it.

Dean Rusk

340. Memorandum From the Executive Secretary of the National Security Council (Smith) to the President's Special Assistant (Moyers)/1/

Washington, March 1, 1965.

/1/Source: Johnson Library, National Security File, Agency File, United Nations, Vol. 1. No classification marking.

SUBJECT

U.S. Pledge to the UN Expanded Program of Technical Assistance and the Special Fund

1. As per our phone conversation on Saturday,/2/ here is the memo from Dean Rusk to the President,/3/ which came to us on Friday and which recommends that we proceed to make our pledge ($60 million) for calendar year 1965 to two UN development programs. The pledge, which normally would have been made in November 1964, was held up to provide us with leverage in the Article 19 negotiations.

/2/February 27.

/3/Document 339.

2. With the General Assembly adjourned and with the Article 19 discussions deferred, I agree that we probably have to go ahead with the pledge. At the same time it might be worthwhile to emphasize to State that they should be careful to explain this one publicly in such a way as to minimize the possibility of a charge that our pledge means that we have given up on Article 19. Accordingly, unless you have any objections, I will pass this word to State if and when you get the President's approval on the Rusk memorandum.

Bromley Smith/4/

/4/Printed from a copy that bears this typed signature.

341. Intelligence Information Cable/1/

TDCS DB-315/00729-65

New York, March 3, 1965.

/1/Source: Johnson Library, National Security File, Country File, United Nations, Article 19, Vol. 2. Secret; No Foreign Dissem; Controlled Dissem; No Dissem Abroad; Background Use Only. Prepared in the Central Intelligence Agency.

COUNTRY

United Nations DATE OF INFO.

Late February 1965

SUBJECT

1. Activities Affecting the United Nations

2. Views of the United Nations Secretary General and Assembly President on Chances for a Successful Negotiation of UN Financial Problem

PLACE & DATE ACQ.

1 March 1965

[less than 1 line of source text not declassified]
[less than 1 line of source text not declassified]

SOURCE AND APPRAISAL
[8 lines of source text not declassified]

1. United Nations General Assembly President Alex Quaison-Sackey and Secretary General U Thant are currently wondering if the newly-formed United Nations Committee on Peace-Keeping Operations (Committee of 33) will be able to operate effectively in the atmosphere created by the Vietnam crisis. United States military operations in Vietnam seem to be bringing about a hardening of the Soviet attitude toward the United States. The situation appears to be getting worse despite the fact that the United States made a major concession to the Soviets by agreeing to exclude Nationalist China from participation on the Committee.

2. U Thant and Quaison-Sackey originally planned to contact personally the French, Soviet, British and United States permanent missions to the United Nations in order to lay a solid groundwork for the Committee of 33 prior to the Committee's meetings. However, U Thant and Quaison-Sackey now feel that in view of the Vietnam crisis, it is pointless to approach the Soviet Union because the Soviets will probably not be very cooperative. Under these circumstances, Quaison-Sackey and U Thant feel that the Committee of 33 will not accomplish anything. (*[less than 1 line of source text not declassified]* Comment: According to the intermediate source, *[less than 1 line of source text not declassified]* heard that an unknown country has already advised U Thant and Quaison-Sackey that the Soviets will not be receptive to any approaches on peace-keeping matters at this time.)

3. Field Dissem: Sent USUN.

—wbloh might have rivalled his and his party's prestige: lee bad, therefore given instructions; to limit the granting of credit ud the issue of import licences; to African businessmen, so that they would be forced to buy through large firms or Government attencies.

As a result of Mr. Ayeh-Kumi's disclosures, the N.L.C. appointed a commission of inquiry to investigate (a) the circumstances surrounding the establishment of Nadeco Ltd. (the National Development Company) and its relationship with the C.P.P., and (6) alleged malpractices in the granting of import licences during the past three years.

A decree signed by General Ankrah on March 10 prohibited Dr. -nd Mrs. Nkrumah and his former aides from withdrawing money and other assets from Ghanaian banks without the consent of the N.L.C., the penalty being a fine of £1,250 or two years' imprisonment or both. The persons named in the decree included all former Cabinet Ministers, Mr. Ayeh-Kumi, Mr. W. M. O. Halm (the former Governor of the Bank of Ghana), and Mr. A. R. Boakye (the former chairman of the State-owned Black Star Line). The decree was later extended to cover also the assets of party officials, district commissioners, former M.P.s, the C.P.P., the Young Pioneers, and other organizations.

Dr. Nkrumah's Promise to return to Ghana as Head of State. - Appointment as Head of State of Guinea.

As stated above, Dr. Nkrumah was on a visit to China when the coup took place. Accompanied by a suite of 60 persons, including Mr. Alex Quaison-Sackey (the Ghanaian Foreign Minister) and Mr. Kwesi Armah (the Minister of Trade), he had left Accra on Feb. 21 to travel via Cairo to Peking, with the intention of later visiting Hanoi at the invitation of President Ho Chi Minn of North Vietnam. Reaching Peking from Rangoon late on Feb. 24, he was officially welcomed by President Liu Shao-chi and was later informed of the coup, the news of which was, however, not at first published in China. In a statement read by Mr. Quaison-Sackey the next day (Feb. 25), Dr. Nkrumah declared that he was still the head of State of Ghana and that he would return there soon, in the knowledge that the people of Ghana were loyal to him.

The same day President Sekou Toure of Guinea, after a special meeting of the Democratic Party of Guinea condemning the coup in Ghana, offered the ex-President political asylum in Guinea. The North Vietnam News Agency stated on Feb. 26 that his visit to Hanoi had been postponed.

A statement issued by Dr. Nkrumah in Peking on Feb. 28 read as follows: "I am sure you have all heard that some men of my Armed Forces in Ghana have attempted to usurp political power in Ghana while I was on my way from Ghana on a mission to Hanoi. What they have done is in fact an act of rebellion against the Government of the Republic of Ghana. This rebellion does not deserve the support of any government. I am determined to stamp out the rebellion without delay and in this I count on the support of the Ghanaian people and friends of Ghana all over the world.

"By the arrest, detention, and murder of Ministers, party officials, and trade unionists, and by indiscriminate killing of defenceless meh and women, the perpetrators of these wanton acts of brigandage, violence, and lawlessness have added brutality to treason. Never in the history of our new Ghana have citizens, men and women, been murdered in cold blood and their children orphaned for political reasons. Never have our Ghanaian people been riddled with bullets because of their political convictions.

"This is a tragedy of monstrous proportions. The inordinate personal ambitions and wanton acts of these military adventurers, if not checked now, would not only destroy the political, economic, and social gains which Ghana has made in recent years but also turn the tide of the African revolution.

"All that the people of Ghana have achieved in the way of economic and social progress, with the assistance of friends all over the world, is now in jeopardy because of the foolhardy act of a few military adventurers. As I go back to Ghana I know that friendly nations and men of good will will support any action I take to restore the Constitution of the Republic of Ghana. —"

After cabling the O. A.U. Foreign Ministers' meeting in Addis Ababa that he would be represented there by Mr. Quaison-Sackey, Dr. Nkrumah left Peking for Moscow in a Soviet aircraft on Feb. 28 and from the Soviet capital flew to Conakry (the capital of Guinea) where he was welcomed by President Toure on March 2.

At a large open-air meeting Dr. Nkrumah declared : " I have come here purposely to use Guinea as a platform to tell the world that very soon I shall be in Accra, in Ghana. I am not going to say anything against anyone, because I understand perfectly well the factors at work in the world today. What has happened in Algeria has happened in Ghana. We are not surprised—we understand the problems. . . . All we have to do is to stand firm and see how we can counteract these factors."

President Toure' announced at the same meeting that Dr. Nkrumah had been appointed head of State of Guinea and

secretary-general of the Guinean People's Party, the country's sole political party [see 21260 A].

It was explained in Addis Ababa on March 3 by M. Abdoulaye Diallo (the roving ambassador of Guinea) that Dr. Nkrumah had been a Guinean citizen since the union of Guinea and Ghana in 1958 [see 16630 A], just as President Toure had been a Ghanaian citizen. [The proposed union of the two States had, however, never been implemented.] M. Abdoulaye said on the following day that President Toure would remain Guinea's chief excutive.

The immediate result of this development was the decision by the N.L.C. in Accra to close the Ghanaian Embassy in Conakry, to recall Ghana's diplomatic mission, and to send a sharp protest to the Guinean Government. The Note alleged that the Ghanaian Embassy staff had been under house arrest since March 1, accused President Nkrumah of harbouring " one of the most notorious tyrants and criminals in Africa, Kwame Nkrumah," and reminded Guinea that it still owed Ghana £5,000,000 lent by Dr. Nkrumah in 1958.

Speaking over the Guinean radio on March 6, Dr. Nkrumah again said that he would soon be back in Ghana as leader of the Ghanaian people and would put to death all the military leaders now in power, as well as all those who had helped to bring about the coup. He added : " I know that when the time comes you will crush the new regime. I know the Ghanaian people will remain faithful to me as well as to my party and my Government."

On March 7 President Toure and Dr. Nkrumah flew to Bamako for talks with President Modibo Keita of Mali.

The Foreign Minister of Mali, M. Oumane Ba, said in Paris the same day that " President Nkrumah's revolutionary work cannot be replaced, and we do not accept that some musical comedy general, helped by policemen, should question the Ghanaian people's 20 years of struggle." Although he expressed his country's " total and resolute support " for Dr. Nkrumah, he did not consider it necessary for other countries " to be summoned to liberate Ghana," as " the Ghanaian people are sufficiently strong and aware of their responsibility to solve the problem."

President Toure stated on March 10 that " 20,000 Guinean ex-servicemen who had been in the French Army, as well as 50,000 soldiers recruited from women members and youths of the Guinean Democratic Party " would be going to Ghana " in military convoys to help the Ghanaian people free itself from the dictatorship of the military traitors." [Guinea is separated from Ghana by 300 miles of Ivory Coast territory.]

Measures to protect the Ivory Coast frontier with Guinea were taken immediately by President Houphouet-Boigny, who announced on March 17 that troops of the Ivory Coast had been moved to the frontier with Guinea with orders to repulse any attempts by Guinean troops and volunteers to march through to Ghana ; on the previous day he had described any such attempt as " a fatal adventure " and had reminded Guinea that the Ivory Coast had a defence agreement with France, which would immediately come to her assistance if she was attacked. A statement by Radio Conakry on March 17 that " so-called French teachers, professors, and engineers " who had been " flooding " the Ivory Coast were " in reality soldiers in civilian clothes," and that " thousands of French troops " were " pouring in " as "« new forces of French colonial conquest," were dismissed in Paris as merely a reaction to President Houphouet-Boigny's attitude towards the Guinean plans.

In Accra Mr. Harley (the vice-chairman of the N.L.C.) said on March 10 that he had " initiated certain actions aimed at recapturing the former President and bringing him back to Ghana to stand trial."

Dr. Nkrumah, in a broadcast on March 13, urged the people of Ghana to " prepare to revolt " against the N.L.C, but the Ghana Trades Union Congress the next day warned President Toure that the workers and all the people of Ghana did " not want Kwame Nkrumah or anything of him " and would " stand solidly by our new progressive Government." The T.U.C. at the same time threatened to disaffiliate itself from the All-African Trade Unions Federation unless the latter ended its recognition of Dr. Nkrumah. [The other trade unions affiliated to the Federation are in Algeria, the Congo (Brazzaville), Guinea, Mali, Morocco, Tanzania, and the U.A.R., the Ghanaian trade unions accounting for about one-third of the Federation's total membership].

Mr. Quaison-Sackey's Return to Ghana.

Mr. Quaison-Sackey left Peking on Feb. 27 for Hong Kong where he stated that Dr. Nkrumah had been unwilling to believe the news of the coup until it had been confirmed by Mr. Chou En-lai, the Chinese Prime Minister. He added that he did not know what Dr. Nkrumah was going to do, as " he has his own mind and does not tell us about his plans." On Feb. 28 Mr. Quaison-Sackey flew to Frankfurt, whence he did not, as expected, proceed to Addis Ababa, but instead flew to

Excerpt from Keesing's Contemporary Archives

Image / **Ambassador Alex Quaison-Sackey, Prime Minister Nnamdi Azikiwe, Ambassador Diallo Telli and...**

THE TALK OF THE TOWN

Notes and Comment

FOR various reasons, we watched the eclipse of the sun from a small park in the Bronx overlooking the Polo Grounds. We were almost alone, because the barrage of ophthalmological warnings from the press and television led most people to lock themselves up in their apartments until the eclipse was over, lest exposure to sunlight cause total blindness. Following instructions, we had drilled a tiny hole in a piece of cardboard, and after a few minutes of jiggling about we focussed the image of the sun as projected through the hole onto another piece of cardboard. We saw many eclipses, since the sunlight was obstructed not only by the moon but by clouds, a pigeon, and a small boy. As the tiny spot of light on our cardboard changed from a circle to a crescent, a

group of children gathered around us to watch, while the pigeons began settling down in trees for what they must have thought was the evening. Actually, it was five-thirty in the afternoon, but the mosquitoes were also confused, and began to whine about as if it were twilight. We felt very important, like an emperor's soothsayer, as we revealed the Blotting Out of the Sun with our mystic cardboards. But just as the moon reduced the sun to a hairline, our spectators left, and one announced he was going home to look at the eclipse on television. We sat there doggedly watching our own solar eclipse until we were quite certain the moon was not going to back up, and then we also went home and watched a Videotape of the eclipse. Television had gone all out and sent crews of astronomers, cameramen, and general-practice savants to Canada,

where the eclipse was total, rather than our local eighty-nine per cent, and we thought there was a gloating tone in their presentation of "the diamond ring" and "Baily's beads"—ecliptic phenomena that were beyond anything we could hope to see in the Bronx. On several occasions, we were invited "to watch the eclipse on your television cameras, where the picture is always clear and the danger is taken out." The danger of possible blindness in watching an eclipse seemed particularly fascinating to the television reporters, and was again dwelt on by Carol Reed in her weather forecast (after the eclipse was over). Perhaps we had been made unduly sensitive when our spectators abandoned us, but we thought we detected a tone of pique among the television reporters that anyone should ever consider seeing an eclipse for himself, rather than on television, and we picked up an implication, never explicit, that blindness was just what was coming to any scab who tried looking at the Universe directly instead of through Authorized Sources.

Unchangeable

BECAUSE, in the course of showing strangers about town, we're accustomed to pointing out the Music Hall as one of our newer marvels, it gives us a considerable shock to realize that its thirtieth anniversary is being commemorated this year. Can it possibly be so long ago that this department was advising its readers "The best way to get to the new Music Hall is via the Sixth Avenue 'L' "? That dingy, celebrated railway, which was dismantled in 1938, would seem to belong to a period much earlier than Rockefeller Center, but it's certainly true that our advice was offered a few days after we had attended, in a terrible rainstorm, the opening night of the Music Hall. The date was December 27, 1932—one of the final, gloomy days of an exceptionally gloomy year. The opening-

night program was an extravagant vaudeville, lasting until the small hours; among the sixteen acts making up the program were the Wallenda aerial ballet, the Tuskegee Choir, Ray Bolger, Martha Graham's dance group, Weber and Fields, Dr. Rockwell, and the Roxyettes (who had first been known as the Missouri Rockets and were eventually transmogrified into Rockettes).

The Music Hall—indeed, the whole Rockefeller Center complex—had been conceived with the idea of providing a new home for the Metropolitan Opera (after three decades, the new home is still a couple of years away); when the opera project fell through, it was decided to make the Music Hall a sort of super vaudeville theatre, under the direction of a super-showman, Samuel Lionel (Roxy) Rothafel. Vaudeville being on the way down and sound pictures on the way up, the program proved to be an instant flop, and the Music Hall hastily switched to a policy of showing

a feature movie and a fifty-minute stage show—a policy so successful that it has remained unaltered over the years. As for Roxy, he resigned after a few months, and in 1933 the management of the Hall was taken over by Rockefeller Center, Inc., which still runs it. The Hall, which grosses about eight million dollars a year, went into the black in 1935 and has been there ever since. This is all the more remarkable because its prices are so low; until noon, general admission on weekdays is ninety-five cents, which makes the greatest movie house on earth one of the cheapest movie houses in town.

The Music Hall isn't, of course, just a place of entertainment; it's a national object of pride, like the Grand Canyon,

417

"As long as you're up, get me a little cold lobster and some champagne."

• •

name was Quaison, meaning 'the son of Kwei.' I have another uncle, Nana Ayirebi-Acquah III, who is a chief, or traditional ruler; around 1925, he helped establish the Joint Provincial Council of Chiefs, which worked with Sir Gordon Guggisberg, the British Governor, to develop the country. He's now chairman of the Ghana Educational Trust."

The Ambassador went on to say that Winneba was a very old fishing port and that many of his relatives were fishermen. "I spent my childhood on the beach," he said. "The fishermen used dugout boats and nets, and went as far as Liberia after herring, mackerel, and so forth. Every Winneba child is a very good swimmer." In 1949, after a year as president of the Political Youth Organization in Winneba, he won a scholarship to Oxford, where he took an honors degree in philosophy, politics, and economics. "It was the first time I had been outside of Africa," he said. "It was a wonderful experience. Three stimulating years; I began to question so many things. I sometimes just shut

myself up in my room and ruminated."

Back home in 1952, Mr. Quaison-Sackey was appointed Labour Officer, a position involving the organization of trade unions and the conciliation of strikes. 1957, the year of independence, found him in the Ghana High Commissioner's Office in London, where he later became Head of Chancery and Official Secretary; his U.N. post dates from the summer of 1959. "I believe in the concept of Negritude—an acceptance and affirmation of the quality of 'blackness,'" he said. "It is a psychological gathering together of all black peoples in the spiritual bonds of brotherhood. Its geographical boundaries are only those of the lands in which black people dwell. Africans and their descendants may well be proud of their past. The great empires of Ghana, Mali, and Songhai and the powerful kingdoms of Ashanti, Ife, and Benin all flourished centuries before the Europeans arrived in Africa. Timbuktu, in Mali, formerly the Sudan, was a seat of advanced learning in the fifteenth century; the records of the old uni

versity are still there. People tend to forget that Africa once was free, and that the modern movement toward independence is actually a reëmergence into independence, a movement toward both past and future glories at once. The policy of Apartheid—the view of the white South African that the African was made by God to be a hewer of wood and a drawer of water—has produced much sadness. You know, after three years of friendship with a white South African at Oxford, I was told by him that he could invite me to his home only if I posed as his shoeshine boy."

Looking anything but sad, the Ambassador informed us that he and his wife, a girl from his home town, live in New Rochelle with four sons—Egya, Nana Bodo, Kweku Bondzi, and Nenyi, and a daughter, Awo. "One and a half years old up to twelve," he said. "I wrote my book in longhand. Its editor, Thomas Goethals, a grandson of your bridge builder, was a great help. He kept urging me to explain things more and to expand my thoughts. I tended to assume that the reader knew more than

THE NEW YORKER

place the pots with Westinghouse electric frying pans, she said, "All right, girls. We're going to fry some marbles now, and later on we're going to make beautiful jewelry out of them."

The madras princesses giggled, but, on cue, they all went diligently to work on the marbles; the judges, nodding appreciatively, peered down into the hot pans. Then, clustering prettily for the A.B.C. crew around one large skillet, the girls turned to the more practical lively homemaking art of Frying Eggs. One by one, twelve eggs were cracked into the pan with enormous care. Two yolks broke. None of the eggs cooked. Miss Bowie, blushing beneath her turban, hurriedly confessed to A.B.C. that she had forgotten to pre-heat the skillet, and then apologized to the head chef of the Tavern, who had been standing by with a pepper mill. "If any of you news photographers want pictures of the finished eggs, wait here," she said.

The twelve beautiful braintrusters meanwhile had moved on to tackle the art of Mixing Drinks, in a Westinghouse blender. Having each been presented with another egg, pineapple juice, milk, watercress, and chocolate sauce, they were told to combine the elements in whatever way they saw fit. "We're testing your imagination, girls," Miss Bowie said.

Miss University of Oklahoma switched on her blender, which, being empty, roared. This frightened Miss University of Washington, who jumped, and Miss University of Denver, who screamed.

"Ah'm puttin' in pineapple juice to make it fruitlike, and then Ah'm puttin' in watercress for health," Miss Florida State University informed us.

"I'm just adding chocolate till I get a color I like," Miss Quincy Junior College said.

Miss Manhattanville again tasted her handiwork and again made a face.

We had just begun to sample an egg-and-pineapple-juice at the blender of Miss Bucknell when Miss Bowie announced that the next lively homemaking art would involve the decoration of Westinghouse Beauty Bonnet Home Hair Dryers with various feminine odds

"I liked her better in 'National Velvet.'"

•   •

and ends. We observed that Miss Bucknell put flowers on her bonnet, Miss University of Minnesota and Miss University of Washington preferred feathers, and Miss Florida State was partial to balloons, even though balloons, as she soon discovered, pop when sewed.

"These girls are pretty enough, but *my* daughter should be here," a woman who had dropped by at the Tavern for brunch told a man from Grey. "She's Miss Syracuse, you know."

"Syracuse University?" ventured the Grey man.

"I should say not! Miss Syracuse-the-whole-town," the Tavern guest replied, walking away.

It was now time for a "forum discussion" on the challenging art of Gracious Entertaining, and for this the twelve brainy beauties forsook their blue-and-gold cardboard in favor of glittering rhinestone crowns.

"What would you do," one of the judges inquired, after some thought, "if you gave a party and your chief rival arrived wearing *your* dress?"

"Oh, that's a good one! Let's play with that," Miss Bowie said enthusiasti-

cally. She called first on Miss University of Washington, who said that a gracious hostess makes the best of any tragedy, and then on Miss Purdue, who suggested that in some cases it is the girl, and not the dress, that counts.

"And what *makes* a good party?" asked another judge.

Miss Minnesota had her hand up first. "Snacks," she said.

"I'd like to add, though, that the snacks should be good, all-round American snacks," said Miss Florida State.

Admonition

A FRIEND of ours reports that he was on a Madison Avenue bus late one rainy night recently when a man boarded it and told the driver that the only money he had with him was fourteen cents and a twenty-dollar bill. After a few moments, apparently taking the downpour and the lateness of the hour into account, the driver agreed to accept the fourteen cents. Then, as the man took his seat, the driver turned his head and said, "Next time, Mister, think ahead!"

A COLLISION IN THE CITY

WHATEVER a person may think of himself, he *has* to think he is nice. The conviction, I have discovered rather suddenly, is precious, and an injury to it can be an almost intolerable hurt. Niceness, of the sort I am talking about, is a part of the code in the city. It has often been remarked how well we all get along here—millions of us crowded together but managing somehow to follow our private paths without serious collisions. Intent on my own business, I walk along the sidewalk, crisscrossing the paths of others, sidestepping, hastening ahead or falling behind, but rarely do I bump into anyone. In elevators, I stand inches from others but manage, mostly, not to touch them. The system works, and the city survives, because we are all nice. I take care that I do not touch others. Everyone else takes care, too. When two people do bump, there may be a flash of irritation, sometimes even of real anger, because someone has not been nice, but usually the bump is small, unintentional, and quickly forgotten. To violate the code, to be not nice—even for good reason—and then to find that you have struck a person in a vital spot, is not so easily forgotten.

I found all this out when I was in what might be called a collision in the city. The episode concerned me, my sister and her newborn baby, and a cab-driver who cried. I made him cry. Of a number of things I said, only one made him cry. The episode showed me why we are all so careful, all of us nice people who are strangers to each other, not to touch each other in passing.

Some months ago, my sister had a baby girl in Lenox Hill Hospital. She had the bad luck to have it while her husband was away, and in his absence it was arranged that I was to fetch her from the hospital. I would go there and pick her and the baby up; we would take a cab to Grand Central Station, and then I would put her on a train to her home in the country. In prospect, this plan seemed simple and unlikely to involve strain for anyone; certainly it promised nothing that would be particularly emotional. I was surprised, then, at how I felt, standing in my sister's room while she shakily put on her clothes, when the nurse came in and put the baby on the bed. She stuffed a few oddments of equipment into a bag and told us that we were on our own. The baby on the bed was so small that it reminded me of a newborn mouse with big, red feet. It didn't seem particularly happy. I looked at my sister, who was working into her stockings as though it were a very difficult task, and found no comfort there. Suddenly the small stage of the journey of which I was in charge—the distance from Lenox Hill to Grand Central—appeared strangely larger. But I told myself not to be silly. I made myself go to the bed and touch the baby and wrap around it the blanket I had brought that was to protect it on the journey. The nurse carried the baby down in the elevator with us, and I carried the suitcase. The nurse went as far as the final glass door. With an encouraging pat and a farewell smile, she put the baby in my sister's arms, and at that moment, I think we both realized, all official responsibility ceased.

It wasn't snowing on the other side of the door, but snow might have been better. It was late afternoon, and a chill, smoggy rain darkened the winter twilight. People were hurrying along the side street, and cars were hurrying when they could, or, stopped by the light at the end of the block, they snorted white fumes while they waited. My sister stood under the door canopy with the baby, and I stood out in the street with my hand held out, waving, ungloved and cold, to signal a cab. At first there were no cabs, just cars, and then several cabs full of people, and then, darting furtively, it seemed, a whole flock of empty cabs that didn't stop. Most of them had "Off Duty" signs propped inside their windshields, and with a sinking feeling I realized it was the time of day when cabs change shifts. One after another, I glimpsed the gray, waxwork faces of the drivers who wouldn't look at us, and it was clear that they were not looking on purpose. I glanced at my sister, who had moved back up on the steps so that she could lean against the building, and I thought that if only I had a sign that said "Newborn Baby," then of course the drivers would know how important our journey was and they would stop. I also regretted that I hadn't lined up a particular cab or a hired car, but I hadn't thought of that sort of fussy precau-

tion since the days, long ago, when my mother would telephone the station-master at Grand Central to make sure a redcap would meet her when she planned to take a train. Standing on the wet street, I realized that if we didn't get a cab soon the whole simple plan would fall into completely unmanageable pieces.

I went back to my sister and said, "The side street is bad for cabs. How are you feeling?"

"Not bad," she said rather whitely.

I said, "Maybe I'd do better on the corner of Park."

"I don't think you'd be able to hold the cab while I walked up there," she said. "And we're late already. I'd better go, too."

"Can you make it?"

"I guess I can."

She slung the baby up on her shoulder, pulled the wrap over its head, and put a foot, brave and trembly, down on the sidewalk, making final the break with the official, protective bulk of the hospital. It seemed to me that she was as dramatic as a heroine in a silent film—that everyone passing should have looked and stopped and said, "A newborn baby! Out in the rain! Let us help you! Let us find you a cab!" Several men and women went by and didn't look at me or my sister and the baby. But there was no way for them to know, and I excused them.

We walked the half block to the corner of Park Avenue and Seventy-seventh Street. My sister again leaned against the building, and I stepped into the avenue. The pavements glistened like coal. Streams of yellow headlights and cold, gleaming bodies of cars went past me on their way uptown. The stop light turned red and green, and red and green, but very few cabs went by. Most of them were going fast and hugging the lane nearest the center island. Then I saw one on our side, going rather slow; the driver was looking my way. I waved hard, and the cab slowed some more, but it was still moving a little as it came abreast of me. The driver leaned across to roll down the front window and say something.

I guess I knew exactly what he was going to say, because I put my hand quickly on the door handle while the cab was still moving and pulled the back door open wide. "Come on, quick!" I called to my sister, and the cab had to stop, because the door was open and the handle was in my hand.

My sister made it across the sidewalk and bent over and got in with her bundle. While she

INDEX

421

N

Nana Ayirebi-Acquah 3, 6, 326
National Liberation Council 282, 283,
    286, 288, 292, 340
Nelson-Williams 66, 67
New York xi, 70, 72, 90, 122, 133, 141,
    150, 166, 167, 196, 197, 198,
    199, 201, 209, 211, 215, 216,
    221, 227, 229, 231, 232, 236,
    238, 243, 267, 270, 271, 284,
    291, 295, 321, 322, 324, 325,
    327, 330, 331, 332, 334, 336,
    337, 338, 339, 341, 346, 352,
    353, 355, 358, 361, 363, 369,
    371, 373, 374, 375, 383, 384,
    389, 390, 402, 403, 405, 406,
    410, 413
Ngu Forocha 180
Nii Kwabena Bonne 43
Nikita Khrushchev 197, 198, 201, 228
Nnamdi Azikiwe 48, 70
Non-aligned 145, 188, 200, 201, 239,
    241, 243, 317, 357, 363, 381, 382

O

OAU 243, 245, 254, 293
Obetsebi Lamptey 42, 43
Ofori Atta 42, 43
Ohene Djan 151, 152
Organization of African Unity 286, 328
Oxford v, 13, 24, 29, 48, 49, 52, 53, 57,
    58, 59, 60, 61, 62, 63, 64, 65, 66,
    67, 68, 69, 70, 71, 72, 74, 75, 76,
    77, 79, 80, 81, 84, 85, 86, 87, 91,
    94, 95, 108, 119, 123, 141, 149,
    168, 169, 171, 186, 293, 296,
    299, 301, 316, 319, 320, 322,
    325, 339

P

Paa Grant 42
Pandit Nehru 197, 198, 200
Patrice Lumumba 319, 326
Peace 5, 47, 63, 77, 146, 160, 170, 174,
    176, 189, 190, 206, 207, 220,
    226, 228, 233, 234, 235, 237,
    238, 241, 244, 255, 256, 259,
    262, 264, 265, 267, 268, 273,
    275, 296, 297, 302, 317, 321,
    322, 323, 324, 329, 330, 332,
    336, 353, 354, 355, 358, 390,
    391, 393, 394, 396, 397, 399,
    401, 408, 409, 414
Peter Barker 71, 72, 73, 76, 135
Politics 39, 42, 44, 46, 48, 49, 52, 57,
    62, 64, 65, 70, 91, 103, 106, 110,
    116, 123, 129, 146, 162, 163,
    171, 184, 230, 242, 262, 293,
    296, 299, 300, 309, 314, 316,
    320, 325, 329
Power 41, 43, 99, 101, 129, 146, 161,
    167, 182, 194, 199, 200, 203,
    204, 228, 262, 280, 283, 309,
    329, 338, 385, 387, 398, 399,
    401, 408, 410
President xii, 7, 8, 13, 23, 42, 47, 48, 67,
    68. 69, 70, 100, 101, 103, 115,
    125, 136, 143, 146, 157, 160,
    161, 162, 163, 164, 168, 174,
    176, 177, 183, 186, 187, 189,
    191, 197, 198, 199, 200, 201,
    205, 206, 208, 221, 222, 224,
    225, 227, 228, 229, 230, 231,
    234, 235, 236, 237, 239, 242,
    243, 244, 245, 251, 255, 256,
    257, 258, 259, 263, 264, 265,
    269, 270, 271, 273, 274, 275,
    277, 278, 279, 280, 281, 282,
    283, 289, 290, 292, 293, 295,
    296, 315, 316, 319, 323, 325,
    326, 327, 330, 332, 334, 336,
    338, 339, 340, 343, 344, 366,
    367, 368, 371, 372, 373, 374,

V

Vote 69, 109, 183, 251, 255, 322, 323,
331, 333, 336, 337, 338, 345,
347, 349, 350, 356, 366, 368,
369, 370, 374, 379, 383, 384,
385, 386, 387, 392, 394, 408

W

West Africa 4, 24, 30, 49, 59, 70, 162,
163, 180, 186, 189, 206, 313,
314, 326
Western 1, 99, 115, 192, 251, 269, 286,
320, 326, 384, 407

Winneba xii, 1, 2, 3, 4, 5, 6, 7, 8, 9, 10,
12, 14, 15, 28, 52, 53, 71, 73, 91,
101, 113, 114, 288, 296, 298,
301, 302, 311, 316, 320
World War 9, 39, 43, 48, 51, 94, 124,
173, 177, 240, 298

Y

Yacine Diallo 162, 163